Europe
Europa

		Currency	SOS	🛣				MAUT/TOLL	‰
Österreich / Austria	A	1 Euro (EUR) = 100 Cent	133 / 144	130	100	100	50	▣	0,5 ‰
Shqipëria / Albania	AL	1 Lek (ALL) = 100 Quindarka	129 /126	120	100	80	40		0,0 ‰
België/Belgique / Belgium	B	1 Euro (EUR) = 100 Cent	101 / 100	120	120	90	50		0,5 ‰
Bålgarija / Bulgaria	BG	1 Lew (BGN) = 100 Stótinki	166 / 150	130	90	90	50	▣	0,5 ‰
Bosna i Hercegovina / Bosnia and Herzegovina	BIH	Konvert. Marka (BAM) = 100 Fening	92 / 94	120	100	80	60		0,3 ‰
Schweiz/Suisse/Svizzera / Switzerland	CH	1 Franken (CHF) = 100 Rappen	117 / 144	120	100	80	50	▣	0,5 ‰
Kýpros/Kibris / Cyprus	CY	1 Euro (EUR) = 100 Cent	199	100	80	80	50		0,5 ‰
Česká Republika / Czech Republic	CZ	1 Koruna (CZK) = 100 Haliru	112 / 155	130	130	90	50	▣	0,0 ‰
Deutschland / Germany	D	1 Euro (EUR) = 100 Cent	110 / 112	⬭	⬭	100	50		0,5 ‰
Danmark / Denmark	DK	1 Krone (DKK) = 100 Øre	112	130	80	80	50		0,5 ‰
España / Spain	E	1 Euro (EUR) = 100 Cent	112	120	100	90	50	▣	0,5 ‰
Eesti / Estonia	EST	1 Euro (EUR) = 100 Cent	110 / 112	110	110	90	50		0,0 ‰
France / France	F	1 Euro (EUR) = 100 Cent	112	130	110	90	50	▣	0,5 ‰
Suomi/Finland / Finland	FIN	1 Euro (EUR) = 100 Cent	112	120	100	100	50		0,5 ‰
United Kingdom / United Kingdom	GB	1 Pound Sterling (GBP) = 100 Pence	999 / 112	70 mph (112)	70 mph (112)	60 mph (96)	30 mph (48)		0,8 ‰
Elláda (Hellás) / Greece	GR	1 Euro (EUR) = 100 Cent	100 / 166	120	110	90	50	▣	0,5 ‰
Magyarország / Hungary	H	1 Forint (HUF) = 100 Filler	112	130	110	90	50	▣	0,0 ‰
Hrvatska / Croatia	HR	1 Kuna (HRK) = 100 Lipa	112 / 94	130	110	90	50	▣	0,5 ‰
Italia / Italy	I	1 Euro (EUR) = 100 Cent	112 / 118	130	110	90	50	▣	0,5 ‰
Éire/Ireland / Ireland	IRL	1 Euro (EUR) = 100 Cent	999 / 112	120	100	60 / 100	50		0,5 ‰
Ísland / Iceland	IS	1 Krona (ISK) = 100 Aurar	112			80 / 90	50		0,5 ‰
Luxembourg / Luxembourg	L	1 Euro (EUR) = 100 Cent	113 / 112	130	90	80	50		0,5 ‰
Lietuva / Lithuania	LT	1 Euro (EUR) = 100 Cent	02 / 03 / 112	110	90	90	50		0,4 ‰
Latvija / Latvia	LV	1 Euro (EUR) = 100 Cent	02 / 03 / 112	110	90	90	50		0,5 ‰
Makedonija / Macedonia	MK	1 Denar (MKD) = 100 Deni	192 / 194	120	100	40 / 60	50	▣	0,5 ‰
Norge / Norway	N	1 Krone (NOK) = 100 Øre	112 / 113	90	90	80	50	▣	0,2 ‰
Nederland / Netherlands	NL	1 Euro (EUR) = 100 Cent	112	120	100	80	50	▣	0,5 ‰
Portugal / Portugal	P	1 Euro (EUR) = 100 Cent	112	120	100	80	50	▣	0,5 ‰
Polska / Poland	PL	2 Zloty (PLN) = 100 Groszy	112 / 999	130 / 140	100 / 120	90	50	▣	0,2 ‰
Kosovo / Kosovo	RKS	1 Euro (EUR) = 100 Cent	112 / 92	130	110	80	50		0,5 ‰
România / Romania	RO	1 Leu (RON) = 100 Bani	112	130	100	90	50	▣	0,0 ‰
Rossija / Russia	RUS	1 Rubel (RUB) = 100 Kopeek	02 / 03	110	90	90	60		0,0 ‰
Sverige / Sweden	S	1 Krona (SEK) = 100 Öre	112	110	110/90	70 / 90	50		0,2 ‰
Slovenská Republika / Slovakia	SK	1 Euro (EUR) = 100 Cent	112 / 155	130	90	90	50	▣	0,0 ‰
Slovenija / Slovenia	SLO	1 Euro (EUR) = 100 Cent	113 / 112	130	100	90	50	▣	0,5 ‰
Srbija / Crna Gora / Serbia / Montenegro	SRB MNE	1 Dinar (CSM) = 100 Para ; Euro	92 / 94	120	100	80	50	▣	0,5 ‰
Türkiye / Turkey	TR	1 Lira (TRY) = 100 Kurus	155 / 112	120	90	90	50	▣	0,5 ‰
Ukrajina / Ukraine	UA	1 Griwna (UAH) = 100 Kopijken	02 / 03	130	110	90	60		0,0 ‰

© Kunth Verlag GmbH & Co. KG 2016
Königinstraße 11, D-80539 München,
phone +49-89-458020-0, fax +49-89-458020-21
e-mail: info@kunth-verlag.de
www.kunth-verlag.de

© AA Media Limited 2016
Fanum House, Basing View,
Basingstoke, Hampshire RG21 4EA, UK
ISBN 9780749577551
A05371

Hill shading 1:2 000 000 / 1:4 000 000:
Produced using SRTM data from Heiner Newe,
GeoKarta, Altensteig

Printed in China

Reykjavik ● (IS) 🕇 319.575 / ▢ 103.125 km²

N o r w e

(AL)	🕇 2.831.741 / ▢ 28.748 km²
(AND)	🕇 85.015 / ▢ 468 km²
(BIH)	🕇 4.621.598 / ▢ 51.129 km²
(FL)	🕇 36.476 / ▢ 160 km²
(HR)	🕇 4.480.043 / ▢ 56.542 km²
(RKS)	🕇 1.733.872 / ▢ 10.887 km²
(L)	🕇 524.853 / ▢ 2.586 km²
(M)	🕇 417.608 / ▢ 316 km²
(MC)	🕇 35.881 / ▢ 1,6 km²
(MD)	🕇 3.560.000 / ▢ 33.800 km²
(MK)	🕇 2.057.284 / ▢ 25.713 km²
(MNE)	🕇 625.266 / ▢ 13.812 km²
(RSM)	🕇 32.284 / ▢ 61 km²
(SLO)	🕇 2.057.660 / ▢ 20.253 km²
(V)	🕇 836 / ▢ 0,44 km²

North

(IRL)
🕇 4.581.269 / ▢ 70.182 km² ● Dublin (GB)

🕇 61.792.000 / ▢ 244.820 km²

London ●   Amsterdam

Brussel/Bruxelles ●
🕇 10.951.266 (B)
▢ 30.528 km²

Paris ●

(F)
🕇 62.793.432 / ▢ 543.965 km²

ATLANTIC OCEAN

🕇 10.602.000 / ▢ 92.212 km²
(P)

Andorra la Vella ● (AND)

Madrid ●

Lisboa ●

(E)
🕇 47.212.990 / ▢ 504.645 km²

M e d i t e r r a n e a n

Al Jaza'ir (Alger) ●

Ar-Ribat (Rabat) ● (MA)   (DZ)

Distances/Enfernungen/Distances/Afstanden

	Amsterdam	Athina	Barcelona	Belfast	Beograd	Berlin	Bern	Birmingham	Bordeaux	Bratislava	Bruxelles/Brussel	Bucureşti	Budapest	Calais	Dublin	Edinburgh	Frankfurt a.M.	Genova	Hamburg	Helsinki	Istanbul	København	Köln	Kyjiv	Le Havre	Lisboa
Amsterdam		2827	1566	1286	1720	656	833	734	1082	1211	210	2267	1398	363	1125	1196	443	1216	466	1953	2693	788	263	1943	598	2241
Athina	2827		2612	3758	1106	2338	2010	3206	2682	1662	2598	1168	1466	2844	3598	3668	2386	1780	2627	3227	1094	2767	2568	2307	2744	3768
Barcelona	1566	2612		2280	1988	1877	915	1728	637	1894	1376	2574	1926	1365	2120	2190	1336	857	1776	3263	2961	2099	1383	3048	1251	1259
Belfast	1286	3758	2280		2800	1850	1745	594	1784	2349	1119	3415	2545	925	166	319	1521	2119	1676	3161	3773	1999	1331	3244	1191	2941
Beograd	1720	1106	1988	2800		1236	1334	2248	2031	560	1680	592	363	1877	2639	2709	1287	1159	1525	2125	979	1665	1469	1472	1971	3147
Berlin	656	2338	1877	1850	1236		956	1298	1632	683	774	1751	881	927	1689	1760	549	1177	289	1649	2320	434	576	1325	1148	2791
Bern	833	2010	915	1745	1334	956		1167	889	950	637	1920	1136	796	1564	1629	429	450	910	2397	2307	1232	583	2205	752	2044
Birmingham	734	3206	1728	594	2248	1298	1167		1232	1797	566	2794	1924	373	385	472	968	1567	1124	2609	3221	1447	779	2582	432	2233
Bordeaux	1082	2682	637	1784	2031	1632	889	1232		1936	891	2616	1967	869	1470	1540	1167	997	1483	2970	3003	1806	1065	2998	686	1162
Bratislava	1211	1662	1894	2349	560	683	950	1797	1936		1203	1071	201	1388	2151	2221	799	1063	968	1751	1640	1109	987	1256	1521	3052
Bruxelles/Brussel	210	2598	1376	1119	1680	774	637	566	891	1203		2227	1357	195	958	1028	402	1023	601	2088	2653	923	212	2163	406	2049
Bucureşti	2267	1168	2574	3415	592	1751	1920	2794	2616	1071	2227		874	2426	3196	3256	1833	1746	2035	2183	625	2175	2015	947	2585	3735
Budapest	1398	1466	1926	2545	363	881	1136	1924	1967	201	1357	874		1577	2315	2386	963	1094	1165	1776	1350	1305	1152	1123	1685	3083
Calais	363	2844	1365	925	1877	927	796	373	869	1388	195	2426	1577		764	777	600	1189	754	2241	2851	1077	410	2213	273	2025
Dublin	1125	3598	2120	166	2639	1689	1564	385	1470	2151	958	3196	2315	764		450	1326	1926	1480	2979	3578	1803	1136	2939	789	2616
Edinburgh	1196	3668	2190	319	2709	1760	1629	472	1540	2221	1028	3256	2386	777	450		1430	2021	1586	3071	3683	1909	1241	3043	894	2697
Frankfurt a.M.	443	2386	1336	1521	1287	549	429	968	1167	799	402	1833	963	600	1326	1430		808	496	1968	2261	818	189	1841	772	2306
Genova	1216	1780	857	2119	1159	1177	450	1567	997	1063	1023	1746	1094	1189	1926	2021	808		1244	2746	2123	1566	971	2210	1104	2013
Hamburg	466	2627	1776	1676	1525	289	910	1124	1483	968	601	2035	1165	754	1480	1586	496	1244		1502	2646	338	425	1603	997	2639
Helsinki	1953	3227	3263	3161	2125	1649	2397	2609	2970	1751	2088	2183	1776	2241	2979	3071	1968	2746	1502		3081	1713	1910	1546	2482	4125
Istanbul	2693	1094	2961	3773	979	2320	2307	3221	3003	1640	2653	625	1350	2851	3578	3683	2261	2123	2646	3081		2642	2442	1475	2944	4121
København	788	2767	2099	1999	1665	434	1232	1447	1806	1109	923	2175	1305	1077	1803	1909	818	1566	338	1713	2642		748	1744	1320	2962
Köln	263	2568	1383	1331	1469	576	583	779	1065	987	212	2015	1152	410	1136	1241	189	971	425	1910	2442	748		1947	580	2223
Kyjiv	1943	2307	3048	3244	1472	1325	2205	2582	2998	1256	2163	947	1123	2213	2939	3043	1841	2210	1603	1546	1475	1744	1947		2532	4183
Le Havre	598	2744	1251	1191	1971	1148	752	432	686	1521	406	2585	1685	273	789	894	772	1104	997	2482	2944	1320	580	2532		1845
Lisboa	2241	3768	1259	2941	3147	2791	2044	2233	1162	3052	2049	3735	3083	2025	2616	2697	2306	2013	2639	4125	4121	2962	2223	4183	1845	
Ljubljana	1234	1633	1462	2316	534	997	809	1764	1503	447	1156	1122	460	1382	2106	2183	803	1184	1226	1508	1390	984	1560	1437	2617	261
London	532	2952	1526	776	2046	1096	965	191	1030	1557	364	2592	1722	171	546	650	766	1364	922	2407	3019	1245	575	2379	298	2187
Luxembourg	360	2414	1180	1347	1500	743	453	357	995	1031	230	2077	1195	414	1145	1256	231	828	623	2106	2449	944	207	2048	531	212
Lyon	923	2115	639	1672	1464	1238	305	1120	588	1368	732	2052	1399	759	1479	1582	700	475	1140	2625	2438	1463	746	2480	658	174
Madrid	1770	3215	627	2474	2594	2320	1543	1768	691	2498	1578	3182	2529	1554	2146	2230	1835	1459	2169	3654	3567	2492	1752	3629	1374	626
Málaga	2321	3619	1031	3009	2998	2879	1947	2302	1242	2902	2129	3586	2933	2105	2717	2764	2341	1863	2720	4205	3971	3043	2303	4033	1925	683
Marseille	1235	2156	508	1983	1535	1549	573	1431	648	1439	1044	2122	1470	1070	1792	1893	1012	400	1452	2937	2508	1775	1058	2570	970	166
Milano	1076	1691	987	2057	1036	1038	318	1498	1014	940	884	1624	971	1023	1751	1959	668	140	1109	2424	2909	1432	826	2071	1044	213
Minsk	1768	2583	2989	2957	1480	1150	1992	2405	2744	1201	1884	1357	1132	2038	2770	2866	1663	2196	1428	882	2006	1104	1683	560	2261	390
Moskva	2469	3283	3690	3660	2181	1850	2693	3108	3445	1902	2585	1790	1832	2738	3470	3569	2364	2897	2128	1107	2524	1786	2384	852	2962	460
München	826	2039	1343	1856	940	588	433	1317	1276	490	737	1525	655	935	1677	1765	393	628	776	1974	1914	981	575	1749	1022	243
Oslo	1268	3440	2578	2478	2338	1031	1723	1926	2285	1705	1403	2713	1901	1556	2288	2387	1308	2057	814	1019	3314	607	1224	2343	1802	344
Paris	502	2554	1071	1206	1771	1053	561	654	586	1350	311	2356	1491	288	1019	1116	573	914	892	2387	2745	1215	485	2336	197	174
Praha	883	1991	1715	2025	889	355	806	1460	1549	333	902	1399	529	1100	1826	1922	510	1081	646	1641	1866	785	692	1405	1230	270
Riga	1873	2830	3093	3062	1728	991	2183	2608	2829	1353	1775	1786	1356	1929	2874	2971	1768	2348	1280	396	2569	912	1575	1045	2153	379
Roma	1662	1267	1366	2651	1296	1163	540	2099	1506	1069	1884	912	1143	2466	2342	2536	1522	1669	2879	1743	1911	1411	2331	1638	252	
Rotterdam	76	2834	1525	1226	1735	693	802	674	1039	1237	151	2286	1411	304	1030	893	456	1177	501	1986	2708	824	257	1977	540	219
Sankt-Peterburg	2424	3381	3645	3601	2279	1711	2648	2913	3249	1904	2389	2366	1907	2543	3272	3375	2319	2899	1893	389	2948	1473	2138	1378	2715	434
Sarajevo	1743	1175	2014	2864	305	1418	1271	2278	2059	723	1702	915	545	1905	2618	2682	1299	1068	1684	2334	1168	1832	1493	1652	2006	317
Skopje	2155	701	2422	3241	439	1687	1767	2682	2463	1007	2113	690	810	2311	3040	3143	1721	1583	2104	2570	787	2117	1910	1645	2404	357
Sofija	2113	798	2380	3193	398	1714	1726	2641	2422	1034	2072	383	769	2270	3033	3102	1680	1542	2063	2476	580	2144	1862	1320	2363	353
Stockholm	1435	3415	2746	2647	2312	1082	1879	2095	2453	1756	1570	2764	1952	1724	2450	2556	1465	2213	985	517	3289	658	1392	1591	1970	361
Strasbourg	602	2170	1130	1540	1314	753	238	988	964	831	434	1906	1067	617	1343	1450	223	703	623	2189	2287	1026	354	2003	688	211
Tallinn	2183	3140	3450	3373	2038	1486	2320	2615	2944	1664	2094	2096	1666	2237	2969	3070	1882	2674	1588	88	2879	1139	1883	1461	2461	410
Tiranë	2217	713	2360	3296	748	1967	1706	2730	2389	1316	2177	923	1119	2332	3101	3206	1785	1482	2170	2879	1015	2360	1967	1859	2432	347
Vilnius	1665	2622	2886	2864	1520	1026	1943	2312	2641	1146	1781	1756	1148	1934	2672	2773	1560	2141	1324	689	2361	919	1580	751	2158	379
Warszawa	1209	2343	2430	2401	1051	590	1448	1849	2185	684	1325	1338	687	1478	2204	2310	1104	1679	868	1062	1943	1009	1124	767	1702	334
Wien	1148	1705	1829	2227	603	686	867	1675	1870	65	1107	1113	243	1305	2031	2137	715	991	976	1754	1580	1116	897	1343	1436	298
Zagreb	1330	1493	1597	2405	395	1053	943	1853	1639	442	1289	982	344	1487	2213	2315	897	759	1280	2121	1368	1472	1079	1444	1580	275

All distances in kilometres. Road/ferry distance chart.

Ljubljana	London	Luxembourg	Lyon	Madrid	Málaga	Marseille	Milano	Minsk	Moskva	München	Oslo	Paris	Praha	Riga	Roma	Rotterdam	Sankt-Peterburg	Sarajevo	Skopje	Sofija	Stockholm	Strasbourg	Tallinn	Tiranë	Vilnius	Warszawa	Wien	Zagreb
1234	532	360	923	1770	2321	1235	1076	1768	2469	826	1268	502	883	1873	1662	76	2424	1743	2155	2113	1435	602	2183	2217	1665	1209	1148	1330
1633	2952	2414	2115	3215	3619	2156	1691	2583	3283	2039	3440	2554	1991	2830	1267	2834	3381	1175	701	798	3415	2170	3140	713	2622	2343	1705	1493
1462	1526	1180	639	627	1031	508	978	2989	3690	1343	2578	1071	1715	3093	1366	1525	3645	2014	2422	2380	2746	1130	3450	2360	2886	2430	1829	1597
2316	776	1347	1672	2474	3009	1983	2057	2957	3660	1856	2478	1206	2025	3062	2651	1226	3601	2864	3241	3193	2647	1540	3373	3396	2864	2401	2227	2405
534	2046	1500	1464	2594	2998	1535	1036	1480	2181	940	2338	1771	889	1728	1296	1735	2279	305	439	398	2312	1314	2038	748	1521	1051	603	395
997	1096	743	1238	2320	2879	1549	1038	1150	1850	588	1031	1053	355	991	1518	693	1711	1418	1687	1714	1082	753	1486	1967	1026	590	686	1053
809	965	453	305	1543	1947	573	318	1992	2693	433	1723	561	806	2183	903	802	2648	1271	1767	1726	1879	238	2320	1706	1943	1448	867	943
1764	191	795	1120	1768	2302	1431	1498	2405	3108	1317	1926	654	1460	2608	2099	674	2913	2278	2682	2641	2095	988	2615	2730	2312	1849	1675	1853
1503	1030	995	588	691	1242	648	1014	2744	3445	1276	2285	586	1549	2829	1506	1039	3249	2059	2463	2422	2453	964	2944	2389	2641	2185	1870	1639
447	1551	1031	1368	2498	2902	1439	940	1201	1902	490	1705	1350	333	1353	1200	1237	1904	723	1007	1034	1756	893	1664	1316	1146	684	65	442
1156	364	230	732	1578	2129	1044	884	1884	2585	737	1403	311	902	1775	1469	151	2389	1702	2113	2072	1570	434	2094	2177	1781	1325	1107	1289
1122	2592	2077	2052	3182	3586	2122	1624	1357	1790	1525	2713	2356	1399	1786	1884	2286	2366	915	690	383	2764	1906	2096	923	1756	1338	1113	982
460	1722	1195	1399	2529	2933	1470	971	1132	1832	655	1901	1491	529	1356	1231	1411	1907	545	810	769	1952	1067	1666	1119	1148	687	273	344
1382	171	414	759	1554	2105	1070	1023	2038	2738	935	1556	288	1100	1929	1608	304	2543	1905	2311	2270	1724	617	2237	2332	1934	1478	1305	1487
2106	546	1145	1479	2146	2717	1792	1751	2770	3470	1677	2288	1019	1826	2874	2342	1030	3272	2618	3040	3033	2450	1343	2969	3101	2672	2204	2031	2213
2183	650	1256	1582	2230	2764	1893	1959	2866	3569	1765	2387	1116	1922	2971	2553	893	3375	2682	3143	3102	2556	1450	3070	3206	2773	2310	2137	2315
801	766	231	700	1835	2341	1012	668	1663	2364	393	1308	573	510	1768	1254	456	2319	1299	1721	1680	1465	223	1882	1785	1560	1104	715	897
623	1364	828	475	1459	1863	400	140	2196	2897	560	2057	914	1081	2348	522	1177	2899	1068	1583	1542	2213	613	2674	1482	2141	1679	991	759
1184	922	623	1140	2169	2720	1452	1109	1428	2128	776	814	892	646	1280	1669	501	1893	1684	2104	2063	985	703	1588	2170	1324	868	976	1280
2126	2407	2106	2625	3654	4205	2937	2424	882	1107	1974	1019	2387	1641	396	2879	1986	389	2334	2570	2476	517	2189	88	2879	689	1062	1754	2121
1508	3019	2449	2438	3567	3971	2508	2009	2006	2524	1914	3314	2745	1866	2569	1743	2708	2948	1168	787	580	3289	2287	2879	1015	2361	1943	1580	1368
1390	1245	944	1463	2492	3043	1775	1432	1104	1786	981	607	1215	785	912	1911	824	1473	1832	2117	2144	658	1026	1139	2360	919	1009	1116	1472
984	575	207	746	1752	2303	1058	826	1683	2384	575	1224	485	692	1575	1411	257	2138	1493	1910	1862	1392	354	1883	1967	1580	1124	897	1079
1560	2379	2048	2480	3629	4033	2570	2071	560	862	1749	2343	2336	1405	1045	2331	1977	1378	1652	1645	1320	1591	2003	1461	1859	751	767	1343	1444
1437	298	531	658	1374	1925	970	1044	2261	2962	1022	1802	197	1320	2153	1638	540	2715	2006	2404	2363	1970	688	2461	2432	2158	1702	1436	1580
2616	2187	2128	1742	626	683	1662	2132	3901	4602	2430	3442	1743	2702	3793	2520	2196	4347	3175	3576	3535	3610	2118	4101	3474	3798	3342	2983	2751
	1538	942	939	2068	2472	1009	510	1588	2289	409	1999	1240	708	1741	770	1251	2245	554	965	924	2038	782	2051	949	1533	1072	383	140
1538		587	918	1720	2254	1229	1260	2202	2905	1120	1724	452	1270	2098	1897	472	2661	2067	2479	2438	1892	786	2098	2542	2109	1646	1473	1651
942	587		517	1634	2158	829	669	1878	2579	523	1427	372	732	1788	1254	355	2352	1494	1906	1864	1595	219	2096	1969	1774	1319	938	1081
939	918	517		1242	1646	317	448	2354	3044	733	1943	468	1080	2265	983	849	2958	1473	1897	1856	2111	495	2573	1823	2251	1795	1304	1072
2068	1720	1634	1242		545	1105	1576	3434	4135	1941	2975	1275	2312	3538	1964	1728	3887	2605	3028	2987	3140	1733	3630	2923	3334	2871	2433	2200
2472	2254	2158	1646	545		1506	1977	3898	4689	2342	3577	1810	2713	4092	2365	2263	4596	2979	3420	3379	3420	2129	4206	3193	3884	3428	2368	2596
1009	1229	829	317	1105	1506		521	2577	3278	1010	2255	779	1382	2729	909	1160	3234	1544	1965	1924	2422	806	2884	1863	2522	2060	1372	1140
510	1260	669	448	1576	1977	521		2077	2778	493	1921	853	865	2229	584	1041	2732	1045	1465	1423	2078	477	2365	1400	2022	1512	872	540
1588	2202	1878	2354	3434	3988	2577	2077		720	1627	1516	2159	1281	484	2338	1800	783	2447	1926	1744	1030	1791	794	2235	191	550	1213	1473
2289	2905	2579	3044	4135	4689	3278	2778	720		2362	1997	2863	1873	917	3041	2503	697	2382	2496	2265	1464	2570	1014	2938	908	1253	1916	2176
409	1120	523	733	1941	2342	1010	493	1627	2362		1588	822	381	1608	928	824	2166	962	1374	1332	1627	364	1916	1435	1594	992	406	549
1999	1724	1427	1943	2975	3577	2255	1921	1516	1997	1588		1703	1382	1069	2507	1302	1341	2430	2713	2741	523	1516	986	2956	1331	1605	1712	2068
1240	452	372	468	1275	1810	779	853	2159	2863	822	1703		1030	2055	1445	458	2619	1805	2204	2163	1873	488	2363	2262	2061	1605	1237	1377
708	1270	732	1080	2312	2713	1382	865	1281	1873	381	1382	1030		1282	1296	917	2044	1334	1427	1044	1752	606	1593	1542	1075	613	333	654
1741	2098	1788	2265	3538	4092	2729	2229	484	917	1608	1069	2055	1282		2482	1905	561	1916	2173	2078	547	1752	310	2482	291	664	1356	1723
770	1897	1254	983	1964	2365	909	584	2338	3041	928	2507	1445	1296	2482		1626	2993	892	1190	1686	2556	1062	2803	975	2284	1823	1135	903
1251	472	355	849	1728	2263	1160	1041	1800	2503	824	1302	458	909	1905	1626		2260	1757	2167	2126	1469	566	2002	2231	1699	1243	1161	1343
2245	2661	2352	2958	3887	4596	3234	2732	783	697	2166	1341	2619	1777	561	2993	2260		2447	2665	2571	899	2317	361	2975	714	1157	1849	2216
554	2067	1494	1473	2605	2979	1544	1045	2447	2382	962	2430	1805	1044	1916	892	1757	2447		459	586	2482	1340	2249	498	1691	1250	759	414
965	2479	1906	1897	3028	3420	1965	1465	1926	2496	1374	2713	2204	1334	2173	1190	2167	2665	459		229	2750	1747	2475	311	1957	1488	1040	828
924	2438	1864	1856	2987	3379	1924	1423	1744	2265	1332	2741	2163	1362	2078	1686	2126	2571	586	229		2709	1706	2389	540	1916	1447	999	787
2038	1892	1595	2111	3140	3677	2422	2078	1030	1464	1627	523	1873	1427	547	2556	1469	899	2482	2750	2709		1674	482	3008	838	1198	1764	2120
782	786	219	495	1733	2129	806	477	1791	2570	364	1516	488	606	1752	1062	566	2317	1340	1747	1706	1674		2090	1815	1767	1311	769	927
2051	2098	2096	2573	3630	4206	2884	2365	794	1014	1916	986	2363	1593	310	2803	2002	361	2249	2475	2389	482	2090		2793	602	975	1667	2034
949	2542	1969	1823	2923	3319	1863	1400	2235	2938	1435	2956	2262	1542	2482	975	2231	2975	498	311	540	3008	1815	2793		2268	1799	1264	910
1533	2109	1774	2251	3334	3884	2522	2022	191	908	1594	1331	2061	1075	291	2284	1699	714	1691	1957	1916	838	1767	602	2268		466	1158	1525
1072	1646	1319	1795	2871	3428	2060	1512	550	1253	992	1605	1605	613	664	1823	1243	1157	1250	1488	1447	1198	1311	975	1799	466		689	1056
383	1473	938	1304	2433	2828	1372	872	1213	1916	406	1712	1237	333	1356	1135	1161	1849	759	1040	999	1764	769	1667	1264	1158	689		376
140	1651	1081	1072	2200	2596	1140	640	1473	2176	549	2068	1377	654	1723	903	1343	2216	414	828	787	2120	927	2034	910	1525	1056	376	

All distances in this chart are in kilometres and include any part of the route taken by ferry.

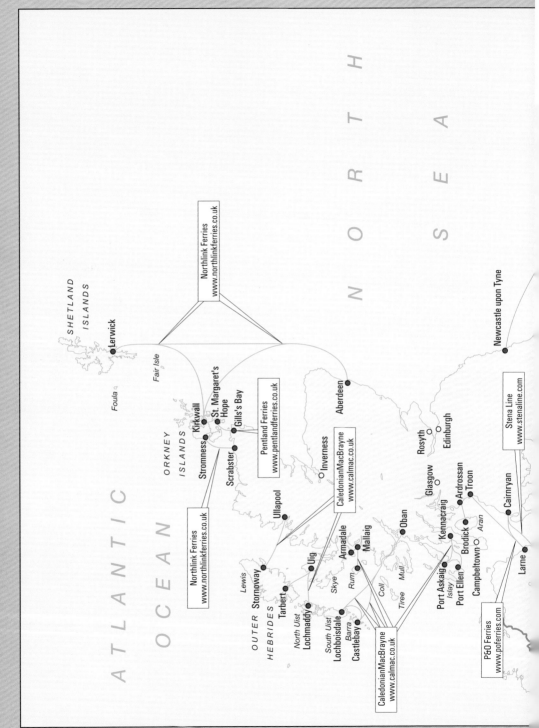

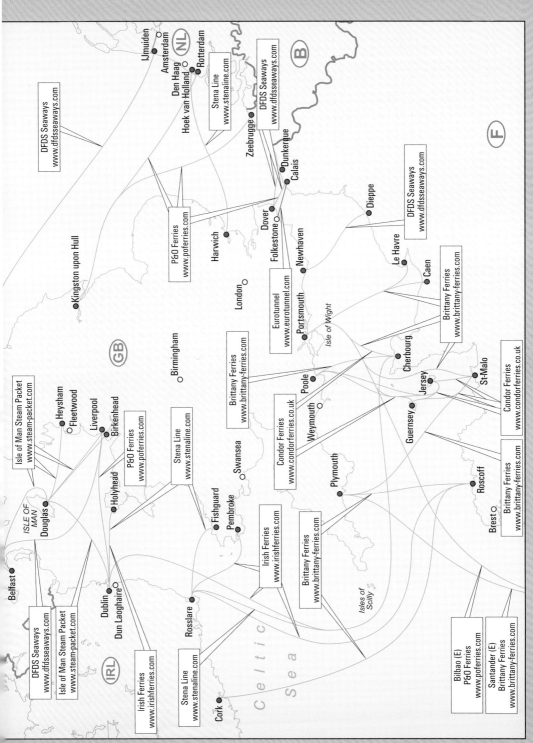

IJmuiden
Amsterdam
NL
Den Haag
Hoek van Holland
Rotterdam

B

F

DFDS Seaways
www.dfdsseaways.com

Stena Line
www.stenaline.com

DFDS Seaways
www.dfdsseaways.com

Zeebrugge
Dunkerque
Calais

Kingston upon Hull

P&O Ferries
www.poferries.com

Harwich

Dover
Folkestone
Newhaven

Dieppe

DFDS Seaways
www.dfdsseaways.com

Le Havre
Caen

Eurotunnel
www.eurotunnel.com

London

Portsmouth

Isle of Wight

Brittany Ferries
www.brittany-ferries.com

Birmingham

GB

Cherbourg

Brittany Ferries
www.brittany-ferries.com

St-Malo

Condor Ferries
www.condorferries.co.uk

Isle of Man Steam Packet
www.steam-packet.com

Heysham
Fleetwood

Liverpool
Birkenhead

Poole

Jersey

Weymouth

Guernsey

Condor Ferries
www.condorferries.co.uk

P&O Ferries
www.poferries.com

Stena Line
www.stenaline.com

Brittany Ferries
www.brittany-ferries.com

Holyhead

Swansea

Plymouth

Roscoff

ISLE OF
MAN
Douglas

Fishguard
Pembroke

Brest

Brittany Ferries
www.brittany-ferries.com

Belfast

Irish Ferries
www.irishferries.com

Brittany Ferries
www.brittany-ferries.com

Isles of
Scilly

DFDS Seaways
www.dfdsseaways.com

Isle of Man Steam Packet
www.steam-packet.com

Dublin
Dun Laoghaire

Rosslare

C e l t i c

IRL

Irish Ferries
www.irishferries.com

Stena Line
www.stenaline.com

S e a

Bilbao (E)
P&O Ferries
www.poferries.com

Santander (E)
Brittany Ferries
www.brittany-ferries.com

Cork

9

(GB)	(D)		(F)	(NL)

Significant points of interest · Herausragende Sehenswürdigkeiten · Curiosités remarquables · Opvallende bezienswaardigheden

(GB)	(D)		(F)	(NL)
Major tourist route	Autoroute		Circuit touristique important	Autoroute
Major tourist railway	Bahnstrecke		Ligne ferroviaire touristique	Spoorwegtraject
Highspeed train	Hochgeschwindigkeitszug		Train à Grande Vitesse	Hogesnelheidstrein
Shipping route	Schiffsroute		Itinéraire de navigation	Scheepsroute
UNESCO World Natural Heritage	UNESCO-Weltnaturerbe		Patrimoine naturel de l'humanité de l'UNESCO	UNESCO wereldnatuurerfgoed
Mountain landscape	Gebirgslandschaft		Paysage de montagne	Berglandschap
Rock landscape	Felslandschaft		Paysage rocheux	Rotslandschap
Ravine/canyon	Schlucht/Canyon		Gorge/canyon	Kloof/canyon
Glacier	Gletscher		Glacier	Gletsjer
Active volcano	Vulkan, aktiv		Volcan actif	Actieve vulkaan
Extinct volcano	Vulkan, erloschen		Volcan éteint	Dode vulkaan
Geyser	Geysir		Geyser	Geiser
Cave	Höhle		Grotte	Grotten
River landscape	Flusslandschaft		Paysage fluvial	Rivierlandschap
Waterfall/rapids	Wasserfall/Stromschnelle		Cascade/rapide	Waterval/stroomversnelling
Lake country	Seenlandschaft		Paysage de lacs	Merenlandschap
Desert	Wüstenlandschaft		Désert	Woestijnlandschap
Fossil site	Fossilienfundstätte		Site fossilifère	Fossielenplaats
Nature park	Naturpark		Parc naturel	Natuurpark
National park (landscape)	Nationalpark (Landschaft)		Parc national (paysage)	Nationaal park (landschap)
National park (flora)	Nationalpark (Flora)		Parc national (flore)	Nationaal park (flora)
National park (fauna)	Nationalpark (Fauna)		Parc national (faune)	Nationaal park (fauna)
National park (culture)	Nationalpark (Kultur)		Parc national (site culturel)	Nationaal park (cultuur)
Biosphere reserve	Biosphärenreservat		Réserve de biosphère	Biosfeerreservaat
Wildlife reserve	Wildreservat		Réserve animale	Wildreservaat
Protected area for sea-lions/seals	Schutzgeb. für Seelöwen/Seehunde		Rés. naturelle d'otaries/de phoques	Besch. geb. v. zeeleeuwen/-honden
Zoo/safari park	Zoo/Safaripark		Zoo/Parc Safari	Dierentuin/safaripark
Coastal landscape	Küstenlandschaft		Paysage côtier	Kustlandschap
Beach	Strand		Plage	Strand
Island	Insel		Île	Eiland
Underwater reserve	Unterwasserreservat		Réserve sous-marine	Onderwaterreservaat
UNESCO World Cultural Heritage	UNESCOWeltkulturerbe		Patrimoine culturel de l'humanité de l'UNESCO	UNESCO wereldcultuurerfgoed
Remarkable city	Außergewöhnliche Metropole		Métropole d'exception	Buitengewone metropolen
Pre-and early history	Vor- und Frühgeschichte		Préhistoire et protohistoire	Prehistorie en vroegste geschiedenis
Prehistoric rockscape	Prähistorische Felsbilder		Peintures rupestres préhistoriques	Prehistorische rotstekeningen
The Ancient Orient	Alter Orient		Ancien Orient	Oud-Oriënt
Minoan site	Minoische Kultur		Civilisation minoenne	Minoïsche cultuur
Phoenecian site	Phönikische Kultur		Civilisation phénicienne	Fenicische cultuur
Etruscan site	Etruskische Kultur		Civilisation étrusque	Etruskische cultuur
Greek antiquity	Griechische Antike		Antiquité grecque	Griekse oudheden
Roman antiquity	Römische Antike		Antiquité romaine	Romeinse oudheden
Vikings	Wikinger		Vikings	Vikingen

Significant points of interest · Herausragende Sehenswürdigkeiten · Curiosités remarquables · Opvallende bezienswaardigheden

GB	D		F	NL
Places of Jewish cultural interest	Jüdische Kulturstätte	✡	Site d'intérêt culturel juif	Joodse cultuurhist. plaatsen
Places of Christian cultural interest	Christliche Kulturstätte	▲	Site d'intérêt culturel chrétien	Christelijke cultuurhist. plaatsen
Places of Islamic cultural interest	Islamische Kulturstätte	☾	Site d'intérêt culturel islamique	Islamitische cultuurhist. plaatsen
Cultural landscape	Kulturlandschaft	∞	Paysage culturel	Cultuurlandschap
Historical city scape	Historisches Stadtbild	▲	Cité historique	Historisch stadsgezicht
Impressive skyline	Imposante Skyline	▥	Gratte-ciel impressionnant	Imposante skyline
Castle/fortress/fort	Burg/Festung/Wehranlage	▉	Château/forteresse/remparts	Burcht/vesting/verdedigingswerk
Palace	Palast/Schloss	▲	Palais	Paleis
Technical/industrial monument	Techn./industrielles Monument	▣	Monument technique/industriel	Technisch/industrieel monument
Disused mine	Bergwerk geschlossen	✕	Mine fermée	Mijn buiten bedrijf
Dam	Staumauer	▨	Barrage	Stuwdam
Impressive lighthouse	Sehenswerter Leuchtturm	▤	Très beau phare	Bezienswaardige vuurtoren
Notable bridge	Herausragende Brücke	▥	Pont remarquable	Opvallende brug
Tomb/grave	Grabmal	▣	Tombeau	Grafmonument
Monument	Denkmal	▮	Monument	Monument
Memorial	Mahnmal	▯	Mémorial	Gedenkteken
Theatre of war/battlefield	Kriegsschauplatz/Schlachtfeld	✕	Champs de bataille	Strijdtoneel/slagvelden
Space telescope	Weltraumteleskop	◩	Télescope astronomique	Ruimtetelescoop
Market	Markt	✿	Marché	Markt
Caravanserai	Karawanserei	▢	Caravansérail	Karavanserai
Festivals	Feste und Festivals	♫	Fêtes et festivals	Feesten en festivals
Museum	Museum	▥	Musée	Museum
Theatre	Theater	◉	Théâtre	Theater
World exhibition/World Fair	Weltausstellung	⊕	Exposition universelle	Wereldtentoonstelling
Olympics	Olympische Spiele	∞	Site olympique	Olympiade
Arena/stadium	Arena/Stadion	⬭	Arène/stade	Arena/stadion
Race track	Rennstrecke	▨	Circuit automobile	Circuit
Golf	Golf	▸	Golf	Golf
Horse racing	Pferdesport	▲	Centre équestre	Paardensport
Skiing	Skigebiet	▧	Station de ski	Skigebied
Sailing	Segeln	▲	Port de plaisance	Zeilen
Wind surfing	Windsurfen	▲	Planche à voile	Surfen
Surfing	Wellenreiten	◀	Surf	Surfriding
Diving	Tauchen	▨	Plongée	Duiken
Canoeing/rafting	Kanu/Rafting	✦	Canoë/rafting	Kanoën/rafting
Waterskiing	Wasserski	▨	Ski nautique	Waterskiën
Beach resort	Badeort	▨	Station balnéaire	Badplaats
Mineral/thermal spa	Mineralbad/Therme	▨	Station hydrothermale	Mineraalbad/thermen
Leisure park	Freizeitpark	◉	Parc de loisirs	Recreatiepark
Casino	Spielcasino	♠	Casino	Casino
Seaport	Seehafen	⚓	Port	Zeehaven

Legend/Zeichenerklärung/Légende/Legenda

(GB)	(D)		(F)	(NL)
Motorway	Autobahn	═══════	Autoroute	Autosnelweg
Toll motorway	Gebührenpflichtige Autobahn	━━━━━━━	Autoroute à péage	Tolautosnelweg
Tunnel motorway	Autobahn mit Tunnel	═⊏ ⊐═	Autoroute avec tunnel	Autosnelweg met tunnel
Motorway under construction	Autobahn im Bau	═ ═ ═ ═ ═	Autoroute en construction	Autosnelweg in aanleg
Dual carriageway	4-oder mehrspurige Straße	═══════	Double chaussée	Hoofdroute, tweebaans
Tunnel dual carriageway	Tunnel mehrspurige Straße	═⊏ ⊐═	Tunnel double chaussée	Hoofdroute, tweebaans met tunnel
Dual carriageway under construction	4-oder mehrspurige Straße im Bau	═ ═ ═ ═ ═	Double chaussée en construction	Hoofdroute, tweebaans in aanleg
Primary route	Fernstraße	━━━━━━	Route primaire	Hoofdroute
Tunnel primary route	Fernstraßentunnel	━⊏ ⊐━	Route primaire	Hoofdroute met tunnel
Primary route under construction	Fernstraße im Bau	▪ ▪ ▪ ▪ ▪	Route primaire en construction	Hoofdroute in aanleg
Important main road	Wichtige Hauptstraße	━━━━━━	Route principale importante	Belangrijke verbindingsweg
Main road	Hauptstraße	━━━━━	Route départementale	Regionale verbindingsweg
Secondary road	Nebenstraße	────────	Route secondaire	Overige wegen
Track	Piste	────	Piste	Onverharde weg
Touristic/historic route	Touristenstraße	▬▬▬▬▬▬▬	Route touristique	Toeristische route
Railway	Eisenbahn	─┼─┼─	Chemin de fer	Spoorweg
Distances in kilometres (within UK in miles)	Kilometrierung (in UK in Meilen)	◥ 25 ◤	Distances kilométriques (au sein du RU en miles)	Afstand in km (in het VK in mijlen)
Ferry	Autofähre	───────	Ferry	Veerdienst
European road number	Europastraßennummer	E20	Numéro des routes européennes	Nummering Europaroutes
Motorway number	Autobahnnummer	10 M3 A16	Numéros des autoroutes	Nummering Autosnelwegen
Other road numbers	Andere Straßennummern	80 56 3 62	Autre numéro de routes	Wegnummers
Major airport	Wichtiger Flughafen	✈	Grand aéroport	Belangrijke luchthaven
Airport	Flughafen	✈	Aéroport	Luchthaven
International boundary	Staatsgrenze	━ ▪ ━ ▪ ━	Frontière de l'État	Staatsgrens
Administrative boundary	Bundesland-/Provinzgrenze	━ ━ ━ ━	Limite administrative	Deelstaat- en provinciegrens
National or nature park	National- und Naturpark	▭	Parc national, parc naturel	Nationaal park, natuurpark
Restricted area	Sperrgebiet	▭	Zone restreinte	Verboden gebied
Mountain summit with height in metres	Berg mit Höhenangabe in Metern	*Grand Ballon* 1424 ▲	Sommet avec cote d'altitude	Bergnaam met hoogte-indicatie in meters
Place of interest	Sehenswerter Ort	**Oxford**	Ville très intéressante	Bezienswaardig

12

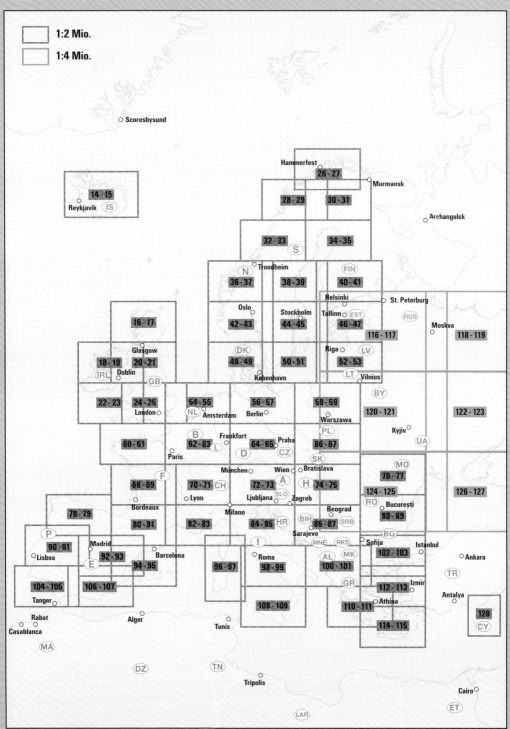

1:2 Mio.

1:4 Mio.

Scoresbysund

Hammerfest

26 - 27

Murmansk

28 - 29   30 - 31

Archangelsk

14 - 15
Reykjavik IS

32 - 33   34 - 35

S

Trondheim

N   38 - 39

FIN

36 - 37

40 - 41

Helsinki

St. Peterburg

16 - 17

Oslo

Stockholm

Tallinn EST

RUS   Moskva

42 - 43   44 - 45

46 - 47

116 - 117   118 - 119

Glasgow

DK

Riga   LV

Dublin

18 - 19 20 - 21

48 - 49   50 - 51

52 - 53

IRL

GB

København

LT   Vilnius

22 - 23 24 - 25

54 - 55   56 - 57

58 - 59

BY

122 - 123

London

NL Amsterdam   Berlin

Warszawa

120 - 121

Kyjiv

B Frankfurt

Praha

PL

UA

60 - 61

62 - 63

64 - 65

66 - 67

L

D

CZ

Paris

SK

München   Wien Bratislava

MD

76 - 77

68 - 69

F

70 - 71 CH

72 - 73

A

H 74 - 75

124 - 125   126 - 127

Lyon

Ljubljana SLO Zagreb

RO Bucureşti

Bordeaux

Beograd

88 - 89

78 - 79

80 - 81

82 - 83

84 - 85 HR

BIH 86 - 87 SRB

Milano

Sarajevo

BG

P

Madrid

I

MNE   RKS

Sofija   Istanbul

90 - 91

Barcelona

AL MK

102 - 103

Lisboa

92 - 93

Roma

100 - 101

Ankara

E

94 - 95

96 - 97

98 - 99

GR

TR

104 - 105 106 - 107

112 - 113 Izmir

Tanger

108 - 109

110 - 111 Athína

Antalya

Rabat

Alger

114 - 115

128

Casablanca

Tunis

CY

MA

DZ

TN

Tripolis

Cairo

LAR

ET

13

Scale 1:2 250 000

0 10 20 30 kilometres
0 10 20 miles

Ba   Bb   Bc   Bd

Straumnes

Vestfirðir

Suðureyri   Hornbjarg
Sæból   Bolungarvík   Breiðaskarðs-hnúkur
Mýrar   Ísafjörður   709
Neðribær   60 IFJ
Breiðavík   TEY   48   Súðavík   Drangajökull
Bjargtangar   Þingeyri   957   925
Patreksfjörður   Hrafnseyri   Ögur
Hnjótur   Bíldudalur   64   178   Reykjanes
Látrabjarg   BÍU   Gláma   Munaðarnes
Reykjafjörður   Dynjandifoss   61   Árnes
663   (Fjallfoss)   130   Gjögur
Hagi   Reiphólsfjöll   53
881   121
Gufudalur   Hólmavík   Skagi
Breiðafjörður   Flatey   Húnaflói   Hof
Reykhólar   Drangsnes
Öndverðarnes   Hellissandur   Króksfjarðarnes   26   Skagaströnd
Ólafsvík   Staðarhóll   Kollafjarðarnes
Þjóðgarðurinn   SYK   Hindisvík   Blönduós
Snæfellsjökull   1446   Stykkishólmur   Hafratindur   60   Þingeyrar   BLO
Tröllakirkja   51   Grundarfjörður   923   Staðarfell   57   1052
Malarrif   Brokey   Prestbakki   Hvammstangi   998   52   50
Hellnar   Snæfellsnes   Buðardalur   Laugarbakki   Svinavatn
Búðir   930   Gerðuberg   Borðeyri   Kolufoss
54   72   57   Eiríkstaðir   Brú   33   Dalfoss
Barðagrunn   820   Staðarskáli   1138
Akrar   82   21   Blöndulón
Mýrar   Hvammur   47
Hjörsey   34   110
Faxaflói   1   Hraunfossar   Einksjökull
Borgarnes   Hvanneyri   Viðgelmir   1675
Skarðshéði   Reykholt   Langjökull
Akranes   45   Húsafell   1420
Garðskagi   Garður   1041   Pyrill   Hveravellir
Sandgerði   Svið   Glymur   Kjölur   Hofsjökull
KEF   Keflavík   Hofsvík   Skjaldbreiður   92   1800
Hafnir   Esja   1060   Hvítárvatn   Snækollur
Hafnaberg   Hafnarfjörður   914   Þingvellir   1477   Í S
Bláa lónið   46   Kópavogur   Mosfellsbær   Þjóðgarðurinn   1204   Jökulkvísl
Reykjanestá   Brúnir   Pingvellir   Strokkur   Hvanngiljafoss   Kvíslavatn
Grindavík   Kleifarvatn   36   Laugarvatn   Geysir   Gullfoss
Heiðin há   44   Reykholt   Vatnleysufoss   141
Strandarkirkja   19   12   Hveragerði   66   Gljúfurleitarfoss
Þorlákshöfn   Selfoss   67   Flúðir   Þórisvatn
Eyrarbakki   Skálholt   84   Stöng   Tangafoss
Stokkseyri   32   Þjóðveldisbærinn
Eyrarbakkabugur   Holt   62   Hekla
Þykkvibær   Hella   1491
Hvolsvöllur   Keldur   Friðland að   Tungnaá
Kross   Fjallabaki   Landmannalaugar   Langisjór
1462   Kaldaklofsfjöll   Laki
Heimaey   1666   1278   Eldgjá
Vestmannaeyjar   98   Þórsmörk
Surtsey   Heimaey   Mýrdalsjökull   Prestbakki
VEY   Skógafoss   Systrafoss
Eyjafjalladjúp   1450   Kirkjubæjarklaustur
Skógar   80
ATLANTIC   Dyrhólaey   Vík   Hraungerði
OCEAN   Mýrnatangi

Denmark Strait

Arnarfjörður   Skorargrunn

Breiðafjörður

Ba   Bb   Bc   Bd

14

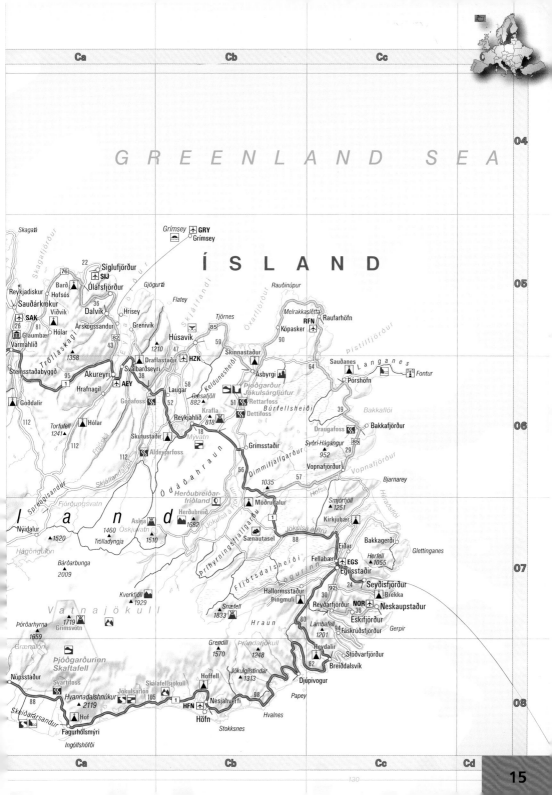

Scale 1:2 000 000

0 10 20 30 kilometres

0 10 20 miles

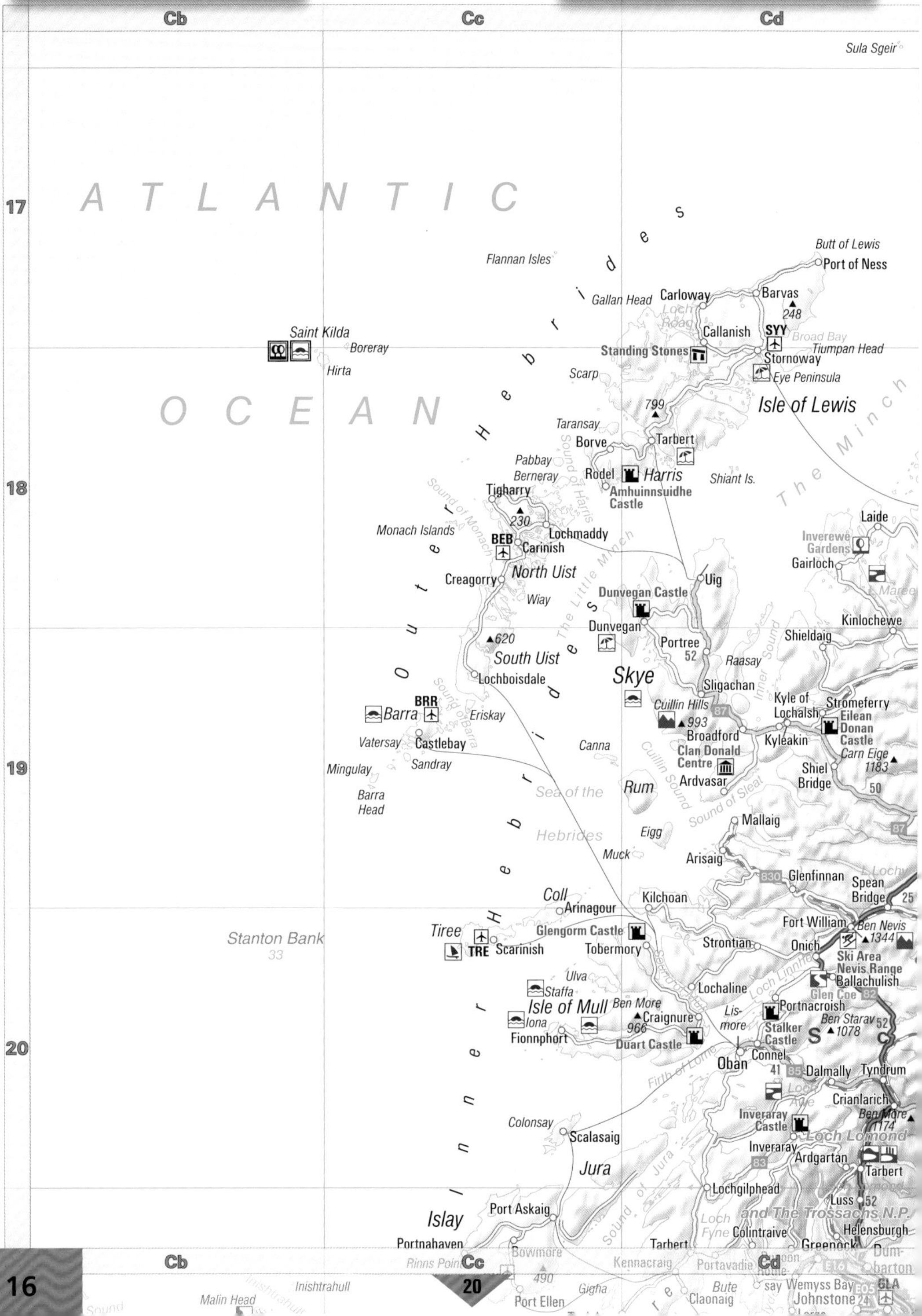

Cb
Cc
Cd
17
18
19
20
Sula Sgeir
ATLANTIC
OCEAN
Outer Hebrides
Inner Hebrides
Flannan Isles
Butt of Lewis
Port of Ness
Gallan Head
Carloway
Loch Roag
Barvas
248
Callanish
SYY
Broad Bay
Tiumpan Head
Standing Stones
Stornoway
Eye Peninsula
Saint Kilda
Boreray
Hirta
Scarp
799
Isle of Lewis
The Minch
Taransay
Borve
Tarbert
Sound of Harris
Pabbay
Berneray
Rodel
Harris
Shiant Is.
Amhuinnsuidhe Castle
Tigharry
Sound of Monach
230
Lochmaddy
Monach Islands
BEB
Carinish
The Little Minch
Laide
Inverewe Gardens
Gairloch
Creagorry
North Uist
Uig
Loch Maree
Wiay
Dunvegan Castle
Kinlochewe
Dunvegan
Shieldaig
620
Portree
52
South Uist
Raasay
Inner Sound
Lochboisdale
Skye
Sligachan
BRR
Barra
Sound of Barra
Eriskay
Cuillin Hills
993
87
Kyle of Lochalsh
Stromeferry
Eilean Donan Castle
Broadford
Kyleakin
Vatersay
Castlebay
Canna
Clan Donald Centre
Carn Eige
1183
Mingulay
Sandray
Cuillin Sound
Shiel Bridge
Ardvasar
Rum
50
Barra Head
Sea of the Hebrides
Sound of Sleat
Mallaig
Eigg
87
Muck
Arisaig
830
Glenfinnan
Loch Lochy
Spean Bridge
Coll
Arinagour
Kilchoan
25
Fort William
Ben Nevis
1344
Stanton Bank
33
Tiree
TRE
Scarinish
Glengorm Castle
Tobermory
Strontian
Onich
Ski Area Nevis Range
Ballachulish
Sound of Mull
Loch Linnhe
Glen Coe
82
Ulva
Staffa
Lochaline
Portnacroish
Isle of Mull
Ben More
966
Craignure
Iona
Lismore
Stalker Castle
Ben Starav
1078
52
Fionnphort
Duart Castle
Connel
Oban
41
85
Dalmally
Tyndrum
Firth of Lorne
Loch Awe
Crianlarich
Inveraray Castle
Ben More
1174
Loch Lomond
Colonsay
Scalasaig
Inveraray
Ardgartan
Jura
Sound of Jura
83
Tarbert
Lochgilphead
Luss
52
Loch Fyne
and The Trossachs N.P.
Islay
Port Askaig
Sound of Islay
Colintraive
Helensburgh
Portnahaven
Tarbert
Greenock
Dumbarton
Rinns Point
Bowmore
Kennacraig
Portavadie
Dunoon
E16
490
Inishtrahull
Gigha
Bute
Wemyss Bay
E05
GLA
Malin Head
Port Ellen
Claonaig
Johnstone
24
20

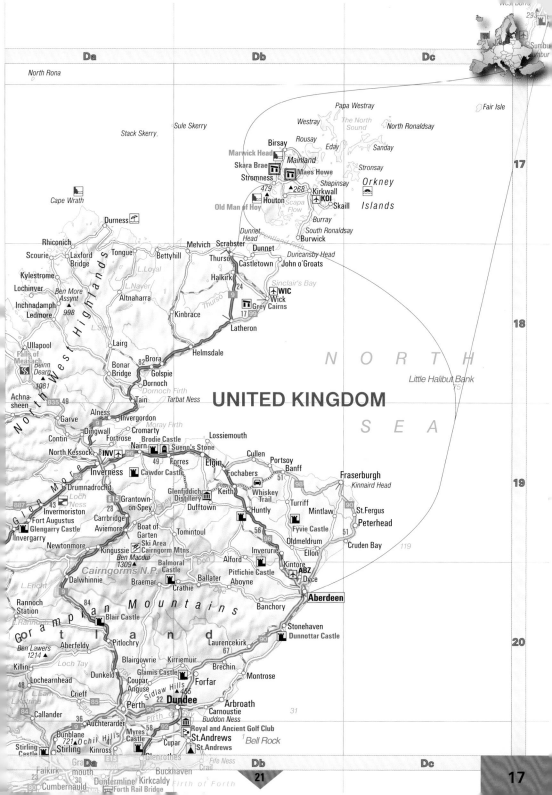

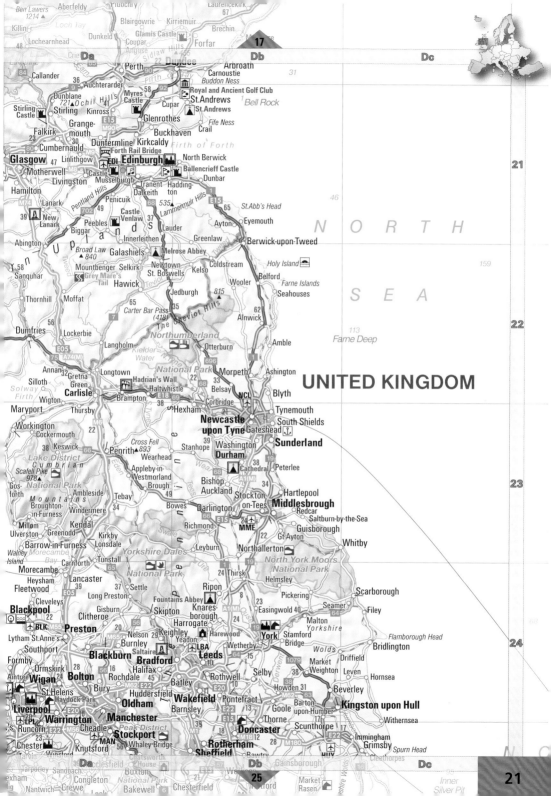

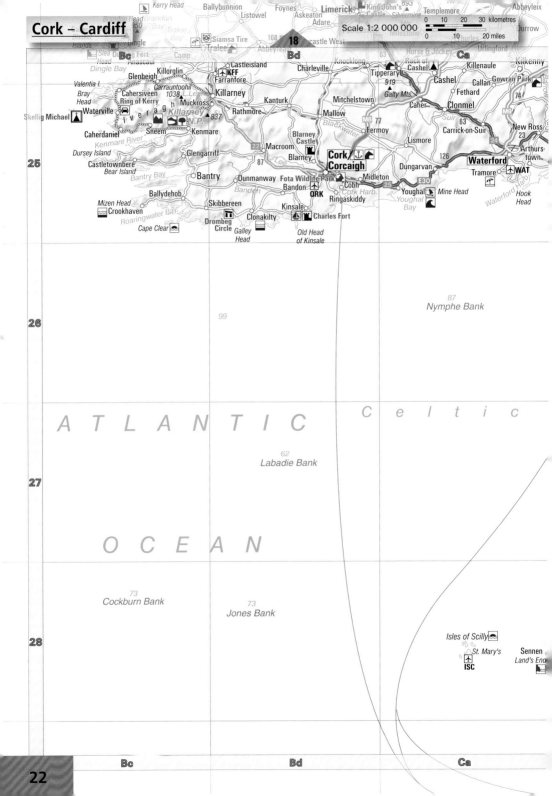

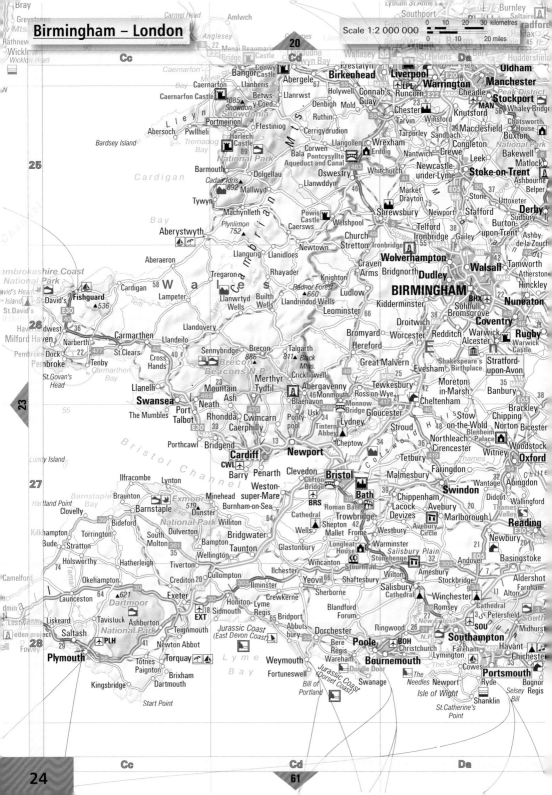

Scale 1:2 000 000

0 10 20 30 kilometres
0 10 20 miles

Fd **Ga** **Gb**

2639

NORWEGIAN

SEA

Fjordgård
Bergsfjord
Gryllefjord
Andenes · Gunnfarnes · Senja
Bleik · ANX
Åndalsnes nasjonalpark
Andøya · Andfjorden
Nordmela
Myre · Skrolsvika · Stonglandet · Dyrøya
Risøyhamn · Bjarkøya · Sandsøya
Grøtavær · Grytøya · Andørja · Reifet
Myre · Myrland · Bjørna · Årbostad
Langøya · Harstad · Rolla · Hamnvik
Breivika · Myrlandshaugen
Straumsnes · Sortland · Flesnes · 26 53 · Sørrollnes · Grov
Steine · Revsnes · Evenskjer
Stokmarknes · 74 · Hinnøya · 65 · 59
SKN · Møysalen · Gullesfjordbotn · Bogen · Narvik
Hadseløya · Melbu · 1262 E10 · Tjeldøya · EVE · NVK
Fiskebøl · Hanøy 50 Lødingen · Tjeldnes
Austvågøya · 146 · Digermulen · Kjeldebotn
Vestvågøy · 135 · Svolvær · Rindbø · 88 · Ballangen
LKN · Leknes · SVJ · Kabelvåg · Tranøya · NORGE
Flakstad · Stamsund · Henningsvær · Bognes · Skarberget
Moskenesøya · Ballstad · Hamarøya · Ulvsvåg · Kjøpsvik
Reine · Flakstadøya · Skutvika · Presteid · Drag · Skarstekojan · Bjørntoppen 1520
Sørvågen · Engeløya · Finnøya · Tømmerneset
Steigen · Åstad · Rautåive 1578 · Ritsem
Værøy · Sørland · Helnessund · Nordfold · Mørsvik · Reinoksfjellet 1472 · Akka 2016
RET · Røst · Laukvika · 1361 · 160 · Elvkroken · Rago nasjonalpark · Padjelanta
Misten · Tårnvika · Røsvik · Staloluokta
Helligvær · Landegode · Festvåg · Straumen · Staloluokta fjällstation
Bodø · 63 · E06 · Blåmannsisen · nationalpark
BOO · Løding · Fauske · Sulitjelma
Saltstraumen · Straumen · Sulitjelma 1914 · Tsähkkok · Tärrekaise 1829
Sandhornøy · Horsdal · Rognan · 61 · Nuort-Saulo 1768 · Mavas
Fugløya · Tverrvika · Vesterli · 1564
Inndyr · 1405 · Riepentjåkkå 1551
Meløya · Ørnes · Glomfjord · Ørfjellet · Storjord 1709 · 1627
Åmnøya · Forøya · Leirmoen · 1751 · Guikultjårro 1276 · 100
Vågaholmen · Storjorda · Saltfjellet-Svartisen nasjonalpark · Vuoggatjålme
Agskardet · Snøtinden 1594 · Saltfjellet 1416 · Riebnas
Nesøya · Jektvika · 1572 · Stødi
Trænstaven · Melfjorden
Kilboghamn · Lurøya · Grønnfjell

Fd **Ga** 33 **Gb**
28
Stokkvågen · MQN

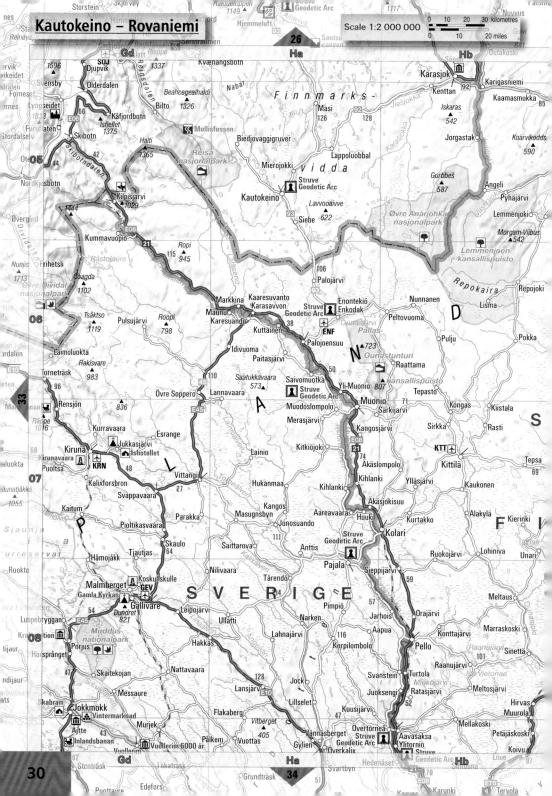

Scale 1:2 000 000

Scale 1:2 000 000

0 10 20 30 kilometres
0 10 20 miles

Fb **Fc** **Fd**

Åmnoy
Vågaholmen

Nesøya
Trænstaven
Kilboghamn
Lurøya
Stokkvågen
Tomma

09 *N O R W E G I A N*
Nordøyvågen Nesna
Dønna Bjørn Låveng
Sandnessjøen
Silvalen
SSJ Alsta Sju søstre

Tjøtta Mosjøen
MJF

S E A
Gladstad Igerøy
Vega Forvika/Vevelstad
Vegaøyan Lakfors
Ylvingen Ånddalsvågen
Horn
Brønnøysund
BNN Hommelstø Blåfjelle
Berg Sømna 92 1293
10 Tosbotn

N O R G E
Vennesund
Holm Majaklumpen
Leka Skei 1021
Sør-Gutvika Terråk
Foldereid Blåfjellet
905 13D
Valøy Namsskogan
Vikna Rørvik
RVK Kolvereid Kongsmoen
Salsbruket **E06**
96 Abelvær Lund
11 Halten Bank Jøa
Utvorda Høylandet Skorovatn
Otterøya
Hamnes Ranemsletta Harran
Sør-Flatanger Grong
Namsos 45 Nyneset 70 **74**
OSY 8
Osen Bangsund Formofoss Bukvassfjellet
Sjøåsen 1004

Hofstad Tørring 68 Snåsa
Gressåmoen
Finnvollheia nasjonalpark
Harsvika 675 Malm Prestesætra Blåfjell
1332
12 Follafors Bølareinen Steinkjer Skjækerhatten
Å Skjelstad 1139
Lysøysundet 516 28 Straumen Sparbu Skäcker-
Hellesvikan fjällen
Fröya Ytterøy Verdalsøra Åkran Anjeskutan Sösjö
Titran Hammarvika Botngård Rødsjøen Skogn 1201 Kolåsen
Brekstad Leksvik Vuku Søre Moen Anjan
Fillan Levanger
Valset Rissa Frosta Markabygd 53 Sandvika
Hopen Hitra Vanvikan Kråfjell Skalstugan
Forsnes Sondstad Rørvika Skatval Okkelberg 905 Tänn- Åre-
Smøla Selbekken Vikhammer Stjørdal E06 forsen Duved Kall
Korsvoll Snillfjord Trondheim **TRD** Meråker Middagsfjället Åre
Dyrnes Hommelvik Kopperå 912

Aure Kyrksæterøra Orkanger Melhus Storlien Duved Järpe
Vinje Fannrem Lstad Annn Undersåker
Svorkmo Korsvegen Selbu Ramfjellet Ånnsjön

Scale 1:2 000 000

0 10 20 30 kilometres
0 10   20 miles

Ec   Ed   Fa

N O R W E G I A N

S E A

13

14

15

16

Dyrnes
Tømmervåg
Kristiansund KSU
Reinsvik Frei
Averøya
Bud Eide
Elnesvågen Nordmøre
Steinshamn
Gossen Molde Hjelset Eidsvåg
Austnes MOL 63 Kleive
Nordøyane Otrøy Vestnes Sølsnes
AES Midsund Åfarnes
Vigra Brattvåg Tomrefjord Isfjorden
Godøy Ålesund Vatne Andalsnes
Atlanterhavsparken Spjelkavik E39 E136 Sjøholt Tresfjord 60 Trolltindan
Runde Langevåg Sykkylven Mardalen
Hareid Stordalen 1797
Fosnavåg Ulsteinvik Stranda Troll- Øverdalen
Stad Sandsøy Vartdal Linge stigen
Hurtigruten Sørøyane Ørsta Sunnmøre Sæbø Leknes Eidsdalen Puttega Stuguflåten
Leikanger Årvik Volda 1999
Koparnes HOV Kvitegga Sjusystre
Vågsøy Selje Folkestad 1691 Hellesylt Geiranger
Raudeberg Aheim Geirangerfjorden
Måløy 52 Stårheim Sjung- 16 Grotli 73
Bremangerlandet dalsvatn Stryn 50 Videsæter
Oldeide Isane Nordfjordeid 44 N O
Frøya Svelgen Staume Olden Sotasæter
Kalvåg 1385 SDN Byrkjelo Jostedals-
Hovden Norddal Sandane Briksdal breen 1958 Fåberg Galdhøpiggen
Skorpa Florø 59 Skei nasjonalpark Sognefjellsvegen 2469
Askrova FRO Eikefjord 67 Bruheim Skjolden Jotunheimen
Svanøy Naustdal 43 Nes Jotun
Askvoll Dale FDE Norsk Bre- Gaupne Øvre Årdal
Atløy Sande museum Fjærland Urnes Årdalstangen
Førde 63 Lustrafjorden Kaupanger Høgeset
Buefjorden Sula Vadheim Høyanger Hella Sogndal 140 Øye
Krakhella Rysjedalsvika Balestrand Leikanger SOG 30 Lærdalsøyri Høgeloft
Ytre Sula Lavik 55 Vangsnes 1920
175 Rutledalen Ytre Oppedal Ortnevik Viksøyri Borlaug Borgund 52
Eivindvik 162 13 1670 Aurlands- Store Hånos stavkirke
Hurtigruten Leirvåg Nærøyfjorden vangen 1836
Fedje Halsvik Gudvangen 109
Fosnøy Duesund Vinje Flåmsbana Flåm
Lindås Masfjorden Myrdal Geilo
Alvøy Radøy Nesheim 1412 Bergensbanen Å
Holsnøy Manger Evanger Finse Hol
Blomøy Herdla Stamnes 40 Voss 37 Geilo 50
Toftøy Tyssebotn Bergensbanen Ulvik
Solsvik Salhus Lonevåg Dale 13 Granvin Finse
Bryggen Kvanndal Haugastøl
291 Ytre Arna E16 Ålvik Steinsdals- 100
Kleppestø Indre Arna 60 fossen Brimnes Eidfjord Fossli
Bergen 137 Espeland Utne Kinsarvik Vøringsfossen Dagali
BGO 7 Lofthus Dyranut 40
Sotra Nesttun Norheimsund Jondal Hårteigen Skrekken
Klokkarvik Fana 28 Strandebarm 1690 1429
Hatrik E39 Hardanger-
Osøyro Fusa Hardangervidda
Korsfjorden Sævareid 98 nasjonalpark
Austevoll Gjermundshamn Tyssedal
Huftarøy 1660 Odda
Tysnes strand
Sandvikvåg

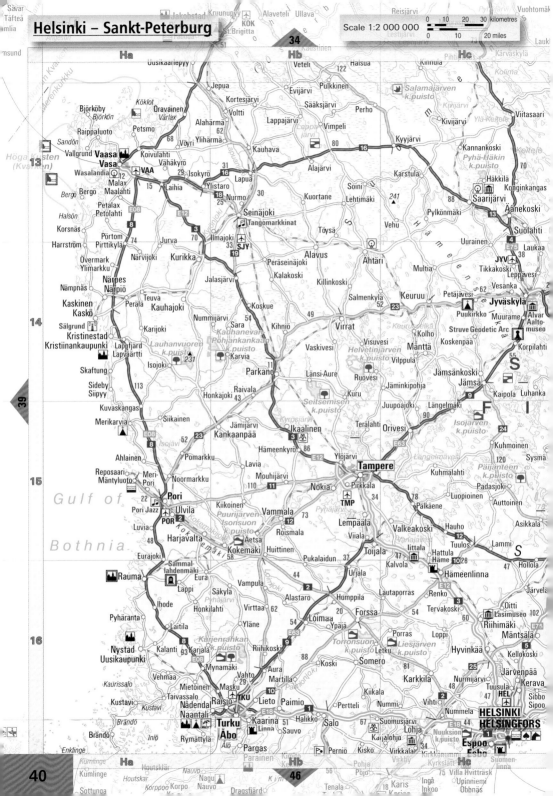

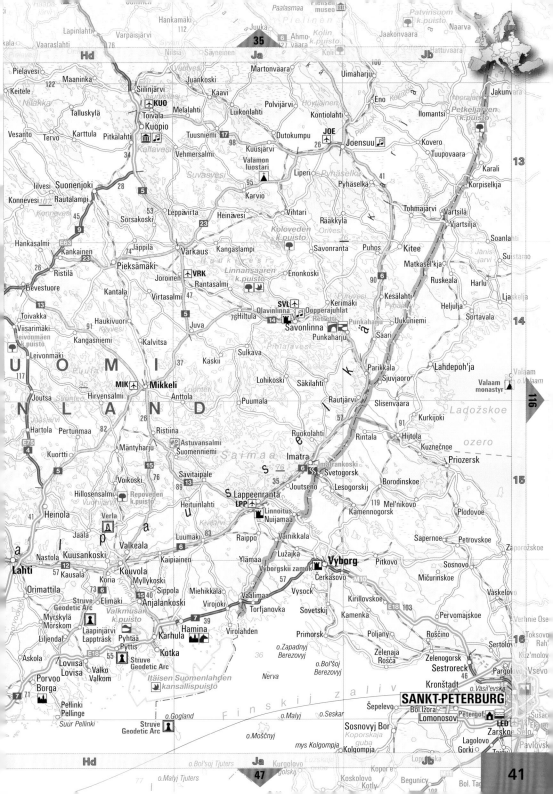

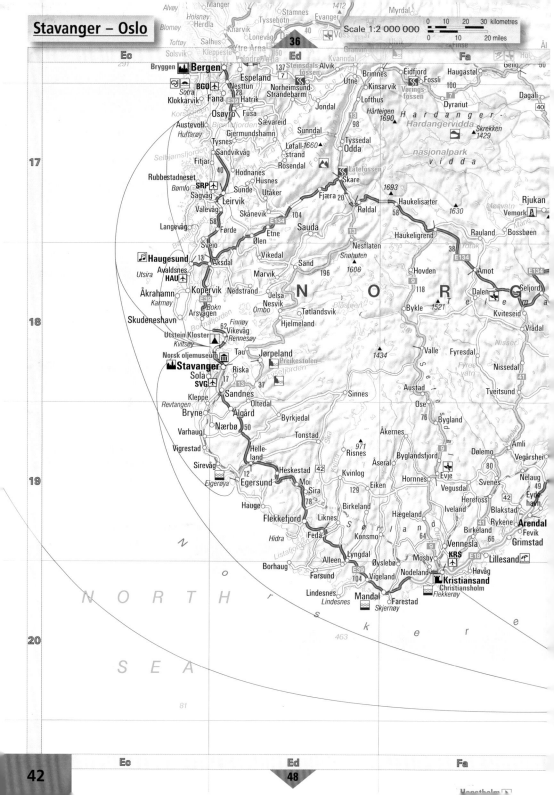

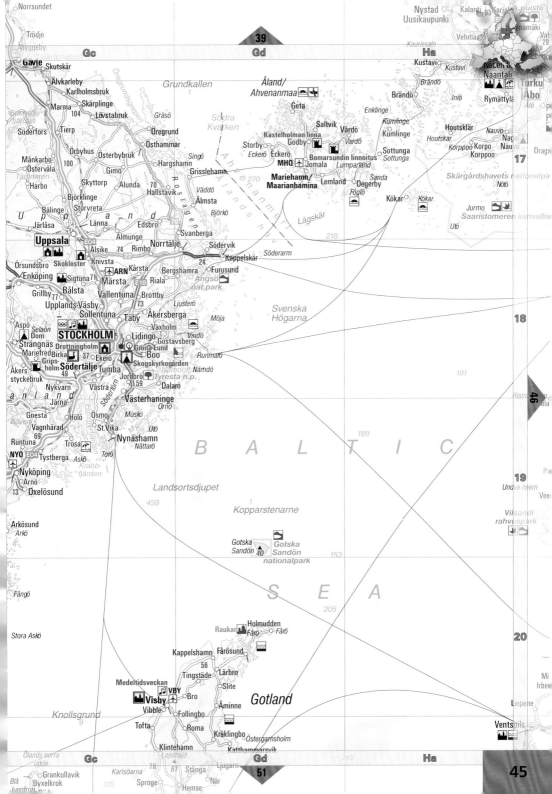

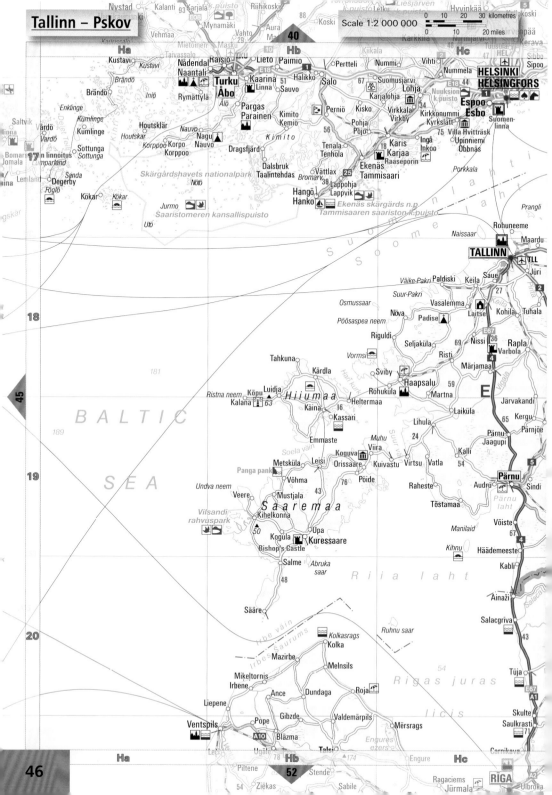

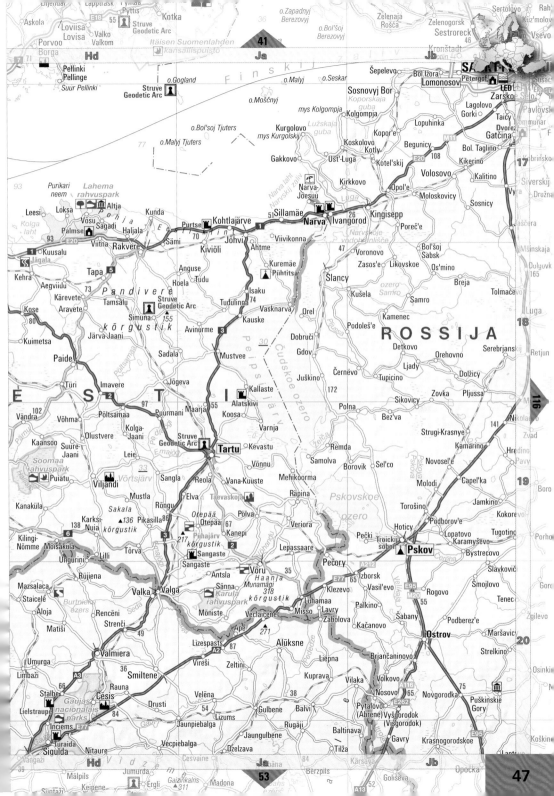

Scale 1:2 000 000

0   10   20   30 kilometres
0   10   20 miles

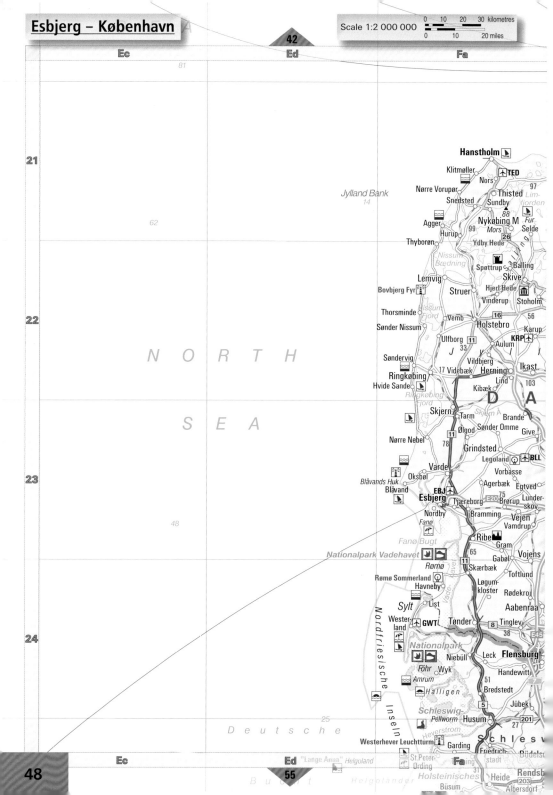

Ec   Ed   Fa

81

Hanstholm

Klitmøller
Nørre Vorupør   Nors   TED
Snedsted   Sundby   Thisted   Lim-
            88   fjorden   97
Agger   Nykøbing M   Fur   Selde
        Hurup   Mors   26
Thyborøn   Ydby Hede
                    99
Jylland Bank   Spøttrup   Balling
14   Skive

Lemvig   Hjerl Hede
Bovbjerg Fyr   Struer   Vinderup   Stoholm

Thorsminde   Vemb   Holstebro   16   56
Sønder Nissum   Karup
Ulfborg   11   Aulum   KRP

Søndervig   17 Videbæk   Vildbjerg   Ikast
Ringkøbing   Herning
Hvide Sande   Lind   103
                    Kibæk

Skjern   Tarm   Brande
        11   Sønder Omme   Give
Nørre Nebel   Ølgod   78
            Grindsted
Varde   Legoland   BLL
        Oksbøl   Vorbasse
Blåvands Huk   Agerbæk   Egtved
    Blåvand   75
        EBJ   Lunder-
    Esbjerg   Tjæreborg   E20   Brørup   skov
    Nordby   Vejen
    Fanø   Bramming   Vamdrup
            Ribe   Gram
Fanø Bugt   65   Gabøl   Vojens
Nationalpark Vadehavet   11
                Skærbæk   Toftlund
        Rømø   Løgum-
Rømø Sommerland   kloster   Rødekro
    Havneby
Sylt   List   Aabenraa
    Wester-   Tønder   Tinglev
    land   GWT   8   38   E45

Nationalpark   Niebüll   Leck   Flensburg
Föhr   Wyk   Handewitt
    Amrum   51
    Halligen   Bredstedt
                    Jübek
Schleswig-   Husum   201
    Pellworm   27
Westerhever Leuchtturm   Garding   Schlesw
        Lange Anna   Helgoland   Friedrich-   Büdelsd
Ec   St.Peter-   stadt   31
        Ording   Fa   Rendsb
Ed   55   Heide   203
Büsum   Heligoländer   Holsteinisches   Albersdorf

N O R T H

S E A

62

48

25

Deutsche

Nordfriesische   Inseln

Heverstrom

Bucht

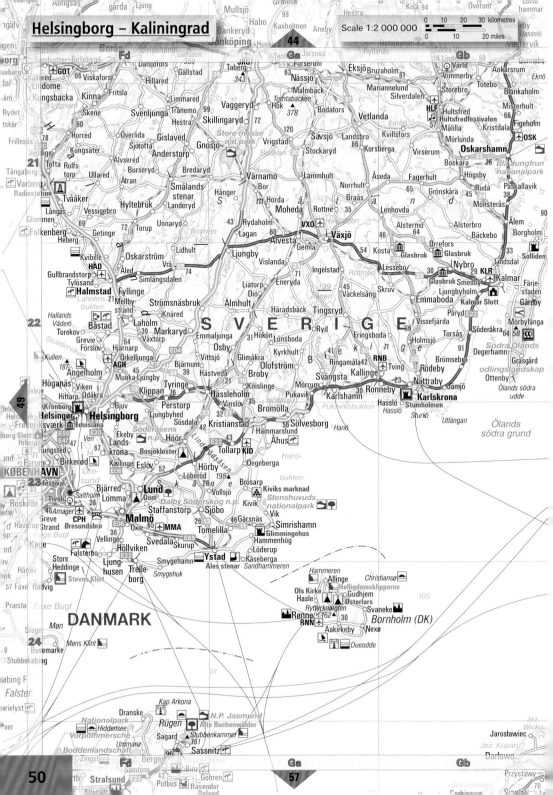

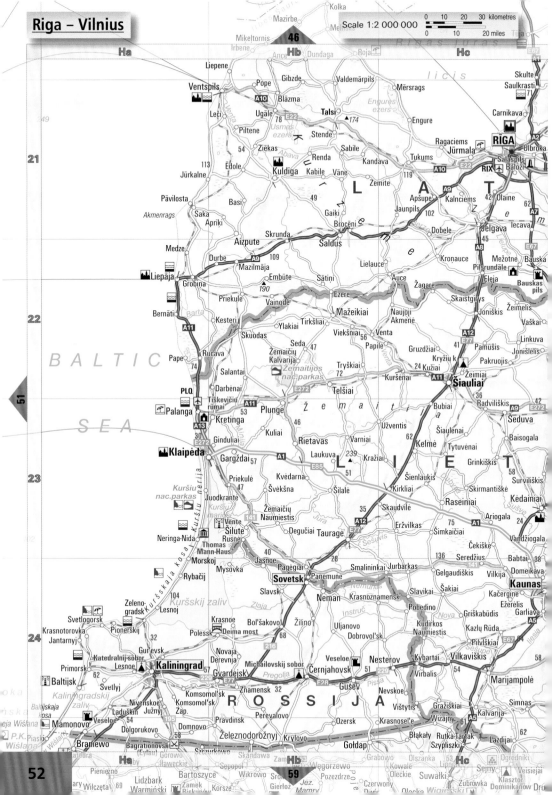

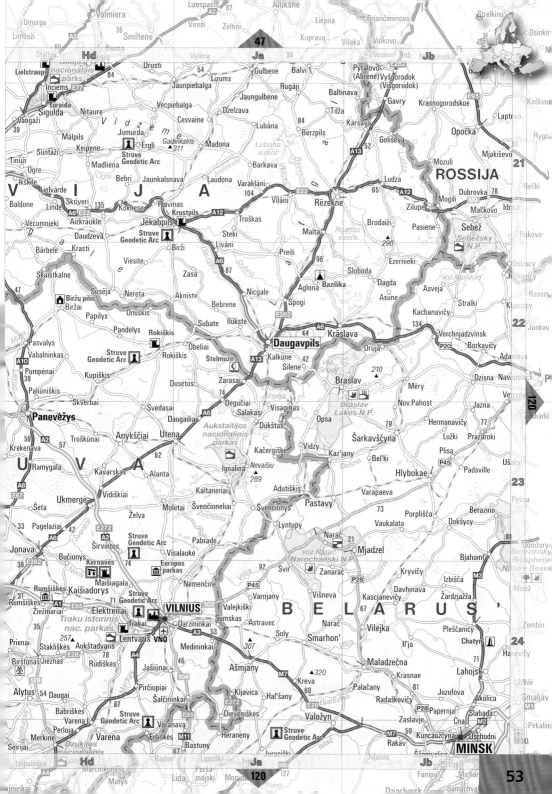

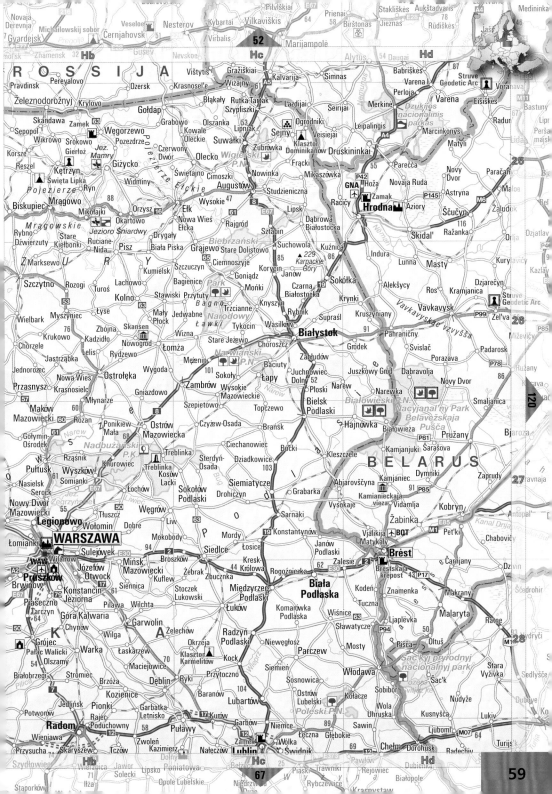

St. Mary's   Sennen   Camborne   Marazion   Penryn   St.Austell   Fowey   29   Newton Abbot
Land's End   St.Michael's Mount   Helston   Plymouth   Kingsbridge   Brixham   Dartmouth
Penzance   Mount's Bay

Lizard Point   Start Point

A T L A N T I C   122   87

O C E A N   Gu   St.P

Ouessant   Les Abers   Côte de Granit Rose
Plouguerneau   Brignogan-Plages   Roscoff   Cairn de Barnenez   Trégastel-Plage   Perros-Guirec   Tréguier   Bréhat
Ploudalmézeau   Plouescat   St-Pol-de-Léon   Plougasnou   Lannion   Paimpol
Plabennec   Lesneven   Carantec   Plestin-les-Grèves   Bégard   Plouha   St-Quay-Portrieux   Baie de
St-Renan   Guipavas   Landivisiau   Morlaix   Guingamp   Pléneuf-Val-André   Erquy   Cô
Le Conquet   Océanopolis   Enclos paroissial   St-Thégonnec   N12   Bourbriac   Plouagat   St-Brieuc   Lamb
Pte.de St-Mathieu   Landerneau   Guimiliau   102   E50   Callac   35   St-Brieuc   le
Camaret-sur-Mer   Brest   N165   Sizun   Enclos paroissial   Maël-Carhaix   Quintin   Ploeuc-sur-Lié   E50
Fortifications de Vauban   Le Faou   Huelgoat   Carhaix-Plouguer   Corlay   700   Lamb
Pte.de Penhir   Presqu'île de Crozon   46   Pleyben   Châteaulin   104   Rostrenen   Mur-de-Bretagne   43   Moncontour
Parc Nat.Rég. d'Armorique   Châteauneuf-du-Faou   N164   Broon
Île de Sein   Baie de Douarnenez   Gourin   Guémené-sur-Scorff   Loudéac   Merdrignac
Pointe du Raz   Douarnenez   26   Briec   Scaër   Le Faouët   Rohan   La Chèze   56
Audierne   44   Locronan   Quimper   Rosporden   Pontivy   La Trinité-Porhoët
Baie d'Audierne   Plozévet   Cathédrale   Bannalec   79   Josselin   Ploërmel
Ploneour-Lanvern   39   Bénodet   Quimperlé   Plouay   768   88
Pont-l'Abbé   Concarneau   N165   Hennebont   N24   Malestroit
St-Guénolé   Loctudy   Baie de Concarneau   Lorient   Baud   Locminé   St-Jean-Brévelay   46
Penmarc'h   Guilvinec   Îles de Glénan   Ploemeur   E60 41   Pluvigner   Elven   Gu
Larmor-Plage   Port-Louis   Auray   Vannes   Questembert   La
Groix   Groix   Erdeven   Alignements   Carnac   Muzillac   Redon
Presqu'île de Quiberon   27   Port-Navalo   Sarzeau   45   La-Roche-Bernard   St-Gilda-des-Boi
Quiberon   Houat   Baie de Quiberon   Herbignac   N165   Pontch
Le Palais   Parc Naturel Régional de Brière   44   Guérande   E60
Hoedic   Marais Salants   Le Croisic   Trignac   Donges
Belle-Île   La Baule   29   St-Nazaire   Paimb
St-Brévin-les-Pins   28   St-Pè-en-Re   Pornic   55
Baie de Bour

Noirmoutier-en-l'Île   Bourgneuf-en-Retz   47
Noirmoutier   Mach
Beauvoir-s.-Mer

Scale 1:2 000 000

0 10 20 30 kilometres

0 10 20 miles

Calais · Gravelines · Dunkerque · Coudekerque-Branche · Diksmuide · Torhout · **Gent** · Beveren · **Antwerpen**

Cap Gris-Nez · Wimereux · **Boulogne-sur-Mer** · Marck · Guînes · Ardres · Audruicq · Bergues · Poperinge · Ieper · Roeselare · Aalter · Tielt · Deinze · Wetteren · Lokeren · St.-Niklaas · Lier · **Mechelen**

Le Portel · Hardelot-Plage · St-Omer · Cassel · Steenvoorde · Kortrijk · Menen · Waregem · Oudenaarde · Ninove · Aalst · Dendermonde

Le Touquet-Paris-Plage · Étaples · Desvres · Samer · Hazebrouck · Bailleul · **Tourcoing** · Mouscron · Zottegem · Anderlecht · **BRU** · Grand Place

Berck-Plage · Montreuil · Aire-s-la-Lys · Armentières · **Lille** · Ronse · Geraardsbergen · **Bruxelles/Brussel**

Fort-Mahon-Plage · Le Crotoy · Rue · Fruges · Lillers · **Béthune** · La Bassée · Seclin · Tournai · Ath · Beloeil · Soignies · Nivelles · Waterloo · Wavre · Tubize · Six Flags

Cayeux-sur-Mer · Ault · Le Tréport · St-Valery-sur-Somme · Abbeville · Bernaville · Bruay-la-Buissière · Lens · Carvin · Douai · St-Amand-les-Eaux · Anzin · **Mons** · **Charleroi** · Gembloux

Varengeville-sur-Mer · **Dieppe** · Eu · Envermeu · Blangy-s.-Bresle · Airaines · Picquigny · Villers-Bocage · Albert · Bapaume · Cambrai · **Valenciennes** · Bavay · Maubeuge · Florennes · Binche · La Louvière

St-Valery-en-Caux · Doudeville · Yerville · Neufchâtel-en-Bray · Aumale · Grandvilliers · **Amiens** · Corbie · Bray-s-Somme · Combles · Le Catelet · Denain · Le Quesnoy · Avesnes-sur-Helpe · Chimay · Couvin · Givet

Rouen · Forges-les-Eaux · Marseille-en-Beauvaisis · Poix-de-Picardie · Ailly-sur-Noye · Santerre · Ham · Péronne · St-Quentin · La Capelle · Hirson · Rocroi · Revin

Gournay-en-Bray · Lyons-la-Forêt · Les Andelys · Beauvais · Crèvecœur-le-Grand · Breteuil · Montdidier · Guiscard · La Fère · Guise · Vervins · Bogny-s.-Meuse · **Charleville-Mézières** · Sedan

Vernon · Gisors · Auneuil · Clermont · Noyon · Tergnier · Chauny · **Laon** · Marle · Rozoy-sur-Serre · Flize

Mantes-la-Jolie · Magny-en-Vexin · Méru · Creil · Pont-Ste-Maxence · Ribécourt · **Compiègne** · Soissons · Bourg-et-Comin · Château-Porcien · Rethel · Le Chesne · Buzancy

Meulan · Pontoise · L'Isle-Adam · Chantilly · Senlis · Crépy-en-Valois · Pierrefonds · Braine · Fismes · **Reims** · Machault · Vouziers

Argenteuil · St-Germain-en-Laye · Nanterre · St-Denis · Bobigny · **PARIS** · Meaux · La Ferté-Milon · Villers-Cotterêts · Fère-en-Tardenois · Tinqueux · Alsace

Dreux · Houdan · **Boulogne-Billancourt** · Versailles · Palaiseau · Louvre · Notre Dame · Créteil · Roissy · Lagny-s.-M. · Disneyland · Coulommiers · La Ferté-sous-Jouarre · Montmirail · Épernay · Ste-Menehould

Rambouillet · Les Ulis · **ORY** · Orly · Brie-Comte-Robert · Fontenay-Trésigny · La Ferté-Gaucher · Avize · Vertus · **Châlons-en-Champagne**

Chartres · Auneau · Dourdan · Arpajon · Corbeil-Essonnes · Melun · Rozay-en-Brie · Villiers-St-Georges · Esternay · Fère-Champenoise · Sommesous · Vitry-le-François · St-Dizier

Étampes · Angerville · Fontainebleau · Bois-le-Roi · Nangis · Provins · Sézanne · Mailly-le-Camp · Arcis-sur-Aube · Brienne-le-Château · Ancerville · Wassy

Voves · Janville · Malesherbes · Nemours · Moret-sur-Loing · Montereau · Nogent-sur-Seine · Romilly-sur-Seine · Piney · Vendeuvre-sur-Barse · Bar-sur-Aube · Montier-en-Der · Joinville

Artenay · Pithiviers · Puiseaux · Château-Landon · Bray-s-Seine · Sergines · Aix-en-Othe · Ste-Savine · **Troyes** · Bar-sur-Seine · Colombey-les-Deux-Églises · Chaumont

Orléans · Jargeau · Montargis · Courtenay · Joigny · Saint-Florentin · Chaource · Essoyes · Château-villain

Olivet · Châteauneuf-sur-Loire · Lorris · Amilly · Migennes · Sens · Villeneuve-sur-Yonne · T.G.V. Paris-Marseille · Flogny-la-Chapelle · Les Riceys · Mussy-s-Seine

La Ferté-St-Cyr · Abbaye de St-Benoît-sur-Loire · Sully-sur-Loire · Ouzouer-sur-Loire · Châtillon-Coligny · Charny · Tonnerre · Arc-en-Barrois · Langres

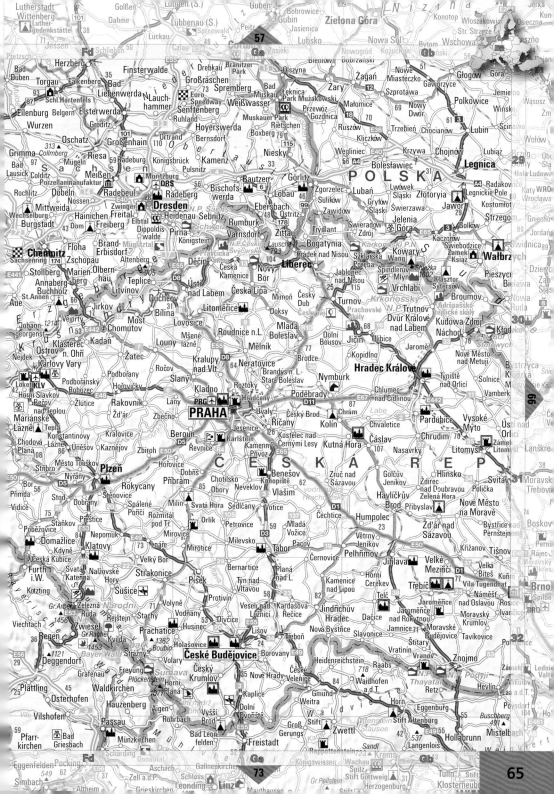

Scale 1:2 000 000

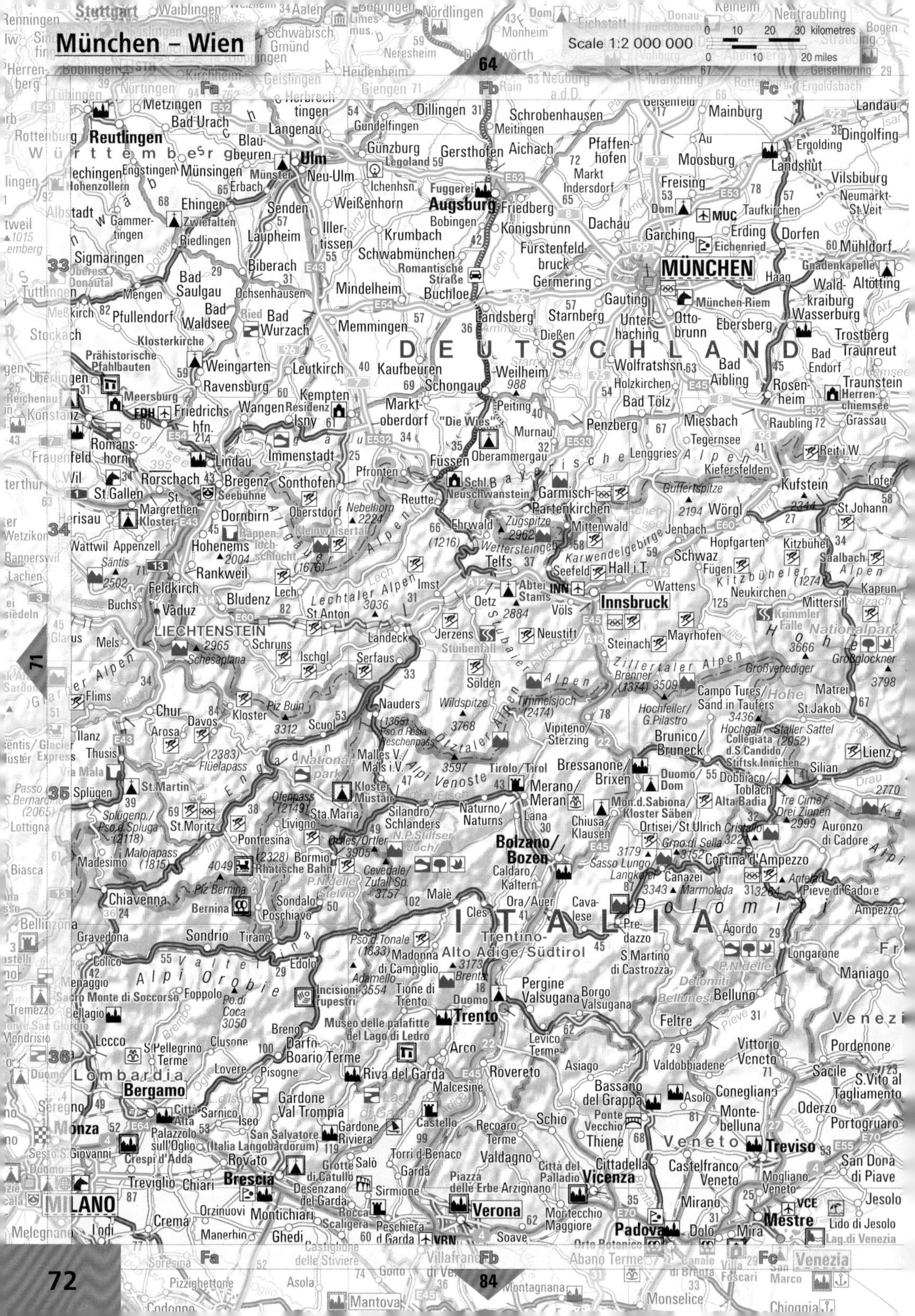

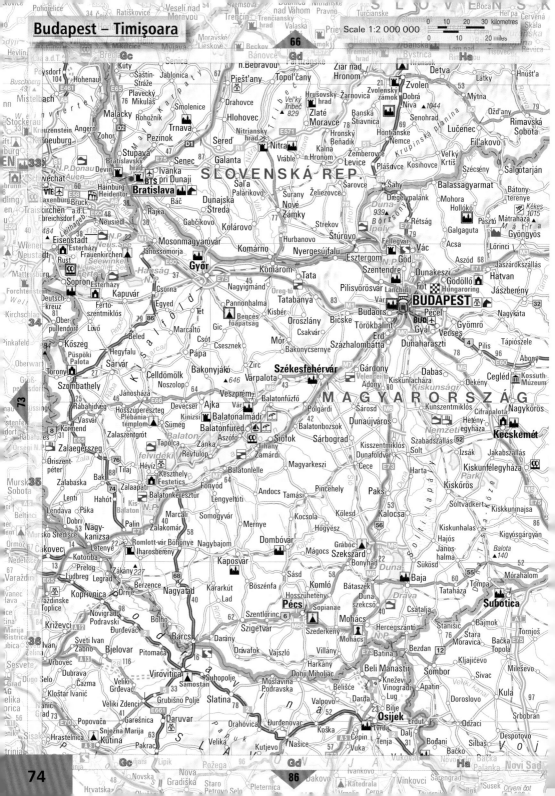

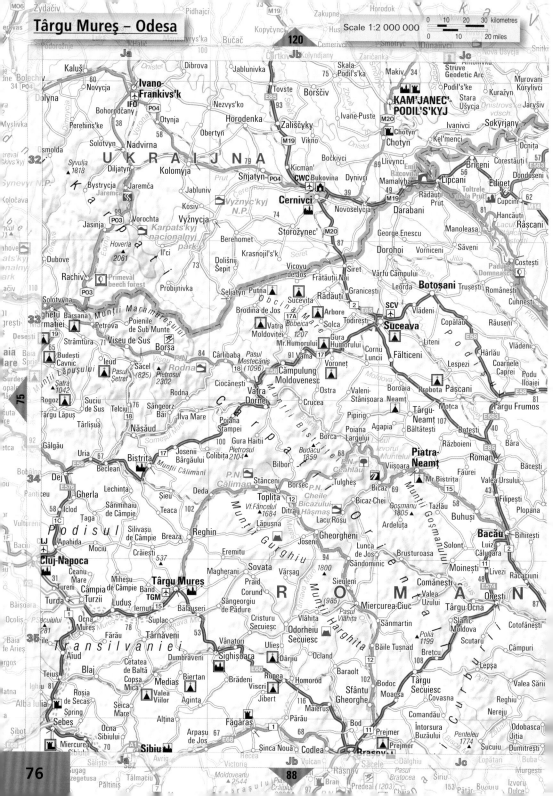

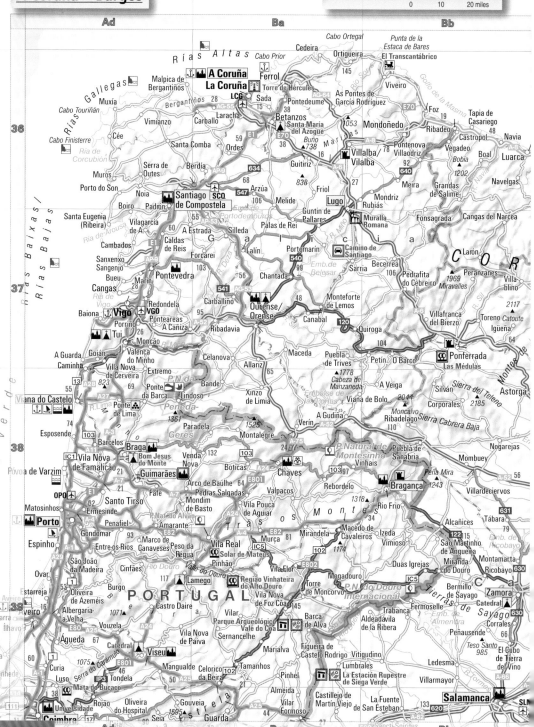

Scale 1:2 000 000

0   10   20   30 kilometres
0   10   20 miles

91

Zaragoza – Toulouse

Scale 1:2 000 000

0 10 20 30 kilometres
0 10 20 miles

Cap Ferret · Arcachon · Pessac
Pyla-sur-Mer · Dune du Pilat · Mestras · Biscarrosse

Cb · **Cc** · **Cd**

Golfo de Vizcaya

Etang de Biscarrosse et de Parentis · Parentis-en-Born · Hostens · Roquetaillade · Villandraut · Langon · La Réole · Marmande · A65 · Bazas · Casteljaloux

Mimizan · Labouheyre · Pissos · Sore · Captieux · Houeillès · Lavardac · Mézos · Sabres · Labrit · Roquefort · Mézin

Costa Vasca · St-Girons-en-Marensin · Morcenx · Mont-de-Marsan · Grenade-sur-l'Adour · Cazaubon · Eauze

Puente Colgante de Vizcaya · Cabo Matxitxako · Bermeo · Castets · Chemins de Compostelle Via Turonensis · Tartas · N124 · St-Justin

Hossegor · Capbreton · Soustons · St-Paul-lès-Dax · Dax · St-Sever · Aire-sur-l'Adour · Riscle · Marciac

Mungia · Lekeitio · Ondarroa · Labenne · Bayonne · Peyrehorade · Hagetmau · Chemins de Compostelle Via Lemovicensis · Boueilho

Bilbao/Bilbo · Gernika · Biarritz · BIQ · Hendaye · St-Jean-de-Luz · Hasparren · Amou · Orthez · A65 · Lembeye · Mirande · N21 · Miélan

Durango · Donostia/S.Sebastián · EAS · Irun · A63 · 900 · Rhune · Ainhoa · Cambo-les-Bains · Sauveterre-de-Béarn · Mourenx · PUF · Chemins de Compostelle Via Tolosana · Maubourguet · Trie-sur-Baïse

Arrasate/Mondragon · Azpeitia · Loyola · Zarautz · Andoain · Irurita · Chemin de St-Jacques-de-Compostelle · Navarrenx · Monein · Morlaàs · Vic-en-Bigorre

Bergara · Santuario de Arantzazu · Zumarraga · Tolosa · Santesteban · St-Jean-Pied-de-Port · Mauléon-Licharre · Oloron-Ste-Marie · Pau · Gan · Pontacq · Tarbes · Castelnau-Magnoac

Vitoria/Gasteiz · Legutiano · Alsasua · Leiza · Puerto de Ibañeta (1057) · Roncesvalles · Aramits · Louvie-Juzon · Nay · LDE · Bagnères-de-Bigorre · Lannemezan

Salvatierra/Agurain · Zudaire · Irurzun · Pic d'Orhy 2017 · Errô · La Colegiata · Escároz · Pic d'Anie 2504 · Grotte de Bétharram · Lourdes · Argelès-Gazost · St-Bertrand-de-Comminges

Peñacerrada · Sta. Cruz de Campezo · Camino de Santiago · Pamplona (Iruña) · PNA · Sanfermines · Aoiz · Isaba · Bisaurín 2668 · Lescun · Col d'Aubisque · Pic du Midi d'Ossau · Luz-Ardiden · Luz-St-Sauveur · Pic du Midi de Bigorre 2872 · Montréjeau

Laguardia · Los Arcos · Estella · Allo · Navascués · Burgui · Candanchú · Col du Pourtalet (1794) · Cauterets · Col du Tourmalet (2115) · La Mongie · Arreau · Bagnères-de-Luchon

Viana · Logroño · Lerín · Puente la Reina · Campanas · Lumbier · Monasterio de Leyre · Sigüés · Canfranc · Est.del Formigal · Balneario de Panticosa · Gavarnie · Monte Perdido 3355 · St-Lary-Soulan

Torrecilla en Cameros · La Rioja · Tafalla · Berbinzana · Aibar · Sangüesa · Castillo de Javier · Jaca · Biescas · Sabiñánigo · P.N.de Ordesa y Monte-Perdido · Bielsa · Baños de Benasque · Est.Cerler · Vall de Boí

Los Arnedo · Lodosa · Olite · Sos del Rey Católico · Puente la Reina de Jaca · Monasterio de San Juan de la Peña · Broto · Pico de Aneto 3408 · Cottiella 2912 · Campo

El Villar de Arnedo · Calahorra · Caparroso · Carcastillo · Biel · Santa María de la Peña · Puerto de Monrepós (1262) · Laguarta · Boltaña · Ainsa · el Pont de Suert

Arnedo · Milagro · Uncastillo · Santa Maria de la Peña · Guara 2077 · Lecina · Embalse de Mediano · Embalse de El Grado

Enciso · Alfaro · Sádaba · Castillo de Loarre · Ayerbe · Castillo de Montearagón · Alquézar · Graus

Cervera del Río Alhama · Corella · Arguedas · Ejea de los Caballeros · Erla · Ardisa · Huesca · Almudévar · Angües · El Grado · Benabarre · Panta de Canelles

Almarza · Cascante · Tudela · Fustiñana · Castejón de Valdejasa · Tauste · Granén · Barbastro · Monzón · Tamarite de Litera · Fontdepou

Ágreda · Tarazona · Mallén · Zuera · Villanueva de Gállego · Leciñena · Venta de Ballerias · Sariñena · Binéfar · Alfarràs · Camarasa

Soria · Olvega · Borja · Monasterio de Veruela · ESPAÑA · Villamayor · Lanaja · Almacelles · Balaguer

Gómara · Serón de Nágima · Aranda de Moncayo · Tabuenca · Alagón · ZAZ · Zaragoza · Fuentes de Ebro · Chalamera · Seu Vella · Lleida

Almazán · Deza · Illueca · Épila · Catedral La Seo · Muel · Villanueva del Huerva · Quinto · Bujaraloz · Zaidín · Alcarràs · Mollerussa

Villarroya de la Sierra · Colegiata de Santa Maria · La Almunia de Doña Godina · Arquitectura mudéjar · Belchite · Azaila · Fraga · Seròs · Castelldans

Ariza · Alhama de Aragón · Ateca · Calatayud · Cariñena · Herrera de los Navarros · Sástago · Híjar · Maials · Reial Monestir de Poblet

Monasterio de Piedra · Montón · Daroca · Moyuela · Lécera · Chiprana · Caspe · la Granadella · Prades

Cubel · Cillas · Mequinenza · Mazaleón · Maella · Batea · Ascó · Falset

Cb · **Cc** · **Cd**

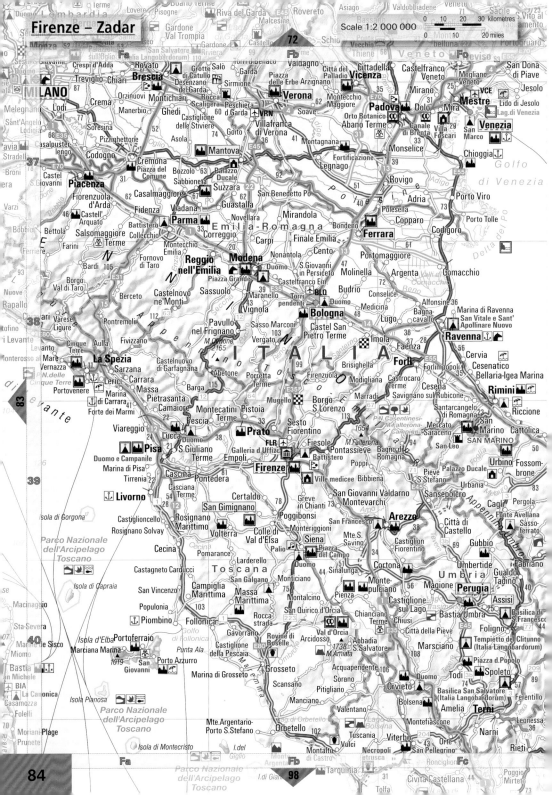

Scale 1:2 000 000

0   10   20   30 kilometres
0   10   20 miles

74

Gc   Gd   Ha

BOSNA I HERCEGOVINA

CRNA GORA

Major places: Osijek, Novi Sad, Vukovar, Vinkovci, Bijeljina, Tuzla, Zenica, Banja Luka, Bosanski Brod, Slavonski Brod, Doboj, Sarajevo, Mostar, Split, Dubrovnik, Trebinje, Podgorica, Kotor, Nikšić, Cetinje

Daruvar, Kutina, Pakrac, Nova Gradiška, Staro Petrovo Selo, Požega, Đakovo, Ivankovo, Ilok, Ruma, Sremska Mitrovica, Šabac, Loznica, Zvornik, Srebrenica, Gradačac, Brčko, Gračanica, Modriča, Derventa, Prnjavor, Kotor Varoš, Teslić, Maglaj, Zavidovići, Žepče, Travnik, Vitez, Busovača, Kakanj, Visoko, Kiseljak, Kreševo, Hadžići, Pale, Goražde, Foča, Čajniče, Pljevlja, Prijepolje, Bijelo Polje

Prijedor, Bosanska Gradiška, Bosanska Dubica, Bosanski Novi, Sanski Most, Ključ, Jajce, Mrkonjić Grad, Bugojno, Donji Vakuf, Gornji Vakuf, Livno, Tomislavgrad, Drvar, Bosansko Grahovo, Glamoč, Kupres, Prozor, Jablanica, Konjic, Kalinovik, Gacko, Bileća, Nevesinje, Stolac, Čapljina, Metković, Ploče, Makarska, Neum

N.P. Kozara, N.P. Fruška Gora, N.P. Sutjeska, N.P. Durmitor, N.P. Biogradska Gora, N.P. Tara, Nacionalni park Mljet, N.P. Skadarsko jezero

86

Gc   Gd   Ha

100

85

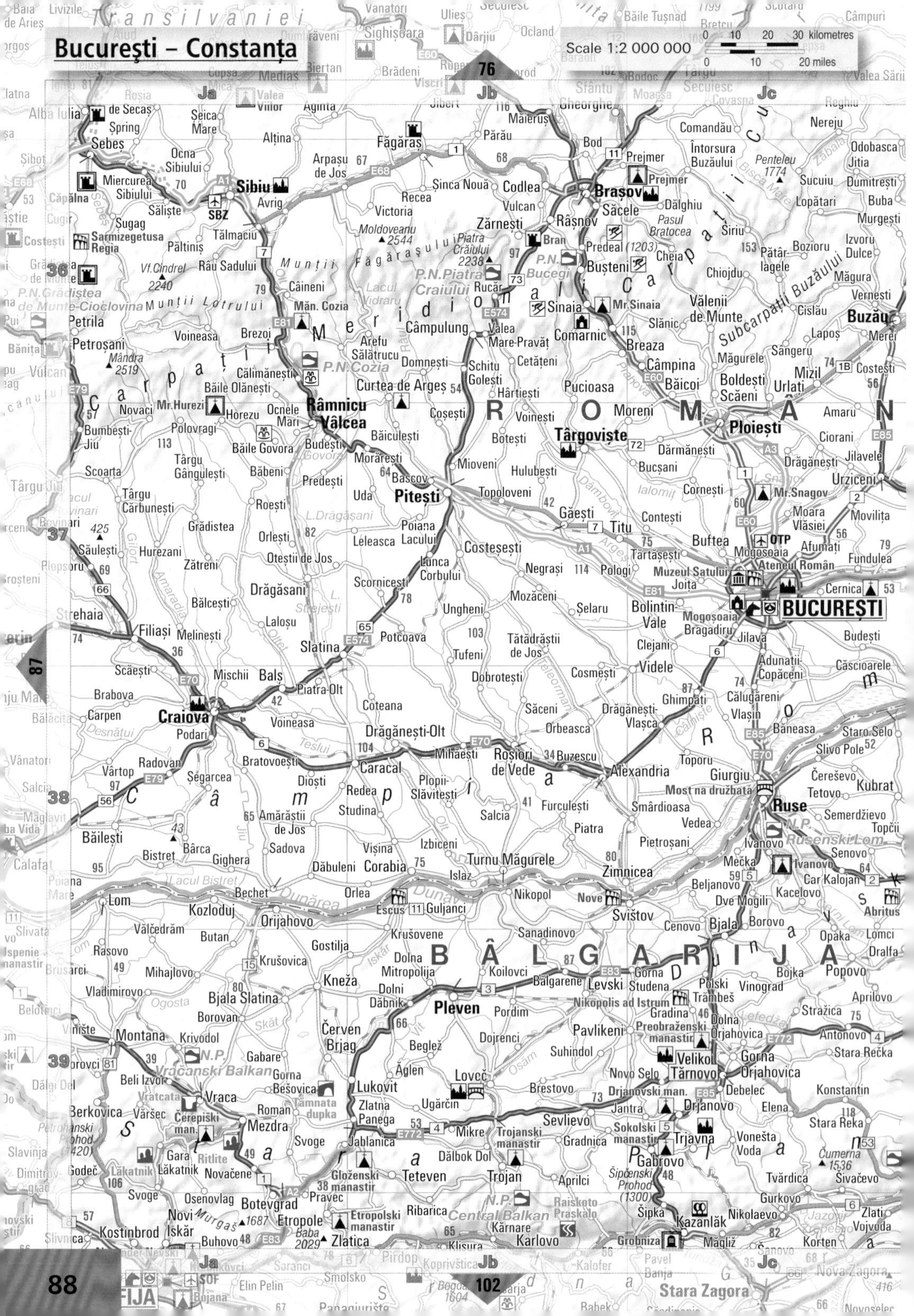

Scale 1:2 000 000

0 10 20 30 kilometres
0 10 20 miles

76

Ja **Jb** **Jc**

BÂLGARIJA

ROMÂN

BUCUREȘTI

Sibiu · Brașov · Predeal · Sinaia · Câmpina · Ploiești · Buzău

Craiova · Pitești · Slatina · Caracal · Alexandria · Giurgiu · Ruse

Pleven · Vraca · Montana · Lovec · Gabrovo · Tărnovo · Kazanlăk

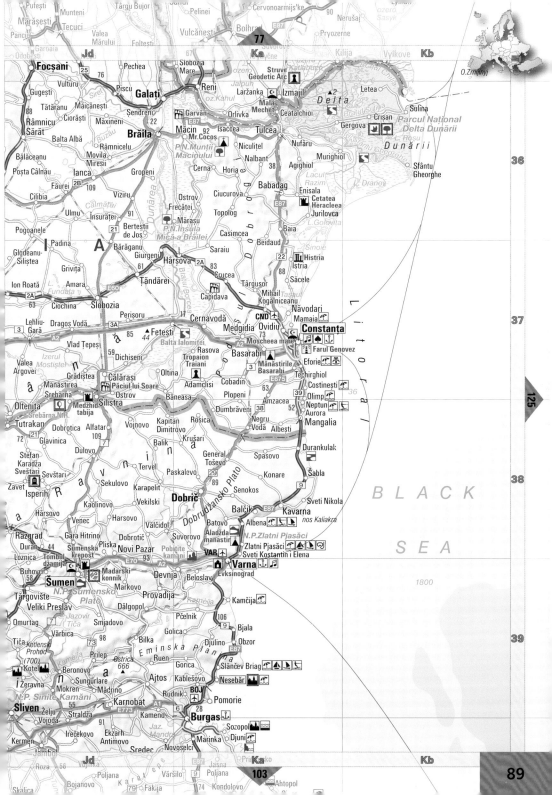

Scale 1:2 000 000

0 10 20 30 kilometres
0 10 20 miles

Ab Ac Ad

ATLANTIC OCEAN

39
40
41
42

Matosinhos
Ermesinde
de Basto
Porto
Gondomar
Penafiel
Amarante
Espinho
Entre-os-Rios
Marco de Canaveses
E82
São João da Madeira
93
Cinfães
Rio Douro
Ovar
Oliveira de Azeméis
Burgo
Lamego
Estarreja
Albergaria-a-Velha
Castro Daire
Ria de Aveiro
Aveiro
16
Vouzela
1071
r
Praia da Barra
E80
Águeda
67
Vila Nova de Paiva
Ílhavo
Mangualde
Praia de Mira
Curia
Serra do Caramulo
Viseu
Mira
60
1
1075
46
50
Cantanhede
Luso
IP3
Tondela
A25
Mata do Bucaco
Oliveira do Hospital
Gouveia
Figueira da Foz
Rojão
Seia
1595
Universidade
Coja
90
Coimbra
17
Serra da Estrela
P.N. da
112
Arganil
Covilhã
Praia da Vieira
52
Conimbriga
Espinhal
Góis
163
Porto da Balsa
E802
Marinha Grande
Pombal
38
Castanheira de Pira
Pampilhosa da Serra
Fundão
IC8
55
Pontão
1227
45
Leiria
Figueiró dos Vinhos
Oleiros
PORTUGA
Mosteiro da Batalha
45
Sertã
95
1084
Sarzedas
112
A23
Nazaré
68
8
Escalos de Cima
Mosteiro de Alcobaça
Fátima
113
Convento de Cristo
Vila de Rei
Castelo Branco
Farilhões
Caldas da Reinha
P.N. das Serras Aire e Candeeiros
40 Torres Novas
241
Berlenga
Tomar
Vila Velha de Ródão
P.N. do Tejo Internacional
Cabo Carvoeiro
Peniche
Óbidos
Alcanede
16
Perdigão
Cedillo
Lourinhã
366
Rio Maior
18
118
Gardete
Santiago de Alcântara
Bombarral
26
79
Abrantes
Gavião
IP2
Nisa
Torres Vedras
Alcoentre
Santarém
Alpiarça
Castelo de Vide
Almeirim
246
Valencia de Alcántara
P.N. de Sintra-Cascais
Alenquer
Cartaxo
Alpalhão
863
Ericeira
114
Crato
Marvão
Mafra
Vila Franca de Xira
118
Portalegre
San Vicente de Alcántara
Cabo da Roca
Sintra
A13
Alter do Chão
P.N. da Serra de S.Mamede
Paisagem Cultural
Loures
Amadora
Porto Alto
Avis
Albu-querque
Cascais
Coruche
Montargil
IP2
Estoril
LIS
LISBOA
Infantado
Monforte
55
Arronches
Mosteiro dos Jerónimos
Torre de Belém
Mora
Pavia
18
Santa Eulalia
Almada
Montijo
Cruzamento de Pegões
Lavre
Sousel
Cidade-Quartel Fronteirica de Elvas e as suas Fortificações
Barreiro
48
Vendas Novas
Vimieiro
67
Estremoz
Campo Maior
P.N. da Arrábida
Palmela
E90
Arraiolos
Evoramonte
Borba
60
Elvas
Cabo Espichel
Sesimbra
Setúbal
36
Montemor-o-Novo
Badajoz
1722
Costa Bela
Tróia
34
114
Évora Romana/Cidade Medieval
44
Vila Viçosa
79
Baia de Setúbal
Comporta
50
2
Évora
Redondo
Olivenza
La Albuera
Alcácer do Sal
16
48
Valverde de Leganés
Melides
Alcáçovas
IP2
256
Monsaraz
Cheles
Almendral
Alconchel
435
52
IP8
Grândola
16
Viana do Alentejo
Reguengos de Monsaraz
Mourão
Villanueva del Fresno
Sines
Torrão
Alvito
Portel
Barcarrota
Cabo de Sines
29
259
62
E802
Vidigueira
Barragem do Alqueva
Jerez de los Caballeros
IC4
Santiago do Cacém
23
Póvoa de São Miguel
35
Alvalade
59
Ferreira do Alentejo
IP8
Amareleja
Oliva de la Frontera
Cercal
58
2
Moura
24
435
Vila Nova de Milfontes
Aljustrel
46
Beja
260
Safara
P.N. do Sudoeste Alentejano e Costa Vicentina
Garvão
Albernoa
Serpa
IP8
58
Barrancos
Fregenal de la Sierra
São Teotónio
Odemira
Ourique
Vila Verde de Ficalho
Rosal de la Frontera
435
39

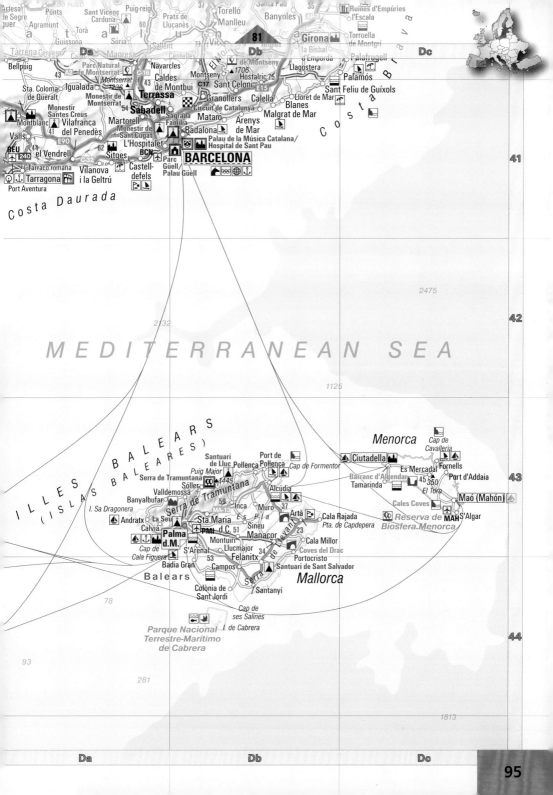

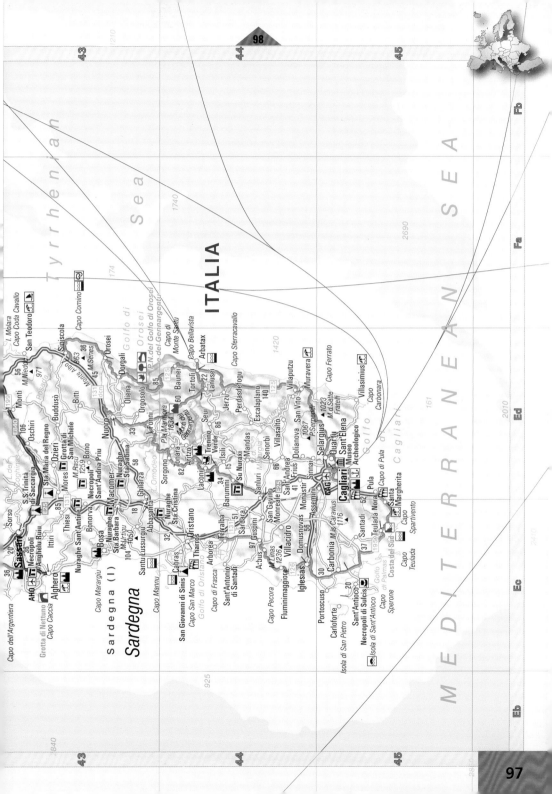

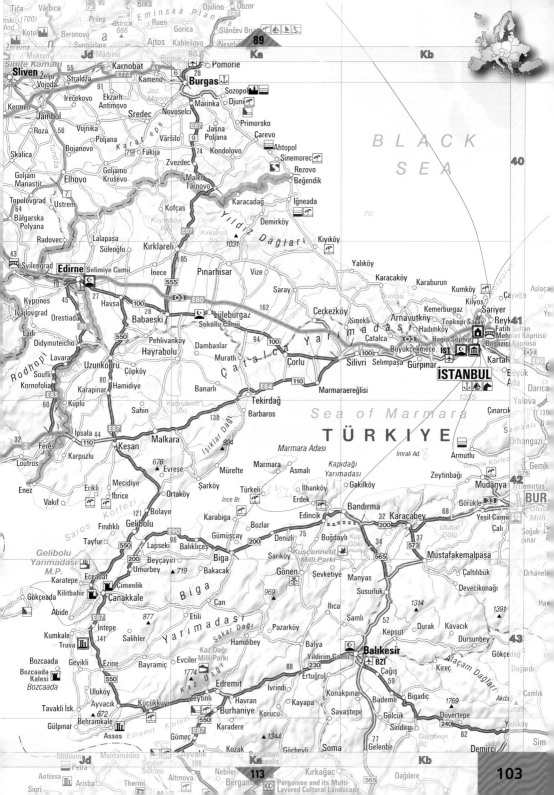

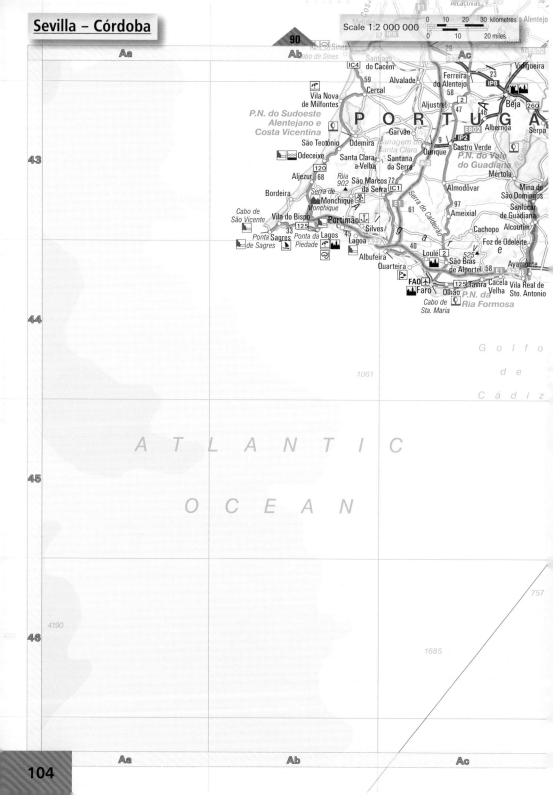

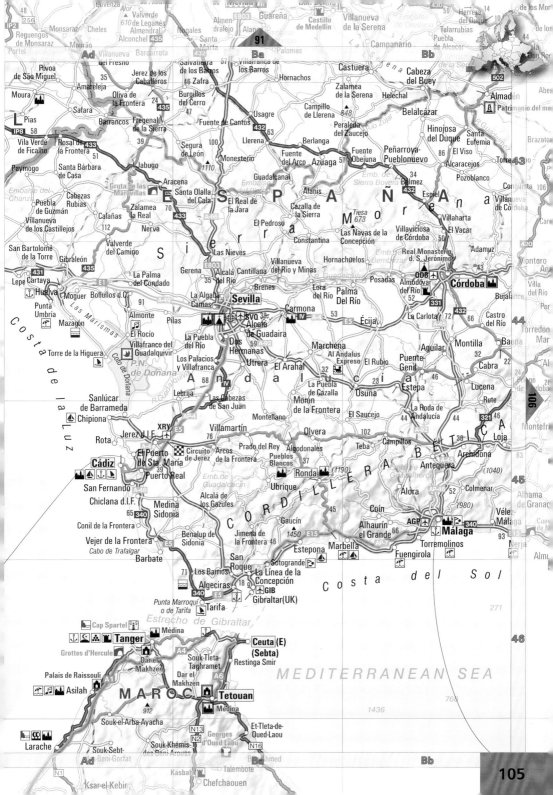

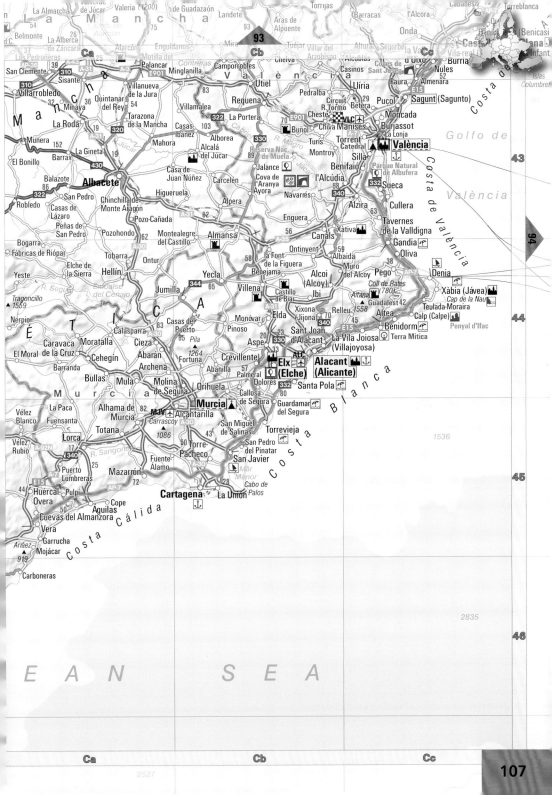

Scale 1:2 000 000

| 0 | 10 | 20 | 30 kilometres |
| 0 | | 10 | 20 miles |

Tyrrhenian Basin

Fb | Fc | Fd

45

T y r r h e n i a n 3500

I.di Ustica

46

S e a

Capo San Vito
San Vito lo Capo
Punta Raisi
Capo Gallo
Mondello
PMO Carini
Palermo

Grotta del Genovese
Erice
Castellammare del Golfo
Monreale Duomo
42
La Martorana
Bagheria
Cefalù

Í.Marettimo
I.di Levanzo
I.Favignana
Trapani
13
28
Partinicio
Cappella Palatina
19
Termini Imerese
E90

Isole Egadi
Favignana
I.dello Stagnone
TRS
Segesta
Alcamo
Piana d. Albanesi
Marineo
Caccamo
40
Duomo
1979

Mozia
Calatafimi
29
Roccamena
Corleone
Alia
Petralia Sottana

Capo Boeo
Marsala
Salemi
41
Gibellina Nuova
Sambuca di Sicilia
Prizzi
134
Lercara Friddi
67
19

Castelvetrano
E90
Partanna
115
Cammarata
Mussomeli

47
995
11
Mazara del Vallo
43
Menfi
Selinunte
Caltabellotta
97
Bivona
Castel-termini
Caltanissetta
San Cataldo

535
Marinella
Capo Granitola
Capo San Marco
Sciacca
Ribera
Racalmuto
69
Canicattì
Riesi

20
Eraclea Minoa
Aragona
Agrigento
Favara
Ravanusa

Porto Empedocle
Valle dei Templi
SICILIA
Palma di Montechiaro
115
74
Licata

Zembretta
Cap Bon
aria
M E D I T E R R A N E A N
53

Dar Allouche
Kerkouane
25
Rass el Melah
ne
Kelibia
Menzel Termime
48

Pantelleria
I.di Pantelleria (I)
Vite ad alberello dello Zibibbo di Pantelleria

a
S E A
1650
ane
82

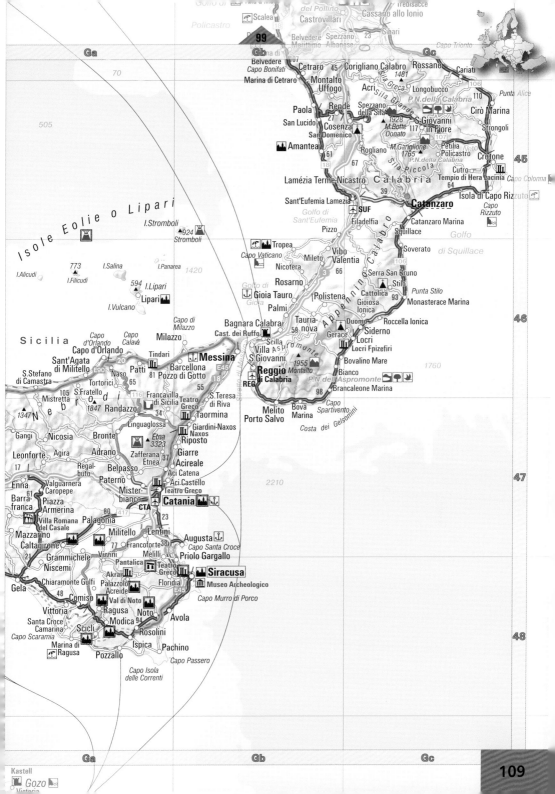

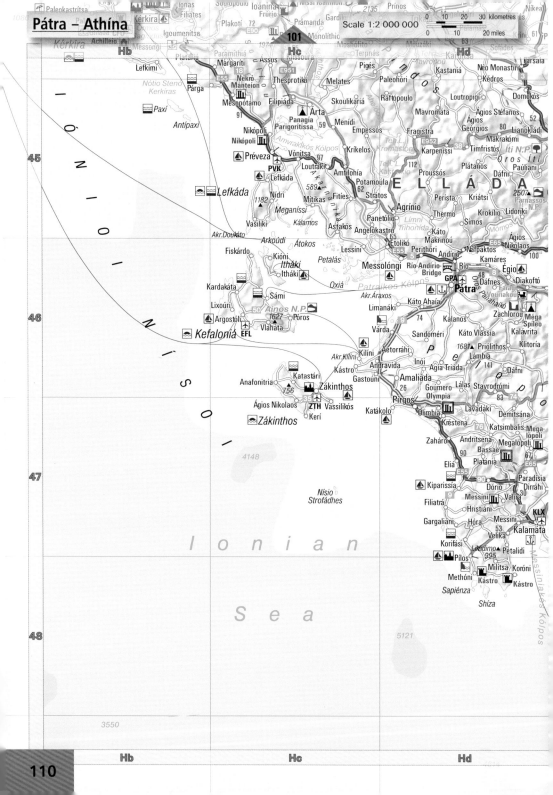

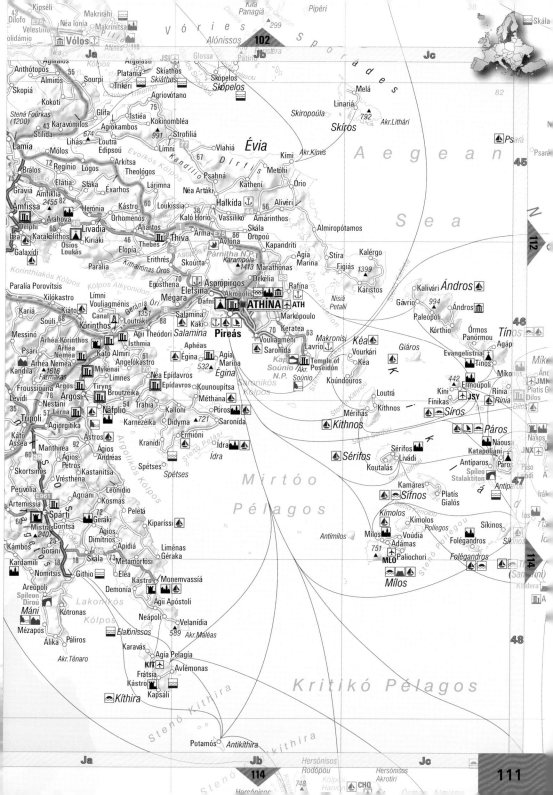

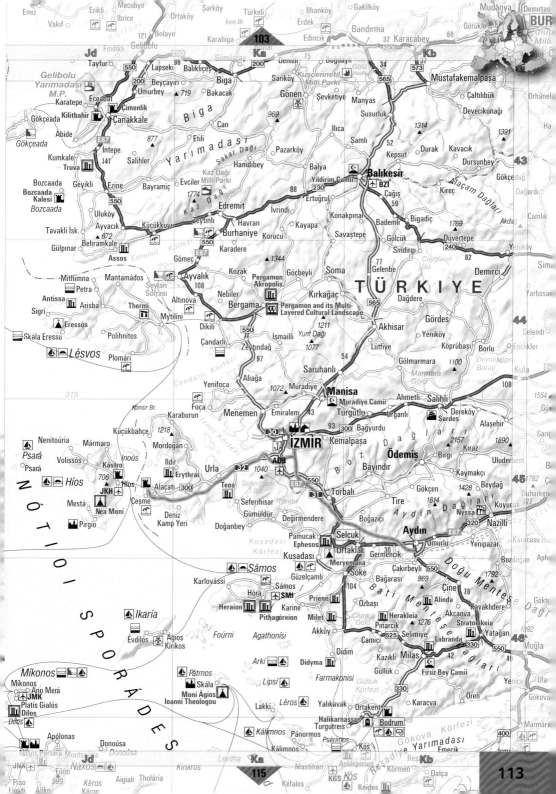

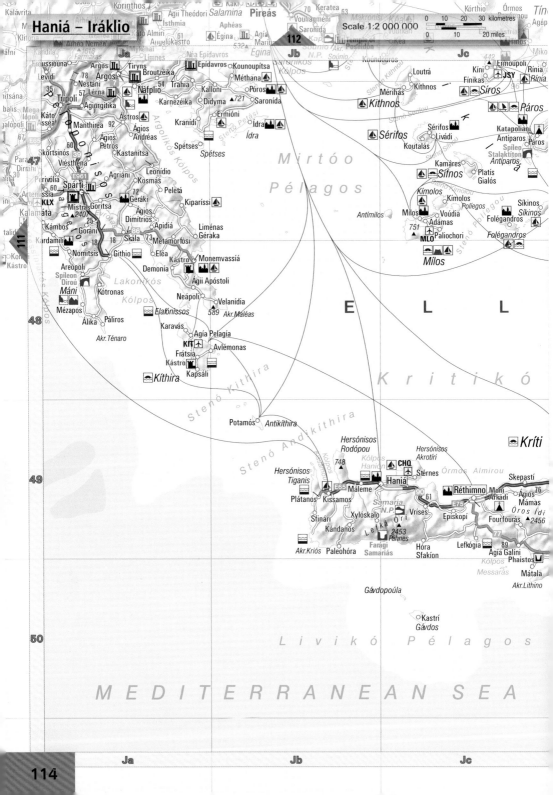

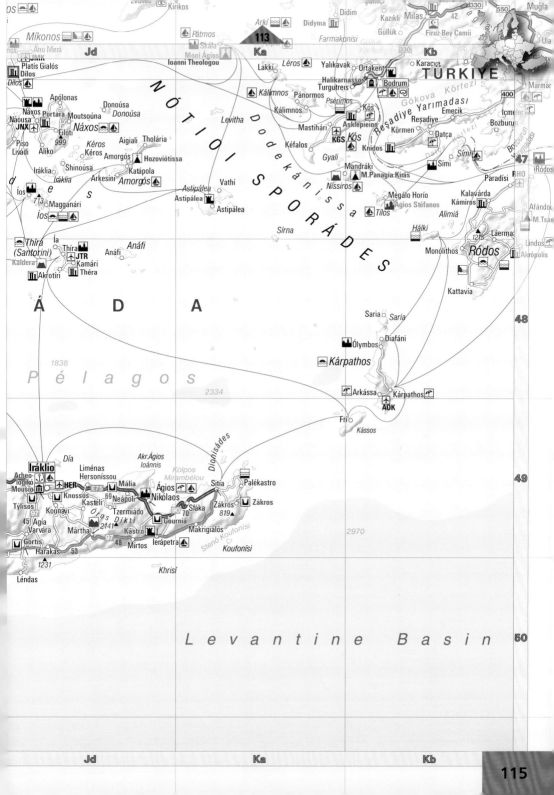

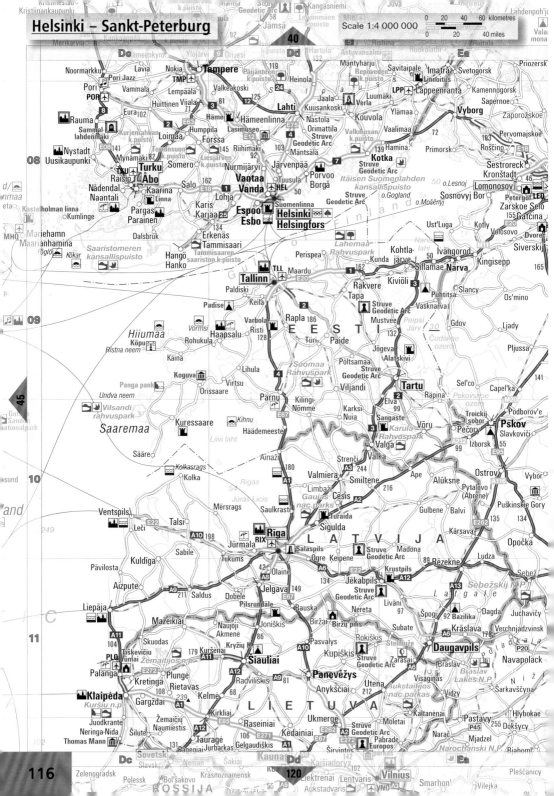

o.Valaam

Olonec   Pogost   Mosnikovskaja   Zubovo   Lipin Bor   Bol'šaja   kij Sever
am   Podporož'e   Mosnikovskaja   Ferapontovo   nal Park
tyr   Makar'evskaja   Bolezersk   Kirillov   Borisovo   Sokol   dnikov

Lodejenoe
Pole   108   Alëhovščina   Korbeniči   Lavrovo   Annino   Vologda
Paša   E105   Alëhovščina   Borisovo-   Kaduj   A114   Grjaz
Novaja   Sjas'stroj   Usadišče   Sudskoe   Čerepovec   126
Ladoga   M18   Timohino   Andorskaja grjada   08
Mor'e   Kobona   Volhov   90   Tihvin   Babaevo   Mjaksa   Prečist
Vsevoložsk   Pikalevo   Efimovskij   Lent'evo   102   Gajutino   150
Šlisselburg Kirovsk   111   Čerencovo   A114   Čagoda   Čaevo   Pošehon'   Transsil
SANKT-PETERBURG   Ustjužna   15
Kolpino   211   102
Ekaterinskij dvorec   Ruguj   Ves'egonsk   Rybinskoe   Rybinsl
Pavlovsk   Tosno   Budogošč'   Nebolči   vodohranilišče   Legkovo   Korovnik
Ljuban'   Koboža   Sandovo   Jaroslav
Vyrica   1961   Šar'ja   Brejtovo   Krasnyj Holm   Bol.Selo
Čudovo   Ljubytino   Pestovo   Dviniščenskaja   Volga   09
Malaja   E105   Grjady   Lesnoe   vozv.   Voskresenskoe   Borissogleb Rostov
Višera   Podberez'e   Petrovo   Sonkovo   monasty Kremi
Oredež   Borovenka   Udomlja   Bežeck   Uglič   Petrovskoe
Luga   Kreml   Okulovka   Boroviči   Maksatiha   Kašin   Kaljazin Zolo   monasty
Sofijskij sobor Novgorod   Bežeck   Nerl'   Gorizkij monasty
E95   Jurjev monastyr   Krestcy   231   Bologoe   Udomlja   Goricy   Pereslavsky N.F
A116   oz.Il'men   M10   Rameški   Nagor   Peres   Niki
18   Valdaj   Vypolzovo   Vyšnij   Spirovo   Kušalino   Taldom   Zales   118
Sol'cy   Simsk   Staraja Russa   Voloček   Kimry   Dvon
240   Valdaisky   Krasnomajskij   Redkino   Liho slavl'   Dubna   Sergiev Posad
Dno   National Park   M11   Toržok   134   Tver'   Konakovo   Troize-Sergieva Lavra   Krasnoar
Porhov   Demjansk   Firovo   Uspenskij sobor   164   Dmitrov   Fjanovo
R O S S I J A   Zaluč'e   Valdajskaja   Klin   Dedenevo   97
Poddor'e   Marevo   vozvyšennost'   Kuvšinovo   Torzžok   Solnečnogorsk   Istra Kremi   Nog
Dedoviči   Ostaškov   Seližárovo   Vysokovsk   Zelenograd   mow   85
Holm   Peno   Lukovnikovo   Lotošino   Nudol'   104   Himki   10
Novoržev   Bežanicy   Bologovo   Okovcy   Starica   Vysokovsk   Zvenigorod   Istra Kremi   Balaši
Loknja   Podberez'e   Andreapol'   Rzžev   Zubcov   Volokolamsk   Novodewitschi   MOSK
Bežanickaja vozv.   Ploskoš'   241   Olenino   129   Ruza   monastyr   MOSK
Toropec   Nelidovo   M9   Zvenigorod   Golicyno   Odincovo   DM
Novosokol'niki   Velikie Luki   Zapadnaja   Belyj   Syčevka   Možajsk   Naro-Fominsk   Podol'sk   Domode
Pustoška   E22   65   Dvina   Il'ino   Gžatsk   244   Borovsk   107   Klimovsk   Mi
M9   138   Holm-   Egor'e   Balabanovo   110   Čehov
M20   48   Usvjaty   Žirkovskij   Vjaz'ma   E30   Malojaroslavec   Obninsk   Stupin
Nevel'   Veliž   Prečistoe   244   Kondrovo   82   Serpuho   E105
Drětun'   E95   Demidov   Vjaz'ma   Juhnov   Tarusa   Aleksi   Jas
St.Sophia   100   166   Safonovo   Ugra   Kaluga   90   11
Polack   M8   Haradok   Ruba   Jarcevo   274   Leninski   DN
St.Efrasinnia   monastyr   105   Lëzna   Smolensko-   Mosal'sk   Suvorov   Dubn
Usjačy   Bešankoviči   P20   Rudnja   Ol'ša   El'nja   Erši   Kirov   Sosnenskij   Ščel
Witebsk   Slavic   130   Smolensk   Suhiniči   216   Kozel'sk   Plavsk
bazaar   69   Uspenskij sobor   Počinok   Ekimoviči   Belev   Čerg
Čašniki   Sjanno   Monastyrščina   107   A141   M3   Starica
Lepel'   Novalukoml'   Orša   Horki   Hislaviči   A101
Berezinsky Biosphere   E30   Talačyn   Ljudinovo   Djat'kovo
Nature Reserve   M1   Eb   Mscislav   Ec   Ed
Barysav   238   Bobr   Sklov   90   121   Hvastovič   Ž

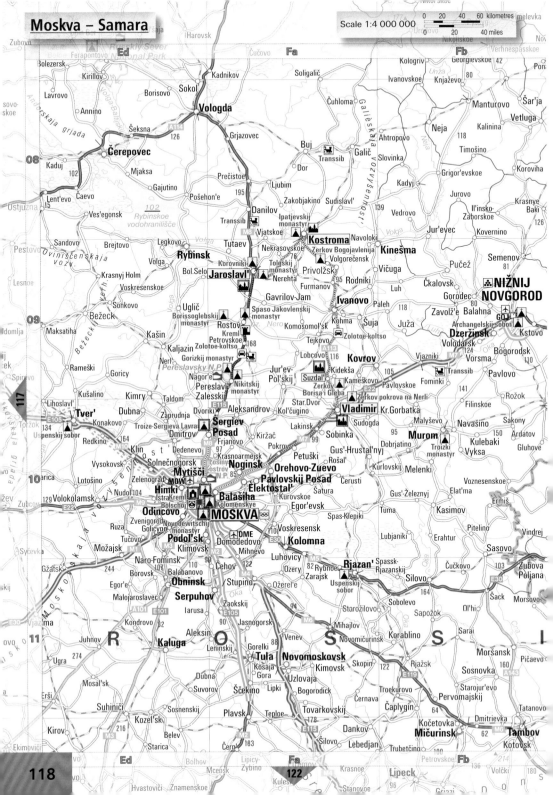

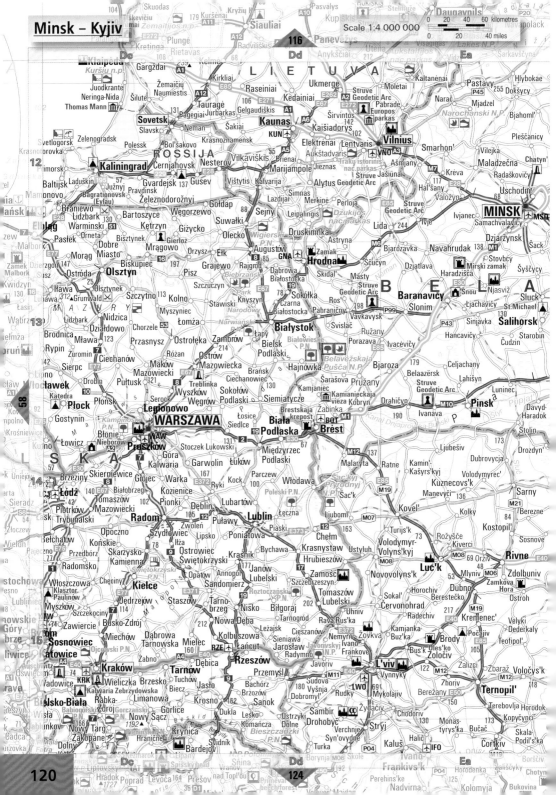

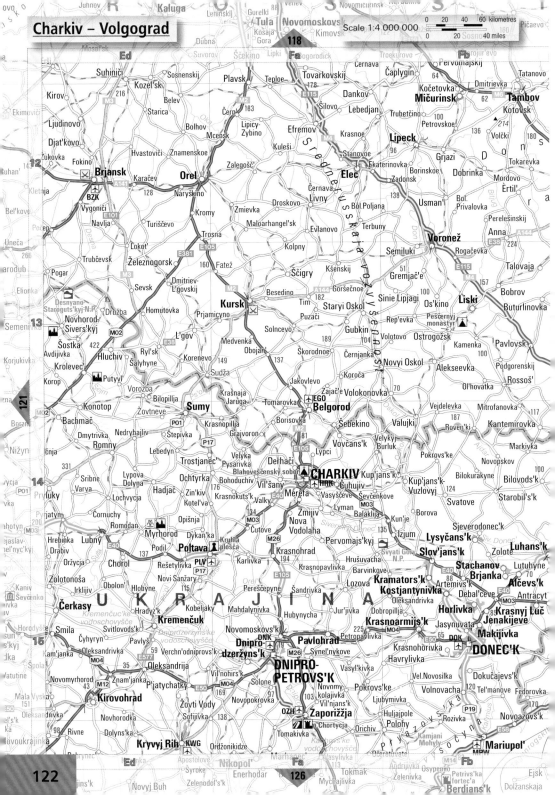

Beograd – Odesa

Scale 1:4 000 000

0 20 40 60 kilometres
0 20 40 miles

120
Dc   Dd   Ea

Sosnowiec Tarnowska Mielec
RZE Łańcut
Jarosław Javorivsky Ivano
Tarnów Dębica Rzeszów
Přemyśl Javoriv Mykolajiv teotipol
Volocys'k

Bielsko-Biała Rabka Limanowa Krosno Sanok Sambir Żydacziv Terebovlja Horodok
Zdroj Gorlice Chodoriv Monastyrys'ka Kopyčynci
Nowy Sącz Dukla Lesko Ustryki Drohobyč Verchnje Stryj Bučač
Nowy Targ 1192 Krynica Kománcza Dolne Syn'ovydno Halič Skala Podil's'ka
Zakopane Turka Kaluš Čortkiv
Svidník Sina Borynja Skole Ivano- Borščiv
Liptovský Bardejov Lipany Vel'ke nad Toplou Frankivs'k Zališčyky Chotyn
TAT Spišská Levoča Perehins'k Nadvirna Kolomyja Bukovina
Poprad 164 Michalovce Perečyn Svaljava Diljatyn Vyžnyts'kyj Snjatyn Černivci

SLOVENSKO Košice Užhorod Mukačeve Karpaty Vyžnycja Storožynec'
Banská Rožňava Kapušany Palanok Dovhe Iršava Siret
Bystrica Moldava Záhony Berehove Chust Rachiv Rädäuti
Detva Hnúšťa nad Bodvou Kisvárda Tjačiv Seljatyn
Zvolen Tornal'a Encs Vásárosnamény Sighetu Gura Humorului
Rimavská Kazincbarcika Marmatiei Voronet
Lučenec Sobota Ózd Szerencs Tokaj hegyalja Mátészalka Negresti-Oas Borsa Poiana
Salgótarján MCQ Tokaj Fehérgyarmat Viseu Vatra Teiului
Kékes Eger Tiszavasvári de Sus Dornei
1015 Hollókő Mezőkövesd Nyíregyháza Satu Mare Seini Näsäud 266 Cârlibaba
Gyöngyös 149 SUJ Carei BAY Baia Mare Rogoz Bistrita P.N.Ceahläu
Hatvan Újfehértó Valea lui Beltiug 1C 149 Rodna Deda Toplita
BUDAPEST Hajdúböszörmény Mihai Tăsnad Jibou Dej Gherla Teaca Gheorgheni
Hortobágy Debrecen Marghita Zalău Zimbor Sovata Bicazului
Jászapáti 178 1F Sălaj Reghin Târgu Mures
Szolnok 169 Püspökladány 82 42 Oradea Silvaniei Huedin CLJ Apahida Praid 196 12
Karcag Biharia Ciucea Turda 115 Miercurea
MAGYARORSZÁG Kenderes Aleşd Bratca 155 Cluj-Napoca Ludus Medias Ciuc
Kecskemét Törökszentmiklós Salonta Beiuş Blaj Sighisoara Odorheiu
Mezőtúr OMR Stei Câmpeni Zlatna Teius Biertan Secuiesc
Körösladány Sarkad P.N.Munţii Alba Iulia Sfântu Gheorghe
Szarvas Békés keresztur Apuseni Albac 113 ROM
Csongrád Szentes 79 117 Sintea Brad Sebes SBZ Sibiu Făgăras Brasov
Kiskőrös Békéscsaba Gyula Mare 206 Metaliferi Câpâlna 159 Säcele
Kiskun- Hódmező- Curtici Ineu 76 Deva 49 Tălmaciu Zărnesti
félegyháza Vásárhely Gurahont Muntii Zarndului Simeria P.N.Cozia 168 Sinaia
Paks Szeged Makó 101 Arad Hunedoara Haţeg Carpatii Meridionali Curtea 73 Câmpulung
Solt Kiskunhalas Nădlac Pecica 53 Lipova E68 66 P.N.Grădiştea de Brezoi de Arges Târgoviste
Szekszárd Sânnicolau Periam E671 Giarmata Lugoj Munte-Cioclovina Râmnicu A1
Baja Mare Biled 6 Recas Otelu Rosu 102 Vâlcea Pitesti Găesti
Bajmok Bácka Kikinda Jimbolia Timisoara Caransebes Petrosani Târgu Jiu Drăgăsani
Subotica Topola Bečej Jáša Jebel 59 Gătaia Bocsa P.N.Cerna Hurezani Slatina
Sombor Srbobran Tornic 164 Resita Parcul 235 Mr.Hurezi A1 Roşiori
Osijek Bačka Zabalj Zrenjanin Anina National Drobeta-Turnu Balcesti de Vede
Vukovar Palanka Kovačica Vršac 164 Oravita Retezat Severin Filiaşi 122 65 Potcoava
Ilok Novi Odžaci Alibunar 10 114 P.N.Cerna Strehaia Bals
Vinkovci Sad Moldova Nouă Domogled Hurezani Slatina
Sremska BEOGRAD Orsova Craiova Caracal Alexandria
Brčko Mitrovica 111 BEG Kladovo 113 Vânju Mare Drăgănesti Olt Turnu
Bijeljina Šabac Smederevo Golubac N.P.Derdap Radovan Vişina Corabia Mägurele
Tuzla Loznica Obrenovac Mladenovac Požarevac Rudna 33 Negotin Višina Orjahovo Nikopol Zimnicea
Živinice Kamenica Petrovac Glava Vidin Calafat Lom Gulianci Svištov
Zvornik Ljubovija Ljig Rudnik Topola Lapovo Despotovac Bor Belogradčik Kozloduj Kneža Bălgarene
Vlasenica Valjevo Gornji Svetozarevo 148 Zaječar 14 Borovan Pleven
Bajina Milanovac Kragujevac Ćuprija Gamzigrad Oriahovo Levski
Bašta Čačak Paraćin 36 Boljevac 141 Montana Loveč Pavliken
Užice Požega Trstenik E75 Aleksinac 35 Vračanski Balkan Vraca Lukovit Mikre Sevlievo
Višegrad Kremna Kraljevo Aleksandrovac Knjaževac 98 Berkovica Mezdra Trojan 208 Gabr
Gorazde Ustiprača 117 Kruševac Svoge
Foča Bistrica Nova Varos Blace Kopaonik Pirot Godeč Ponaravski

87

SRBIJA

SOFIJA

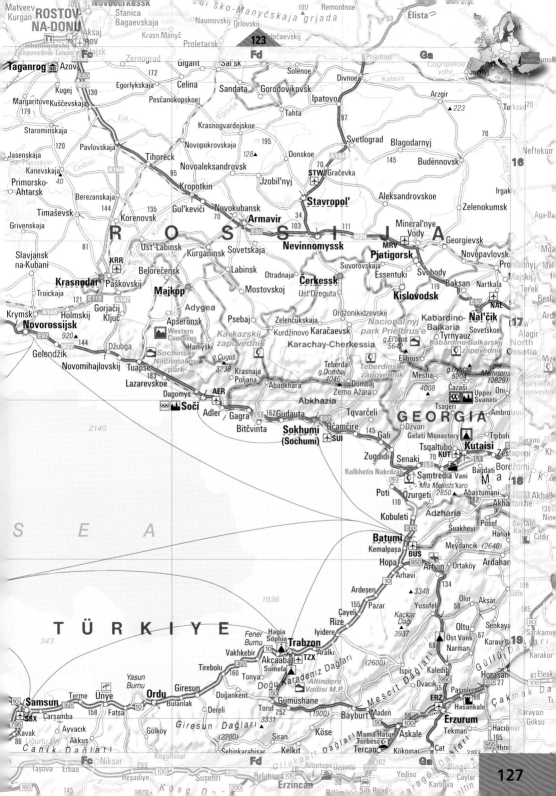

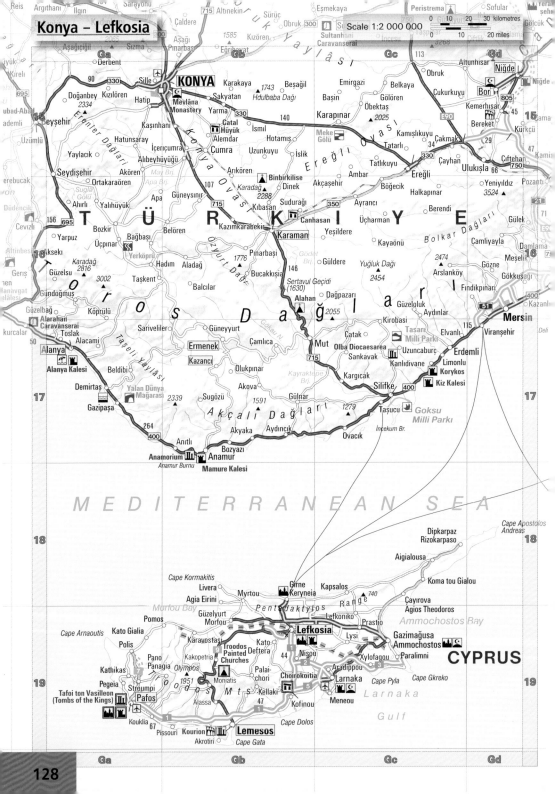

The index explained

All of the places named on the maps in the atlas are listed in the atlas index. The place names are listed alpabetically. Special symbols and letters including accents and umlauts are ignored in the order of the index. For example, the letters Á, Ä, Â are all categorized under A, and Ž, Ż, ź are all treated as the standard Latin letter Z. Written characters consisting of two letters joined together (ligatures) are treated as two separate characters in the index: for example, words beginning with the character Æ would be indexed under A E.

The grid references for towns and cities identify the location of the place name on the map. The place names are followed by international vehicle registration codes and the page numbers of relevant maps as well as a number-letter combination indicating the area's location in the map. Letters indicate the east-west position and numbers the north-south position of an area.

International vehicle registration codes of Europe

AL	Albania	**LV**	Latvia
GBA	Alderney	**FL**	Liechtenstein
AND	Andorra	**LT**	Lithuania
A	Austria	**L**	Luxembourg
BY	Belarus'	**MK**	Macedonia
B	Belgium	**M**	Malta
BIH	Bosnia and Herzegovina	**MD**	Moldova
BG	Bulgaria	**MC**	Monaco
HR	Croatia	**MNE**	Montenegro
CY	Cyprus	**NL**	Netherlands
CZ	Czech Republic	**N**	Norway
DK	Denmark	**PL**	Poland
EST	Estonia	**P**	Portugal
FIN	Finland	**RO**	Romania
F	France	**RUS**	Russia
D	Germany	**RSM**	San Marino
GBZ	Gibraltar	**SRB**	Serbia
GR	Greece	**SK**	Slovakia
GBG	Guernsey	**SLO**	Slovenia
H	Hungary	**E**	Spain
IS	Iceland	**S**	Sweden
IRL	Ireland	**CH**	Switzerland
GBM	Isle of Man	**TR**	Turkey
I	Italy	**UA**	Ukraine
GBJ	Jersey	**GB**	United Kingdom
RKS	Kosovo	**V**	Vatican City

Å – Akova

A

Å N 32 Fc12
Aabenraa DK 48 Fa24
Aabybro DK 49 Fb21
Aachen D 63 Ec29
Aakirkeby DK 50 Ga24
Aalborg DK 49 Fb21
Aalen D 64 Fa32
Aalestrup DK 49 Fb22
Aalst B 62 Ea29
Aalter B 54 Ea28
Äänekoski FIN 40 Hc13
Aapua S 30 Ha08
Aarau CH 71 Ed34
Aareavaara S 30 Ha07
Aarhus DK 49 Fb22
Aars DK 49 Fb21
Aarschot B 63 Eb29
Aarup DK 49 Fb23
Aavasaksa FIN 34 Hb09
Abanilla E 107 Cb44
Abano Terme I 84 Fc37
Abarán E 107 Ca44
Abbadia San Salvatore I 84 Fb40
Abbasanta I 97 Ec43
Abbeville F 62 Dc30
Abbeyfeale IRL 18 Bd24
Abbeyleix IRL 18 Ca24
Abbiategrasso I 83 Ed37
Abborrträsk S 34 Gd10
Abbotsbury GB 24 Cd28
Abejar E 79 Ca39
Abelvær N 32 Fc11
Abenójar E 106 Bc43
Abensberg D 64 Fc32
Aberaeron GB 23 Cc26
Aberdeen GB 17 Db20
Aberfeldy GB 17 Da20
Abergavenny GB 24 Cd26
Abergele GB 20 Cd24
Abersoch GB 23 Cc25
Aberystwyth GB 23 Cc25
Abetone I 84 Fb38
Abganerovo RUS 123 Fd14
Abide TR 103 Jd43
Abingdon GB 24 Da27
Abington GB 21 Da22
Abisko S 29 Gc06
Abjarovščyna BY 59 Hc27
Åbo FIN 40 Hb16
Abony H 74 Ha34
Aboyne GB 17 Db20
Abrantes P 90 Ac41
Abraur S 33 Gc09
Abrene RUS 47 Jb20
Abrud RO 75 Hd35
Åby S 44 Ga20
Åby S 44 Gb19
Åbyggeby S 39 Gc16
Åbyn S 34 Ha10
Åbytorp S 44 Ga18
A Cañiza E 78 Ad37
Acceglio I 83 Eb38

Acerenza I 99 Gb43
Achim D 56 Fa26
Achnasheen GB 17 Da19
Aci Castello I 109 Ga47
Aci Catena I 109 Ga47
Acireale I 109 Gb47
Acle GB 25 Dd26
A Coruña E 78 Ba36
Acqua Doria F 96 Ed41
Acquapendente I 84 Fb40
Acquasanta Terme I 85 Fd40
Acquaviva delle Fonti I 99 Gc43
Acqui Terme I 83 Ed37
Acri I 109 Gc45
Acsa H 74 Ha33
Ada SRB 75 Hb36
Adak S 33 Gc10
Ådalsbruk N 37 Fc16
Adámas GR 111 Jc47
Adamclisi RO 89 Ka37
Adamova BY 53 Jb22
Adamsfjord N 27 Hb03
Adamuz E 105 Bb44
Adare IRL 18 Bd24
Ademuz E 93 Cb42
Adenau D 63 Ec30
Adjud RO 77 Jd35
Adliswil CH 71 Ed34
Admjany BY 53 Ja24
Admont A 73 Ga34
Adolfsström S 33 Gb09
Adony H 74 Ha34
Adorf D 64 Fc30
Adra E 106 Bc46
Adrall E 81 Da40
Adrano I 109 Ga47
Adria I 84 Fc37
Adunaţii-Copăceni RO 88 Jc37
Adutiškis LT 53 Ja23
Aegviidu EST 47 Hd18
A Estrada E 78 Ad37
Aetorráhi GR 110 Hd46
Äetsä FIN 40 Hb15
Afándou GR 115 Kc47
Åfarnes N 36 Fa14
Afétes GR 101 Ja44
Afumaţi RO 88 Jc37
Agápi GR 112 Jc46
Agapia RO 76 Jc34
Agde F 81 Dc39
Agen F 81 Da37
Agerbæk DK 48 Fa23
Agger DK 48 Fa21
Aggtelek H 75 Hb33
Aghireşu RO 75 Hd34
Agiá GR 101 Ja44
Agia Eirini CY 128 Gb18
Agía Galíni GR 114 Jc49
Agía Marína GR 112 Jb46
Agía Marína GR 112 Jb46
Agía Pelagía GR 111 Ja48
Agía Triáda GR 110 Hd46
Agía Varvára GR 115 Jd49

Agighiol RO 89 Ka36
Ágii Apóstoli GR 111 Ja48
Ágii Theódori GR 111 Ja46
Aginta RO 76 Ja35
Agiókambos GR 101 Ja44
Agiokambos GR 111 Ja45
Agiorgítika GR 111 Ja47
Ágios Andréas GR 111 Ja47
Agios Charalampos GR 102 Jc42
Ágios Dimítrios GR 101 Hd43
Ágios Dimítrios GR 111 Ja47
Ágios Efstrátios GR 113 Jc44
Ágios Geórgios GR 110 Hd45
Ágios Kírikos GR 113 Jd46
Ágios Mámas GR 114 Jc49
Ágios Nikolaos GR 110 Hc47
Ágios Nikólaos GR 110 Hd46
Ágios Nikólaos GR 115 Jd49
Ágios Pétros GR 111 Ja47
Ágios Stéfanos GR 110 Hd45
Agios Theódori GR 101 Hc44
Agios Theodoros CY 128 Gc18
Agira I 109 Ga47
Ãglen BG 88 Jb39
Aglona LV 53 Ja22
Agnantiá GR 101 Hc44
Agnone I 99 Ga41
Ágordo I 72 Fc36
Agramunt E 81 Da40
Ágreda E 80 Cb39
Agreliá GR 101 Hd44
Agriáni GR 111 Ja47
Agrigento I 108 Fd47
Agrínio GR 110 Hd45
Agriovótano GR 111 Ja45
Agrópoli I 99 Ga43
Ågskardet N 28 Ga08
A Guarda E 78 Ad37
A Gudiña E 78 Ba38
Agudo E 91 Bb42
Águeda P 78 Ad39
Aguilar E 105 Bb44
Aguilar de Campóo E 79 Bd38
Águilas E 107 Ca45
Ahaus D 55 Ec28
Åheim N 36 Ed14
Ahırlı TR 128 Ga16
Ahladiá GR 102 Jb41
Ahladhóri GR 101 Ja42
Ahlainen FIN 40 Ha15
Ahlbeck D 57 Ga25
Ahlen D 55 Ed28
Ahmalahti RUS 27 Hd04
Ahmetli TR 113 Kb45
Ahmovaara FIN 35 Ja12

Ahrensbök D 56 Fb25
Ahrensburg D 56 Fb26
Ãhtäri FIN 40 Hb14
Ahtme EST 47 Ja17
Ahtopol BG 103 Ka40
Ahtropovo RUS 118 Fb08
Ahtubinsk RUS 123 Ga14
Ahun F 69 Db35
Åhus S 50 Ga23
Ahvenselkä FIN 31 Hd07
Aibar E 80 Cc39
Aichach D 72 Fb33
Aigen A 65 Fd32
Aigen A 73 Ga34
Aigiali GR 113 Jd47
Aigialousa CY 128 Gc18
Aigle CH 71 Ec35
Aignay-le-Duc F 70 Ea33
Aigre F 69 Da35
Aigrefeuille-d'Aunis F 68 Cd34
Aiguebelle F 71 Eb36
Aigues-Mortes F 82 Dd38
Aiguilles F 83 Eb37
Aiguillon F 81 Da37
Aigurande F 69 Db34
Ailefroide F 83 Eb37
Ailly-sur-Noye F 62 Dc30
Ainaži LV 46 Hc20
Ainhoa F 80 Cc38
Ainsa E 80 Cd39
Airaines F 62 Dc30
Airasca I 83 Ec37
Aire-sur-l'Adour F 80 Cd37
Aire-sur-la-Lys F 62 Dd29
Airolo CH 71 Ed35
Airvault F 69 Da33
Aiud RO 76 Ja35
Aix-en-Othe F 62 Dd32
Aix-en-Provence F 82 Ea39
Aixe-sur-Vienne F 69 Db35
Aix-les-Bains F 71 Eb36
Aizenay F 68 Cd33
Aizkräukle LV 53 Hd21
Aizpute LV 52 Hb21
Ajaccio F 96 Ed41
Ajaureforsen S 33 Gb10
Ajka H 74 Gc35
Ajtos BG 89 Jd39
Äkäsjokisuu FIN 30 Ha07
Äkäslompolo FIN 30 Hb07
Akçaabat TR 127 Fd19
Akçaova TR 113 Kb46
Akçaşehir TR 128 Gc16
Akcjabrski BY 121 Eb13
Aken D 56 Fc28
Åkernes N 42 Fa19
Åkersberga S 45 Gc18
Åkersjön S 33 Ga12
Akhisar TR 113 Kb44
Akkerfjord N 26 Ha03
Akköy TR 113 Ka46
Akniste LV 53 Ja22
Akolica BY 53 Jb24
Akören TR 128 Ga15
Akova TR 128 Gb17

Åkran N 32 Fd12
Akranes IS 14 Bc06
Åkrestrømmen N 37 Fc15
Akrotiri CY 128 Gb19
Akrotíri GR 115 Jd48
Aksaj RUS 123 Fc15
Akşar TR 127 Ga19
Aksdal N 42 Ed18
Aksubaevo RUS 119 Ga09
Aktarsk RUS 123 Fd12
Akureyri IS 15 Ca06
Akyaka TR 128 Gb17
Ål N 37 Fb16
Ala S 39 Gc16
Alaçam TR 126 Fb19
Alacami TR 128 Ga17
Alacant (Alicante) E 107
Cb44
Alaçatı TR 113 Jd45
Aladağ TR 128 Gb16
Alaejos E 79 Bc39
Alagna Valesia I 71 Ec36
Alagón E 80 Cc40
Alahärmä FIN 40 Hb13
Alajärvi FIN 40 Hb13
Alakurtti RUS 31 Ja07
Alakylä FIN 30 Hb07
Alakylä FIN 35 Hc10
Alanäs S 33 Gb12
Ålandsbro S 39 Gc14
Alange E 91 Ba42
Alanis E 105 Ba43
Alanta LT 53 Hd23
Alanya TR 128 Ga17
Alaraz E 91 Bc40
Alarcón E 92 Ca42
Alaşehir TR 113 Kb45
Ålåsen S 33 Ga12
Alassio I 83 Ec38
Alassio CY 128 Gb19
Alastaro FIN 40 Hb16
Alatri I 98 Fd42
Alatyr' RUS 119 Fd09
Alaveteli FIN 34 Hb12
Alavieska FIN 34 Hb11
Alavus FIN 40 Hb14
Alba I 83 Ec37
Albac RO 75 Hd35
Albacete E 92 Ca43
Alba de Tormes E 91 Bb40
Ålbæk DK 43 Fb20
Albaida E 107 Cb44
Alba Iulia RO 76 Ja35
Albalate del Arzobispo E
93 Cc41
Albalate de Zorita E 92
Ca41
Alban F 81 Db38
Albano Laziale I 98 Fc42
Albanyà E 81 Db40
Albarracín E 93 Cb41
Albena BG 89 Ka38
Albenga I 83 Ec38
Albentosa E 93 Cb42
Albergaria-a-Velha P 78
Ad39

Albernoa P 104 Ac43
Alberobello I 99 Gc43
Albersdorf D 56 Fa25
Albert F 62 Dd30
Albertville F 71 Eb36
Albeşti RO 77 Jd34
Albeşti RO 89 Ka38
Albi F 81 Db38
Albocàsser E 93 Cc42
Alborea E 93 Cb43
Albox E 106 Bd45
Albstadt D 71 Ed33
Albufeira P 104 Ac44
Albuñol E 106 Bc45
Albuquerque E 90 Ad41
Alcácer do Sal P 90 Ac42
Alcáçovas P 90 Ac42
Alcalá de Guadaira E 105
Ba44
Alcalá de Henares E 92 Bd41
Alcalá del Júcar E 93 Cb43
Alcalá de los Gazules E 105
Ba45
Alcalá del Río E 105 Ba44
Alcalà de Xivert E 93 Cc42
Alcalá la Real E 106 Bc44
Alcamo I 108 Fc46
Alcanar E 93 Cd42
Alcanede P 90 Ac41
Alcañices E 78 Bb38
Alcañiz E 93 Cc41
Alcántara E 91 Ba41
Alcantarilla E 107 Cc45
Alcaracejos E 105 Bb43
Alcarràs E 80 Cd40
Alcaudete E 106 Bc44
Alcaudete de la Jara E 91
Bc41
Alcázar de San Juan E 92
Bd42
Alcester GB 24 Da26
Alčevs'k UA 122 Fb15
Alcoba de los Montes E 91
Bc42
Alcoentre P 90 Ac41
Alcoi (Alcoy) E 107 Cb44
Alcolea del Pinar E 92 Ca40
Alconchel E 90 Ad42
Alcorisa E 93 Cc41
Alcoutim P 104 Ac43
Alcublas E 93 Cc42
Alcúdia E 95 Db43
Aldeadávila de la Ribera E
78 Bb39
Aldea del Rey E 92 Bc43
Aldeburgh GB 25 Dc27
Aldenueva del Codonal E
91 Bc40
Aldershot GB 24 Da28
Åled S 49 Fd22
Alëhovščina RUS 117 Eb08
Aleksandro Gaj RUS 123
Ga12
Aleksandrov RUS 118 Fa10
Aleksandrovac SRB 87
Hc38

Aleksandrovac SRB 87
Hc39
Aleksandrovskoe RUS 127
Ga16
Aleksandrów Kujawski PL
58 Gd27
Aleksandrów Łódzki PL 58
Ha28
Alekseevka RUS 122 Fb13
Alekseevka RUS 123 Fc12
Alekseevskaja RUS 123
Fc13
Alekseevskoe RUS 119
Ga09
Aleksin RUS 117 Ed11
Aleksinac SRB 87 Hc39
Alekšycy BY 59 Hd26
Ålem S 50 Gb21
Alemdar TR 128 Gb15
Ålen N 37 Fc13
Alençon F 61 Da31
Alenquer P 90 Ac41
Alès F 82 Dd38
Aleşd RO 75 Hc34
Alessandria I 83 Ed37
Ålesund N 36 Ed14
Alexándria GR 101 Hd43
Alexandria RO 88 Jb38
Alexandroupoli GR 102
Jc42
Alfaro E 80 Cb39
Alfarràs E 80 Cd40
Alfatar BG 89 Jd38
Alfeld D 56 Fb28
Alfonsine I 84 Fc38
Alford GB 17 Db19
Alford GB 25 Dc25
Alfta S 38 Gb16
Ålgård N 42 Ed19
Algeciras E 105 Ba46
Alghero I 97 Ec43
Algodonales E 105 Ba45
Alhama de Aragón E 80
Cb40
Alhama de Granada E 106
Bc45
Alhama de Murcia E 107
Ca45
Alhambra E 92 Bd43
Alhaurín el Grande E 105
Bb45
Alia I 108 Fd47
Aliaga E 93 Cc41
Aliağa TR 113 Ka44
Alíartos GR 111 Ja45
Alıbeyhüyüğü TR 128 Gb15
Alibunar SRB 87 Hb37
Alicante E 107 Cb44
Álika GR 111 Ja48
Alíki GR 102 Jb42
Alíko GR 115 Jd47
Alingsås S 43 Fd20
Aliseda E 91 Ba41
Alivéri GR 112 Jb45
Aljezur P 104 Ab43
Aljustrel P 104 Ac43

Alkmaar NL 55 Eb27
Allanche F 69 Dc36
Allariz E 78 Ba37
Allauch F 82 Ea39
Alleen N 42 Ed20
Allersberg D 64 Fb32
Allevard F 71 Eb36
Allinge DK 50 Ga24
Allo E 80 Cb39
Allones F 61 Da32
Allos F 83 Eb38
Almacelles E 80 Cd40
Almada P 90 Ab41
Almadén E 105 Bb43
Almagro E 92 Bc43
Almansa E 93 Cb43
Almanza E 79 Bc38
Almaraz E 91 Bb41
Almarza E 80 Cb39
Almazán E 92 Ca40
Almdalen N 33 Ga10
Almeida P 91 Ba40
Almeirim P 90 Ac41
Almelo NL 55 Ec27
Almenara E 93 Cc42
Almenar de Soria E 80 Cb40
Almendral E 90 Ad42
Almendralejo E 91 Ba42
Almere NL 55 Eb27
Almería E 106 Bd46
Almerimar E 106 Bd46
Al'met'evsk RUS 119 Ga08
Älmhult S 50 Ga22
Almiropótamos GR 112
Jb45
Almirós GR 101 Ja44
Almodôvar P 104 Ac43
Almodóvar del Campo E
92 Bc43
Almodóvar del Río E 105
Bb44
Almoharín E 91 Ba42
Almonte E 105 Ad44
Älmsta S 45 Gd17
Almudévar E 80 Cc40
Almuñécar E 106 Bc45
Almunge S 45 Gc17
Alnaši RUS 119 Ga08
Alness GB 17 Da19
Alnwick GB 21 Db22
Aloja LV 47 Hd20
Álora E 105 Bb45
Alpalhão P 90 Ad41
Alpera E 93 Cb43
Alphen a/d Rijn NL 55 Eb27
Alpiarça P 90 Ac41
Alpua FIN 35 Hc11
Alquézar E 80 Cd39
Als DK 49 Fb22
Alsasua E 80 Cb38
Alsfeld D 64 Fa29
Alsike S 45 Gc18
Alsterbro S 50 Gb21
Alstermo S 50 Gb21
Alta N 26 Ha04
Altamura I 99 Gc43

Altdorf **CH** 71 Ed35
Altdorf **D** 64 Fb31
Altea **E** 94 Cc44
Altenberg **D** 65 Fd30
Altenburg **D** 64 Fc29
Altenkirchen **D** 63 Ed29
Altenmarkt **A** 73 Fd34
Altenmarkt **A** 73 Ga34
Altensteig **D** 63 Ed32
Altentreptow **D** 57 Fd26
Alter do Chão **P** 90 Ad41
Altheim **A** 73 Fd33
Althofen **A** 73 Ga35
Alţina **RO** 76 Ja35
Altınova **TR** 113 Ka44
Altkirch **F** 71 Ec33
Altnaharra **GB** 17 Da18
Altn Bulg **RUS** 123 Ga14
Alton **GB** 24 Da28
Altötting **D** 72 Fc33
Altunhisar **TR** 128 Gc15
Altura **E** 93 Cc42
Alūksne **LV** 47 Ja20
Alunda **S** 45 Gc17
Alupka **UA** 126 Fa18
Alušta **UA** 126 Fa18
Alvalade **P** 90 Ac42
Älvängen **S** 43 Fc20
Alvdal **N** 37 Fc14
Älvdalen **S** 38 Ga16
Alvesta **S** 50 Ga21
Ålvho **S** 38 Ga15
Ålvik **N** 36 Ed16
Alvito **P** 90 Ac42
Älvkarleby **S** 45 Gc17
Älvros **S** 38 Fd15
Älvros **S** 38 Ga15
Älvsbyn **S** 34 Gd10
Älvsered **S** 49 Fd21
Alytus **LT** 53 Hd24
Alzey **D** 63 Ed31
Alzira **E** 93 Cc43
Ämådalen **S** 38 Ga16
Amadora **P** 90 Ab41
Åmål **S** 43 Fd19
Amalfi **I** 99 Ga43
Amaliáda **GR** 110 Hd46
Amandola **I** 85 Fd40
Amantea **I** 109 Gb45
Amara **RO** 89 Jd37
Amarante **P** 78 Ad38
Amărăştii de Jos **RO** 88 Ja38
Amareleja **P** 105 Ad43
Amárinthos **GR** 112 Jb45
Amaru **RO** 88 Jc37
Amatrice **I** 85 Fd40
Ambar **TR** 128 Gc15
Ambazac **F** 69 Db35
Ambelákia **GR** 101 Ja44
Ambelóna **GR** 100 Hb44
Ambelónas **GR** 101 Hd44
Amberg **D** 64 Fc31
Ambérieu-en-Bugey **F** 70 Ea35
Ambert **F** 70 Dd36

Ambjörby **S** 44 Fd17
Amble **GB** 21 Db22
Ambleside **GB** 21 Da23
Amboise **F** 69 Db33
Ameixial **P** 104 Ac43
Amelia **I** 84 Fc40
Amélie-les-Bains **F** 81 Db40
Amelinghausen **D** 56 Fb26
Amendolara **I** 99 Gc44
Amersfoort **NL** 55 Eb27
Amesbury **GB** 24 Da28
Amfíklia **GR** 111 Ja45
Amfilohía **GR** 110 Hc45
Ámfissa **GR** 111 Ja45
Amiens **F** 62 Dc30
Amilly **F** 62 Dc32
Amindeo **GR** 101 Hd43
Åminne **S** 45 Gd20
Åmli **N** 42 Fa19
Amlwch **GB** 20 Cd24
Ämmänsaari **FIN** 35 Ja10
Ammarnäs **S** 33 Gb09
Ammochostos **CY** 128 Gc19
Amoliani **GR** 102 Jb43
Amorgós **GR** 115 Jd47
Åmot **N** 37 Fb16
Åmot **N** 42 Fa18
Åmot **N** 43 Fb17
Åmot **S** 38 Gb16
Åmotfors **S** 43 Fd18
Amou **F** 80 Cd38
Ampezzo **I** 72 Fc35
Amplepuis **F** 70 Dd35
Amposta **E** 93 Cd41
Åmsele **S** 34 Gd11
Amsterdam **NL** 55 Eb27
Amstetten **A** 73 Ga33
Amusquillo **E** 79 Bd39
Amzacea **RO** 89 Ka37
Anáfi **GR** 115 Jd48
Anafonitria **GR** 110 Hc46
Anagni **I** 98 Fd42
Anaharavi **GR** 100 Hb44
Anamur **TR** 128 Gb17
Anan'iv **UA** 77 Ka32
Anapa **RUS** 126 Fb17
Anascaul **IRL** 18 Bc24
Ånäset **S** 34 Ha11
Ance **LV** 46 Hb20
Ancenis **F** 68 Cd33
Ancerville **F** 62 Ea32
Ancona **I** 85 Fd39
Ancy-le-Franc **F** 70 Ea33
Åndalsnes **N** 36 Fa14
Ånddalsvågen **N** 32 Fd10
Andebu **N** 43 Fb18
Andelot **F** 63 Eb32
Andenes **N** 28 Gb05
Anderlecht **B** 62 Ea29
Andermatt **CH** 71 Ed35
Andernach **D** 63 Ed30
Andernos-les-Bains **F** 68 Cc36
Anderstorp **S** 49 Fd21
Andírio **GR** 110 Hd46
Andoain **E** 80 Cb38

Andocs **H** 74 Gd35
Andorra **E** 93 Cc41
Andorra la Vella **AND** 81 Da39
Andover **GB** 24 Da28
Andratx **E** 95 Da43
Andravída **GR** 110 Hc46
Andreapol' **RUS** 117 Ec10
Andria **I** 99 Gc42
Andrievo-Ivanivka **MD** 77 Kb32
Andrijevica **MNE** 87 Hb40
Andrijivka **UA** 126 Fb16
Andrítsena **GR** 110 Hd47
Ándros **GR** 112 Jc46
Andruševka **UA** 121 Eb15
Andrychów **PL** 67 Ha31
Andselv **N** 26 Gc05
Andújar **E** 106 Bc44
Anduze **F** 82 Dd38
Aneby **S** 44 Ga20
Änge **S** 38 Ga13
Ånge **S** 38 Gb14
Ängelholm **S** 49 Fd22
Angeli **FIN** 27 Hb05
Angelókastro **GR** 110 Hc45
Angelókastro **GR** 111 Ja46
Ängelsberg **S** 44 Gb17
Angermünde **D** 57 Ga27
Angern **A** 74 Gc33
Angers **F** 69 Da33
Angerville **F** 62 Dc32
Anglès **E** 81 Db40
Angles **F** 68 Cd34
Anglure **F** 62 Dd32
Angoulême **F** 69 Da35
Angüés **E** 80 Cd40
Anguse **EST** 47 Ja18
Anina **RO** 87 Hc37
Anıtlı **TR** 128 Gb17
Anjalankoski **FIN** 41 Hd16
Anjan **S** 32 Fd12
Ankarsrum **S** 44 Gb20
Ankarvattnet **S** 33 Ga11
Anklam **D** 57 Fd26
Ånn **S** 38 Fd13
Anna **RUS** 122 Fb12
Annaberg-Buchholz **D** 65 Fd30
Annan **GB** 21 Da22
Anna Paulowna **NL** 55 Eb26
Annecy **F** 71 Eb36
Annemasse **F** 71 Eb35
Annino **RUS** 117 Ed08
Annonay **F** 70 Dd36
Annopol **PL** 67 Hc29
Annot **F** 83 Eb38
Áno Poróia **GR** 101 Ja42
Áno Vrondoú **GR** 101 Ja42
Anröchte **D** 55 Ed28
Ans **B** 63 Eb29
Ansbach **D** 64 Fb31
Antequera **E** 105 Bb45
Anthótopos **GR** 101 Ja44
Antibes **F** 83 Eb39
Antíparos **GR** 111 Jc47

Antnäs **S** 34 Ha10
Antonin **PL** 66 Gc29
Antonovo **BG** 88 Jc39
Antracyt **UA** 122 Fb15
Antrim **GB** 20 Cc22
Antrodoco **I** 98 Fd41
Antsla **EST** 47 Ja20
Anttis **S** 30 Ha07
Anttola **FIN** 41 Ja14
Antwerpen **B** 54 Ea28
Anykščiai **LT** 53 Hd23
Anzin **F** 62 Ea29
Anzio **I** 98 Fc42
Aoiz **E** 80 Cc38
Aosta **I** 71 Ec36
Apa **TR** 128 Gc16
Apagy **H** 75 Hc33
Apahida **RO** 76 Ja34
Apastovo **RUS** 119 Fd09
Apatin **SRB** 74 Ha36
Ape **LV** 47 Ja20
Apeldoorn **NL** 55 Ec27
Apen **D** 55 Ed26
Apidiá **GR** 111 Ja47
Apolda **D** 64 Fc29
Apólonas **GR** 115 Jd47
Apostolove **UA** 125 Ed16
Äppelbo **S** 44 Ga17
Appenzell **CH** 72 Fa34
Appingedam **NL** 55 Ed26
Appleby-in-Westmorland **GB** 21 Da23
Apricena **I** 99 Gb42
Apriķi **LV** 52 Hb21
Aprilci **BG** 88 Jb39
Aprilia **I** 98 Fc42
Aprilovo **BG** 88 Jc39
Apšeronsk **RUS** 127 Fc17
Apšupe **LV** 52 Hc21
Apt **F** 82 Ea38
Aquileia **I** 73 Fd36
Aracena **E** 105 Ad43
Arad **RO** 75 Hc35
Aradippou **CY** 128 Gc19
Aragona **I** 108 Fd47
Aráhova **GR** 111 Ja45
Aralkı **TR** 127 Fd19
Aramits **F** 80 Cc38
Aranda de Duero **E** 79 Bd39
Aranda de Moncayo **E** 80 Cb40
Arandjelovac **SRB** 87 Hb38
Aranjuez **E** 92 Bd41
Arantzazu **E** 80 Cb38
Aras de Alpuente **E** 93 Cb42
Aravete **EST** 47 Hd18
Arbatax **I** 97 Ed44
Arboga **S** 44 Gb18
Arbois **F** 71 Eb34
Arborea **I** 97 Ec44
Årbostad **N** 28 Gb06
Arbrå **S** 38 Gb15
Arbroath **GB** 17 Db20
Arbus **I** 97 Ec44
Arbuzinka **MD** 77 Kb32
Arcachon **F** 68 Cc36

Aubenas F 82 Dd37
Aubergenville F 62 Dc31
Auberive F 70 Ea33
Aubiet F 81 Da38
Aubigny-sur-Nère F 69 Dc33
Aubin F 81 Db37
Aubusson F 69 Dc35
Auce LV 52 Hc22
Auch F 81 Da38
Auchterarder GB 21 Da21
Audierne F 60 Cb31
Audincourt F 71 Ec34
Audru EST 46 Hc19
Audruicq F 62 Dd29
Aue D 65 Fd30
Auer I 72 Fb35
Auerbach D 64 Fc30
Auerbach D 64 Fc31
Aughnacloy GB 20 Cb22
Augsburg D 72 Fb33
Augusta I 109 Gb47
Augustów PL 59 Hc25
Aukštadvaris LT 53 Hd24
Auktsjaur S 34 Gd10
Aulla I 84 Fa38
Aullène F 96 Ed41
Aulnay F 68 Cd34
Ault F 62 Dc29
Aulum DK 48 Fa22
Aumale F 62 Dc30
Aumont-Aubrac F 81 Dc37
Aunay-sur-Odon F 61 Da31
Auneau F 62 Dc32
Auneuil F 62 Dc31
Auning DK 49 Fb22
Aups F 83 Eb39
Aura FIN 40 Hb16
Auray F 60 Cc32
Aurdal N 37 Fb16
Aure N 37 Fb13
Aurich D 55 Ed26
Aurillac F 69 Dc36
Auriol F 82 Ea39
Aurlandsvangen N 36 Fa16
Auronzo di Cadore I 72 Fc35
Aurora RO 89 Ka38
Austad N 42 Fa18
Austevoll N 42 Ec17
Austmarka N 43 Fd17
Austnes N 36 Ed13
Auterive F 81 Da38
Authon-du-Perche F 61 Db32
Auttoinen FIN 40 Hc15
Autun F 70 Dd34
Auvillar F 81 Da37
Auxerre F 70 Dd33
Auxi-le-Château F 62 Dc29
Auxonne F 70 Ea34
Auzances F 69 Dc35
Availles-Limouzine F 69 Da35
Avaldsnes N 42 Ec18
Avallon F 70 Dd33
Avaviken S 33 Gc10

Avdijivka UA 121 Ed13
Ávdira GR 102 Jc42
Avebury GB 24 Da27
A Veiga E 78 Bb38
Aveiro P 78 Ad39
Avellino I 99 Ga43
Aversa I 99 Ga43
Avesnes-sur-Helpe F 62 Ea30
Avesta S 44 Gb17
Avezzano I 98 Fd41
Avgustivka UA 77 Kb34
Aviemore GB 17 Da19
Avigliana I 83 Ec37
Avigliano I 99 Gb43
Avignon F 82 Dd38
Ávila E 91 Bc40
Avilés E 79 Bc36
Avinurme EST 47 Ja18
Avion F 62 Dd29
Avis P 90 Ad41
Avize F 62 Ea31
Avlémonas GR 111 Jb48
Avliotes GR 100 Hb44
Avlóna GR 112 Jb46
Avola I 109 Ga48
Avram Iancu RO 75 Hc35
Avram Iancu RO 75 Hd35
Avranches F 61 Cd31
Avrig RO 88 Ja36
Avrillé F 61 Da32
Ax-les-Thermes F 81 Db39
Axmarby S 39 Gc16
Axvall S 44 Fd19
Ayamonte E 104 Ac44
Ayancık TR 126 Fb19
Aydın TR 113 Kb45
Aydıncık TR 128 Gb17
Aydınlar TR 128 Gc16
Ayerbe E 80 Cc39
Aylesbury GB 25 Db27
Ayllón E 92 Ca40
Aylsham GB 25 Dc26
Ayora E 93 Cb43
Ayr GB 20 Cd21
Ayrancı TR 128 Gc16
Ayton GB 21 Db21
Aytré F 68 Cd34
Ayvacık TR 103 Jd43
Ayverbe E 80 Cc39
Ayvalık TR 113 Ka44
Azaila E 80 Cc40
Azaryčy BY 121 Eb13
Azay-le-Rideau F 69 Da33
Aziory BY 59 Hd25
Aznakaevo RUS 119 Ga08
Azov RUS 123 Fc15
Azpeitia E 80 Cb38
Azuaga E 105 Ba43

B

Babadag RO 89 Ka36
Babaeski TR 103 Jd41
Babaevo RUS 117 Ec08
Babek BG 102 Jb40

Băbeni RO 88 Ja37
Babica PL 67 Hc30
Babilafuente E 91 Bc40
Babriškės LT 53 Hd24
Babrujsk BY 121 Eb13
Babtai LT 52 Hc24
Báč SK 74 Gc33
Bacău RO 76 Jc34
Baccarat F 63 Ec32
Băcești RO 76 Jc34
Bacharach D 63 Ed30
Bachčysaraj UA 126 Fa18
Bachmač UA 121 Ed14
Bachórz PL 67 Hc31
Băcina SRB 87 Hc39
Baciu RO 75 Hd34
Baciuty PL 59 Hc26
Bačka Palanka SRB 86 Ha37
Bačka Topola SRB 74 Ha36
Backe S 33 Gb12
Bäckebo S 50 Gb21
Bäckefors S 43 Fd19
Bäckhammar S 44 Ga18
Backnang D 64 Fa32
Bačko Novo Selo SRB 86 Ha37
Bad Aibling D 72 Fc33
Badajoz E 90 Ad42
Badalona E 95 Db41
Bad Arolsen D 64 Fa29
Bad Aussee A 73 Fd34
Bad Bederkesa D 56 Fa26
Bad Bentheim D 55 Ed27
Bad Bergzabern D 63 Ed32
Bad Berka D 64 Fb29
Bad Berleburg D 63 Ed29
Bad Bevensen D 56 Fb26
Bad Bibra D 64 Fc29
Bad Bramstedt D 56 Fb25
Bad Brückenau D 64 Fa30
Bad Camberg D 63 Ed30
Bad Doberan D 56 Fc25
Bad Driburg D 56 Fa28
Bad Düben D 57 Fd28
Bad Dürkheim D 63 Ed31
Bademli TR 103 Kb43
Baden A 73 Gb33
Baden CH 71 Ed34
Baden-Baden D 63 Ed32
Bad Endorf D 72 Fc33
Bad Fallingbostel D 56 Fa27
Bad Freienwalde D 57 Ga27
Bad Friedrichshall D 64 Fa31
Bad Gandersheim D 56 Fb28
Bad Gastein A 73 Fd34
Bad Gleichenberg A 73 Gb35
Bad Griesbach D 73 Fd33
Bad Hall A 73 Ga33
Bad Hersfeld D 64 Fa29
Bad Hofgastein A 73 Fd34
Bad Homburg D 63 Ed30
Bad Honnef D 63 Ec29

Badia Gran E 95 Db44
Bad Ischl A 73 Fd34
Bad Karlshafen D 56 Fa28
Bad Kissingen D 64 Fb30
Bad Kleinen D 56 Fc26
Bad Königshofen D 64 Fb30
Bad Kreuznach D 63 Ed31
Bad Krozingen D 71 Ec33
Bad Laasphe D 63 Ed29
Bad Langensalza D 64 Fb29
Bad Lausick D 65 Fd29
Bad Lauterberg D 56 Fb28
Bad Leonfelden A 73 Ga33
Bad Liebenwerda D 65 Fd29
Bad Mergentheim D 64 Fa31
Bad Münstereifel D 63 Ec30
Bad Muskau D 65 Ga29
Bad Nauheim D 64 Fa30
Bad Neuenahr-Ahrweiler D 63 Ec30
Bad Neustadt D 64 Fb30
Bad Oeynhausen D 56 Fa28
Bad Oldesloe D 56 Fb25
Badonviller F 63 Ec32
Bad Pyrmont D 56 Fa28
Bad Radkersburg A 73 Gb35
Bad Reichenhall D 73 Fd34
Bad Säckingen D 71 Ed34
Bad Salzuflen D 56 Fa28
Bad Salzungen D 64 Fb29
Bad Sankt Leonhard A 73 Ga35
Bad Saulgau D 72 Fa33
Bad Schönborn D 63 Ed31
Bad Schwalbach D 63 Ed30
Bad Schwartau D 56 Fb25
Bad Segeberg D 56 Fb25
Bad Sobernheim D 63 Ed31
Bad Sülze D 57 Fd25
Bad Tölz D 72 Fc34
Bad Urach D 64 Fa32
Bad Vöslau A 73 Gb33
Bad Waldsee D 72 Fa33
Bad Wildungen D 64 Fa29
Bad Wilsnack D 56 Fc27
Bad Windsheim D 64 Fb31
Bad Wünnenberg D 56 Fa28
Bad Wurzach D 72 Fa33
Bad Zwischenahn D 55 Ed26
Baena E 105 Bb44
Baeza E 106 Bc44
Bafra TR 126 Fb19
Bagà E 81 Da40
Bağarası TR 113 Kb46
Bağbaşı TR 128 Ga16
Bagenalstown IRL 19 Cb24
Bagenkop DK 49 Fb24
Bagheria I 108 Fd46
Bagienice PL 59 Hc26
Bagn N 37 Fb16
Bagnacavallo I 84 Fc38
Bagnara Calabra I 109 Gb46

Bârzava – Berlanga de Duero

Bârzava **RO** 75 Hc35
Bašaid **SRB** 75 Hb36
Basarabeasca **MD** 77 Ka34
Basarabi **RO** 89 Ka37
Bascov **RO** 88 Jb37
Basel **CH** 71 Ec34
Basi **LV** 52 Hb21
Basildon **GB** 25 Db27
Başin **TR** 128 Gc15
Basingstoke **GB** 24 Da28
Baška **HR** 85 Ga37
Bassano del Grappa **I** 72 Fc36
Bassella **E** 81 Da40
Bassum **D** 56 Fa27
Båstad **S** 49 Fd22
Baštanka **UA** 125 Ed16
Bastia **F** 96 Ed40
Bastogne **B** 63 Eb30
Bastuträsk **S** 34 Gd11
Bäta **BG** 102 Jb40
Batajsk **RUS** 123 Fc15
Batak **BG** 102 Jb41
Batanovci **BG** 102 Ja40
Batăr **RO** 75 Hc35
Bátaszék **H** 74 Gd36
Batea **E** 93 Cd41
Bath **GB** 24 Cd27
Batina **HR** 74 Ha36
Batković **BIH** 86 Ha37
Batley **GB** 21 Db24
Bátonyterenye **H** 74 Ha33
Batovo **BG** 89 Ka38
Båtsfjord **N** 27 Hc03
Båtskärsnäs **S** 34 Hb09
Battenberg **D** 64 Fa29
Battipaglia **I** 99 Ga43
Battonya **H** 75 Hb35
Batuša **SRB** 87 Hc38
Batyrevo **RUS** 119 Fd09
Baud **F** 60 Cc32
Baugé **F** 69 Da33
Baume-les-Dames **F** 71 Eb34
Baunatal **D** 64 Fa29
Baunei **I** 97 Ed44
Bauska **LV** 52 Hc22
Băuţar **RO** 75 Hd36
Bautzen **D** 65 Ga29
Bavay **F** 62 Ea30
Bavella **F** 96 Ed41
Bawtry **GB** 25 Db25
Bayburt **TR** 127 Ga19
Bayeux **F** 61 Da30
Bayındır **TR** 113 Kb45
Bayon **F** 63 Eb32
Bayonne **F** 80 Cc37
Bayramiç **TR** 103 Jd43
Bayreuth **D** 64 Fc31
Baza **E** 106 Bd45
Bazarnye Mataki **RUS** 119 Ga09
Bazarnyi Karabulak **RUS** 119 Fd11
Bazas **F** 80 Cd37
Beasain **E** 80 Cb38
Beas de Segura **E** 106 Bd44

Beaucaire **F** 82 Dd38
Beaugency **F** 69 Db33
Beaujeu **F** 70 Ea35
Beaumont **F** 69 Da36
Beaumont-de-Lomagne **F** 81 Da37
Beaumont-Hague **F** 61 Cd29
Beaumont-le-Roger **F** 61 Db31
Beaumont-sur-Sarthe **F** 61 Da32
Beaune **F** 70 Ea34
Beaupréau **F** 68 Cd33
Beauraing **B** 63 Eb30
Beaurepaire **F** 70 Ea36
Beauvais **F** 62 Dc30
Beauvoir-sur-Mer **F** 68 Cc33
Beauvoir-sur-Niort **F** 68 Cd34
Bebra **D** 64 Fa29
Bebrene **LV** 53 Ja22
Bebri **LV** 53 Hd21
Beccles **GB** 25 Dd26
Bečej **SRB** 75 Hb36
Becerreá **E** 78 Bb37
Bechet **RO** 88 Ja38
Becilla de Valderaduey **E** 79 Bc38
Beckum **D** 55 Ed28
Beclean **RO** 76 Ja34
Bečov nad Teplou **CZ** 65 Fd31
Bédarieux **F** 81 Dc38
Bedekovčina **HR** 73 Gb36
Bedford **GB** 25 Db27
Beelitz **D** 57 Fd28
Beeskow **D** 57 Ga28
Bégard **F** 60 Cc30
Beğendik **TR** 103 Ka40
Begleż **BG** 88 Jb39
Begnadalen **N** 37 Fb16
Begovo **BG** 102 Jb40
Begunicy **RUS** 47 Jb17
Behramkale **TR** 113 Jd44
Beidaud **RO** 89 Ka36
Beilen **NL** 55 Ec26
Beilngries **D** 64 Fc32
Beisfjord **N** 29 Gc06
Beiuş **RO** 75 Hc35
Beja **P** 104 Ac43
Béjar **E** 91 Bb40
Békés **H** 75 Hb35
Békéscsaba **H** 75 Hb35
Bekkarfjord **N** 27 Hb03
Belaazёrsk **BY** 120 Ea13
Bélâbre **F** 69 Db34
Bela Crkva **SRB** 87 Hc37
Belaja Kalitva **RUS** 123 Fc14
Belalcázar **E** 105 Bb43
Bela Palanka **SRB** 87 Hd39
Belarus **BY** 120 Ea12
Bełchatów **PL** 67 Ha29
Belchite **E** 80 Cc40
Belcoo **GB** 19 Cb22
Beldibi **TR** 128 Ga17
Beled **H** 74 Gc34

Belev **RUS** 121 Ed12
Belfast **GB** 20 Cc22
Belfir **RO** 75 Hc35
Belford **GB** 21 Db22
Belfort **F** 71 Ec33
Belgern **D** 65 Fd29
Belgodère **F** 96 Ed40
Belgorod **RUS** 122 Fa14
Belica **MK** 101 Hc42
Beli Izvor **BG** 88 Ja39
Beli Manastir **HR** 74 Gd36
Belin-Béliet **F** 68 Cd36
Beliş **RO** 75 Hd35
Belišće **HR** 74 Gd36
Beljanovo **BG** 88 Jc38
Belkaya **TR** 128 Gc15
Bel'ki **BY** 53 Jb23
Bel'kovo **RUS** 121 Ec12
Bellac **F** 69 Db35
Bellagio **I** 71 Ed36
Bellaria-Igea Marina **I** 84 Fc38
Bellegarde **F** 62 Dc32
Bellegarde-sur-Valserine **F** 71 Eb35
Bellême **F** 61 Db32
Belleville **F** 70 Ea35
Belleville-sur-Vie **F** 68 Cd33
Belley **F** 70 Ea36
Bellinzona **CH** 71 Ed36
Bellpuig **E** 81 Da40
Belluno **I** 72 Fc36
Bélmez **E** 105 Bb43
Belmonte **E** 92 Ca42
Belmonte **P** 91 Ba40
Belmullet **IRL** 18 Bd22
Beloci **MD** 77 Ka32
Belœil **B** 62 Ea29
Belogradčik **BG** 87 Hd39
Belorado **E** 79 Ca38
Belorečensk **RUS** 127 Fc17
Belören **TR** 128 Gb16
Beloslav **BG** 89 Ka39
Belotinci **BG** 87 Hd39
Belpasso **I** 109 Ga47
Belper **GB** 24 Da25
Belsay **GB** 21 Db22
Beltinci **SLO** 73 Gb35
Beltiug **RO** 75 Hd34
Belturbet **IRL** 19 Cb23
Belvedere Marittimo **I** 99 Gb44
Belvès **F** 69 Da36
Belyj **RUS** 117 Ec11
Belz **UA** 67 Hd30
Belzig **D** 57 Fd28
Bełżyce **PL** 67 Hc29
Benabarre **E** 80 Cd40
Benalup de Sidonia **E** 105 Ba45
Benamaurel **E** 106 Bd45
Benavente **E** 79 Bc38
Benavides **E** 79 Bc38
Benejama **E** 107 Cb44
Benešov **CZ** 65 Ga31
Benevento **I** 99 Ga42

Bengtsfors **S** 43 Fd19
Benicarló **E** 93 Cd42
Benicàssim (Benicasim) **E** 93 Cc42
Benidorm **E** 94 Cc44
Benifaió **E** 93 Cc43
Benkovac **HR** 85 Gb39
Bénodet **F** 60 Cb31
Bensheim **D** 63 Ed31
Beograd **SRB** 87 Hb37
Beograd-Surcin **SRB** 87 Hb37
Berat **AL** 100 Hb43
Berazino **BY** 53 Jb23
Berazino **BY** 121 Eb12
Berbinzana **E** 80 Cb39
Berceto **I** 84 Fa38
Berchtesgaden **D** 73 Fd34
Berck-Plage **F** 62 Dc29
Berdía **E** 78 Ba36
Berdjans'k **UA** 126 Fb16
Berdyčiv **UA** 121 Eb15
Berehomet **UA** 76 Jb32
Berehove **UA** 75 Hd33
Bereket **TR** 128 Gd15
Berendi **TR** 128 Gc16
Bere Regis **GB** 24 Cd28
Berestečko **UA** 120 Ea15
Bereşti **RO** 77 Jd35
Berettyóújfalu **H** 75 Hc34
Berezanka **UA** 125 Ec16
Berezanskaja **RUS** 127 Fc16
Berežany **UA** 120 Ea15
Berezivka **MD** 77 Kb33
Berezna **UA** 121 Ec13
Berezne **UA** 120 Ea14
Bereznehuvate **UA** 125 Ed16
Berg **N** 32 Fd10
Berga **E** 81 Da40
Bergama **TR** 113 Ka44
Bergamo **I** 72 Fa36
Bergara **E** 80 Cb38
Bergeforsen **S** 39 Gc14
Bergen **D** 56 Fb27
Bergen **D** 57 Fd25
Bergen **N** 36 Ed16
Bergen op Zoom **NL** 54 Ea28
Berger **N** 43 Fc18
Bergerac **F** 69 Da36
Bergheim **D** 63 Ec29
Bergö **FIN** 40 Ha13
Bergsfjord **N** 28 Gb05
Bergshamra **S** 45 Gd18
Bergsjö **S** 38 Gb15
Bergsviken **S** 34 Ha10
Bergues **F** 62 Dd29
Bergviken **S** 33 Gc09
Beringen **B** 63 Eb29
Berja **E** 106 Bd45
Berkåk **N** 37 Fc13
Berkovica **BG** 88 Ja39
Berkovici **BIH** 86 Gd40
Berlanga **E** 105 Ba43
Berlanga de Duero **E** 92 Ca40

136

Bled – Botoşani

Bled **SLO** 73 Ga35
Bleiburg **A** 73 Ga35
Bleik **N** 28 Gb05
Bleikvassli **N** 33 Ga09
Bléneau **F** 70 Dd33
Bleré **F** 69 Db33
Blerick **NL** 55 Ec28
Bletterans **F** 70 Ea34
Blieskastel **D** 63 Ec31
Blinisht **AL** 100 Hb41
Blizne **PL** 67 Hc31
Blois **F** 69 Db33
Blokhus **DK** 49 Fb21
Blombacka **S** 44 Ga18
Blönduós **IS** 14 Bd05
Błonie **PL** 58 Ha28
Błotno **PL** 57 Ga26
Bludenz **A** 72 Fa34
Blumau **A** 73 Gb35
Blumberg **D** 71 Ed33
Blyth **GB** 21 Db22
Bø **N** 43 Fb18
Boal **E** 78 Bb36
Boat of Garten **GB** 17 Da19
Bobâlna **RO** 75 Hd34
Bobbio **I** 83 Ed37
Bobigny **F** 62 Dc31
Bobingen **D** 72 Fb33
Böblingen **D** 64 Fa32
Bobolice **PL** 57 Gb25
Boboševo **BG** 101 Ja41
Bobovdol **BG** 102 Ja40
Bobr **BY** 121 Eb12
Bobrov **RUS** 122 Fb13
Bobrovycja **UA** 121 Ec14
Bobrowice **PL** 57 Ga28
Bobrynec' **UA** 125 Ed16
Bočac **BIH** 86 Gc38
Bochnia **PL** 67 Hb31
Bocholt **D** 55 Ec28
Bochum **D** 55 Ec28
Bockara **S** 50 Gb21
Bockenem **D** 56 Fb28
Bócki **PL** 59 Hc27
Bočkivci **UA** 76 Jb32
Bocşa **RO** 87 Hc37
Bocsig **RO** 75 Hc35
Bod **RO** 88 Jb36
Boda **S** 38 Ga16
Böda **S** 51 Gc21
Boðani **SRB** 86 Ha37
Bodafors **S** 50 Ga21
Boden **S** 34 Ha09
Bodenwerder **D** 56 Fa28
Bodmin **GB** 23 Cb28
Bodø **N** 28 Ga08
Bodoc **RO** 76 Jb35
Bodrost **BG** 101 Ja41
Bodrum **TR** 115 Kb47
Bodsjö **S** 38 Ga14
Bodzentyn **PL** 67 Hb29
Boën **F** 70 Dd36
Bogarra **E** 107 Ca44
Bogatić **SRB** 86 Ha37
Bogatynia **PL** 65 Ga29
Boğaziçi **TR** 113 Kb45

Bogdana **RO** 77 Jd34
Bogë **AL** 100 Hb41
Bögecik **TR** 128 Gc16
Bogen **D** 64 Fc32
Bogen **N** 28 Gb06
Bogense **DK** 49 Fb23
Bogetići **MNE** 86 Ha40
Bognes **N** 28 Gb06
Bognor Regis **GB** 24 Da28
Bogny-sur-Meuse **F** 62 Ea30
Bogorodick **RUS** 118 Fa11
Bogorodsk **RUS** 118 Fb09
Bogova **RO** 87 Hd38
Bogučar **RUS** 123 Fc13
Bogutovac **SRB** 87 Hb39
Bohain-en-Vermandois **F** 62 Dd30
Bohdalov **CZ** 65 Gb31
Bohoduchiv **UA** 122 Fa14
Bohonal de Ibor **E** 91 Bb41
Böhönye **H** 74 Gc35
Bohorodčany **UA** 76 Ja32
Bohuslav **UA** 121 Ec15
Boiro **E** 78 Ad37
Bois-le-Roi **F** 62 Dd32
Boizenburg **D** 56 Fb26
Bojano **I** 99 Ga42
Bojanovo **BG** 103 Jd40
Bojanów **PL** 67 Hc30
Bojanowo **PL** 58 Gc28
Bøjden **DK** 49 Fb24
Bojnik **SRB** 87 Hc40
Boksjön **S** 33 Gb10
Bol **HR** 86 Gc40
Bol.Selo **RUS** 117 Ed09
Bolaños de Calatrava **E** 92 Bc43
Bolayır **TR** 103 Jd42
Bolbec **F** 61 Db30
Boldeşti Scǎeni **RO** 88 Jc36
Bolechiv **UA** 67 Hd31
Bolesławiec **PL** 65 Gb29
Bolewicko **PL** 57 Gb27
Bolhó **H** 74 Gc36
Bolhov **RUS** 121 Ed12
Bolhrad **UA** 77 Ka35
Bolintin-Vale **RO** 88 Jc37
Boljanići **MNE** 86 Ha39
Boljevac **SRB** 87 Hc39
Bolków **PL** 65 Gb29
Bollebygd **S** 43 Fd20
Bollène **F** 82 Dd38
Bollnäs **S** 38 Gb15
Bollstabruk **S** 39 Gc13
Bollullos del Condado **E** 105 Ad44
Bologna **I** 84 Fb38
Bologoe **RUS** 117 Ec09
Bologovo **RUS** 117 Eb10
Bol'šaja Ižora **RUS** 41 Jb16
Bol'šakovo **RUS** 52 Hb24
Bolscno **I** 84 Гc40
Bol'ševik **RUS** 123 Fd12
Bol'šinka **RUS** 123 Fc14
Bol'šoj Sabsk **RUS** 47 Jb18

Bol'šoj Taglino **RUS** 47 Jb17
Bolsward **NL** 55 Ec26
Boltaña **E** 80 Cd39
Bolton **GB** 21 Da24
Bolungarvik **IS** 14 Bc04
Bolzano **I** 72 Fb35
Bombarral **P** 90 Ac41
Boñar **E** 79 Bc37
Bonar Bridge **GB** 17 Da18
Bonäs **S** 38 Ga16
Bondeno **I** 84 Fb37
Bonifacio **F** 96 Ed42
Bonn **D** 63 Ec29
Bonnat **F** 69 Db34
Bonnétable **F** 61 Db32
Bonneval **F** 61 Db32
Bonneville **F** 71 Eb35
Bono **I** 97 Ed43
Bonorva **I** 97 Ec43
Bonyhád **H** 74 Gd36
Boo **S** 45 Gc18
Bopfingen **D** 64 Fb32
Boppard **D** 63 Ed30
Bor **CZ** 65 Fd31
Bor **S** 50 Ga21
Bor **SRB** 87 Hd38
Bor **TR** 128 Gd15
Borås **S** 43 Fd20
Borba **P** 90 Ad42
Borca **RO** 76 Jb34
Bordeaux **F** 68 Cd36
Bordeira **P** 104 Ab43
Bordesholm **D** 56 Fb25
Borðeyri **IS** 14 Bd05
Bordighera **I** 83 Ec39
Borek Wielkopolski **PL** 58 Gc28
Borensberg **S** 44 Gb19
Borga **FIN** 41 Hd16
Borgarnes **IS** 14 Bc06
Borger **NL** 55 Ec26
Borgholm **S** 50 Gb21
Borgomanero **I** 71 Ed36
Borgorose **I** 98 Fd41
Borgo San Dalmazzo **I** 83 Ec38
Borgo San Lorenzo **I** 84 Fb39
Borgosesia **I** 71 Ed36
Borgo Val di Taro **I** 84 Fa38
Borgo Valsugana **I** 72 Fb36
Borhaug **N** 42 Ed20
Borinskoe **RUS** 122 Fb12
Borisoglebsk **RUS** 123 Fc12
Borisovka **RUS** 122 Fa14
Borisovo **RUS** 117 Ed08
Borisovo-Sudskoe **RUS** 117 Ec08
Borja **E** 80 Cb40
Borkavičy **BY** 53 Jb22
Borken **D** 55 Ec28
Borlänge **S** 44 Gb17
Borlaug **N** 36 Fa16
Borlu **TR** 113 Kb44
Bormio **I** 72 Fa35
Borna **D** 64 Fc29

Bornheim **D** 63 Ec29
Boroaia **RO** 76 Jc33
Borobia **E** 80 Cb40
Borodinskoe **RUS** 41 Jb15
Borodjanka **UA** 121 Ec14
Borodyno **UA** 77 Ka34
Borova **UA** 122 Fb14
Borovan **BG** 88 Ja39
Borovany **CZ** 65 Ga32
Borovci **BG** 88 Ja39
Borovec **BG** 102 Ja40
Borovenka **RUS** 117 Ec09
Boroviči **RUS** 117 Ec09
Borovik **RUS** 47 Jb19
Borovsk **RUS** 117 Ed11
Borrisokane **IRL** 18 Ca24
Borşa **RO** 76 Ja33
Boršćiv **UA** 76 Jb32
Borščiv **UA** 124 Ea16
Borsec **RO** 76 Jb34
Børselv **N** 27 Hb03
Borsh **AL** 100 Hb44
Bort-les-Orgues **F** 69 Dc36
Börtnan **S** 38 Ga14
Borup **DK** 49 Fc23
Borve **GB** 16 Cc18
Borvika **UA** 77 Jd32
Borynja **UA** 67 Hd32
Boryslav **UA** 67 Hd31
Boryspil' **UA** 121 Ec14
Borzna **UA** 121 Ec14
Borzysław **PL** 58 Gc25
Bosa **I** 97 Ec43
Bosanci **HR** 85 Gb37
Bosanska Dubica **BIH** 86 Gc37
Bosanska Gradiška **BIH** 86 Gc37
Bosanska Kostajnica **BIH** 86 Gc37
Bosanska Krupa **BIH** 85 Gb37
Bosanski Brod **BIH** 86 Gd37
Bosanski Kobaš **BIH** 86 Gd37
Bosanski Novi **BIH** 86 Gc37
Bosanski Petrovac **BIH** 86 Gc38
Bosanski Šamac **BIH** 86 Gd37
Bosansko Grahovo **BIH** 86 Gc38
Bosilegrad **SRB** 87 Hd40
Boskovice **CZ** 66 Gc31
Bossbøen **N** 42 Fa17
Boston **GB** 25 Db25
Bosut **SRB** 86 Ha37
Böszénfa **H** 74 Gd36
Bote **S** 39 Gc13
Boteşti **RO** 76 Jc34
Boteşti **RO** 88 Jb37
Botevgrad **BG** 102 Ja40
Boticas **P** 78 Ba38
Botiz **RO** 75 Hd33
Botngård **N** 32 Fc12
Botoşani **RO** 76 Jc33

Botsmark **S** 34 Gd12
Bottrop **D** 55 Ec28
Boueilho **F** 80 Cd38
Bouillon **B** 63 Eb30
Bouligny **F** 63 Eb31
Bouloc **F** 81 Dc37
Boulogne-Billancourt **F** 62 Dc31
Boulogne-sur-Gesse **F** 81 Da38
Boulogne-sur-Mer **F** 62 Dc29
Bouloire **F** 61 Db32
Bourbon-Lancy **F** 70 Dd34
Bourbon-l'Archambault **F** 69 Dc34
Bourbonne-les-Bains **F** 71 Eb33
Bourbriac **F** 60 Cc31
Bourdeaux **F** 82 Ea37
Bourganeuf **F** 69 Db35
Bourg-Argental **F** 70 Ea36
Bourg-en-Bresse **F** 70 Ea35
Bourges **F** 69 Dc34
Bourg-et-Comin **F** 62 Dd31
Bourg-Madame **F** 81 Db40
Bourgneuf-en-Retz **F** 68 Cc33
Bourgoin-Jallieu **F** 70 Ea36
Bourg-Saint-Andéol **F** 82 Dd37
Bourg-Saint-Maurice **F** 71 Eb36
Bournemouth **GB** 24 Da28
Boussac **F** 69 Dc34
Boussens **F** 81 Da38
Bouxwiller **F** 63 Ec32
Bovalino Mare **I** 109 Gb46
Bova Marina **I** 109 Gb47
Bovenden **D** 56 Fb28
Boves **F** 62 Dd30
Bovino **I** 99 Gb42
Bowes **GB** 21 Db23
Bowmore **GB** 20 Cc21
Boxberg **D** 65 Ga29
Boxholm **S** 44 Ga20
Boxmeer **NL** 55 Ec28
Boxtel **NL** 55 Eb28
Boyle **IRL** 18 Ca23
Božava **HR** 85 Ga38
Bozburun **TR** 115 Kb47
Bozcaada **TR** 103 Jd43
Bozdoğan **TR** 113 Kb46
Bozen **I** 72 Fb35
Bozioru **RO** 88 Jc36
Bozkir **TR** 128 Ga16
Bozlar **TR** 103 Ka42
Bozouls **F** 81 Dc37
Bozovici **RO** 87 Hc37
Bozyazı **TR** 128 Gb17
Bozzolo **I** 84 Fa37
Bra **I** 83 Ec37
Braås **S** 50 Ga21
Brabova **RO** 88 Ja38
Bracciano **I** 98 Fc41
Brachlewo **PL** 58 Gd25

Bräcke **S** 38 Gb14
Brackley **GB** 24 Da27
Brad **RO** 75 Hd35
Brădeni **RO** 76 Jb35
Bradford **GB** 21 Db24
Brædstrup **DK** 49 Fb23
Braemar **GB** 17 Da20
Braga **P** 78 Ad38
Bragadiru **RO** 88 Jc37
Bragança **P** 78 Bb38
Brăila **RO** 89 Jd36
Braine **F** 62 Dd31
Braintree **GB** 25 Dc27
Brake **D** 56 Fa26
Brakel **D** 56 Fa28
Brålanda **S** 43 Fd19
Brálos **GR** 111 Ja45
Bramming **DK** 48 Fa23
Brampton **GB** 21 Da22
Bramsche **D** 55 Ed27
Brånaberg **S** 33 Gb10
Branäs **S** 38 Fd16
Brancaleone Marina **I** 109 Gb46
Brandbu **N** 43 Fc17
Brande **DK** 48 Fa23
Brandenburg **D** 57 Fd27
Brand-Erbisdorf **D** 65 Fd30
Brändö **FIN** 46 Ha17
Brandon **GB** 25 Dc26
Brandval **N** 43 Fd17
Brandýs nad Labem-Stará Boleslav **CZ** 65 Ga30
Braniewo **PL** 58 Ha25
Bränna **S** 43 Fd19
Brańsk **PL** 59 Hc27
Brantôme **F** 69 Dc35
Braslav **BY** 53 Ja22
Brașov **RO** 88 Jb36
Brastad **S** 43 Fc19
Brzeszcze **PL** 66 Gd29
Brataj **AL** 100 Hb43
Bratca **RO** 75 Hd34
Bratislava **SK** 74 Gc33
Bratovoești **RO** 88 Ja38
Bråttas **S** 34 Ha11
Brattmon **S** 38 Fd16
Brattvåg **N** 36 Fa14
Bratunac **BIH** 86 Ha38
Braunau **A** 73 Fd33
Braunfels **D** 63 Ed30
Braunlage **D** 56 Fb28
Braunschweig **D** 56 Fb28
Braunton **GB** 23 Cc27
Bray **IRL** 19 Cb24
Bray-sur-Seine **F** 62 Dd32
Bray-sur-Somme **F** 62 Dd30
Brazatortas **E** 106 Bc43
Brbinj **HR** 85 Ga39
Brčko **BIH** 86 Ha37
Breaza **RO** 76 Ja34
Breaza **RO** 88 Jc36
Brechin **GB** 17 Db20
Břeclav **CZ** 66 Gc32
Brecon **GB** 24 Cd26
Breda **NL** 55 Eb28

Bredaryd **S** 50 Ga21
Bredbyn **S** 39 Gc13
Bredstedt **D** 48 Fa24
Bree **B** 63 Eb29
Bregenz **A** 72 Fa34
Bregovo **BG** 87 Hd38
Bréhal **F** 61 Cd31
Breiðdalsvik **IS** 15 Cc08
Breidvikeidet **N** 26 Gc04
Breil-sur-Roya **F** 83 Ec38
Breisach **D** 71 Ec33
Breivika **N** 28 Gb06
Breivikbotn **N** 26 Gd03
Breja **RUS** 47 Jb18
Brejtovo **RUS** 117 Ed09
Brekken **N** 37 Fd14
Brekstad **N** 32 Fb12
Bremen **D** 56 Fa26
Bremerhaven **D** 56 Fa26
Bremervörde **D** 56 Fa26
Brem-sur-Mer **F** 68 Cc33
Breń **PL** 57 Gb27
Brenes **E** 105 Ba44
Brenna **N** 33 Ga10
Breno **I** 72 Fa36
Brescia **I** 72 Fa36
Bressanone **I** 72 Fc35
Bressuire **F** 69 Da33
Brëst **BY** 59 Hd27
Brest **F** 60 Cb31
Brestovac **SRB** 87 Hd38
Brestovo **BG** 88 Jb39
Brețcu **RO** 76 Jc35
Bretenoux **F** 69 Db36
Breteuil **F** 62 Dc30
Breteuil-sur-Iton **F** 61 Db31
Bretten **D** 63 Ed32
Breuil-Cervínia **I** 71 Ec36
Breza **BIH** 86 Gd38
Brežice **SLO** 73 Gb36
Breznik **BG** 87 Hd40
Brezno **SK** 67 Ha32
Brezoi **RO** 88 Ja36
Brezovo **BG** 102 Jb40
Briançon **F** 83 Eb37
Briare **F** 69 Dc33
Bribir **HR** 85 Gb39
Briceni **MD** 76 Jc32
Bricquebec **F** 61 Cd30
Bridge End **IRL** 19 Cb21
Bridgend **GB** 24 Cd27
Bridgnorth **GB** 24 Da26
Bridgwater **GB** 24 Cd27
Bridlington **GB** 21 Db24
Bridport **GB** 24 Cd28
Briec **F** 60 Cb31
Brie-Comte-Robert **F** 62 Dc31
Brienne-le-Château **F** 62 Ea32
Brienz **CH** 71 Ed35
Briey **F** 63 Eb31
Brig **CH** 71 Ec35
Brighton **GB** 25 Db28
Brignogan-Plages **F** 60 Cb30

Brignoles **F** 82 Ea39
Brihuega **E** 92 Ca41
Briksdal **N** 36 Fa15
Brilon **D** 64 Fa29
Brimnes **N** 36 Fa16
Brindisi **I** 100 Gd43
Brinje **HR** 85 Ga37
Brinlack **IRL** 19 Cb21
Brintbodarna **S** 38 Ga16
Brionne **F** 61 Db31
Brioude **F** 69 Dc36
Briouze **F** 61 Da31
Brisighella **I** 84 Fb38
Bristol **GB** 24 Cd27
Brive-la-Gaillarde **F** 69 Db36
Briviesca **E** 79 Ca38
Brixen **I** 72 Fc35
Brixham **GB** 23 Cc28
Brjančaninovo **RUS** 47 Jb20
Brjanka **UA** 122 Fb15
Brjansk **RUS** 121 Ed12
Brka **BIH** 86 Ha37
Brnaze **HR** 86 Gc39
Brno **CZ** 66 Gc32
Bro **S** 45 Gd20
Broadford **GB** 16 Cd19
Broadstairs **GB** 25 Dc28
Broby **S** 50 Ga22
Broceni **LV** 52 Hb21
Brochów **PL** 58 Ha27
Brod **BIH** 86 Ha39
Brod **MK** 101 Hc42
Brod **MK** 101 Hc42
Brodaiži **LV** 53 Jb21
Brodarevo **SRB** 87 Hb39
Brodce **CZ** 65 Ga30
Brodec'ke **UA** 121 Eb15
Brodick **GB** 20 Cd21
Brodina de Jos **RO** 76 Jb33
Brodnica **PL** 58 Ha26
Brody **UA** 120 Ea15
Brojce **PL** 57 Gb25
Brokind **S** 44 Gb20
Brome **D** 56 Fb27
Bromölla **S** 50 Ga23
Brömsebro **S** 50 Gb22
Bromsgrove **GB** 24 Da26
Bromyard **GB** 24 Da26
Brønderslev **DK** 49 Fb21
Broni **I** 83 Ed37
Brønnøysund **N** 32 Fd10
Bronte **I** 109 Ga47
Broons **F** 61 Cd31
Brora **GB** 17 Da18
Brørup **DK** 48 Fa23
Brösarp **S** 50 Ga23
Brøstadbotn **N** 26 Gc05
Broșteni **RO** 87 Hd37
Broszków **PL** 59 Hc27
Broto **E** 80 Cd39
Brottby **S** 45 Gc18
Brou **F** 61 Db32
Brough **GB** 21 Da23
Broughton-in-Furness **GB** 21 Da23
Broumov **CZ** 65 Gb30

Broutzéika – Cagnano Varano

Broutzéika **GR** 111 Ja46
Brouwershaven **NL** 54 Ea28
Brovary **UA** 121 Ec14
Brovst **DK** 49 Fb21
Brozas **E** 91 Ba41
Brú **IS** 14 Bd05
Bruay-la-Buissière **F** 62 Dd29
Bruchsal **D** 63 Ed32
Bruck **A** 73 Fd34
Bruck **D** 64 Fc32
Bruck an der Leitha **A** 74 Gc33
Bruck an der Mur **A** 73 Gb34
Brüel **D** 56 Fc26
Brugg **CH** 71 Ed34
Brugge **B** 54 Dd28
Bruheim **N** 36 Fa15
Brûlon **F** 61 Da32
Brumath **F** 63 Ed32
Brumov-Bylnice **CZ** 66 Gd32
Brumunddal **N** 37 Fc16
Brundby **DK** 49 Fb23
Bruneck **I** 72 Fc35
Brunflo **S** 38 Ga13
Brunico **I** 72 Fc35
Brunsbüttel **D** 56 Fa25
Bruntál **CZ** 66 Gc31
Brus **SRB** 87 Hc39
Brusarci **BG** 87 Hd39
Brussel **B** 62 Ea29
Brüssow **D** 57 Ga26
Brusturoasa **RO** 76 Jc34
Bruvno **HR** 85 Gb38
Bruxelles **B** 62 Ea29
Bruyères **F** 71 Ec33
Bruz **F** 61 Cd32
Bruzaholm **S** 44 Ga20
Brvenik **SRB** 87 Hb39
Brwinow **PL** 59 Hb28
Bryne **N** 42 Ec19
Brzeg **PL** 66 Gc29
Brzeg Dolny **PL** 66 Gc29
Brześć Kujawski **PL** 58 Gd27
Brzesko **PL** 67 Hb31
Brzeszcze **PL** 67 Ha31
Brzeziny **PL** 58 Ha28
Brzostek **PL** 67 Hb31
Brzóza **PL** 59 Hb28
Brzozie Lubawskie **PL** 58 Ha26
Brzozów **PL** 67 Hc31
Buba **RO** 88 Jc36
Bubiai **LT** 52 Hc23
Buča **UA** 121 Fc14
Bučač **UA** 124 Ea16
Bucakkışia **TR** 128 Gb16
Buccino **I** 99 Gb43
Buceş **RO** 75 Hd35
Buchen **D** 64 Fa31
Buchholz **D** 56 Fb26
Buchloe **D** 72 Fb33
Buchs **CH** 72 Fa34

Buchy **F** 62 Dc30
Bučionys **LT** 53 Hd24
Buciumi **RO** 75 Hd34
Buckhaven **GB** 21 Da21
Bučovice **CZ** 66 Gc32
Bucşani **RO** 88 Jc37
Bucureşti **RO** 88 Jc37
Buczek **PL** 66 Gd29
Bud **N** 36 Fa13
Budaörs **H** 74 Ha34
Budapest **H** 74 Ha34
Buðardalur **IS** 14 Bc05
Buddusò **I** 97 Ed43
Bude **GB** 23 Cc27
Büdelsdorf **D** 56 Fb25
Budeşti **RO** 88 Ja37
Budeşti **RO** 88 Jc37
Buđevo **SRB** 87 Hb40
Büdingen **D** 64 Fa30
Budogošč' **RUS** 117 Eb08
Budrio **I** 84 Fb38
Budva **MNE** 100 Ha41
Budziszewice **PL** 58 Ha28
Budzyń **PL** 58 Gc27
Buenavista de Valdavia **E** 79 Bd38
Buendía **E** 92 Ca41
Bueu **E** 78 Ad37
Buftea **RO** 88 Jc37
Buğdaylı **TR** 103 Ka42
Bugeat **F** 69 Db35
Bugojno **BIH** 86 Gc39
Bugøyfjord **N** 27 Hd04
Bugøynes **N** 27 Hd04
Bugul'ma **RUS** 119 Ga09
Bühl **D** 63 Ed32
Buhovci **BG** 89 Jd39
Buhovo **BG** 102 Ja40
Buhuşi **RO** 76 Jc34
Builth Wells **GB** 24 Cd26
Buinsk **RUS** 119 Fd09
Buj **RUS** 118 Fa08
Bujalance **E** 105 Bb44
Bujanovac **SRB** 87 Hc40
Bujaraloz **E** 80 Cc40
Buje **HR** 85 Fd37
Bukanovskaja **RUS** 123 Fc13
Bukta **N** 26 Gd04
Buky **UA** 121 Ec15
Bülach **CH** 71 Ed34
Bulanlak **TR** 127 Fd19
Bulgar **RUS** 119 Fd09
Bullas **E** 107 Ca44
Bulle **CH** 71 Ec35
Bumbeşti-Jiu **RO** 88 Ja37
Bunclody **IRL** 23 Cb25
Buncrana **IRL** 19 Cb21
Bünde **D** 56 Fa27
Bundoran **IRL** 18 Ca22
Bunkris **S** 38 Fd15
Buñol **E** 93 Cb43
Bureå **S** 34 Ha11
Buren **NL** 55 Ec26
Burfjord **N** 26 Gd04

Burg **D** 56 Fc25
Burg **D** 56 Fc28
Burgas **BG** 89 Ka39
Burgdorf **CH** 71 Ec34
Burgdorf **D** 56 Fb27
Burgebrach **D** 64 Fb31
Burgess Hill **GB** 25 Db28
Burghausen **D** 73 Fd33
Burgillos del Cerro **E** 105 Ba43
Burglengenfeld **D** 64 Fc32
Burgo **P** 78 Ad39
Burgohondo **E** 91 Bc41
Burgos **E** 79 Ca38
Burgstädt **D** 65 Fd29
Burgsvik **S** 51 Gc21
Burgui **E** 80 Cc39
Burhaniye **TR** 103 Ka43
Burila Mare **RO** 87 Hd38
Burjassot **E** 93 Cc43
Burnham-on-Crouch **GB** 25 Dc27
Burnham-on-Sea **GB** 24 Cd27
Burnley **GB** 21 Da24
Burrel **RKS** 100 Hb42
Burriana **E** 93 Cc42
Burseryd **S** 49 Fd21
Bürstadt **D** 63 Ed31
Burton-upon-Trent **GB** 24 Da25
Burträsk **S** 34 Gd11
Burwick **GB** 17 Db17
Bury **GB** 21 Da24
Bury Saint Edmunds **GB** 25 Dc27
Busalla **I** 83 Ed38
Buşăuca **MD** 77 Ka33
Busca **I** 83 Ec38
Busemarke **DK** 49 Fd24
Buševec **HR** 73 Gb36
Busici **MK** 101 Hd41
Bus'k **UA** 120 Ea15
Busko-Zdrój **PL** 67 Hb30
Busovača **BIH** 86 Gd38
Buşteni **RO** 88 Jb36
Büsum **D** 56 Fa25
Butan **BG** 88 Ja39
Butrint **AL** 100 Hb44
Buttstädt **D** 64 Fc29
Buturlinovka **RUS** 122 Fb13
Butzbach **D** 63 Ed30
Bützow **D** 56 Fc26
Buxtehude **D** 56 Fb26
Buxton **GB** 24 Da25
Buxy **F** 70 Ea34
Büyükçekmece **TR** 103 Kb41
Buzançals **F** 69 Db34
Buzancy **F** 62 Ea31
Buzău **RO** 88 Jc36
Buzescu **RO** 88 Jb38
Buzet **HR** 85 Fd37
Buziaş **RO** 75 Hc36
Bychav **BY** 121 Eb12
Bychawa **PL** 67 Hc29

Byczyna **PL** 66 Gd29
Bydgoszcz **PL** 58 Gc26
Bygdeå **S** 34 Gd12
Bygdisheim **N** 37 Fb15
Bygdsiljum **S** 34 Gd11
Bygland **N** 42 Fa19
Byglandsfjord **N** 42 Fa19
Bykle **N** 42 Fa18
Bykovo **RUS** 123 Fd13
Byrkjedal **N** 42 Ed19
Byrkjelo **N** 36 Ed15
Byske **S** 34 Ha11
Bysław **PL** 58 Gc26
Bystrecovo **RUS** 47 Jb19
Bystřice nad Pernštejnem **CZ** 65 Gb31
Bystrycja **UA** 76 Ja32
Bystrzyca Kłodzka **PL** 66 Gc30
Byszyno **PL** 57 Gb25
Bytča **SK** 66 Gd32
Bytom **PL** 66 Gd30
Bytom Odrzański **PL** 57 Gb28
Bytoń **PL** 58 Gd27
Bytów **PL** 58 Gc25
Byxelkrok **S** 51 Gc21

C

Cabañaquinta **E** 79 Bc37
Cabanes **E** 93 Cc42
Cabeza del Buey **E** 105 Bb43
Cabezas Rubias **E** 105 Ad43
Cabezón de la Sal **E** 79 Bd37
Cabezuela del Valle **E** 91 Bb40
Cabourg **F** 61 Da30
Cabra **E** 105 Bb44
Cabras **I** 97 Ec44
Čačak **SRB** 87 Hb39
Caccamo **I** 108 Fd47
Cacela Velha **P** 104 Ac44
Cáceres **E** 91 Ba41
Čačёrsk **BY** 121 Ec13
Čačіvičy **BY** 121 Eb12
Cachopo **P** 104 Ac43
Cadaqués **E** 81 Dc40
Čadca **SK** 66 Gd31
Cadenet **F** 82 Ea38
Cadillac **F** 68 Cd36
Cádiz **E** 105 Ad45
Caen **F** 61 Da30
Caernarfon **GB** 20 Cd24
Caerphilly **GB** 24 Cd27
Caersws **GB** 24 Cd25
Čaevo **RUS** 117 Ed08
Cagan Aman **RUS** 123 Ga14
Cagan-Nur **RUS** 123 Ga14
Çağış **TR** 103 Kb43
Cagli **I** 84 Fc39
Cagliari **I** 97 Ed45
Cagnano Varano **I** 99 Gb41

140

Cagnes-sur-Mer **F** 83 Eb39
Čagoda **RUS** 117 Ec08
Caher **IRL** 22 Ca25
Caherdaniel **IRL** 22 Bc25
Cahersiveen **IRL** 22 Bc25
Cahors **F** 81 Db37
Cahul **MD** 77 Jd35
Căinari **MD** 77 Ka34
Căinarii Vechi **MD** 77 Jd32
Câineni **RO** 88 Ja36
Cairnryan **GB** 20 Cd22
Cairo Montenotte **I** 83 Ec38
Cajarc **F** 81 Db37
Čajniče **BIH** 86 Ha39
Čakino **RUS** 123 Fc12
Çakırbeyli **TR** 113 Kb46
Çakmak **TR** 128 Gc15
Čakovec **HR** 74 Gc35
Calaceite **E** 93 Cd41
Calaf **E** 81 Da40
Calafat **RO** 87 Hd38
Calahorra **E** 80 Cb39
Calais **F** 54 Dc28
Cala Millor **E** 95 Db43
Calamocha **E** 93 Cb41
Călan **RO** 75 Hd36
Calañas **E** 105 Ad43
Calanda **E** 93 Cc41
Calangianus **I** 96 Ed42
Cala Rajada **E** 95 Db43
Călărași **MD** 77 Jd33
Călărași **RO** 89 Jd37
Calasparra **E** 107 Ca44
Calatafimi **I** 108 Fc47
Calatañazor **E** 79 Ca39
Calatayud **E** 80 Cb40
Calau **D** 57 Ga38
Calbe **D** 56 Fc28
Caldaro **I** 72 Fb35
Caldas da Reinha **P** 90 Ac40
Caldas de Reis **E** 78 Ad37
Caldes de Montbui **E** 95 Db41
Calella **E** 95 Db41
Calenzana **F** 96 Ed40
Caleruega **E** 79 Ca39
Çalı **TR** 103 Kb42
Călimănești **RO** 88 Ja36
Callac **F** 60 Cc31
Callan **IRL** 22 Ca25
Callander **GB** 17 Da20
Callanish **GB** 16 Cd17
Callosa de Segura **E** 107 Cb44
Calp (Calpe) **E** 94 Cc44
Caltabellotta **I** 108 Fd47
Caltagirone **I** 109 Ga47
Caltanissetta **I** 108 Fd47
Çaltılıbük **TR** 103 Kb43
Călugăreni **RO** 88 Jc38
Calvi **F** 96 Ed40
Calvià **E** 95 Da43
Calw **D** 63 Ed32
Calzada de Calatrava **E** 92 Bc43

Camaiore **I** 84 Fa39
Camarasa **E** 80 Cd40
Camarès **F** 81 Dc38
Camaret-sur-Mer **F** 60 Cb31
Camas **E** 105 Ba44
Cambados **E** 78 Ad37
Cambo-les-Bains **F** 80 Cc38
Camborne **GB** 23 Cb28
Cambrai **F** 62 Dd30
Cambridge **GB** 25 Db26
Cambrils **E** 93 Cd41
Camelford **GB** 23 Cb28
Camenca **MD** 77 Jd32
Camerino **I** 85 Fd40
Camerota **I** 99 Gb44
Çamiçi **TR** 113 Kb46
Caminha **P** 78 Ad37
Caminreal **E** 93 Cb41
Çamlıca **TR** 128 Gb17
Çamlıyayla **TR** 128 Gd16
Cammarata **I** 108 Fd47
Camp **IRL** 18 Bc24
Campanario **E** 91 Bb42
Campanas **E** 80 Cb38
Campbeltown **GB** 20 Cc21
Câmpeni **RO** 75 Hd35
Câmpia Turzii **RO** 76 Ja35
Campiglia Marittima **I** 84 Fa40
Campillo de Llerena **E** 105 Ba43
Campillos **E** 105 Bb45
Câmpina **RO** 88 Jc36
Campo **E** 80 Cd39
Campobasso **I** 99 Ga42
Campo de Criptana **E** 92 Bd42
Campo Ligure **I** 83 Ed38
Campo Maior **P** 90 Ad42
Camporrobles **E** 93 Cb42
Campos **E** 95 Db44
Campotéjar **E** 106 Bc45
Campo Tures **I** 72 Fc35
Câmpu lui Neag **RO** 75 Hd36
Câmpulung **RO** 88 Jb36
Câmpulung Moldovenesc **RO** 76 Jb33
Câmpuri **RO** 76 Jc35
Çan **TR** 103 Ka43
Canabal **E** 78 Ba37
Çanakkale **TR** 103 Jd43
Canale **I** 83 Ec37
Canals **E** 93 Cb43
Cañaveral **E** 91 Ba41
Cañaveras **E** 92 Ca41
Canazei **I** 72 Fc35
Cancale **F** 61 Cb31
Cancon **F** 81 Da37
Çandarlı **TR** 113 Ka44
Candé **F** 61 Cd32
Candeleda **E** 91 Bb41
Canelli **I** 83 Ed37
Cañete **E** 93 Cb42
Canet-Plage **F** 81 Dc39
Canfranc **E** 80 Cc39

Cangas **E** 78 Ad37
Cangas del Narcea **E** 78 Bb37
Cangas de Onís **E** 79 Bd37
Canicattì **I** 108 Fd47
Caniles **E** 106 Bd45
Cañizal **E** 79 Bc39
Canjáyar **E** 106 Bd45
Cannes **F** 83 Eb39
Cannobio **I** 71 Ed36
Canosa di Puglia **I** 99 Gb42
Cantalejo **E** 92 Bd40
Cantalpino **E** 91 Bc40
Cantavieja **E** 93 Cc41
Cantemir **MD** 77 Jd35
Canterbury **GB** 25 Dc28
Cantillana **E** 105 Ba44
Cantoria **E** 106 Bd45
Caorle **I** 73 Fd36
Capaccio **I** 99 Ga43
Čapaevskj **RUS** 119 Ga10
Caparroso **E** 80 Cb39
Capbreton **F** 80 Cc37
Cap d'Agde **F** 81 Dc39
Capdenac-Gare **F** 81 Db37
Capel·la **RUS** 47 Jb19
Cap Ferret **F** 68 Cc35
Capidava **RO** 89 Ka37
Capinha **P** 91 Ba40
Čapljina **BIH** 86 Gd40
Čaplygin **RUS** 118 Fb11
Čaplynka **UA** 126 Fa17
Capo d'Orlando **I** 109 Ga46
Capri **I** 99 Ga43
Captieux **F** 80 Cd37
Capua **I** 99 Ga42
Caracal **RO** 88 Jb38
Caraman **F** 81 Db38
Caranga de Abajo **E** 79 Bc37
Caransebeş **RO** 75 Hc36
Carantec **F** 60 Cb30
Caravaca de la Cruz **E** 107 Ca44
Carballiño **E** 78 Ba37
Carballo **E** 78 Ba36
Carboneras **E** 107 Ca46
Carboneras de Guadazaón **E** 93 Cb42
Carbonia **I** 97 Ec45
Carbonne **F** 81 Da38
Carcans **F** 68 Cc35
Carcans-Plage **F** 68 Cc35
Carcassonne **F** 81 Db39
Carcastillo **E** 80 Cc39
Carcelén **E** 93 Cb43
Cardeña **E** 106 Bc43
Cardiff **GB** 24 Cd27
Cardigan **GB** 23 Cc26
Cardona **E** 81 Da40
Carei **RO** 75 Hc33
Carevo **BG** 103 Ka40
Cargèse **F** 96 Ed41
Carhaix-Plouguer **F** 60 Cb31

Cariati **I** 99 Gc44
Carignan **F** 63 Eb31
Cariñena **E** 80 Cb40
Carini **I** 108 Fd46
Carinish **GB** 16 Cc18
Car Kalojan **BG** 88 Jc38
Cârlibaba **RO** 76 Jb33
Carlisle **GB** 21 Da22
Carloforte **I** 97 Ec45
Carlow **IRL** 19 Cb24
Carloway **GB** 16 Cd17
Carmagnola **I** 83 Ec37
Carmanova **MD** 77 Ka33
Carmarthen **GB** 23 Cc26
Carmaux **F** 81 Db37
Cármenes **E** 79 Bc37
Carmona **E** 105 Ba44
Carnac **F** 60 Cc32
Carndonagh **IRL** 19 Cb21
Carnew **IRL** 23 Cb25
Carnforth **GB** 21 Da23
Carnikava **LV** 52 Hc21
Čarnjany **BY** 59 Hd28
Carnoustie **GB** 17 Db20
Carolinensiel **D** 55 Ed25
Carpen **RO** 88 Ja38
Carpentras **F** 82 Ea38
Carpi **I** 84 Fb37
Carquefou **F** 68 Cd33
Carrara **I** 84 Fa38
Carrascosa del Campo **E** 92 Ca42
Carrbridge **GB** 17 Da19
Carrick **GB** 17 Db20
Carrickfergus **GB** 20 Cc22
Carrickmacross **IRL** 19 Cb23
Carrick-on-Shannon **IRL** 18 Ca23
Carrick-on-Suir **IRL** 22 Ca25
Carrión de los Condes **E** 79 Bd38
Carrouges **F** 61 Da31
Carryduff **GB** 20 Cc22
Çarşamba **TR** 127 Fc19
Cartagena **E** 107 Cb45
Cartaxo **P** 90 Ac41
Cartaya **E** 105 Ad44
Cărvarica **BG** 101 Hd41
Carvin **F** 62 Dd29
Casacalenda **I** 99 Ga42
Casa de Juan Núñez **E** 93 Cb43
Casalbordino **I** 99 Ga41
Casale Monferrato **I** 83 Ed37
Casalmaggiore **I** 84 Fa37
Casalpusterlengo **I** 84 Fa37
Casamassima **I** 99 Gc43
Casamozza **F** 96 Ed40
Casarano **I** 100 Gd44
Casas de Lázaro **E** 92 Ca43
Casas del Puerto **E** 107 Cb44
Casas-Ibáñez **E** 93 Cb43
Casavieja **E** 91 Bc41
Cascais **P** 90 Ab41

141

Cascante **E** 80 Cb39
Cascia **I** 85 Fd40
Casciana Terme **I** 84 Fa39
Cascina **I** 84 Fa39
Căscioarele **RO** 88 Jc38
Caselle Torinese **I** 83 Ec37
Caserta **I** 99 Ga42
Cashel **IRL** 18 Ca24
Casimcea **RO** 89 Ka36
Casinos **E** 93 Cb42
Čáslav **CZ** 65 Gb31
Čašniki **BY** 121 Eb12
Casoli **I** 99 Ga41
Casoria **I** 99 Ga43
Caspe **E** 93 Cc41
Cassano allo Ionio **I** 99 Gc44
Cassel **F** 62 Dd29
Cassino **I** 98 Fd42
Cassis **F** 82 Ea39
Castagneto Carducci **I** 84 Fa40
Castañar de Ibor **E** 91 Bb41
Castanheira de Pèra **P** 90 Ad40
Castejón de Valdejasa **E** 80 Cc40
Castel di Sangro **I** 99 Ga42
Castelfidardo **I** 85 Fd39
Castelfranco Emilia **I** 84 Fb38
Castelfranco Veneto **I** 72 Fc36
Casteljaloux **F** 80 Cd37
Castellabate **I** 99 Ga43
Castellammare del Golfo **I** 108 Fc46
Castellane **F** 83 Eb38
Castellaneta **I** 99 Gc43
Castellaneta Marina **I** 99 Gc43
Castellar de Santiago **E** 92 Bd43
Castell' Arquato **I** 84 Fa37
Castelldans **E** 80 Cd40
Castelldefels **E** 95 Da41
Castell de Ferro **E** 106 Bc46
Castelló de la Plana **E** 93 Cc42
Castelnaudary **F** 81 Db38
Castelnau-de-Médoc **F** 68 Cd36
Castelnau-Magnoac **F** 80 Cd38
Castelnovo ne'Monti **I** 84 Fa38
Castelnuovo di Garfagnana **I** 84 Fa38
Castelo Branco **P** 90 Ad40
Castelo de Vide **P** 90 Ad41
Castel San Giovanni **I** 84 Fa37
Castel San Pietro Terme **I** 84 Fb38
Castelsardo **I** 96 Ec42
Castelsarrasin **F** 81 Da37

Casteltermini **I** 108 Fd47
Castelvetrano **I** 108 Fc47
Castets **F** 80 Cc37
Castiglioncello **I** 84 Fa39
Castiglione della Pescaia **I** 84 Fb40
Castiglione delle Stiviere **I** 84 Fa37
Castiglione sul Lago **I** 84 Fc40
Castiglion Fiorentino **I** 84 Fc39
Castilblanco **E** 91 Bb42
Castillejo de Martín Viejo **E** 91 Ba40
Castillon-en-Couserans **F** 81 Da39
Castillonnès **F** 69 Da36
Castlebar **IRL** 18 Bd22
Castlebay **GB** 16 Cc19
Castleblayney **IRL** 19 Cb23
Castle Douglas **GB** 20 Cd22
Castleisland **IRL** 18 Bd24
Castlepollard **IRL** 19 Cb23
Castlerea **IRL** 18 Ca23
Castletown **GB** 17 Db18
Castletown **GBM** 20 Cd23
Castletownbere **IRL** 22 Bc25
Castres **F** 81 Db38
Castricum **NL** 55 Eb27
Castril **E** 106 Bd44
Castrocaro Terme **I** 84 Fc38
Castro Daire **P** 78 Ad39
Castro del Río **E** 105 Bb44
Castrojeriz **E** 79 Bd38
Castropol **E** 78 Bb36
Castro-Urdiales **E** 79 Ca37
Castro Verde **P** 104 Ac43
Castrovillari **I** 99 Gb44
Castuera **E** 91 Bb42
Çatak **TR** 128 Gc17
Çatalca **TR** 103 Kb41
Catania **I** 109 Ga47
Catanzaro **I** 109 Gc45
Catanzaro Marina **I** 109 Gc45
Cateraggio **F** 96 Ed41
Cattolica **I** 84 Fc39
Căuaş **RO** 75 Hd34
Caudry **F** 62 Dd30
Caumont-l'Éventé **F** 61 Da30
Caunes-Minervois **F** 81 Db38
Cauro **F** 96 Ed41
Căuşeni **MD** 77 Ka34
Caussade **F** 81 Db37
Cauterets **F** 80 Cd39
Cava de'Tirreni **I** 99 Ga43
Cavaillon **F** 82 Ea38
Cavalaire-sur-Mer **F** 83 Eb39
Cavalese **I** 72 Fb35
Cavan **IRL** 19 Cb23
Căvăran **RO** 75 Hc36
Cavnic **RO** 76 Ja33

Cavour **I** 83 Ec37
Cavtat **HR** 86 Gd40
Čavusy **BY** 121 Ec12
Çayağzı **TR** 103 Kb41
Çayeli **TR** 127 Ga19
Cayeux-sur-Mer **F** 62 Dc29
Çayhan **TR** 128 Gc15
Çayırova **CY** 128 Gc18
Caylus **F** 81 Db37
Cazalla de la Sierra **E** 105 Ba43
Cazaubon **F** 80 Cd37
Cazin **BIH** 85 Gb37
Čazma **HR** 74 Gc36
Cazorla **E** 106 Bd44
Cea **E** 79 Bc38
Ceadâr-Lunga **MD** 77 Ka35
Ceanu Mare **RO** 76 Ja35
Ceatalchioi **RO** 89 Ka36
Čeboksary **RUS** 119 Fc09
Cebreros **E** 91 Bc41
Cebrikove **MD** 77 Kb33
Čečava **BIH** 86 Gd38
Ceccano **I** 98 Fd42
Cece **H** 74 Gd35
Čečel'nyk **UA** 77 Ka32
Čečel'nyk **UA** 125 Ec16
Čechtice **CZ** 65 Ga31
Cecina **I** 84 Fa39
Cedeira **E** 78 Ba36
Cedillo **E** 90 Ad41
Cedrillas **E** 93 Cc41
Cée **E** 78 Ad36
Cefalù **I** 108 Fd46
Cegléd **H** 74 Ha34
Ceglie Messapica **I** 100 Gd43
Cehegín **E** 107 Ca44
Čehov **RUS** 118 Fa11
Cehu Silvaniei **RO** 75 Hd34
Čejč **CZ** 66 Gc32
Čekiškė **LT** 52 Hc23
Celano **I** 98 Fd41
Celanova **E** 78 Ba37
Celbridge **IRL** 19 Cb24
Čelebići **BIH** 86 Ha39
Čelić **BIH** 86 Ha38
Celina **RUS** 123 Fd15
Čelinac Donji **BIH** 86 Gc38
Celjachany **BY** 120 Ea13
Celje **SLO** 73 Gb36
Cella **E** 93 Cb41
Celldömölk **H** 74 Gc34
Celle **D** 56 Fb27
Celle Ligure **I** 83 Ed38
Celorico da Beira **P** 78 Ba39
Čel'ovce **SK** 67 Hc32
Cemerno **BIH** 86 Ha40
Cenovo **BG** 88 Jc38
Centelles **E** 81 Db40
Cento **I** 84 Fb30
Čepigovo **MK** 101 Hc42
Čepin **HR** 86 Gd37
Cer **MK** 101 Hc42
Cerachovka **BY** 121 Ec13
Cerbère **F** 81 Dc40

Cercal **P** 104 Ab43
Čerdakly **RUS** 119 Fd09
Cerdeira **P** 91 Ba40
Čerencovo **RUS** 117 Eb08
Čerepovec **RUS** 117 Ed08
Čereševo **BG** 88 Jc38
Ceresole Reale **I** 71 Ec36
Céret **F** 81 Db40
Cerezo de Abajo **E** 92 Bd40
Cerfontaine **B** 62 Ea30
Cerignola **I** 99 Gb42
Cérilly **F** 69 Dc34
Cerizay **F** 68 Cd33
Čerkasovo **RUS** 41 Ja16
Čerkasy **UA** 121 Ed15
Čerkessk **RUS** 127 Fd17
Çerkezköy **TR** 103 Ka41
Cerknica **SLO** 73 Ga36
Cermei **RO** 75 Hc35
Čern' **RUS** 122 Fa12
Cerna **HR** 86 Gd37
Cerna **RO** 89 Ka36
Cerna-Sat **RO** 87 Hd37
Černava **RUS** 118 Fa11
Černava **RUS** 122 Fa12
Cernavodă **RO** 89 Ka37
Cernay **F** 71 Ec33
Černégula **E** 79 Ca38
Černëvo **RUS** 47 Jb18
Cernica **RO** 88 Jc37
Černihiv **UA** 121 Ec14
Černivci **UA** 76 Jb32
Černivci **UA** 124 Ea16
Černjachiv **UA** 121 Eb14
Černjahovsk **RUS** 52 Hb24
Černjanka **RUS** 122 Fa13
Černovice **CZ** 65 Ga32
Černyškovskij **RUS** 123 Fd14
Cerovica **SRB** 87 Hd39
Cerrigydrudion **GB** 24 Cd25
Cërrik **RKS** 100 Hb42
Certaldo **I** 84 Fb39
Čertižné **SK** 67 Hc31
Čertkovo **RUS** 123 Fc14
Čerusti **RUS** 118 Fa10
Červen' **BY** 121 Eb12
Červená Skala **SK** 67 Ha32
Červená Voda **CZ** 66 Gc31
Červen Brjag **BG** 88 Ja39
Cervera **E** 81 Da40
Cervera del Río Alhama **E** 80 Cb39
Cervera de Pisuerga **E** 79 Bd37
Cerveteri **I** 98 Fc41
Cervia **I** 84 Fc38
Cervignano del Friuli **I** 73 Fd36
Červonoarmijs'ke **UA** 77 Ka35
Červonohrad **UA** 67 Hd30
Červonoznam'janka **MD** 77 Kb33
Čery6kav **BY** 121 Ec12
Cesena **I** 84 Fc38

Cesenatico I 84 Fc38
Cēsis LV 47 Hd20
Česká Kamenice CZ 65 Ga30
Česká Lípa CZ 65 Ga30
České Budějovice CZ 65 Ga32
České Velenice CZ 65 Ga32
Český Brod CZ 65 Ga31
Český Dub CZ 65 Ga30
Český Krumlov CZ 65 Ga32
Český Těšín CZ 66 Gd31
Çeşme TR 113 Jd45
Cesvaine LV 53 Ja21
Cetatea de Baltă RO 76 Ja35
Cetăţeni RO 88 Jb36
Cetingrad HR 85 Gb37
Cetinje MNE 100 Ha41
Cetraro I 99 Gb44
Ceuta E 105 Ba46
Ceva I 83 Ec38
Cewice PL 58 Gc25
Chabanais F 69 Da35
Chabeuil F 82 Ea37
Chablis F 70 Dd33
Chabovičy BY 59 Hd27
Chabris F 69 Db33
Chagny F 70 Ea34
Chaillé-les-Marais F 68 Cd34
Chalais F 69 Da36
Chalamera E 80 Cd40
Chalamont F 70 Ea35
Châlette-sur-Loing F 62 Dc32
Challans F 68 Cc33
Châlons-en-Champagne F 62 Ea31
Chalon-sur-Saône F 70 Ea34
Châlus F 69 Da35
Cham CH 71 Ed34
Cham D 64 Fc32
Chambéry F 71 Eb36
Chambley F 63 Eb31
Chambly F 62 Dc31
Chamonix-Mont-Blanc F 71 Eb36
Champagne-Mouton F 69 Da35
Champagnole F 71 Eb34
Champlitte-et-le-Prélot F 71 Eb33
Chantada E 78 Ba37
Chantelle F 69 Dc35
Chantilly F 62 Dc31
Chantonnay F 68 Cd33
Chaource F 70 Ea33
Charkiv UA 122 Fa14
Charleroi B 62 Ea29
Charlestown IRL 18 Ca22
Charleville IRL 18 Bd24
Charleville-Mézières F 62 Ea30
Charlieu F 70 Dd35
Charlottenberg S 44 Fd17

Charmes F 63 Eb32
Charny F 70 Dd33
Charolles F 70 Dd35
Charost F 69 Dc34
Chartres F 62 Dc32
Château-Arnoux F 82 Ea38
Châteaubourg F 61 Cd32
Châteaubriant F 61 Cd32
Château-Chinon F 70 Dd34
Château-du-Loir F 61 Da32
Châteaudun F 61 Db32
Châteaugiron F 61 Cd32
Château-Gontier F 61 Da32
Château-Landon F 62 Dc32
Château-la-Vallière F 69 Da33
Château-l'Evêque F 69 Da36
Châteaulin F 60 Cb31
Châteaumeillant F 69 Dc34
Châteauneuf-de-Randon F 82 Dd37
Châteauneuf-du-Faou F 60 Cb31
Châteauneuf-en-Thymerais F 61 Db31
Châteauneuf-la-Forêt F 69 Db35
Châteauneuf-sur-Charente F 69 Da35
Châteauneuf-sur-Cher F 69 Dc34
Châteauneuf-sur-Loire F 62 Dc32
Châteauneuf-sur-Sarthe F 61 Da32
Châteauponsac F 69 Db35
Château-Porcien F 62 Ea31
Château-Renault F 69 Db33
Châteauroux F 69 Db34
Château-Salins F 63 Ec32
Château-Thierry F 62 Dd31
Châteauvillain F 70 Ea33
Châtelaillon-Plage F 68 Cd34
Châtel-Censoir F 70 Dd33
Châtelet B 62 Ea30
Châtelguyon F 69 Dc35
Châtellerault F 69 Da34
Châtelus-Malvaleix F 69 Db35
Châtenois F 63 Eb32
Chatham GB 25 Db28
Châtillon I 71 Ec36
Châtillon-Coligny F 70 Dd33
Châtillon-en-Bazois F 70 Dd34
Châtillon-sur-Chalaronne F 70 Ea35
Châtillon-sur-Indre F 69 Db33
Châtillon-sur-Loire F 69 Dc33
Châtillon-sur-Marne F 62 Ea31
Châtillon-sur-Seine F 70 Ea33

Chaudes-Aigues F 81 Dc37
Chauffailles F 70 Dd35
Chaumergy F 70 Ea34
Chaumont F 70 Ea33
Chauny F 62 Dd30
Chauvigny F 69 Da34
Chaves P 78 Ba38
Chazelles-sur-Lyon F 70 Dd36
Cheadle GB 24 Da25
Cheb CZ 64 Fc31
Checiny PL 67 Ha29
Chef-Boutonne F 69 Da34
Cheia RO 88 Jc36
Cheles E 90 Ad42
Chełm PL 67 Hd29
Chełmno PL 58 Gd26
Chełmża PL 58 Gd26
Cheltenham GB 24 Da26
Chelva E 93 Cb42
Chemillé F 68 Cd33
Chemnitz D 65 Fd30
Chénerailles F 69 Dc35
Chenôve F 70 Ea34
Cheptow GB 24 Cd27
Cherbourg-Octeville F 61 Cd30
Chéroy F 62 Dd32
Cherson UA 125 Ed16
Cheste E 93 Cb43
Chester GB 24 Da25
Chesterfield GB 25 Db25
Chevanceaux F 68 Cd35
Chianciano Terme I 84 Fb40
Chiaramonte Gulfi I 109 Ga48
Chiaravalle I 85 Fd39
Chiari I 72 Fa36
Chiaromonte I 99 Gb44
Chiavari I 83 Ed38
Chiavenna I 72 Fa35
Chichester GB 24 Da28
Chiclana de la Frontera E 105 Ad45
Chieri I 83 Ec37
Chieti I 99 Ga41
Chigwell GB 25 Db27
Chimay B 62 Ea30
Chinchilla de Monte Aragón E 92 Ca43
Chinchón E 92 Bd41
Chinon F 69 Da33
Chioggia I 84 Fc37
Chiojdu RO 88 Jc36
Chipiona E 105 Ad45
Chippenham GB 24 Da27
Chipping Norton GB 24 Da27
Chiprana E 93 Cc41
Chirivel E 106 Bd45
Chişinău MD 77 Ka33
Chişlaz RO 75 Hc34
Chiusa I 72 Fb35
Chiusi I 84 Fc40
Chiva E 93 Cb43

Chivasso I 83 Ec37
Chłudowo PL 58 Gc27
Chlumec nad Cidlinou CZ 65 Gb30
Chmel'nyc'kyj UA 121 Eb15
Chmielnik PL 67 Hb30
Chmil'nyk UA 121 Eb15
Chocianów PL 65 Gb29
Chociwel PL 57 Gb26
Chodoriv UA 120 Ea15
Chodová Planá CZ 65 Fd31
Chodzież PL 58 Gc27
Chojna PL 57 Ga27
Chojnice PL 58 Gc26
Chojniki BY 121 Eb13
Chojnów PL 65 Gb29
Cholet F 68 Cd33
Chomutov CZ 65 Fd30
Chorol UA 121 Ed14
Choroszcz PL 59 Hc26
Chorzele PL 59 Hb26
Chorzów PL 66 Gd30
Choszczno PL 57 Gb26
Chotilsko CZ 65 Ga31
Chotyn UA 76 Jc32
Chr'aščevka RUS 119 Ga10
Chrisi Ammoudiá GR 102 Jb42
Christchurch GB 24 Da28
Christiansfeld DK 49 Fb23
Chrudim CZ 65 Gb31
Chrystynivka UA 121 Ec15
Chrzanów PL 67 Ha30
Chur CH 72 Fa35
Church Stretton GB 24 Cd26
Chust UA 75 Hd33
Chvaletice CZ 65 Gb31
Chwałowice PL 67 Hc29
Chwaszczyno PL 58 Gd25
Chynów PL 59 Hb28
Chyriv UA 67 Hc31
Ćićevac SRB 87 Hc39
Ciechanów PL 58 Ha27
Ciechanowiec PL 59 Hc27
Ciechocinek PL 58 Gd27
Ciemnik PL 57 Gb26
Ciemnoszyje PL 59 Hc26
Čierny Balog SK 67 Ha32
Cieszanów PL 67 Hd30
Cieszyn PL 66 Gd31
Cieza E 107 Ca44
Ciężkowice PL 67 Ha29
Çiftehan TR 128 Gd15
Cifuentes E 92 Ca41
Cigel'ka SK 67 Hb31
Cigliano I 83 Ec37
Cilibia RO 89 Jd36
Cillas E 93 Cb41
Cilleros E 91 Ba40
Čil'na RUS 119 Fd09
Cimljansk RUS 123 Fd15
Cimoszki PL 59 Hc25
Çınarcık TR 103 Kb42
Çine TR 113 Kb46
Ciney B 63 Eb30

Cinfães – Courchevel

Cinfães **P** 78 Ad39
Cingoli **I** 85 Fd39
Cintei **RO** 75 Hc35
Cioara **MD** 77 Jd34
Ciocănești **RO** 76 Jb33
Ciochina **RO** 89 Jd37
Cioclovina **RO** 75 Hd36
Ciolacu Nou **MD** 77 Jd33
Ciorani **RO** 88 Jc37
Ciorăști **RO** 89 Jd36
Cirencester **GB** 24 Da27
Cirey-sur-Vezouze **F** 63
  Ec32
Cirìe **I** 83 Ec37
Ciripcău **MD** 77 Jd32
Cirò **I** 109 Gc45
Cirò Marina **I** 109 Gc45
Čirpan **BG** 102 Jc40
Cislău **RO** 88 Jc36
Cismișlia **MD** 77 Ka34
Cisterna di Latina **I** 98 Fc42
Cistierna **E** 79 Bc37
Čitluk **BIH** 86 Gd40
Cittadella **I** 72 Fc36
Città della Pieve **I** 84 Fc40
Città di Castello **I** 84 Fc39
Città Sant'Angelo **I** 98 Fd41
Ciucea **RO** 75 Hd34
Ciucurova **RO** 89 Ka36
Ciudad Real **E** 92 Bc43
Ciudad Rodrigo **E** 91 Ba40
Ciuperceni **RO** 87 Hd37
Ciutadella **E** 95 Dc43
Ciutești **MD** 77 Jd33
Cividale del Friuli **I** 73 Fd36
Civil'sk **RUS** 119 Fc09
Civita Castellana **I** 98 Fc41
Civitanova Marche **I** 85
  Fd39
Civitavecchia **I** 98 Fb41
Civitella del Tronto **I** 85
  Fd40
Civitella Roveto **I** 98 Fd41
Civray **F** 69 Da34
Cjurupyns'k **UA** 125 Ed17
Čkalovsk **RUS** 118 Fb09
Clacton-on-Sea **GB** 25 Dc27
Clamecy **F** 70 Dd33
Claonaig **GB** 20 Cd21
Claremorris **IRL** 18 Ca23
Clausthal-Zellerfeld **D** 56
  Fb28
Cleethorpes **GB** 25 Dc25
Clejani **RO** 88 Jc37
Clelles **F** 82 Ea37
Clermont **F** 62 Dc31
Clermont-en-Argonne **F** 62
  Ea31
Clermont-Ferrand **F** 69
  Dc35
Clermont-l'Hérault **F** 81
  Dc38
Clerval **F** 71 Eb34
Clervaux **L** 63 Eb30
Cles **I** 72 Fb35
Clevedon **GB** 24 Cd27

Cleveleys **GB** 21 Da24
Clifden **IRL** 18 Bd23
Clisson **F** 68 Cd33
Clitheroe **GB** 21 Da24
Cloghan **IRL** 18 Ca24
Clogherhead **IRL** 19 Cb23
Clonakilty **IRL** 22 Bd25
Clones **IRL** 19 Cb22
Clonmel **IRL** 22 Ca25
Cloppenburg **D** 55 Ed27
Clovelly **GB** 23 Cc27
Cloyes-sur-le-Loir **F** 61
  Db32
Cluj-Napoca **RO** 75 Hd34
Cluny **F** 70 Ea35
Cluses **F** 71 Eb35
Clusone **I** 72 Fa36
Clydebank **GB** 20 Cd21
Coarnele Caprei **RO** 76
  Jc33
Cobadin **RO** 89 Ka37
Cobh **IRL** 22 Bd25
Coburg **D** 64 Fb30
Coca **E** 91 Bc40
Cochem **D** 63 Ec30
Cockermouth **GB** 21 Da23
Codigoro **I** 84 Fc37
Codlea **RO** 88 Jb36
Codogno **I** 84 Fa37
Codroipo **I** 73 Fd36
Codru **MD** 77 Ka33
Coesfeld **D** 55 Ed28
Coevorden **NL** 55 Ec27
Cognac **F** 68 Cd35
Cogne **I** 71 Ec36
Cogolin **F** 83 Eb39
Coimbra **P** 90 Ad40
Coín **E** 105 Bb45
Coja **P** 90 Ad40
Colchester **GB** 25 Dc27
Colditz **D** 65 Fd29
Coldstream **GB** 21 Db22
Colera **E** 81 Dc40
Coleraine **GB** 20 Cc21
Colfontaine **B** 62 Ea29
Colibița **RO** 76 Ja34
Colico **I** 72 Fa36
Colintraive **GB** 20 Cd21
Collado-Villalba **E** 92 Bd40
Collecchio **I** 84 Fa37
Colle di Val d'Elsa **I** 84 Fb39
Colleferro **I** 98 Fc42
Colmar **F** 71 Ec33
Colmars **F** 83 Eb38
Colmenar **E** 105 Bb45
Colmenar Viejo **E** 92 Bd40
Colombey-les-Belles **F** 63
  Eb32
Colombey-les-Deux-Églises
  F 62 Ea32
Colònia de Sant Jordi **E** 95
  Db44
Colunga **E** 79 Bd37
Colwyn Bay **GB** 20 Cd24
Comacchio **I** 84 Fc38
Comandău **RO** 76 Jc35

Comănești **RO** 76 Jc35
Comarnic **RO** 88 Jb36
Combeaufontaine **F** 71
  Eb33
Combles **F** 62 Dd30
Combourg **F** 61 Cd31
Comiso **I** 109 Ga48
Commentry **F** 69 Dc35
Commercy **F** 63 Eb32
Como **I** 71 Ed36
Compiègne **F** 62 Dd31
Comporta **P** 90 Ac42
Comps-sur-Artuby **F** 83
  Eb39
Comrat **MD** 77 Ka34
Concarneau **F** 60 Cb31
Conches-en-Ouche **F** 61
  Db31
Condat **F** 69 Dc36
Condé-en-Brie **F** 62 Dd31
Condé-sur-Noireau **F** 61
  Da31
Condom **F** 81 Da37
Conegliano **I** 72 Fc36
Confolens **F** 69 Da35
Congaz **MD** 77 Ka35
Congleton **GB** 24 Da25
Congostrina **E** 92 Ca40
Conil de la Frontera **E** 105
  Ad45
Connah's Quay **GB** 24 Cd25
Connel **GB** 16 Cc20
Connerré **F** 61 Db32
Conques **F** 81 Db37
Conquista **E** 106 Bc43
Conselice **I** 84 Fc38
Constanța **RO** 89 Ka37
Constantina **E** 105 Ba43
Consuegra **E** 92 Bd42
Contadero **E** 106 Bc43
Contești **RO** 88 Jc37
Contin **GB** 17 Da19
Contres **F** 69 Db33
Contrexéville **F** 71 Eb33
Conversano **I** 99 Gc43
Cookstown **GB** 20 Cb22
Cootehill **IRL** 19 Cb23
Copălău **RO** 76 Jc33
Copalnic-Mănăstur **RO** 75
  Hd33
Cope **E** 107 Ca45
Copertino **I** 100 Gd43
Çöpköy **TR** 103 Jd41
Copparo **I** 84 Fc37
Copșa Mică **RO** 76 Ja35
Corabia **RO** 88 Jb38
Corato **I** 99 Gc42
Corbeil-Essonnes **F** 62
  Dc32
Corbie **F** 62 Dd30
Corbigny **F** 70 Dd34
Corbridge **GB** 21 Db23
Corby **GB** 25 Db26
Corcaigh **IRL** 22 Bd25
Cordes **F** 81 Db37
Córdoba **E** 105 Bb44

Corella **E** 80 Cb39
Corestăuți **MD** 76 Jc32
Coria **E** 91 Ba41
Corigliano Calabro **I** 99
  Gc44
Cork **IRL** 22 Bd25
Corlay **F** 60 Cc31
Corleone **I** 108 Fd47
Corleto Perticara **I** 99 Gb43
Çorlu **TR** 103 Ka41
Čorna **UA** 77 Ka33
Cornea **RO** 87 Hd37
Cornești **MD** 77 Jd33
Cornești **RO** 88 Jc37
Cornimont **F** 71 Ec33
Čornobyl' **UA** 121 Ec14
Čornomors'ke **UA** 125 Ed17
Čornuchy **UA** 121 Ed14
Cornudilla **E** 79 Ca38
Cornu Luncii **RO** 76 Jb33
Çorovodë **AL** 100 Hb43
Corporales **E** 78 Bb38
Corps **F** 83 Eb37
Corral de Almaguer **E** 92
  Bd42
Corral de Calatrava **E** 92
  Bc43
Corrales **E** 78 Bb39
Correggio **I** 84 Fb37
Corridonia **I** 85 Fd40
Corsicana **F** 96 Ed41
Corte **F** 96 Ed41
Cortemilia **I** 83 Ec38
Cortijos Nuevos **E** 106 Bd44
Cortina d'Ampezzo **I** 72
  Fc35
Čortkiv **UA** 124 Ea16
Cortona **I** 84 Fc40
Coruche **P** 90 Ac41
Corund **RO** 76 Jb35
Corwen **GB** 24 Cd25
Cosenza **I** 109 Gc45
Coșești **RO** 88 Jb37
Cosmești **RO** 88 Jb38
Cosne-Cours-sur-Loire **F**
  69 Dc33
Cosne-d'Allier **F** 69 Dc34
Cossato **I** 71 Ed36
Costești **RO** 88 Jb37
Costești **MD** 76 Jc33
Costești **RO** 88 Jc36
Costinești **RO** 89 Ka37
Coswig **D** 56 Fc28
Coteana **RO** 88 Jb38
Cotofănești **RO** 76 Jc35
Cottbus **D** 57 Ga28
Coudekerque-Branche **F**
  54 Dd28
Couflens **F** 81 Da39
Couhé **F** 69 Da34
Couiza **F** 81 Db39
Coulommiers **F** 62 Dd31
Coulonges-sur-l'Autize **F**
  68 Cd34
Coupar Anguse **GB** 17 Da20
Courchevel **F** 71 Eb36

144

Courmayeur I 71 Ec36
Cournon-d'Auvergne F 69 Dc35
Coursan F 81 Dc39
Courseulles-sur-Mer F 61 Da30
Cours-la Ville F 70 Dd35
Courtenay F 62 Dd32
Courtomer F 61 Db31
Coutances F 61 Cd30
Coutras F 68 Cd36
Couvin B 62 Ea30
Covaleda E 79 Ca39
Covasna RO 76 Jc35
Coventry GB 24 Da26
Covilhã P 90 Ad40
Cowes GB 24 Da28
Cózar E 92 Bd43
Cozes F 68 Cd35
Crăiești RO 76 Ja34
Craignure GB 16 Cd20
Crail GB 21 Db21
Crailsheim D 64 Fa32
Craiova RO 88 Ja38
Craiva RO 75 Hc35
Cranbrook GB 25 Db28
Craon F 61 Cd32
Craponne-sur-Arzon F 70 Dd36
Crasna RO 75 Hd34
Crasnoe MD 77 Kb34
Crathie GB 17 Db20
Crato P 90 Ad41
Craven Arms GB 24 Cd26
Crawley GB 25 Db28
Creagorry GB 16 Cc18
Crediton GB 23 Cc28
Creil F 62 Dc31
Crema I 84 Fa37
Crémieu F 70 Ea36
Cremona I 84 Fa37
Créon F 68 Cd36
Crepaja SRB 87 Hb37
Crépy-en-Valois F 62 Dd31
Cres HR 85 Ga37
Crest F 82 Ea37
Créteil F 62 Dc31
Creußen D 64 Fc31
Creutzwald F 63 Ec31
Creuzburg D 64 Fb29
Crèvecœur-le-Grand F 62 Dc30
Crevillente E 107 Cb44
Crewe GB 24 Da25
Crewkerne GB 24 Cd28
Crianlarich GB 16 Cd20
Crickhowell GB 24 Cd26
Cricova MD 77 Ka33
Crieff GB 17 Da20
Crikvenica HR 85 Ga37
Crimmitschau D 64 Fc30
Crişan RO 89 Kb36
Čristopol' RUS 119 Ga08
Cristuru Secuiesc RO 76 Jb35
Criuleni MD 77 Ka33

Crivitz D 56 Fc26
Crna Bara SRB 75 Hb36
Črnomelj SLO 85 Gb37
Crocq F 69 Dc35
Croissilles F 62 Dd30
Cromarty GB 17 Da19
Cromer GB 25 Dc26
Crookhaven IRL 22 Bc25
Cross Hands GB 23 Cc26
Crotone I 109 Gc45
Crozon F 60 Cb31
Crtil' RUS 122 Fb12
Crucea RO 76 Jb34
Crucea RO 89 Ka37
Cruden Bay GB 17 Dc19
Cruzamento de Pegões P 90 Ac41
Csakvár H 74 Gd34
Csánytelek H 75 Hb35
Csaroda H 75 Hc33
Csátalja H 74 Ha36
Csenger H 75 Hd33
Csesznek H 74 Gd34
Csongrád H 75 Hb35
Csorna H 74 Gc34
Csorvás H 75 Hb35
Csót H 74 Gc34
Cubel E 80 Cb40
Čučkovo RUS 118 Fb11
Cucoara MD 77 Jd35
Cudillero E 79 Bc36
Čudniv UA 121 Eb15
Čudovo RUS 117 Eb09
Čudzin BY 120 Ea13
Cuéllar E 79 Bd39
Cuenca E 92 Ca42
Cuers F 82 Ea39
Cuerva E 91 Bc42
Cuevas del Almanzora E 107 Ca45
Cugir RO 75 Hd36
Cugnaux F 81 Da38
Čuhloma RUS 118 Fa08
Cuhnești MD 76 Jc33
Čuhujiv UA 122 Fa14
Cuijk NL 55 Ec28
Cuiseaux F 70 Ea35
Cuisery F 70 Ea35
Çukurkuyu TR 128 Gc15
Culan F 69 Dc34
Culemborg NL 55 Eb28
Cúllar-Baza E 106 Bd45
Cullen GB 17 Db19
Cullera E 93 Cc43
Cullompton GB 23 Cc28
Culoz F 71 Eb36
Cumbernauld GB 21 Da21
Čumić SRB 87 Hb38
Cumnock GB 20 Cd21
Çumra TR 128 Gb15
Cuneo I 83 Ec38
Cunlcea MD 77 Jd32
Cunlhat F 70 Dd36
Cuorgnè I 71 Ec36
Cupar GB 21 Da21
Cupcini MD 76 Jc32

Ćuprija SRB 87 Hc38
Curia P 78 Ad39
Curtea de Argeş RO 88 Jb36
Curtici RO 75 Hc35
Cusset F 70 Dd35
Čuteevo RUS 119 Fd09
Čutove UA 122 Fa14
Cutro I 109 Gc45
Cuxhaven D 56 Fa25
Cwmcarn GB 24 Cd27
Cybinka PL 57 Ga28
Čyhyryn UA 121 Ed15
Czaplinek PL 57 Gb26
Czarna PL 67 Hc31
Czarna Białostocka PL 59 Hc26
Czarna Dąbrówka PL 58 Gc25
Czarnków PL 57 Gb27
Czarny Dunajec PL 67 Ha31
Czechowice-Dziedzice PL 66 Gd31
Czekarzewice PL 67 Hb29
Czermno PL 67 Ha29
Czersk PL 58 Gc26
Czerwieńsk PL 57 Gb28
Czerwionka-Leszczyny PL 66 Gd30
Czerwony Dwór PL 59 Hb25
Częstochowa PL 66 Gd29
Człopa PL 57 Gb27
Człuchów PL 58 Gc26
Czyżew-Osada PL 59 Hc27

D

Dabas H 74 Ha34
Dąbie PL 57 Ga28
Dąbie PL 58 Gd28
Dabilja MK 101 Hd42
Dabravolja BY 59 Hd26
Dąbrowa Białostocka PL 59 Hc25
Dąbrowa Górnicza PL 67 Ha30
Dąbrowa Tarnowska PL 67 Hb30
Dabryn' BY 121 Eb14
Dăbuleni RO 88 Ja38
Dachau D 72 Fb33
Dačice CZ 65 Gb32
Dačne UA 77 Kb34
Dáfnes GR 110 Hd46
Dáfni GR 102 Jb43
Dáfni GR 110 Hd46
Dáfni GR 110 Hd45
Dagali N 42 Fa17
Dagda LV 53 Jb22
Dağdere TR 113 Kb44
Dagomys RUS 127 Fd17
Dağpazarı TR 128 Gc16
Dahme D 57 Fd28
Dahn D 63 Ed31
Daimiel E 92 Bd43

Đakovica RKS 100 Hb41
Đakovo HR 86 Gd37
Dalarö S 45 Gc18
Dalbeattie GB 20 Cd22
Dălbok Dol BG 88 Jb39
Dălbok izvor BG 102 Jc40
Dale N 36 Ed16
Dale N 36 Ed16
Dalen N 42 Fa18
Dalfors S 38 Gb16
Dălghiu RO 88 Jc36
Dălgi Del BG 87 Hd39
Dălgopol BG 89 Jd39
Dalías E 106 Bd46
Dalj HR 86 Ha37
Dalkeith GB 21 Da21
Dalmally GB 16 Cd20
Dalmose DK 49 Fc24
Dalsbruk FIN 46 Hb17
Dalsjöfors S 44 Fd20
Dals Långed S 43 Fd19
Dalvík IS 15 Ca05
Dalwhinnie GB 17 Da20
Damaskinia GR 101 Hc43
Dambaslar TR 103 Ka41
Dammartin-en-Goële F 62 Dd31
Damme D 55 Ed27
Damnica PL 58 Gc25
Dampierre-sur-Salon F 71 Eb33
Danasjö S 33 Gb10
Danilov RUS 118 Fa08
Danilovgrad MNE 86 Ha40
Danilovka RUS 123 Fd13
Dankov RUS 122 Fa12
Dannenberg D 56 Fc26
Darabani RO 76 Jc32
Darány H 74 Gd36
Darbėnai LT 52 Hb22
Darda HR 74 Gd36
Dardesheim D 56 Fb28
Dardhë AL 101 Hc43
Darfo-Boario Terme I 72 Fa36
Dargosław PL 57 Gb25
Đarkavdčyna BY 53 Jb23
Darlington GB 21 Db23
Darłowo PL 57 Gb25
Dărmănești RO 88 Jc37
Darmstadt D 63 Ed31
Darney F 71 Eb33
Daroca E 93 Cb41
Dartford GB 25 Db28
Dartmouth GB 23 Cc28
Daruvar HR 74 Gc36
Darzininkai LT 53 Ja24
Dáski GR 101 Hd43
Dassel D 56 Fa28
Dassow D 56 Fb25
Datça TR 115 Kb47
Daudzeva LV 53 Hd21
Daugai LT 53 Hd24
Daugailiai LT 53 Ja23
Daugavpils LV 53 Ja22
Daun D 63 Ec30

Davhinava – Dolní Dvořiště

Davhinava **BY** 53 Jb24
Davor **BIH** 86 Gc37
Davos **CH** 72 Fa35
Davyd-Haradok **BY** 120 Ea14
Dax **F** 80 Cc37
Deal **GB** 25 Dc28
Deauville **F** 61 Db30
Debal'ceve **UA** 122 Fb15
Debar **MK** 100 Hb42
Debelec **BG** 88 Jc39
Dębica **BG** 58 Gb25
Dębica **PL** 67 Hb30
Dęblin **PL** 59 Hb28
Dębnica Kaszubska **PL** 58 Gc25
Dębno **PL** 57 Ga27
Debrc **SRB** 87 Hb38
Debrecen **H** 75 Hc34
Debrznica **PL** 57 Ga28
Dečani **RKS** 87 Hb40
Decazeville **F** 81 Db37
Děčín **CZ** 65 Ga30
Decize **F** 70 Dd34
De Cocksdorp **NL** 55 Eb26
Deda **RO** 76 Jb34
Dedemsvaart **NL** 55 Ec27
Dedenevo **RUS** 117 Ed10
Dedoviči **RUS** 117 Eb10
Deftera **CY** 128 Gb19
Degeberga **S** 50 Ga23
Degerby **FIN** 46 Ha17
Degerfors **S** 44 Ga18
Degerhamn **S** 50 Gb22
Deggendorf **D** 65 Fd32
Değirmendere **TR** 113 Ka45
Degučiai **LT** 52 Hb23
Degučiai **LT** 53 Ja22
Deinze **B** 62 Ea29
Dej **RO** 76 Ja34
Deje **S** 44 Fd18
Dekélia **GR** 112 Jb46
De Koog **NL** 55 Eb26
Delbrück **D** 56 Fa28
Delčevo **MK** 101 Hd41
Delémont **CH** 71 Ec34
Delft **NL** 54 Ea27
Delfzijl **NL** 55 Ed26
Deligrad **SRB** 87 Hc39
Delitzsch **D** 64 Fc29
Delmenhorst **D** 56 Fa26
Delnice **HR** 85 Ga37
Delsbo **S** 38 Gb15
Delvin **IRL** 19 Cb23
Demidov **RUS** 117 Ec11
Demidove **MD** 77 Kb33
Demirci **TR** 113 Kb44
Demir Kapija **MK** 101 Hd42
Demirköy **TR** 103 Ka40
Demirtaş **TR** 128 Ga17
Demitsána **GR** 110 Hd47
Demjansk **RUS** 117 Eb09
Dem'jas **RUS** 119 Ga11
Demmin **D** 57 Fd25
Demonía **GR** 111 Ja48
Demonte **I** 83 Ec38

Denain **F** 62 Dd29
Denbigh **GB** 24 Cd25
Den Burg **NL** 55 Eb26
Dendermonde **B** 62 Ea29
Den Haag **NL** 54 Ea27
Den Helder **NL** 55 Eb26
Denia **E** 94 Cc44
Deniz Kamp Yeri **TR** 113 Ka45
Denizli **TR** 103 Ka42
Den Oever **NL** 55 Eb26
Derbent **TR** 128 Ga15
Derby **GB** 24 Da25
Dereköy **TR** 113 Kb45
Dereli **TR** 127 Fd19
Dergači **RUS** 119 Ga11
Derhači **UA** 122 Fa14
Derry **GB** 20 Cb21
Derval **F** 61 Cd32
Derventa **BIH** 86 Gd37
Descartes **F** 69 Db33
Desenzano del Garda **I** 84 Fb37
Deskáti **GR** 101 Hd44
Despotovac **SRB** 87 Hc38
Despotovo **SRB** 86 Ha37
Dessau **D** 56 Fc28
Desvres **F** 62 Dc29
Deta **RO** 87 Hc37
Detkovo **RUS** 47 Jb18
Detmold **D** 56 Fa28
Detva **SK** 67 Ha32
Deurne **NL** 55 Eb28
Deutschfeistritz **A** 73 Gb34
Deutschkreuz **A** 74 Gc34
Deutschlandsberg **A** 73 Gb35
Deva **RO** 75 Hd36
Dévaványa **H** 75 Hb34
Devecikonağı **TR** 103 Kb43
Devecser **H** 74 Gc35
Deventer **NL** 55 Ec27
Devizes **GB** 24 Da27
Devnja **BG** 89 Ka39
Deza **E** 80 Cb40
Diafáni **GR** 115 Kb48
Diakoftó **GR** 110 Hd46
Diamante **I** 99 Gb44
Dianalund **DK** 49 Fc23
Diano Marina **I** 83 Ec39
Diavata **GR** 101 Ja42
Dichiseni **RO** 89 Jd37
Didam **NL** 55 Ec28
Didim **TR** 113 Ka46
Dídyma **GR** 111 Ja47
Didymoteicho **GR** 103 Jd41
Die **F** 82 Ea37
Dieburg **D** 64 Fa31
Diekirch **L** 63 Eb30
Diepholz **D** 56 Fa27
Dieppe **F** 62 Dc30
Dierdorf **D** 63 Ed30
Dieren **NL** 55 Ec28
Diest **B** 63 Eb29
Dietikon **CH** 71 Ed34
Dieulefit **F** 82 Ea37

Dieulouard **F** 63 Eb32
Dieuze **F** 63 Ec32
Dieveniškės **LT** 53 Ja24
Differdange **L** 63 Eb31
Digermulen **N** 28 Ga06
Digne-les-Bains **F** 83 Eb38
Digoin **F** 70 Dd35
Dijon **F** 70 Ea34
Dikanäs **S** 33 Gb10
Dikili **TR** 113 Ka44
Diksmuide **B** 54 Dd28
Diljatyn **UA** 76 Ja32
Diljatyn **UA** 124 Ea16
Dillenburg **D** 63 Ed29
Dillingen **D** 63 Ec31
Dillingen **D** 64 Fb32
Dilofo **GR** 101 Ja44
Dimitrie Cantemir **RO** 77 Jd34
Dimitrovgrad **BG** 102 Jc40
Dimitrovgrad **RUS** 119 Ga09
Dimitrovgrad **SRB** 87 Hd39
Dimovo **BG** 87 Hd39
Dinan **F** 61 Cd31
Dinant **B** 63 Eb30
Dinard **F** 61 Cd31
Dinek **TR** 128 Gb16
Dingle **IRL** 18 Bc24
Dingle **S** 43 Fc19
Dingolfing **D** 64 Fc32
Dingwall **GB** 17 Da19
Dinkelsbühl **D** 64 Fb32
Dinklage **D** 55 Ed27
Diö **S** 50 Ga22
Dioşti **RO** 88 Ja38
Dipkarpaz **CY** 128 Gc18
Dipótama **GR** 102 Jb41
Dippoldiswalde **D** 65 Fd29
Dirráhi **GR** 110 Hd47
Disentis **CH** 71 Ed35
Diss **GB** 25 Dc26
Dissen **D** 55 Ed28
Ditrău **RO** 76 Jb34
Divakë **RKS** 100 Hb42
Divčibare **SRB** 87 Hb38
Divčice **CZ** 65 Ga32
Divnoe **RUS** 123 Ga15
Divonne **F** 71 Eb35
Djat'kovo **RUS** 121 Ed12
Djulino **BG** 89 Ka39
Djuni **BG** 103 Ka40
Djúpivogur **IS** 15 Cb08
Djupvik **N** 26 Gd04
Djurås **S** 44 Ga17
Dmitrievka **RUS** 122 Fb12
Dmitriev-L'govskij **RUS** 121 Ed13
Dmitrov **RUS** 117 Ed10
Dmytrivka **UA** 77 Ka35
Dmytrivka **UA** 121 Ed14
Dnestrovsc **MD** 77 Kb34
Dniprodzeržyns'k **UA** 122 Fa15
Dnipropetrovs'k **UA** 122 Fa15
Dniprorudne **UA** 126 Fa16

Dno **RUS** 117 Eb10
Dobbiaco **I** 72 Fc35
Dobczyce **PL** 67 Ha31
Dobele **LV** 52 Hc21
Döbeln **D** 65 Fd29
Dobiegniew **PL** 57 Gb27
Dobieszczyn **PL** 57 Ga26
Doboj **BIH** 86 Gd38
Dobra **PL** 57 Gb26
Dobra **RO** 75 Hd36
Dobra **SRB** 87 Hc37
Dobrá Niva **SK** 74 Ha33
Dobřany **CZ** 65 Fd31
Dobrcz **PL** 58 Gd26
Dobre **PL** 59 Hb27
Dobre Miasto **PL** 58 Ha25
Dobri **H** 74 Gc35
Dobrič **BG** 89 Ka38
Dobrinka **RUS** 122 Fb12
Dobříš **CZ** 65 Ga31
Dobrjanka **UA** 121 Ec13
Dobrjatino **RUS** 118 Fb10
Dobrodzień **PL** 66 Gd30
Dobromyl' **UA** 67 Hc31
Dobropillja **UA** 122 Fb15
Dobro Polje **BIH** 86 Gd39
Dobrosyn **UA** 67 Hd30
Dobroteşti **RO** 88 Jb38
Dobrotič **BG** 89 Jd38
Dobrotica **BG** 89 Jd38
Dobrovol'sk **RUS** 52 Hc24
Dobruči **RUS** 47 Ja18
Dobruš **BY** 121 Ec13
Dobrzeń Wielki **PL** 66 Gd30
Dobšiná **SK** 67 Hb32
Docksta **S** 39 Gc13
Doclin **RO** 87 Hc37
Doetinchem **NL** 55 Ec28
Doğanbey **TR** 113 Ka45
Doğanbey **TR** 128 Ga15
Doğankent **TR** 127 Fd19
Dogliani **I** 83 Ec38
Dojeviće **SRB** 87 Hb40
Dojrenci **BG** 88 Jb39
Dokka **N** 37 Fb16
Dokkum **NL** 55 Ec26
Doksy **CZ** 65 Ga30
Dokšycy **BY** 53 Jb23
Dokšycy **BY** 120 Ea12
Dokučajevs'k **UA** 122 Fb15
Dol-de-Bretagne **F** 61 Cd31
Dole **F** 70 Ea34
Dølemo **N** 42 Fa19
Dolgellau **GB** 24 Cd25
Dolgorukovo **RUS** 59 Ha25
Dolianova **I** 97 Ed44
Dolišnij Šepit **UA** 76 Jb33
Doljani **BIH** 86 Gd39
Dolna Banja **BG** 102 Ja40
Dolna Mitropolija **BG** 88 Jb39
Dolna Orjahovica **BG** 88 Jc39
Dolní Bousov **CZ** 65 Ga30
Dolní Dǎbnik **BG** 88 Jb39
Dolní Dvořiště **CZ** 65 Ga32

Dolni Lom **BG** 87 Hd39
Dolno Dupeni **MK** 101 Hc42
Dolný Kubín **SK** 67 Ha32
Dolo **I** 84 Fc37
Dolores **E** 107 Cb44
Dolyna **UA** 67 Hd32
Dolyna **UA** 67 Hd32
Dolyns'ka **UA** 125 Ed16
Dolyns'ke **UA** 77 Ka33
Dolžanskaja **RUS** 126 Fb16
Dolžicy **RUS** 47 Jb18
Domanivka **MD** 77 Kb32
Domaradz **PL** 58 Gc25
Domaradz **PL** 67 Hc31
Domažlice **CZ** 65 Fd31
Dombaj **RUS** 127 Ga17
Dombås **N** 37 Fb14
Dombóvár **H** 74 Gd35
Dombrád **H** 75 Hc33
Domeikava **LT** 52 Hc24
Domérat **F** 69 Dc35
Domfront **F** 61 Da31
Dömitz **D** 56 Fc26
Domme **F** 69 Da36
Domnești **RO** 88 Jb36
Domnovo **RUS** 59 Ha25
Domodedovo **RUS** 118 Fa10
Domodossola **I** 71 Ed36
Domokós **GR** 110 Hd45
Dompaire **F** 71 Eb33
Dompierre-sur-Besbre **F** 70 Dd34
Domusnovas **I** 97 Ec44
Domžale **SLO** 73 Ga36
Donaueschingen **D** 71 Ed33
Donauwörth **D** 64 Fb32
Don Benito **E** 91 Ba42
Doncaster **GB** 25 Db25
Dondușeni **MD** 76 Jc32
Donec'k **UA** 122 Fb15
Donegal **IRL** 19 Cb22
Donges **F** 60 Cc32
Donja Stubica **HR** 73 Gb36
Donji Dušnik **SRB** 87 Hd39
Donji Kamengrad **BIH** 86 Gc38
Donji Lapac **HR** 85 Gb38
Donji Miholjac **HR** 74 Gd36
Donjin Milanova **SRB** 87 Hd38
Donji Rujani **BIH** 86 Gc39
Donji Stajevac **SRB** 87 Hd40
Donji Striževac **SRB** 87 Hd39
Donji Tovarnik **SRB** 87 Hb37
Donji Vakuf **BIH** 86 Gc38
Donji Žirovac **HR** 85 Gb37
Donostia **E** 80 Cb38
Donoúsa **GR** 115 Jd47
Donskoe **RUS** 127 Fd16
Donzy **F** 70 Dd33
Dor **RUS** 118 Fa08
Đorče Petrov **MK** 101 Hc41
Dorchester **GB** 24 Cd28
Dordrecht **NL** 55 Eb28
Dorfen **D** 72 Fc33

Dorgali **I** 97 Ed43
Dório **GR** 110 Hd47
Dorking **GB** 25 Db28
Dormagen **D** 63 Ec29
Dormánd **H** 75 Hb34
Dormans **F** 62 Dd31
Dornbirn **A** 72 Fa34
Dornes **F** 70 Dd34
Dornoch **GB** 17 Da18
Dorohoi **RO** 76 Jc33
Dorohusk **PL** 67 Hd29
Doroslovo **SRB** 74 Ha36
Dorotea **S** 33 Gb12
Dörpen **D** 55 Ed26
Dorsten **D** 55 Ec28
Dortmund **D** 55 Ed28
Doruchów **PL** 66 Gd29
Dörzbach **D** 64 Fa31
Dos Hermanas **E** 105 Ba44
Dospat **BG** 102 Jb41
Douai **F** 62 Dd29
Douarnenez **F** 60 Cb31
Douchy-les-Mines **F** 62 Dd30
Doudeville **F** 61 Db30
Doué-la-Fontaine **F** 69 Da33
Douglas **GBM** 20 Cd23
Doullens **F** 62 Dd30
Dourdan **F** 62 Dc32
Dover **GB** 25 Dc28
Dovhe **UA** 67 Hd32
Dovre **N** 37 Fb15
Dovsk **BY** 121 Eb13
Downham Market **GB** 25 Dc26
Downpatrick **GB** 20 Cc23
Dowra **IRL** 18 Ca22
Drabiv **UA** 121 Ed14
Drachten **NL** 55 Ec26
Drag **N** 28 Gb07
Dragalj **MNE** 86 Ha40
Drăgănești **MD** 77 Jd33
Drăgănești **RO** 88 Jc37
Drăgănești-Olt **RO** 88 Jb38
Drăgănești-Vlașca **RO** 88 Jc38
Dragaš **RKS** 100 Hb41
Drăgășani **RO** 88 Ja37
Draginac **SRB** 86 Ha38
Draglica **SRB** 87 Hb39
Dragoș Vodă **RO** 89 Jd37
Dragsfjärd **FIN** 46 Hb17
Draguignan **F** 83 Eb39
Drăgușeni **RO** 77 Jd35
Drahičyn **BY** 120 Ea14
Drahovce **SK** 74 Gd33
Drahove **UA** 75 Hd33
Dralfa **BG** 88 Jc39
Dráma **GR** 102 Jb42
Drammen **N** 43 Fb18
Drangedal **N** 43 Fb18
Drangsnes **IS** 14 Bd05
Dranske **D** 50 Fd24
Drávafok **H** 74 Gd36
Drawsko Pomorskie **PL** 57 Gb26

Drebkau **D** 57 Ga28
Drégelypalánk **H** 74 Ha33
Drenovac **SRB** 87 Hd40
Drenovci **HR** 86 Ha37
Drenovo **MK** 101 Hd42
Dresden **D** 65 Fd29
Drëtun' **BY** 117 Eb11
Dretyń **PL** 58 Gc25
Dreux **F** 62 Dc31
Drevsjø **N** 37 Fd15
Drezdenko **PL** 57 Gb27
Drežnica **HR** 85 Ga37
Driebes **E** 92 Bd41
Driffield **GB** 21 Dc24
Drinjača **BIH** 86 Ha38
Drjanovo **BG** 88 Jc39
Drniš **HR** 85 Gb39
Drnje **HR** 74 Gc36
Drøbak **N** 43 Fc18
Drobeta-Turnu Severin **RO** 87 Hd37
Drobin **PL** 58 Ha27
Drochia **MD** 77 Jd32
Drogheda **IRL** 19 Cb23
Drohiczyn **PL** 59 Hc27
Drohobyč **UA** 67 Hd31
Droitwich **GB** 24 Da26
Drolshagen **D** 63 Ed29
Dromore **GB** 20 Cc22
Dronero **I** 83 Ec38
Dronninglund **DK** 49 Fb21
Dronten **NL** 55 Ec27
Droskovo **RUS** 122 Fa12
Drossáto **GR** 101 Ja42
Drosseró **GR** 101 Hc43
Drozdyn' **UA** 120 Ea14
Druja **BY** 53 Jb22
Drumcliff **IRL** 18 Ca22
Drummore **GB** 20 Cd22
Drumnadrochit **GB** 17 Da19
Druskininkai **LT** 59 Hd25
Druskininkai **LT** 59 Hd25
Drusti **LV** 47 Hd20
Druten **NL** 55 Eb28
Družba **UA** 121 Ed13
Družetići **SRB** 87 Hb38
Drvar **BIH** 86 Gc38
Drvenik **HR** 86 Gc40
Drwęczno **PL** 58 Ha25
Drygały **PL** 59 Hb25
Duas Igrejas **P** 78 Bb39
Dubăsari **MD** 77 Ka33
Dubău **MD** 77 Ka33
Dubienka **PL** 67 Hd29
Dubin **PL** 58 Gc28
Dub'jazy **RUS** 119 Fd08
Dublin **IRL** 19 Cb24
Dubna **RUS** 117 Ed10
Dubna **RUS** 118 Fa11
Dub nad Moravou **CZ** 66 Gc31
Dubnica nad Váhom **SK** 66 Gd32
Dubno **UA** 120 Ea15
Dubova **RO** 87 Hd37
Dubove **UA** 76 Ja33

Dubovka **RUS** 123 Fd13
Dubovskoje **RUS** 123 Fd15
Dubovyj Ovrag **RUS** 123 Fd14
Dubrava **HR** 74 Gc36
Dubrivka **UA** 121 Eb15
Dubrovka **RUS** 53 Jb21
Dubrovka **RUS** 123 Fc12
Dubrovnik **HR** 86 Gd40
Dubrovcja **UA** 67 Hd30
Dubrovcja **UA** 120 Ea14
Ducey **F** 61 Cd31
Duchcov **CZ** 65 Fd30
Ducherow **D** 57 Fd26
Dudelange **L** 63 Eb31
Duderstadt **D** 64 Fb29
Dudley **GB** 24 Da26
Dueñas **E** 79 Bd39
Duesund **N** 36 Ed16
Dufftown **GB** 17 Db19
Duga Poljana **SRB** 87 Hb39
Duga Resa **HR** 85 Gb37
Dugo Selo **HR** 73 Gb36
Duhovnickoe **RUS** 119 Ga11
Duisburg **D** 55 Ec28
Dukat **AL** 100 Hb43
Dukla **PL** 67 Hc31
Dūkštas **LT** 53 Ja23
Dülmen **D** 55 Ed28
Dulovo **BG** 89 Jd38
Dulverton **GB** 23 Cc27
Dumbarton **GB** 20 Cd21
Dumbrăveni **RO** 76 Ja35
Dumbrăveni **RO** 89 Ka38
Dumbrăvița **MD** 77 Jd33
Dumfries **GB** 21 Da22
Dumitrești **RO** 88 Jc36
Dunaföldvár **H** 74 Ha35
Dunaharaszti **H** 74 Ha34
Dunajivci **UA** 125 Eb16
Dunajská Streda **SK** 74 Gc33
Dunakeszi **H** 74 Ha34
Dunaszekcső **H** 74 Gd36
Dunaújváros **H** 74 Ha35
Dunbar **GB** 21 Db21
Dunblane **GB** 21 Da21
Dundaga **LV** 46 Hb20
Dundalk **IRL** 19 Cb23
Dundee **GB** 17 Db20
Dunfanaghy **IRL** 19 Cb21
Dunfermline **GB** 21 Da21
Dungannon **GB** 20 Cb22
Dungarvan **IRL** 22 Ca23
Dungiven **GB** 20 Cb22
Dunglow **IRL** 18 Ca21
Dunkeld **GB** 17 Da20
Dunkerque **F** 54 Dd28
Dun Laoghaire **IRL** 19 Cb24
Dunmanway **IRL** 22 Bd25
Dunnet **GB** 17 Db18
Dunoon **GB** 20 Cd21
Dunshaughlin **IRL** 19 Cb23
Dunstable **GB** 25 Db27
Dunster **GB** 24 Cd27
Dun-sur-Auron **F** 69 Dc34

Dun-sur-Meuse – Elvanlı

Dun-sur-Meuse **F** 63 Eb31
Dunvegan **GB** 16 Cd18
Dupnica **BG** 102 Ja40
Durak **TR** 103 Kb43
Duran **BG** 89 Jd38
Durango **E** 80 Cb38
Durankulak **BG** 89 Ka38
Duras **F** 80 Da36
Durbe **LV** 52 Hb22
Durbuy **B** 63 Eb30
Đurđenovac **HR** 86 Gd37
Đurđevac **HR** 84 Gc36
Düren **D** 63 Ec29
Durham **GB** 21 Db23
Durness **GB** 17 Da17
Durrës **AL** 100 Ha42
Durrow **IRL** 18 Ca24
Dursunbey **TR** 103 Kb43
Durtal **F** 61 Da32
Dusetos **LT** 53 Ja22
Dušinci **BG** 87 Hd40
Düsseldorf **D** 63 Ec29
Duved **S** 38 Fd13
Düvertepe **TR** 103 Kb43
Dvor **HR** 85 Gb37
Dvoriki **RUS** 118 Fa10
Dvůr Králové nad Labem **CZ** 65 Gb30
Dyce **GB** 17 Db20
Dydnia **PL** 67 Hc31
Dygowo **PL** 57 Gb25
Dykan'ka **UA** 121 Ed14
Dymer **UA** 121 Ec14
Dymniki **BY** 59 Hd27
Dynivci **UA** 76 Jb32
Dyranut **N** 42 Fa17
Dyrnes **N** 36 Fa13
Džalil' **RUS** 119 Ga08
Džankoj **UA** 126 Fa17
Dzelzava **LV** 53 Ja21
Dzeržinsk **RUS** 118 Fb09
Dziadkowice **PL** 59 Hc27
Działdowo **PL** 58 Ha26
Działoszyce **PL** 67 Ha30
Działoszyn **PL** 66 Gd29
Dziemiany **PL** 58 Gc25
Dzierzgoń **PL** 58 Gd25
Dzierżoniów **PL** 66 Gc30
Dzisna **BY** 53 Jb22
Dzivin **BY** 59 Hd28
Dzjarečyn **BY** 59 Hd26
Dzjaržynsk **BY** 120 Ea12
Dzjatlava **BY** 120 Ea13
Džubga **RUS** 127 Fc17
Džuryn **UA** 125 Eb16

E

Easingwold **GB** 21 Db24
Eastbourne **GB** 25 Db28
East Dereham **GB** 25 Dc26
East Grinstead **GB** 25 Db28
East Kilbride **GB** 20 Cd21
Eauze **F** 80 Cd37
Ebeleben **D** 64 Fb29

Ebeltoft **DK** 49 Fb22
Ebensee **A** 73 Fd34
Eberbach **D** 64 Fa31
Ebern **D** 64 Fb30
Ebersbach **D** 65 Ga29
Ebersberg **D** 72 Fc33
Eberswalde **D** 57 Fd27
Eboli **I** 99 Ga43
Ebreichsdorf **A** 73 Gb33
Eceabat **TR** 103 Jd43
Echternach **L** 63 Ec31
Écija **E** 105 Bb44
Eckernförde **D** 56 Fb25
Eckerö **FIN** 45 Gd17
Écommoy **F** 61 Da32
Ecouché **F** 61 Da31
Ecueillé **F** 69 Db33
Ed **S** 43 Fc19
Edam **NL** 55 Eb27
Edane **S** 43 Fd18
Ede **NL** 55 Eb27
Edebäck **S** 44 Fd17
Edefors **S** 34 Gd09
Edelény **H** 75 Hb33
Edemissen **D** 56 Fb27
Edenderry **IRL** 19 Cb24
Edesbyn **S** 38 Gb15
Édessa **GR** 101 Hd42
Edgeworthstown **IRL** 18 Ca23
Edinburgh **GB** 21 Da21
Edincik **TR** 103 Ka42
Edineţ **MD** 76 Jc32
Edirne **TR** 103 Jd41
Édole **LV** 52 Hb21
Edolo **I** 72 Fa36
Edremit **TR** 103 Ka43
Edsbro **S** 45 Gc17
Edsbruk **S** 44 Gb20
Edsele **S** 38 Gb13
Edsta **S** 38 Gb15
Eeklo **B** 54 Ea28
Eemshaven **NL** 55 Ed26
Efimovskij **RUS** 117 Ec08
Efkarpía **GR** 102 Jb42
Eforie **RO** 89 Ka37
Efremov **RUS** 122 Fa12
Egby **S** 51 Gc21
Egeln **D** 56 Fc28
Eger **H** 75 Hb33
Egersund **N** 42 Ed19
Eggedal **N** 43 Fb17
Eggenburg **A** 65 Gb32
Eggenfelden **D** 73 Fd33
Eggesin **D** 57 Ga26
Egilsstaðir **IS** 15 Cc07
Égina **GR** 112 Jb46
Egínio **GR** 101 Hd43
Égio **GR** 110 Hd46
Égletons **F** 69 Db36
Egmond aan Zee **NL** 55 Eb27
Egor'e **RUS** 117 Ed11
Egor'evsk **RUS** 118 Fa10
Egorlykskaja **RUS** 127 Fc16
Egósthena **GR** 111 Ja46

Egtved **DK** 48 Fa23
Egyed **H** 74 Gc34
Ehingen **D** 72 Fa33
Ehinos **GR** 102 Jc41
Ehrwald **A** 72 Fb34
Eibar **E** 80 Cb38
Eibiswald **A** 73 Gb35
Eichstätt **D** 64 Fb32
Eiðar **IS** 15 Cc07
Eide **N** 36 Fa13
Eidet **N** 26 Gc05
Eidfjord **N** 36 Fa16
Eidsdalen **N** 36 Fa14
Eidsvåg **N** 36 Fa13
Eidsvoll **N** 43 Fc17
Eidvågeid **N** 26 Ha03
Eijsden **NL** 63 Eb29
Eikefjord **N** 36 Ed15
Eiken **N** 42 Ed19
Eilenburg **D** 65 Fd29
Èilgar **RUS** 123 Ga15
Eilsleben **D** 56 Fc28
Eina **N** 37 Fc16
Einbeck **D** 56 Fb28
Eindhoven **NL** 55 Eb28
Eisenach **D** 64 Fb29
Eisenberg **D** 64 Fc29
Eisenerz **A** 73 Ga34
Eisenhüttenstadt **D** 57 Ga28
Eisenstadt **A** 74 Gc34
Eisfeld **D** 64 Fb30
Eišiškės **LT** 59 Hd25
Eišiškės **LT** 59 Hd25
Eitorf **D** 63 Ed29
Eivindvik **N** 36 Ed16
Eivissa (Ibiza) **E** 94 Cd44
Ejea de los Caballeros **E** 80 Cc39
Ejsk **RUS** 126 Fb16
Ekaterinovka **RUS** 122 Fa12
Ekaterinovka **RUS** 123 Fc12
Ekeby **S** 49 Fd23
Ekenäs **FIN** 46 Hb17
Ekenäs **S** 44 Fd19
Ekerö **S** 45 Gc18
Ekimoviči **RUS** 121 Ec12
Ekshärad **S** 44 Fd17
Eksjö **S** 44 Ga20
Ekträsk **S** 34 Gd11
Ekzarh Antimovo **BG** 103 Jd40
Elabuga **RUS** 119 Ga08
Elan' **RUS** 123 Fd12
Elan'-Kolenovskij **RUS** 123 Fc13
El Arahal **E** 105 Ba44
Elassóna **GR** 101 Hd44
El Astillero **E** 79 Ca37
Elátia **GR** 111 Ja45
Elat'ma **RUS** 118 Fb10
Elatohóri **GR** 101 Hc44
Élatos **GR** 101 Hc44
El Barco de Ávila **E** 91 Bb40
Elbasan **RKS** 100 Hb42
Elbeuf **F** 61 Db30
Elbląg **PL** 58 Gd25

El Bonillo **E** 92 Ca43
El'brus **RUS** 127 Ga17
El Burgo de Osma **E** 92 Ca40
Elche **E** 107 Cb44
Elche de la Sierra **E** 107 Ca44
El Cubo de Tierra del Vino **E** 78 Bb39
Elda **E** 107 Cb44
Eléa **GR** 111 Ja48
Elec **RUS** 122 Fa12
Elefsína **GR** 112 Jb46
Eleftheroúpoli **GR** 102 Jb42
Eleja **LV** 52 Hc22
Èlektostal' **RUS** 118 Fa10
Elektrėnai **LT** 53 Hd24
Elena **BG** 88 Jc39
Elgå **N** 37 Fd14
Elgin **GB** 17 Db19
El Grado **E** 80 Cd40
Elhovka **RUS** 119 Ga09
Elhovo **BG** 103 Jd40
Eliá **GR** 110 Hd47
Elimäki **FIN** 41 Hd16
Elin Pelin **BG** 102 Ja40
Elionka **RUS** 121 Ec13
Èlista **RUS** 123 Ga15
Etk **PL** 59 Hc25
Ellon **GB** 17 Db19
Ellös **S** 43 Fc20
Ellwangen **D** 64 Fa32
El Molinillo **E** 91 Bc42
El Moral **E** 107 Ca44
Elmshorn **D** 56 Fb26
Elne **F** 81 Db39
Elnesvågen **N** 36 Fa13
El'nja **RUS** 117 Ec11
Elopía **GR** 111 Ja46
El Pedroso **E** 105 Ba43
El Pilar de la Mola **E** 94 Cd44
El Pobo de Dueñas **E** 93 Cb41
el Pont de Suert **E** 80 Cd39
El Puente del Arzobispo **E** 91 Bb41
El Puerto de Santa María **E** 105 Ad45
El Real de la Jara **E** 105 Ba43
El Real de San Vicente **E** 91 Bc41
El Rocío **E** 105 Ad44
El Rubio **E** 105 Bb44
El Saucejo **E** 105 Bb45
Elsfjord **N** 33 Ga09
Elsfleth **D** 56 Fa26
Elst **NL** 55 Ec28
Elsterwerda **D** 65 Fd29
Eltmann **D** 64 Fb31
El'ton **RUS** 123 Ga13
Eltville **D** 63 Ed30
Elva **EST** 47 Ja19
El Vacar **E** 105 Bb43
Elvanlı **TR** 128 Gc17

148

Elvas **P** 90 Ad42
Elven **F** 60 Cc32
el Vendrell **E** 95 Da41
Elverum **N** 37 Fc16
El Villar de Arnedo **E** 80 Cb39
El Viso **E** 105 Bb43
Elvkroken **N** 28 Gb07
Elx (Elche) **E** 107 Cb44
Ely **GB** 25 Dc26
Elze **D** 56 Fa28
Embrun **F** 83 Eb37
Embūte **LV** 52 Hb22
Emden **D** 55 Ed26
Emecik **TR** 115 Kb47
Emiralem **TR** 113 Ka45
Emirgazi **TR** 128 Gc15
Emlichheim **D** 55 Ec27
Emmaboda **S** 50 Gb22
Emmaljunga **S** 49 Fd22
Emmaste **EST** 46 Hb19
Emmeloord **NL** 55 Ec27
Emmen **NL** 55 Ec27
Emmendingen **D** 71 Ed33
Emmerich **D** 55 Ec28
Empessós **GR** 110 Hc45
Empoli **I** 84 Fb39
Emsdetten **D** 55 Ed27
Ёna **RUS** 31 Ja06
Enånger **S** 38 Gb15
Encekler **TR** 113 Kb44
Enciso **E** 80 Cb39
Encs **H** 75 Hb33
Enerhodar **UA** 126 Fa16
Eneryda **S** 50 Ga22
Enez **TR** 103 Jd42
Enge **N** 37 Fb13
Engelberg **CH** 71 Ed35
Engels **RUS** 123 Fd12
Enger **D** 56 Fa28
Engerneset **N** 37 Fd15
Engstingen **D** 72 Fa33
Enguera **E** 93 Cb43
Enguídanos **E** 93 Cb42
Engure **LV** 52 Hc21
Enisala **RO** 89 Ka36
Enkhuizen **NL** 55 Eb27
Enköping **S** 45 Gc18
Enna **I** 109 Ga47
Ennigerloh **D** 55 Ed28
Ennis **IRL** 18 Bd24
Enniscorthy **IRL** 23 Cb25
Enniskerry **IRL** 19 Cb24
Enniskillen **GB** 19 Cb22
Ennistimon **IRL** 18 Bd24
Enns **A** 73 Ga33
Eno **FIN** 41 Jb13
Enonkoski **FIN** 41 Ja14
Enontekiö Enokadak **FIN** 30 Ha06
Enschede **NL** 55 Ec27
Ensisheim **F** 71 Ec33
Entraygues-sur-Truyère **F** 81 Dc37
Entre-os-Rios **P** 78 Ad39
Entrevaux **F** 83 Eb38

Envermeu **F** 62 Dc30
Enviken **S** 38 Gb16
Épernay **F** 62 Ea31
Épila **E** 80 Cb40
Épinal **F** 71 Eb33
Epískopí **GR** 114 Jc49
Eppingen **D** 64 Fa32
Epsom **GB** 25 Db28
Eptahóri **GR** 101 Hc43
Équeurdreville-Hainneville **F** 61 Cd30
Erahtur **RUS** 118 Fb10
Erátira **GR** 101 Hc43
Erba **I** 71 Ed36
Erbach **D** 64 Fa31
Erbach **D** 72 Fa33
Erd **H** 74 Ha34
Erdek **TR** 103 Ka42
Erdemli **TR** 128 Gc17
Erdeven **F** 60 Cc32
Erding **D** 72 Fc33
Erdut **HR** 86 Ha37
Eregli **TR** 128 Gc15
Eremiivka **MD** 77 Kb33
Eremitu **RO** 76 Jb34
Erfurt **D** 64 Fb29
Ērgli **LV** 53 Hd21
Ergolding **D** 72 Fc33
Ergoldsbach **D** 64 Fc32
Erice **I** 108 Fc46
Ericeira **P** 90 Ab41
Erikli **TR** 103 Jd42
Eringsboda **S** 50 Gb22
Erithrés **GR** 111 Ja46
Erka **N** 37 Fb14
Erkelenz **D** 63 Ec29
Erkner **D** 57 Fd27
Erla **E** 80 Cc39
Erlangen **D** 64 Fb31
Ermakovo **RUS** 119 Ga09
Ermenek **TR** 128 Gb17
Ermesinde **P** 78 Ad38
Ermióni **GR** 111 Jb47
Ermiš **RUS** 118 Fb10
Ermoúpoli **GR** 112 Jc46
Ernée **F** 61 Da31
Erquy **F** 60 Cc31
Erro **E** 80 Cc38
Ersekë **AL** 101 Hc43
Erši **RUS** 117 Ed11
Ersmark **S** 34 Gd12
Ersmark **S** 34 Gd11
Erstein **F** 63 Ec32
Ertuğrul **TR** 103 Ka43
Ervenik **HR** 85 Gb38
Ervy-le-Châtel **F** 70 Dd33
Erwitte **D** 55 Ed28
Erzurum **TR** 127 Ga19
Eržvilkas **LT** 52 Hc23
Esbjerg **DK** 48 Fa23
Esbo **FIN** 46 Hc17
Escalada **E** 79 Ca38
Escalaplano **I** 97 Ed44
Escalona **E** 91 Bc41
Escalos de Cima **P** 90 Ad40
Escároz **E** 80 Cc38

Eschede **D** 56 Fb27
Eschenburg **D** 63 Ed29
Esch-sur-Alzette **L** 63 Eb31
Esch-sur-Sûre **L** 63 Eb30
Eschwege **D** 64 Fb29
Eschweiler **D** 63 Ec29
Esens **D** 55 Ed26
Eskifjörður **IS** 15 Cc07
Eskilstuna **S** 44 Gb18
Eslohe **D** 63 Ed29
Eslöv **S** 49 Fd23
Es Mercadal **E** 95 Dc43
Espalion **F** 81 Dc37
Espeland **N** 36 Ed16
Espiel **E** 105 Bb43
Espinama **E** 79 Bd37
Espinhal **P** 90 Ad40
Espinho **P** 78 Ad39
Espinosa de los Monteros **E** 79 Ca38
Espoo **FIN** 46 Hc17
Esposende **P** 78 Ad38
Esrange **S** 29 Gd07
Essen **B** 54 Ea28
Essen **D** 55 Ec28
Essentuki **RUS** 127 Ga17
Esslingen **D** 64 Fa32
Essoyes **F** 70 Ea33
Estaing **F** 81 Dc37
Estarreja **P** 78 Ad39
Estella **E** 80 Cb38
Estepa **E** 105 Bb44
Estepona **E** 105 Ba45
Estercuel **E** 93 Cc41
Esternay **F** 62 Dd32
Esterri d'Àneu **E** 81 Da39
Estissac **F** 62 Dd32
Estoril **P** 90 Ab41
Estremoz **P** 90 Ad42
Esztergom **H** 74 Gd34
Étain **F** 63 Eb31
Étampes **F** 62 Dc32
Étaples **F** 62 Dc29
Etili **TR** 103 Ka43
Etne **N** 42 Ed17
Etoliko **GR** 110 Hd46
Etrépagny **F** 62 Dc31
Étretat **F** 61 Db30
Etropole **BG** 102 Ja40
Ettelbruck **L** 63 Eb30
Ettenheim **D** 71 Ed33
Etten-Leur **NL** 55 Eb28
Ettlingen **D** 63 Ed32
Eu **F** 62 Dc30
Eupen **B** 63 Eb29
Eura **FIN** 40 Ha16
Eurajoki **FIN** 40 Ha15
Euskirchen **D** 63 Fc29
Eutin **D** 56 Fb25
Evanger **N** 36 Ed16
Evaux-les-Bains **F** 69 Dc35
Evciler **TR** 103 Ka43
Évdilos **GR** 113 Jd46
Evenskjer **N** 28 Gb06
Evergem **B** 54 Ea28
Evertsberg **S** 38 Ga16

Evesham **GB** 24 Da26
Évian-les-Bains **F** 71 Eb35
Evijärvi **FIN** 40 Hb13
Evisa **F** 96 Ed41
Evje **N** 42 Fa19
Evlanovo **RUS** 122 Fa12
Evolène **CH** 71 Ec35
Évora **P** 90 Ac42
Évoramonte **P** 90 Ad42
Evreşe **TR** 103 Jd42
Évreux **F** 61 Db31
Évron **F** 61 Da32
Évry **F** 62 Dc32
Éxarhos **GR** 111 Ja45
Exeter **GB** 23 Cc28
Extremo **P** 78 Ad38
Eydehavn **N** 42 Fa19
Eyemouth **GB** 21 Db21
Eygurande **F** 69 Dc35
Eymoutiers **F** 69 Db35
Eyrarbakki **IS** 14 Bc07
Ezcaray **E** 79 Ca39
Ezere **LV** 52 Hb22
Eželis **LT** 52 Hc24
Ezernieki **LV** 53 Jb22
Ezine **TR** 103 Jd43

F

Faaborg **DK** 49 Fb24
Fåberg **N** 36 Fa15
Fåberg **N** 37 Fc16
Fábiánsebestyén **H** 75 Hb35
Fäboda **FIN** 34 Ha12
Fabriano **I** 84 Fc39
Fábricas de Riópar **E** 107 Ca44
Faenza **I** 84 Fc38
Fafe **P** 78 Ad38
Fãgãraş **RO** 88 Jb36
Fågelsjö **S** 38 Ga15
Fagerås **S** 44 Fd18
Fagerhult **S** 43 Fc19
Fagerhult **S** 50 Gb21
Fagernes **N** 26 Gc05
Fagernes **N** 37 Fb16
Fagersta **S** 44 Gb17
Fãget **RO** 75 Hc36
Fagurhólsmýri **IS** 15 Ca08
Fakenham **GB** 25 Dc26
Fåker **S** 38 Ga13
Fakija **BG** 103 Jd40
Falaise **F** 61 Da31
Falconara Marittima **I** 85 Fd39
Falerum **S** 44 Gb20
Fãleşti **MD** 77 Jd33
Falkenberg **D** 65 Fd29
Falkenberg **S** 49 Fd21
Falkensee **D** 57 Fd27
Falkenstein **D** 64 Fc30
Falkirk **GB** 21 Da21
Falköping **S** 44 Fd20
Fällfors **S** 34 Gd10
Fälloheden **S** 33 Gc10

Falmouth – Forøya

Forres **GB** 17 Da19
Fors **S** 44 Gb17
Forserum **S** 44 Ga20
Forshaga **S** 44 Fd18
Förslöv **S** 49 Fd22
Forsmark **S** 33 Gb10
Forsmo **S** 39 Gc13
Forsnäs **S** 33 Gc09
Forsnes **N** 37 Fb13
Forssa **FIN** 40 Hb16
Forst **D** 57 Ga28
Forsvik **S** 44 Ga19
Fort Augustus **GB** 17 Da19
Forte dei Marmi **I** 84 Fa39
Fort-Mahon-Plage **F** 62 Dc29
Fortrose **GB** 17 Da19
Fortuna **E** 107 Cb44
Fortunes-well **GB** 24 Cd28
Fort William **GB** 16 Cd20
Forvika **N** 32 Fd10
Fosnavåg **N** 36 Ed14
Fossacesia Marina **I** 99 Ga41
Fossano **I** 83 Ec38
Fossbakken **N** 29 Gc06
Fosses-la-Ville **B** 62 Ea30
Fossli **N** 36 Fa16
Fossombrone **I** 84 Fc39
Fos-sur-Mer **F** 82 Dd39
Fót **H** 74 Ha34
Fougères **F** 61 Cd31
Fourchambault **F** 70 Dd34
Fourfourás **GR** 114 Jc49
Fourmies **F** 62 Ea30
Fours **F** 70 Dd34
Foústani **GR** 101 Hd42
Fowey **GB** 23 Cb28
Foxford **IRL** 18 Ca22
Foynes **IRL** 18 Bd24
Foz **E** 78 Bb36
Foz de Odeleite **P** 104 Ac44
Frącki **PL** 59 Hc25
Fraga **E** 80 Cd40
Fragístra **GR** 110 Hd45
Framlev **DK** 49 Fb22
Frammersbach **D** 64 Fa30
Frampol **PL** 67 Hc29
Francardo **F** 96 Ed41
Francavilla al Mare **I** 99 Ga41
Francavilla di Sicilia **I** 109 Ga47
Francavilla Fontana **I** 100 Gd43
Francoforte **I** 109 Ga47
Franeker **NL** 55 Ec26
Frankenberg **D** 64 Fa29
Frankenthal **D** 63 Ed31
Frankfurt (Main) **D** 63 Ed30
Frankfurt (Oder) **D** 57 Ga28
Fränsta **S** 38 Gb14
Františkovy Lázně **CZ** 64 Fc30
Frascati **I** 98 Fc41
Fraserburgh **GB** 17 Db19

Frashër **AL** 100 Hb43
Frătăuţii Noi **RO** 76 Jb33
Frátsia **GR** 111 Ja48
Frauenfeld **CH** 71 Ed34
Frauenkirchen **A** 74 Gc34
Frecăţei **RO** 89 Ka36
Fredericia **DK** 49 Fb23
Frederikshavn **DK** 49 Fb21
Frederikssund **DK** 49 Fc23
Frederiksværk **DK** 49 Fc23
Fredrika **S** 33 Gc12
Fredriksberg **S** 44 Ga17
Fredrikstad **N** 43 Fc18
Fregenal de la Sierra **E** 105 Ad43
Freiberg **D** 65 Fd29
Freiburg **D** 71 Ed33
Freilassing **D** 73 Fd34
Freising **D** 72 Fc33
Freistadt **A** 73 Ga33
Freital **D** 65 Fd29
Fréjus **F** 83 Eb39
Frenštát pod Radhoštěm **CZ** 66 Gd31
Freren **D** 55 Ed27
Fresnay-sur-Sarthe **F** 61 Da32
Fresno-Alhándiga **E** 91 Bb40
Fresno de Caracena **E** 92 Ca40
Fretigney **F** 71 Eb34
Freudenberg **D** 63 Ed29
Freudenstadt **D** 63 Ed32
Frévent **F** 62 Dd29
Freyburg **D** 64 Fc29
Freyming-Merlebach **F** 63 Ec31
Freyung **D** 65 Fd32
Frí **GR** 115 Kb49
Fribourg **CH** 71 Ec35
Friedberg **A** 73 Gb34
Friedberg **D** 64 Fa30
Friedberg **D** 72 Fb33
Friedewald **D** 64 Fa29
Friedland **D** 57 Fd26
Friedland **D** 57 Ga28
Friedland **D** 64 Fb29
Friedrichshafen **D** 72 Fa34
Friedrichstadt **D** 56 Fa25
Friesach **A** 73 Ga35
Friesack **D** 57 Fd27
Friesoythe **D** 55 Ed26
Friggesund **S** 38 Gb15
Frihetsli **N** 29 Gc06
Frillesås **S** 49 Fc21
Friol **E** 78 Ba36
Fristad **S** 44 Fd20
Fritsla **S** 49 Fd21
Fritzlar **D** 64 Fa29
Friville-Escarbotin **F** 62 Dc30
Frjanovo **RUS** 118 Fa10
Frohnleiten **A** 73 Gb34
Frolovo **RUS** 123 Fd13
Frombork **PL** 58 Ha25

Frome **GB** 24 Cd27
Frómista **E** 79 Bd38
Frontignan **F** 81 Dc38
Frosinone **I** 98 Fd42
Frosta **N** 32 Fc12
Froussioúna **GR** 111 Ja46
Frövi **S** 44 Gb18
Fruges **F** 62 Dc29
Frunzivka **UA** 77 Ka33
Frunzivka **UA** 125 Ec16
Frutigen **CH** 71 Ec35
Frýdek-Místek **CZ** 66 Gd31
Frýdlant **CZ** 65 Ga29
Fuengirola **E** 105 Bb45
Fuensalida **E** 91 Bc41
Fuensanta **E** 107 Ca45
Fuente-Álamo **E** 107 Ca45
Fuente de Cantos **E** 105 Ba43
Fuente del Arco **E** 105 Ba43
Fuente el Fresno **E** 91 Bc42
Fuente Obejuna **E** 105 Bb43
Fuentesaúco **E** 79 Bc39
Fuentes de Ebro **E** 80 Cc40
Fügen **A** 72 Fc34
Fulda **D** 64 Fa30
Fulunäs **S** 38 Fd16
Fumay **F** 62 Ea30
Fumel **F** 81 Da37
Funäsdalen **S** 38 Fd14
Fundão **P** 90 Ad40
Fundulea **RO** 88 Jc37
Furculeşti **RO** 88 Jb38
Furmanov **RUS** 118 Fa09
Fürstenau **D** 55 Ed27
Fürstenberg **D** 57 Fd26
Fürstenfeld **A** 73 Gb35
Fürstenfeldbruck **D** 72 Fb33
Fürstenwalde **D** 57 Ga28
Furta **H** 75 Hc34
Fürth **D** 64 Fb31
Furth im Wald **D** 65 Fd32
Furtwangen **D** 71 Ed33
Furudal **S** 38 Ga16
Furuflaten **N** 26 Gd05
Furusund **S** 45 Gd18
Fusa **N** 42 Ed17
Fushë-Muhur **AL** 100 Hb41
Füssen **D** 72 Fb34
Fustiñana **E** 80 Cb39
Füzesabony **H** 75 Hb33
Füzesgyarmat **H** 75 Hb34
Fyllinge **S** 49 Fd22
Fynshav **DK** 49 Fb24
Fyresdal **N** 42 Fa18

G

Gabare **BG** 88 Ja39
Gabčíkovo **SK** 74 Gc33
Gabøl **DK** 48 Fa23
Gabrovo **BG** 88 Jc39
Gacé **F** 61 Db31
Gacko **BIH** 86 Gd40
Gäddede **S** 33 Ga11

Gadebusch **D** 56 Fc26
Gádor **E** 106 Bd46
Gærum **DK** 49 Fb21
Găeşti **RO** 88 Jb37
Gaeta **I** 98 Fd42
Gafsele **S** 33 Gc12
Gaggenau **D** 63 Ed32
Gagince **SRB** 87 Hc40
Gagino **RUS** 119 Fc09
Gagnef **S** 44 Ga17
Gaiki **LV** 52 Hb21
Gaildorf **D** 64 Fa32
Gailey **GB** 24 Da25
Gaillac **F** 81 Db38
Gaillon **F** 62 Dc31
Gainsborough **GB** 25 Db25
Gairloch **GB** 16 Cd18
Gajutino **RUS** 117 Ed08
Gajvoron **UA** 77 Ka32
Gakilköy **TR** 103 Kb42
Gakkovo **RUS** 47 Ja17
Gălăbovo **BG** 102 Jc40
Galanta **SK** 74 Gd33
Galashiels **GB** 21 Da22
Galaţi **RO** 89 Jd36
Galatina **I** 100 Gd44
Galátista **GR** 101 Ja43
Galaxídi **GR** 111 Ja46
Galera **E** 106 Bd44
Galéria **F** 96 Ed40
Galgaguta **H** 74 Ha33
Gălgău **RO** 76 Ja34
Galič **RUS** 118 Fa08
Gallarate **I** 71 Ed36
Gallipoli **I** 100 Gd44
Gällivare **S** 29 Gd08
Gallneukirchen **A** 73 Ga33
Gällö **S** 38 Ga13
Gällstad **S** 44 Fd20
Galtström **S** 39 Gc14
Galway **IRL** 18 Bd23
Gaming **A** 73 Ga33
Gamleby **S** 44 Gb20
Gammelbo **S** 44 Gb18
Gammelstaden **S** 34 Ha10
Gammertingen **D** 72 Fa33
Gamvik **N** 27 Hc02
Ganderkesee **D** 56 Fa26
Gandesa **E** 93 Cd41
Gandia **E** 94 Cc44
Gandvik **N** 27 Hc04
Ganges **F** 81 Dc38
Gangi **I** 109 Ga47
Gannat **F** 69 Dc35
Gap **F** 83 Eb37
Gara Hitrino **BG** 89 Jd38
Gara Lăkatnik **BG** 88 Ja39
Garbatka-Letnisko **PL** 59 Hb28
Gârbou **RO** 75 Hd34
Garbów **PL** 67 Hc29
Garbsen **D** 56 Fa27
Garching **D** 72 Fc33
Garda **I** 72 Fb36
Gardanne **F** 82 Ea39

Gårdby – Gniechowice

Gårdby **S** 50 Gb22
Gardelegen **D** 56 Fc27
Gardermoen **N** 43 Fc17
Gardete **P** 90 Ad41
Gardíki **GR** 101 Hc44
Garding **D** 56 Fa25
Gärdnäs **S** 33 Ga12
Gardone Riviera **I** 72 Fb36
Gardone Val Trompia **I** 72 Fa36
Gárdony **H** 74 Gd34
Garður **IS** 14 Bb06
Garešnica **HR** 74 Gc36
Garessio **I** 83 Ec38
Gargaliáni **GR** 110 Hd47
Gargnäs **S** 33 Gc10
Gargždai **LT** 52 Hb23
Garlasco **I** 83 Ed37
Garliava **LT** 52 Hc24
Gärljano **BG** 101 Hd41
Garmisch-Partenkirchen **D** 72 Fb34
Garoaia **RO** 77 Jd35
Garphyttan **S** 44 Ga18
Garrovillas **E** 91 Ba41
Garrucha **E** 107 Ca45
Gärsnäs **S** 50 Ga23
Gartz **D** 57 Ga26
Garvão **P** 104 Ac43
Garve **GB** 17 Da19
Garwolin **PL** 59 Hb28
Gasteiz **E** 80 Cb38
Gastoúni **GR** 110 Hc46
Gätaia **RO** 75 Hc36
Gatčina **RUS** 47 Jb17
Gatehouse of Fleet **GB** 20 Cd22
Gateshead **GB** 21 Db23
Gattinara **I** 71 Ed36
Gaucín **E** 105 Ba45
Gaupne **N** 36 Fa15
Gauting **D** 72 Fb33
Gavarnie **F** 80 Cd39
Gavião **P** 90 Ad41
Gävle **S** 39 Gc16
Gavorrano **I** 84 Fb40
Gavray **F** 61 Cd31
Gavrilov-Jam **RUS** 118 Fa09
Gávrio **GR** 112 Jc46
Gávros **GR** 101 Hc43
Gavry **RUS** 53 Jb21
Gaworzyce **PL** 57 Gb28
Gazimağusa **CY** 128 Gc19
Gazipaşa **TR** 128 Ga17
Gdańsk **PL** 58 Gd25
Gdov **RUS** 47 Ja18
Gdynia **PL** 58 Gd25
Gedser **DK** 49 Fc25
Geel **B** 63 Eb29
Geeste **D** 55 Ed27
Geesthacht **D** 56 Fb26
Gefell **D** 64 Fc30
Geilenkirchen **D** 63 Ec29
Geilo **N** 36 Fa16
Geiranger **N** 36 Fa14
Geiselhöring **D** 64 Fc32

Geisenfeld **D** 64 Fc32
Geisingen **D** 71 Ed33
Geislingen **D** 64 Fa32
Geithus **N** 43 Fb17
Gela **I** 109 Ga48
Geldern **D** 55 Ec28
Geldrop **NL** 55 Eb28
Geleen **NL** 63 Eb29
Gelenbe **TR** 113 Kb44
Gelendžik **RUS** 127 Fc17
Gelgaudiškis **LT** 52 Hc24
Gelibolu **TR** 103 Jd42
Gelnhausen **D** 64 Fa30
Gelsenkirchen **D** 55 Ec28
Gelting **D** 49 Fb24
Gelu **RO** 75 Hb36
Gembloux **B** 62 Ea29
Gemla **S** 50 Ga22
Gemona del Friuli **I** 73 Fd36
Gemünden **D** 64 Fa29
Gemünden **D** 64 Fa30
Gençay **F** 69 Da34
Generalski Stol **HR** 85 Gb37
General Toševo **BG** 89 Ka38
Genève **CH** 71 Eb35
Gengenbach **D** 63 Ed32
Genk **B** 63 Eb29
Genlis **F** 70 Ea34
Gennep **NL** 55 Ec28
Génolhac **F** 82 Dd37
Genova **I** 83 Ed38
Gent **B** 62 Ea29
Genthin **D** 56 Fc27
Genzano di Lucania **I** 99 Gb43
George Enescu **RO** 76 Jc32
Georgievsk **RUS** 127 Ga17
Gera **D** 64 Fc29
Geraardsbergen **B** 62 Ea29
Gerace **I** 109 Gc46
Gerakaroú **GR** 101 Ja43
Geráki **GR** 111 Ja47
Gerakiní **GR** 101 Ja43
Gérardmer **F** 71 Ec33
Gerena **E** 105 Ba44
Gérgal **E** 106 Bd45
Gergova **RO** 89 Ka36
Germencik **TR** 113 Kb45
Germering **D** 72 Fb33
Germersheim **D** 63 Ed31
Gernika **E** 80 Cb37
Gernsheim **D** 63 Ed31
Gerolstein **D** 63 Ec30
Gerolzhofen **D** 64 Fb31
Gersfeld **D** 64 Fa30
Gersthofen **D** 72 Fb33
Gescher **D** 55 Ec28
Gesunda **S** 38 Ga16
Gèsves **B** 63 Eb30
Geta **FIN** 45 Gd17
Getafe **E** 92 Bd41
Getinge **S** 49 Fd21
Gettorf **D** 56 Fb25
Getxo **E** 79 Ca37
Gevgelija **MK** 101 Hd42
Gex **F** 71 Eb35

Geyikli **TR** 103 Jd43
Ghedi **I** 84 Fa37
Gheorgheni **RO** 76 Jb34
Gherla **RO** 76 Ja34
Gherţa Mică **RO** 75 Hd33
Ghilarza **I** 97 Ed43
Ghimpaţi **RO** 88 Jc38
Ghisonaccia **F** 96 Ed41
Ghisoni **F** 96 Ed41
Gianitsá **GR** 101 Hd42
Giardini-Naxos **I** 109 Gb47
Giarmata **RO** 75 Hc36
Giarre **I** 109 Gb47
Gibellina Nuova **I** 108 Fc47
Gibostad **N** 26 Gc05
Gibraleón **E** 105 Ad44
Gibraltar **GBZ** 105 Ba46
Gibzde **LV** 52 Hb21
Gic **H** 74 Gd34
Gideå **S** 39 Gc13
Gideåkroken **S** 33 Gc11
Gieboldehausen **D** 56 Fb28
Gien **F** 69 Dc33
Giengen **D** 64 Fb32
Giens **F** 82 Ea39
Giera **RO** 87 Hb37
Gießen **D** 63 Ed30
Gieten **NL** 55 Ec26
Gietrzwałd **PL** 58 Ha26
Gifhorn **D** 56 Fb27
Gigant **RUS** 123 Fd15
Gighera **RO** 88 Ja38
Gignac **F** 81 Dc38
Gijón **E** 79 Bc36
Gilău **RO** 75 Hd35
Gilavë **AL** 100 Hb43
Gilleleje **DK** 49 Fd22
Gimåfors **S** 38 Gb14
Gimo **S** 45 Gc17
Gimone **F** 81 Da38
Ginduliai **LT** 52 Hb23
Ginosa **I** 99 Gc43
Gioia del Colle **I** 99 Gc43
Gioia Tauro **I** 109 Gb46
Gioiosa Ionica **I** 109 Gc46
Giraltovce **SK** 67 Hb32
Giresun **TR** 127 Fd19
Girne **CY** 128 Gb18
Giromagny **F** 71 Ec33
Girona **E** 81 Db40
Girvan **GB** 20 Cd22
Gisburn **GB** 21 Da24
Gislaved **S** 49 Fd21
Gisors **F** 62 Dc31
Githio **GR** 111 Ja48
Giulianova **I** 85 Fd40
Giulvăz **RO** 75 Hb36
Giurgeni **RO** 89 Jd37
Giurgiu **RO** 88 Jc38
Give **DK** 48 Fa23
Givet **F** 62 Ea30
Givors **F** 70 Ea36
Givry **F** 70 Ea34
Givry-en-Argonne **F** 62 Ea31
Giżałki **PL** 58 Gc28
Giżycko **PL** 59 Hb25

Gjermundshamn **N** 42 Ed17
Gjerstad **N** 43 Fb19
Gjersvik **N** 33 Ga11
Gjesvær **N** 27 Hb02
Gjirokastër **AL** 100 Hb44
Gjøra **N** 37 Fb14
Gjøvik **N** 37 Fc16
Gladenbach **D** 63 Ed29
Gladstad **N** 32 Fd10
Glamoč **BIH** 86 Gc39
Glamsbjerg **DK** 49 Fb24
Glandorf **D** 55 Ed28
Glarus **CH** 71 Ed34
Glasgow **GB** 21 Da21
Glastonbury **GB** 24 Cd27
Glavatićevo **BIH** 86 Gd39
Glavinica **BG** 89 Jd38
Głębokie **PL** 67 Hc29
Gleisdorf **A** 73 Gb34
Glenariff **GB** 20 Cc22
Glenarm **GB** 20 Cc22
Glenbeigh **IRL** 18 Bc24
Glencolumbkille **IRL** 18 Ca21
Glenfinnan **GB** 16 Cd19
Glengarriff **IRL** 22 Bc25
Glenluce **GB** 20 Cd22
Glenrothes **GB** 21 Da21
Glenties **IRL** 18 Ca21
Glífa **GR** 111 Ja45
Glifáda **GR** 100 Hb44
Glimåkra **S** 50 Ga22
Glina **HR** 85 Gb37
Glinojeck **PL** 58 Ha27
Gliwice **PL** 66 Gd30
Glodeanu-Siliştea **RO** 89 Jd37
Glodeni **MD** 76 Jc33
Gloggnitz **A** 73 Gb34
Glogovac **RKS** 87 Hc40
Głogów **PL** 57 Gb28
Głogówek **PL** 66 Gd30
Głogów Małopolski **PL** 67 Hc30
Glomfjord **N** 28 Ga08
Glommen **S** 49 Fd21
Glommersträsk **S** 34 Gd10
Glöte **S** 38 Fd15
Gloucester **GB** 24 Da27
Główczyce **PL** 51 Gc24
Głowno **PL** 58 Ha28
Głubczyce **PL** 66 Gd30
Glubokij **RUS** 123 Fc14
Głuchołazy **PL** 66 Gc30
Głuchowo **PL** 58 Gc28
Glücksburg **D** 49 Fb24
Glückstadt **D** 56 Fa25
Gluhove **RUS** 118 Fb10
Gmünd **A** 65 Ga32
Gmünd **A** 73 Fd35
Gmunden **A** 73 Fd33
Gnarp **S** 39 Gc15
Gnarrenburg **D** 56 Fa26
Gnesta **S** 45 Gc19
Gniazdowo **PL** 59 Hb26
Gniechowice **PL** 66 Gc29

152

Gniew PL 58 Gd25
Gniezno PL 58 Gc27
Gnjilane RKS 87 Hc40
Gnoien D 57 Fd25
Gnosjö S 50 Ga21
Gobesh AL 100 Hb43
Göçbeyli TR 113 Ka44
Goce Delčev BG 101 Ja41
Goce Delčev BG 101 Ja41
Goch D 55 Ec28
Göd H 74 Ha34
Godby FIN 45 Gd17
Godeanu RO 87 Hd37
Godeč BG 88 Ja39
Goderville F 61 Db30
Gödöllő H 74 Ha34
Goes NL 54 Ea28
Gogolin PL 66 Gd30
Göhren D 57 Fd25
Goián E 78 Ad37
Góis P 90 Ad40
Goito I 84 Fb37
Gójsk PL 58 Ha27
Gökçeada TR 103 Jd43
Gökçen TR 113 Kb45
Gökkuşağı TR 128 Gd16
Gol N 37 Fb16
Golce PL 57 Gb26
Gölcük TR 103 Kb43
Golčův Jeníkov CZ 65 Gb31
Golczewo PL 57 Ga26
Gołdap PL 59 Hb25
Goldberg D 56 Fc26
Göle TR 127 Ga19
Goleniów PL 57 Ga26
Golfo Aranci I 96 Ed42
Golica BG 89 Ka39
Golicyno RUS 117 Ed10
Gološeva LV 53 Jb21
Goljam Manastir BG 103 Jd40
Goljamo Kruševo BG 103 Jd40
Gölmarmara TR 113 Kb44
Gölören TR 128 Gc15
Golspie GB 17 Da18
Golßen D 57 Fd28
Golubac SRB 87 Hc37
Golub-Dobrzyń PL 58 Gd26
Gołymin-Ośrodek PL 59 Hb27
Gómara E 80 Cb40
Gömeç TR 113 Ka44
Gommern D 56 Fc28
Gomulin PL 67 Ha29
Goncelin F 71 Eb36
Gondomar P 78 Ad39
Gondrecourt-le-Château F 63 Eb32
Gönen TR 103 Ka43
Goniądz PL 59 Hc26
Goole GB 21 Db24
Goor NL 55 Ec27
Göppingen D 64 Fa32
Góra PL 57 Gb28
Góra PL 58 Ha27

Góra Kalwaria PL 59 Hb28
Goráni GR 111 Ja47
Goražde BIH 86 Ha39
Gorban RO 77 Jd34
Gördalen S 38 Fd15
Gördes TR 113 Kb44
Gorelki RUS 118 Fa11
Gorey IRL 23 Cb25
Gorica BG 89 Ka39
Goricë AL 101 Hc42
Goricy RUS 117 Ed09
Gorinchem NL 55 Eb28
Goritsá GR 111 Ja47
Gorizia I 73 Fd36
Gorjačij Ključ RUS 127 Fc17
Gorki RUS 47 Jb17
Gørlev DK 49 Fc23
Gorlice PL 67 Hb31
Görlitz D 65 Ga29
Gormanstown IRL 19 Cb23
Gorna Bešovica BG 88 Ja39
Gorna Orjahovica BG 88 Jc39
Gorni Okol BG 102 Ja40
Gornjackij RUS 123 Fc14
Gornja Radgona SLO 73 Gb35
Gornja Sabanta SRB 87 Hc38
Gornje Peulje BIH 86 Gc38
Gornji Jabolčište MK 101 Hc41
Gornji Milanovac SRB 87 Hb38
Gornji Vakuf-Uskoplje BIH 86 Gd39
Górno PL 67 Hb29
Gornyj RUS 119 Ga11
Gorodec RUS 118 Fb09
Gorodišče RUS 119 Fd11
Gorodovikovsk RUS 127 Fd16
Górowo Iławeckie PL 58 Ha25
Gorron F 61 Da31
Goršečnoe RUS 122 Fa13
Gort IRL 18 Bd24
Görükle TR 103 Kb42
Görvik S 38 Gb13
Gorzkowice PL 67 Ha29
Gorzków-Osada PL 67 Hc29
Gorzów Wielkopolski PL 57 Gb27
Gorzyń PL 57 Gb27
Gosau A 73 Fd34
Gościkowo Jordanowo PL 57 Gb27
Gosforth GB 21 Da23
Goslar D 56 Fb28
Gospić HR 85 Gb38
Gostilja BG 88 Ja39
Gostivar MK 101 Hc41
Göstling A 73 Ga34
Gostomia PL 57 Gb26
Gostyń PL 58 Gc28
Gostynin PL 58 Ha27

Göteborg S 43 Fc20
Götene S 44 Fd19
Gotha D 64 Fb29
Götlunda S 44 Gb18
Göttingen D 56 Fb28
Gottskär S 49 Fc21
Gouda NL 55 Eb27
Gouménissa GR 101 Hd42
Goúmero GR 110 Hd46
Gourdon F 69 Db36
Gourin F 60 Cb31
Gournay-en-Bray F 62 Dc30
Gouveia P 90 Ad40
Gouzon F 69 Dc35
Goveđari HR 86 Gc40
Gowidlino PL 58 Gc25
Gozdnica PL 65 Ga29
Gözne TR 128 Gd16
Grabarka PL 59 Hc27
Graben-Neudorf D 63 Ed32
Grabovica SRB 87 Hb38
Grabovica SRB 87 Hd38
Grabow D 56 Fc26
Grabów nad Prosną PL 66 Gd29
Grabowno PL 58 Gc26
Grabowo PL 59 Hb25
Gračac HR 85 Gb38
Gračanica BIH 86 Gd39
Gračanica BIH 86 Gd38
Gračanica RKS 87 Hc40
Graçay F 69 Dc33
Gračevka RUS 127 Fd16
Gradac HR 85 Gb37
Gradačac BIH 86 Gd37
Gradec BG 87 Hd38
Gradešnica MK 101 Hd42
Gradina BG 88 Jc39
Grădinari RO 87 Hc37
Gradište HR 86 Ha37
Grădiştea RO 89 Jd37
Grădiştea RO 88 Ja37
Grădiştea de Munte RO 75 Hd36
Gradnica BG 88 Jb39
Grado I 73 Fd36
Gradojević SRB 86 Ha38
Grafenau D 65 Fd32
Gräfenberg D 64 Fb31
Gräfenhainichen D 56 Fc28
Grafenwöhr D 64 Fc31
Graiguenamanagh IRL 23 Cb25
Grajduri RO 77 Jd34
Grajewo PL 59 Hc26
Grajvoron RUS 122 Fa14
Gram DK 48 Fa23
Gramat F 69 Db36
Grammichele I 109 Ga47
Gramsh AL 100 Hb43
Gramzow D 57 Ga26
Gran N 43 Fc17
Granada E 106 Bc45
Granard IRL 19 Cb23
Grandas de Salime E 78 Bb36

Grandcamp-Maisy F 61 Da30
Grândola P 90 Ac42
Grandrieu F 82 Dd37
Grandvillars F 71 Ec34
Grandvilliers F 62 Dc30
Grañén E 80 Cc40
Grangärde S 44 Ga17
Grangemouth GB 21 Da21
Grängesberg S 44 Ga17
Graniceşti RO 76 Jb33
Graninge S 38 Gb13
Granitis GR 102 Jb42
Grankullavik S 51 Gc21
Granliden S 33 Gb11
Gränna S 44 Ga20
Grannäs S 33 Gb10
Granö S 34 Gd12
Granollers E 95 Db41
Gransee S 57 Fd27
Gransherad N 43 Fb18
Grantham GB 25 Db25
Grantown-on-Spey GB 17 Da19
Granville F 61 Cd31
Granvin N 36 Ed16
Grapska BIH 86 Gd38
Gräsgård S 50 Gb22
Grassano I 99 Gc43
Grassau D 72 Fc34
Grasse F 83 Eb39
Gråsten DK 49 Fb24
Grästorp S 43 Fd20
Gratwein A 73 Gb34
Graulhet F 81 Db38
Graus E 80 Cd40
Grávavencsellő H 75 Hc33
Gravberget N 37 Fd16
Gravedona I 72 Fa36
Gravelines F 54 Dd28
Gravesend GB 25 Db28
Graviá GR 111 Ja45
Gravina in Puglia I 99 Gc43
Gray F 71 Eb34
Graz A 73 Gb35
Gražiškiai LT 52 Hc24
Great Ayton GB 21 Db23
Great Malvern GB 24 Da26
Great Yarmouth GB 25 Dd26
Grebbestad S 43 Fc19
Grebenhain D 64 Fa30
Grębocin PL 58 Gd26
Greenlaw GB 21 Db21
Greenock GB 20 Cd21
Greenodd GB 21 Da23
Greetsiel D 55 Ed26
Greifenburg A 73 Fd35
Greifswald D 57 Fd25
Grein A 73 Ga33
Greiz D 64 Fc30
Gremjač'e RUS 122 Fb13
Grenaa DK 49 Fc22
Grenade F 81 Da38
Grenade-sur-l'Adour F 80 Cd37

Hainfeld **A** 73 Gb33
Hainichen **D** 65 Fd29
Hajdúböszörmény **H** 75 Hc33
Hajdúnánás **H** 75 Hc33
Hajdúsámson **H** 75 Hc34
Hajdúszoboszló **H** 75 Hc34
Hajnówka **PL** 59 Hd27
Hajós **H** 74 Ha35
Hajsyn **UA** 121 Ec15
Håkafot **S** 33 Ga11
Hakkas **S** 30 Ha08
Häkkilä **FIN** 40 Hc13
Halástra **GR** 101 Ja43
Halberstadt **D** 56 Fb28
Halden **N** 43 Fc18
Haldensleben **D** 56 Fc28
Halesworth **GB** 25 Dc27
Halič **UA** 124 Ea16
Halifax **GB** 21 Da24
Halikko **FIN** 40 Hb16
Haljala **EST** 47 Hd17
Halkapınar **TR** 128 Gc16
Halkida **GR** 112 Jb45
Halkirk **GB** 17 Db18
Hälla **S** 33 Gc12
Halle (Saale) **D** 64 Fc29
Hällefors **S** 44 Ga18
Hälleforsnäs **S** 44 Gb18
Hallein **A** 73 Fd34
Hällekis **S** 44 Fd19
Hallen **S** 38 Ga13
Hällesjö **S** 38 Gb13
Hall in Tirol **A** 72 Fb34
Hällnäs **S** 34 Gd11
Hallormsstaður **IS** 15 Cb07
Hallsberg **S** 44 Ga19
Hållsta **S** 44 Gb18
Hallstahammar **S** 44 Gb18
Hallstatt **A** 73 Fd34
Hallstavik **S** 45 Gc17
Hallviken **S** 33 Gb12
Halmstad **S** 49 Fd22
Hals **DK** 49 Fb21
Halsa **N** 37 Fb13
Hal'dany **BY** 53 Ja24
Hal'šany **BY** 120 Ea12
Halstead **GB** 25 Dc27
Halsteren **NL** 54 Ea28
Halsua **FIN** 34 Hb12
Halsvik **N** 36 Ed16
Haltern **D** 55 Ed28
Haltwhistle **GB** 21 Da22
Halvarsgårdarna **S** 44 Gb17
Ham **F** 62 Dd30
Hamar **N** 37 Fc16
Hamburg **D** 56 Fb26
Hamdibey **TR** 103 Ka43
Hämeenkyrö **FIN** 40 Hb15
Hämeenlinna **FIN** 40 Hc16
Hameln **D** 56 Fa28
Hamidiye **TR** 103 Jd41
Hamilton **GB** 21 Da21
Hamina **FIN** 41 Ja16
Hamm **D** 55 Ed28
Hammar **S** 44 Ga19

Hammarslund **S** 50 Ga23
Hammarstrand **S** 38 Gb13
Hammarvika **N** 32 Fb12
Hammel **DK** 49 Fb22
Hammelburg **D** 64 Fa30
Hammenhög **S** 50 Ga23
Hammerdal **S** 38 Ga13
Hammerfest **N** 26 Ha03
Hamminkeln **D** 55 Ec28
Hamneidet **N** 26 Gd04
Hamnes **N** 32 Fc11
Hamnvik **N** 28 Gb06
Håmojåkk **S** 29 Gd07
Hamyški **RUS** 127 Fd17
Hanak **TR** 127 Ga18
Hanau **D** 64 Fa30
Hancǎuți **MD** 76 Jc32
Hancaviçy **BY** 120 Ea13
Hâncești **MD** 77 Ka34
Handewitt **D** 48 Fa24
Handlová **SK** 66 Gd32
Hanestad **N** 37 Fc15
Haneviçy **BY** 53 Jb24
Hånger **S** 50 Ga21
Hangö **FIN** 46 Hb17
Haniá **GR** 114 Jc49
Haniótis **GR** 101 Ja43
Hankamäki **FIN** 35 Ja12
Hankasalmi **FIN** 41 Hd14
Hanko **FIN** 46 Hb17
Hann. Münden **D** 64 Fa29
Hannover **D** 56 Fa27
Hannut **B** 63 Eb29
Hanøy **N** 28 Ga06
Han Pijesak **BIH** 86 Ha38
Hansnes **N** 26 Gc04
Hanstholm **DK** 48 Fa21
Han-sur-Nied **F** 63 Ec32
Hanušovce nad Topl'ou **SK** 67 Hb32
Hanušovice **CZ** 66 Gc31
Haparanda **S** 34 Hb09
Haradok **BY** 117 Eb11
Harads **S** 34 Gd09
Häradsbäck **S** 50 Ga22
Haradzišča **BY** 120 Ea13
Hárakas **GR** 115 Jd49
Harasiuki **PL** 67 Hc30
Harbo **S** 45 Gc17
Harborg **N** 37 Fc14
Hardelot-Plage **F** 62 Dc29
Hardenberg **NL** 55 Ec27
Harderwijk **NL** 55 Ec27
Hardheim **D** 64 Fa31
Hareid **N** 36 Ed14
Haren (Ems) **D** 55 Ed27
Hargshamn **S** 45 Gc17
Harjavalta **FIN** 40 Ha15
Harkány **H** 74 Gd36
Hârlǎu **RO** 76 Jc33
Hårlev **DK** 49 Fc24
Harlingen **NL** 55 Eb26
Harlow **GB** 25 Db27
Harlu **RUS** 41 Jb14
Harmånger **S** 39 Gc15
Härmänkyla **FIN** 35 Ja11

Harmanli **BG** 102 Jc41
Harnes **F** 62 Dd29
Härnösand **S** 39 Gc14
Haro **E** 79 Ca38
Harran **N** 32 Fd11
Harrogate **GB** 21 Db24
Harrsjö **S** 33 Gb11
Harrström **FIN** 40 Ha14
Harsefeld **D** 56 Fa26
Hârșova **RO** 89 Ka37
Harsovo **BG** 89 Jd38
Härsovo **BG** 89 Jd38
Harsprånget **S** 29 Gd08
Harstad **N** 28 Gb06
Harsum **D** 56 Fb28
Harsvika **N** 32 Fc12
Harta **H** 74 Ha35
Hartberg **A** 73 Gb34
Hårtiești **RO** 88 Jb36
Hartlepool **GB** 21 Db23
Hartola **FIN** 41 Hd15
Harwich **GB** 25 Dc27
Harzgerode **D** 56 Fb28
Haselünne **D** 55 Ed27
Haskovo **BG** 102 Jc41
Hasle **DK** 50 Ga24
Haslev **DK** 49 Fc24
Hasparren **F** 80 Cc38
Hassela **S** 38 Gc14
Hasselt **B** 63 Eb29
Haßfurt **D** 64 Fb30
Hässleholm **S** 49 Fd22
Hasslö **S** 50 Gb22
Hastings **GB** 25 Db28
Hästveda **S** 50 Ga22
Hasvik **N** 26 Gd03
Haţeg **RO** 75 Hd36
Hatherleigh **GB** 23 Cc28
Hatip **TR** 128 Ga15
Hatrik **N** 42 Ed17
Hattfjelldal **N** 33 Ga10
Hattingen **D** 55 Ec28
Hattula **FIN** 40 Hc15
Hattuselkonen **FIN** 35 Ja12
Hattuvaara **FIN** 41 Jb12
Hatunsaray **TR** 128 Ga15
Hatvan **H** 74 Ha34
Haugastøl **N** 36 Fa16
Hauge **N** 42 Ed17
Hauho **FIN** 40 Hc15
Haukeligrend **N** 42 Fa17
Haukelisæter **N** 42 Fa17
Haukipudas **FIN** 35 Hc10
Haukivuori **FIN** 41 Hd14
Hausach **D** 71 Ed33
Hautajärvi **FIN** 31 Hd08
Hautefort **F** 69 Da36
Hautmont **F** 62 Ea30
Hauzenberg **D** 65 Fd32
Havant **GB** 24 Da28
Havdhem **S** 51 Gd21
Havdrup **DK** 49 Fc23
Havelberg **D** 56 Fc27
Haverfordwest **GB** 23 Cc26
Haverhill **GB** 25 Dc27
Håverud **S** 43 Fd19

Havířov **CZ** 66 Gd31
Havlíčkův Brod **CZ** 65 Gb31
Havneby **DK** 48 Fa24
Havøysund **N** 26 Ha03
Havran **TR** 103 Ka43
Havrylivka **UA** 122 Fb15
Havsa **TR** 103 Jd41
Hawick **GB** 21 Da22
Hayange **F** 63 Eb31
Hayrabolu **TR** 103 Ka41
Haywards Heath **GB** 25 Db28
Hazebrouck **F** 62 Dd29
Heanor **GB** 25 Db25
Heberg **S** 49 Fd21
Heby **S** 44 Gb17
Hechingen **D** 71 Ed33
Hedalen **N** 37 Fb16
Heddal **N** 43 Fb18
Hédé **F** 61 Cd31
Hede **S** 38 Fd14
Hedemora **S** 44 Gb17
Hedenäset **S** 34 Hb09
Hedensted **DK** 49 Fb23
Hedesunda **S** 44 Gb17
Hedeviken **S** 38 Ga14
Heek **D** 55 Ed28
Heerenveen **NL** 55 Ec26
Heerhugowaard **NL** 55 Eb27
Heerlen **NL** 63 Ec29
Hegyfalu **H** 74 Gc34
Heide **D** 56 Fa25
Heidelberg **D** 63 Ed31
Heidenau **D** 65 Fd29
Heidenheim **D** 64 Fa32
Heidenreichstein **A** 65 Ga32
Heikendorf **D** 56 Fb25
Heikkylä **FIN** 35 Ja09
Heilbronn **D** 64 Fa32
Heiligenblut **A** 73 Fd35
Heiligenhafen **D** 56 Fc25
Heiligenstadt **D** 64 Fb29
Heimaey **IS** 14 Bc08
Heimdal **N** 37 Fc13
Heinävesi **FIN** 41 Ja13
Heinola **FIN** 41 Hd15
Heinsberg **D** 63 Ec29
Heituinlahti **FIN** 41 Ja15
Heksem **N** 37 Fc13
Hel **PL** 51 Gd24
Heldrungen **D** 64 Fb29
Helechal **E** 105 Bb43
Helensburgh **GB** 20 Cd21
Heljulja **RUS** 41 Jb14
Hella **IS** 14 Bc07
Hella **N** 36 Ed15
Helleland **N** 42 Ed19
Hellesvikan **N** 32 Fb12
Hellesylt **N** 36 Fa14
Hellevoetsluis **NL** 54 Ea28
Hellín **E** 107 Ca44
Hellissandur **IS** 14 Bb05
Hellnar **IS** 14 Bb05
Helmond **NL** 55 Eb28
Helmsdale **GB** 17 Db18
Helmsley **GB** 21 Db24

Helmstedt **D** 56 Fb28
Helnessund **N** 28 Ga07
Hel'pa **SK** 67 Ha32
Helshan **AL** 100 Hb41
Helsingborg **S** 49 Fd23
Helsinge **DK** 49 Fc23
Helsingfors **FIN** 46 Hc17
Helsingør **DK** 49 Fd23
Helsinki **FIN** 46 Hc17
Helston **GB** 23 Cb28
Heltermaa **EST** 46 Hb19
Hemau **D** 64 Fc32
Hemavan **S** 33 Ga10
Hemel Hempstead **GB** 25 Db27
Hemer **D** 63 Ed29
Hemling **S** 33 Gc12
Hemmingsmark **S** 34 Ha10
Hemmoor **D** 56 Fa26
Hemnes **N** 43 Fc18
Hemnesberget **N** 33 Ga09
Hemse **S** 51 Gd21
Hemsedal **N** 37 Fb16
Hemsö **S** 39 Gc14
Henån **S** 43 Fc20
Hendaye **E** 80 Cb38
Hengelo **NL** 55 Ec27
Heničes'k **UA** 126 Fa17
Hénin-Beaumont **F** 62 Dd29
Hennan **S** 38 Gb15
Hennebont **F** 60 Cc32
Hennef **D** 63 Ec29
Hennigsdorf **D** 57 Fd27
Henningsvær **N** 28 Ga07
Henrichemont **F** 69 Dc33
Heradsbygd **N** 37 Fc16
Herbignac **F** 60 Cc32
Herborn **D** 63 Ed30
Herbrechtingen **D** 64 Fa32
Herbstein **D** 64 Fa30
Herby **PL** 66 Gd30
Herceg-Novi **MNE** 100 Ha41
Hercegszántó **H** 74 Ha36
Herdla **N** 36 Ec16
Hereford **GB** 24 Cd26
Herefoss **N** 42 Fa19
Herentals **B** 63 Eb29
Herford **D** 56 Fa28
Héricourt **F** 71 Ec33
Heringsdorf **D** 57 Ga25
Herisau **CH** 72 Fa34
Hérisson **F** 69 Dc33
Herl'any **SK** 67 Hb32
Herleshausen **D** 64 Fb29
Hermagor **A** 73 Fd35
Hermanavicy **BY** 53 Jb23
Hermannsburg **D** 56 Fb27
Hermsdorf **D** 64 Fc29
Herne **D** 55 Ed28
Herne Bay **GB** 25 Dc28
Herning **DK** 48 Fa22
Herónia **GR** 111 Ja45
Herrera del Duque **E** 91 Bb42
Herrera de los Navarros **E** 80 Cc40

Herrera de Pisuerga **E** 79 Bd38
Herreruela **E** 91 Ba41
Herrestad **S** 43 Fc19
Herrljunga **S** 44 Fd20
Herrskog **S** 39 Gc13
Hersbruck **D** 64 Fc31
Herstal **B** 63 Eb29
Hertford **GB** 25 Db27
Hervás **E** 91 Bb40
Herzberg **D** 56 Fb28
Herzberg **D** 57 Fd28
Herzogenaurach **D** 64 Fb31
Herzogenburg **A** 73 Gb33
Hesdin **F** 62 Dc29
Hesel **D** 55 Ed26
Heskestad **N** 42 Ed19
Hessisch Lichtenau **D** 64 Fa29
Hestra **S** 44 Ga20
Hestra **S** 49 Fd21
Hetekylä **FIN** 35 Hc10
Hetényegyháza **H** 74 Ha35
Hettstedt **D** 56 Fc28
Heves **H** 75 Hb34
Héviz **H** 74 Gc35
Hevlin **CZ** 65 Gb32
Hexham **GB** 21 Db23
Heyrieux **F** 70 Ea36
Heysham **GB** 21 Da24
Hickstead **GB** 25 Db28
Hidasnémeti **H** 67 Hb32
Hieflau **A** 73 Ga34
Hietapera **FIN** 35 Ja11
High Wycombe **GB** 25 Db27
Higueruela **E** 93 Cb43
Hiisijärvi **FIN** 35 Hd11
Hijar **E** 93 Cc41
Hijtola **RUS** 41 Jb15
Hildburghausen **D** 64 Fb30
Hilden **D** 63 Ec29
Hildesheim **D** 56 Fb28
Hillared **S** 44 Fd20
Hillerød **DK** 49 Fd23
Hillesøy **N** 26 Gc05
Hillosensalmi **FIN** 41 Hd15
Hilpoltstein **D** 64 Fb32
Hiltula **FIN** 41 Ja14
Hilvarenbeek **NL** 55 Eb28
Hilversum **NL** 55 Eb27
Himanka **FIN** 34 Hb12
Himki **RUS** 117 Ed10
Hinckley **GB** 24 Da26
Hinojosa del Duque **E** 105 Bb43
Hios **GR** 113 Jd45
Hirschaid **D** 64 Fb31
Hirson **F** 62 Ea30
Hirtshals **DK** 43 Fb20
Hirvas **FIN** 30 Hb08
Hirvensalmi **FIN** 41 Hd15
Hisarja **BG** 102 Jb40
Hisingen **S** 43 Fc20
Hislavici **RUS** 121 Ec12
Hittarp **S** 49 Fd22
Hitzacker **D** 56 Fb26

Hjallerup **DK** 49 Fb21
Hjärnarp **S** 49 Fd22
Hjelmeland **N** 42 Ed18
Hjelset **N** 36 Fa13
Hjerkinn **N** 37 Fb14
Hjo **S** 44 Ga20
Hjørring **DK** 49 Fb21
Hjortkvarn **S** 44 Gb19
Hlevacha **UA** 121 Ec14
Hlinsko **CZ** 65 Gb31
Hlobyne **UA** 121 Ed15
Hlohovec **SK** 74 Gd33
Hluchiv **UA** 121 Ed13
Hlusk **BY** 121 Eb13
Hlybokae **BY** 53 Jb23
Hnivan' **UA** 121 Eb15
Hnjótur **IS** 14 Bb04
Hnúšt'a **SK** 67 Ha32
Hobro **DK** 49 Fb22
Höchstadt **D** 64 Fb31
Hódmező-Vásárhely **H** 75 Hb35
Hodnanes **N** 42 Ed17
Hodonín **CZ** 66 Gc32
Hoek van Holland **NL** 54 Ea27
Hof **D** 64 Fc30
Hof **N** 43 Fb18
Hofgeismar **D** 56 Fa28
Hofheim **D** 64 Fb30
Höfn **IS** 15 Cb08
Hofors **S** 44 Gb17
Hofsós **IS** 15 Ca05
Hofstad **N** 32 Fc12
Hofsvík **IS** 14 Bc06
Höganäs **S** 49 Fd22
Høgeset **N** 36 Fa16
Högland **S** 33 Gb11
Höglekardalen **S** 38 Ga13
Högsäter **S** 43 Fc19
Högsby **S** 50 Gb21
Högsjö **S** 44 Gb19
Hőgyész **H** 74 Gd35
Hohenau **A** 66 Gc32
Hohenems **A** 72 Fa34
Hohenwestedt **D** 56 Fb25
Hok **S** 50 Ga21
Hokksund **N** 43 Fb17
Hökmark **S** 34 Ha11
Hökön **S** 50 Ga22
Hol **N** 36 Fa16
Hola Prystan' **UA** 125 Ed17
Hólar **IS** 15 Ca05
Holasovice **CZ** 66 Gc31
Holbæk **DK** 49 Fb22
Holbæk **DK** 49 Fb20
Holbeach **GB** 25 Db26
Holešov **CZ** 66 Gc31
Holíč **SK** 66 Gc32
Höljes **S** 38 Fd16
Hollabrunn **A** 73 Gb33
Hollfeld **D** 64 Fb31
Hollókő **H** 74 Ha33
Hollola **FIN** 40 Hc15
Hollum **NL** 55 Ec26
Höllviken **S** 49 Fd23

Hollywood **IRL** 19 Cb24
Holm **N** 32 Fd10
Holm **RUS** 117 Eb10
Holm **S** 38 Gb14
Hólmavík **IS** 14 Bd05
Holmestrand **N** 43 Fb18
Holmsjö **S** 50 Gb22
Holmskij **RUS** 127 Fc17
Holmsund **S** 34 Gd12
Holmsveden **S** 38 Gb16
Holmudden **S** 45 Gd20
Holm-Žirkovskij **RUS** 117 Ec11
Hölö **S** 45 Gc19
Holovec'ke **UA** 67 Hd31
Holøydal **N** 37 Fc14
Holstebro **DK** 48 Fa22
Holsworthy **GB** 23 Cc27
Holwerd **NL** 55 Ec26
Holyhead **GB** 20 Cc24
Holywell **GB** 24 Cd25
Holywood **GB** 20 Cc22
Holzkirchen **D** 72 Fc33
Holzminden **D** 56 Fa28
Homberg (Efze) **D** 64 Fa29
Homberg (Ohm) **D** 64 Fa29
Homburg (Saar) **D** 63 Ec31
Homel' **BY** 121 Ec13
Hommelstø **N** 32 Fd10
Hommelvik **N** 37 Fc13
Homoroade **RO** 75 Hd33
Homorod **RO** 76 Jb35
Homps **F** 81 Db39
Homutovka **RUS** 121 Ed13
Hønefoss **N** 43 Fb17
Honfleur **F** 61 Db30
Høng **DK** 49 Fc23
Honiton **GB** 24 Cd28
Honkajoki **FIN** 40 Ha14
Honkilahti **FIN** 40 Ha16
Honningsvåg **N** 27 Hb03
Hönö **S** 43 Fc20
Hontianske Nemce **SK** 74 Ha33
Hontivka **UA** 77 Jd32
Hoogeveen **NL** 55 Ec27
Hoogezand-Sappemeer **NL** 55 Cc26
Hoogstraten **B** 55 Eb28
Höör **S** 49 Fd23
Hoorn **NL** 55 Eb27
Hopa **TR** 127 Ga19
Hopen **N** 37 Fb13
Hopfgarten **A** 72 Fc34
Hopseidet **N** 27 Hc03
Hóra **GR** 110 Hd47
Hóra **TR** 113 Ka46
Horasan **TR** 127 Ga19
Hóra Sfakíon **GR** 114 Jc49
Horb **D** 63 Ed32
Hörby **S** 49 Fd23
Horcajo de los Montes **E** 91 Bc42
Horcajo de Santiago **E** 92 Bd42
Horda **S** 50 Ga21

I

Ilok – Järva-Jaani

Ilok **HR** 86 Ha37
Ilomantsi **FIN** 41 Jb13
Ilükste **LV** 53 Ja22
Ilva Mare **RO** 76 Ja34
Iłża **PL** 67 Hb29
Imatra **FIN** 41 Ja15
Imavere **EST** 47 Hd18
Immenstadt **D** 72 Fa34
Immingham **GB** 25 Dc25
Imola **I** 84 Fb38
Imotski **HR** 86 Gc39
Imperia **I** 83 Ec39
Imphy **F** 70 Dd34
Imst **A** 72 Fb34
Inari **FIN** 27 Hc05
Inca **E** 95 Db43
Inchnadamph **GB** 17 Da18
Inciems **LV** 53 Hd21
Indal **S** 38 Gb14
Indija **SRB** 87 Hb37
Indre Arna **N** 36 Ed16
Indre Billefjord **N** 27 Hb03
Indura **BY** 59 Hd26
Inebolu **TR** 126 Fa19
İnece **TR** 103 Jd41
Ineu **RO** 75 Hc35
Infantado **P** 90 Ac41
Ingå **FIN** 46 Hc17
Ingelheim **D** 63 Ed30
Ingelstad **S** 50 Ga22
Ingolstadt **D** 64 Fb32
Inkoo **FIN** 46 Hc17
Innbygda **N** 37 Fd16
Inndyr **N** 28 Ga08
Innerleithen **GB** 21 Da21
Innfield **IRL** 19 Cb24
Innsbruck **A** 72 Fb34
Innset **N** 29 Gc06
Innset **N** 37 Fc14
Inói **GR** 110 Hd46
Inowłódz **PL** 58 Ha28
Inowrocław **PL** 58 Gd27
Insar **RUS** 119 Fc10
Insjön **S** 38 Ga16
Însurăţei **RO** 89 Jd36
İntepe **TR** 103 Jd43
Interlaken **CH** 71 Ec35
Întorsura Buzăului **RO** 88 Jc36
Inveraray **GB** 16 Cd20
Invergarry **GB** 17 Da19
Invergordon **GB** 17 Da19
Invermoriston **GB** 17 Da19
Inverness **GB** 17 Da19
Inverurie **GB** 17 Db19
Inza **RUS** 119 Fd10
Inžavino **RUS** 123 Fc12
Ioánina **GR** 101 Hc44
Ion Roată **RO** 89 Jd37
Íos **GR** 115 Jd47
Ipatovo **RUS** 127 Fd16
İpsala **TR** 103 Jd42
Ipswich **GB** 25 Dc27
Iráklia **GR** 101 Ja42
Iráklia **GR** 115 Jd47
Iráklio **GR** 115 Jd49

Irbene **LV** 46 Hb20
Irečekovo **BG** 103 Jd40
Irklijiv **UA** 121 Ed15
Irmath **RKS** 100 Hb42
Ironbridge **GB** 24 Da25
Iršava **UA** 75 Hd33
Irsina **I** 99 Gb43
Irsta **S** 44 Gb18
Irun **E** 80 Cb38
Iruñea **E** 80 Cb38
Irurita **E** 80 Cc38
Irurzun **E** 80 Cb38
Irvine **GB** 20 Cd21
Irvinestown **GB** 19 Cb22
Isaba **E** 80 Cc38
Isaccea **RO** 89 Ka36
Ísafjörður **IS** 14 Bc04
Isaku **EST** 47 Ja18
Isane **N** 36 Ed14
Iscar **E** 79 Bc39
Ischgl **A** 72 Fa35
Ischia **I** 98 Fd43
Iseo **I** 72 Fa36
Iserlohn **D** 63 Ed29
Isernia **I** 99 Ga42
Isfjorden **N** 36 Fa14
Isigny-sur-Mer **F** 61 Da30
Isili **I** 97 Ed44
Islaz **RO** 88 Jb38
İslik **TR** 128 Gb15
İsmailli **TR** 113 Ka44
İsmıl **TR** 128 Gb15
Isny **D** 72 Fa34
Isojoki **FIN** 40 Ha14
Isokylä **FIN** 31 Hc08
Isokyrö **FIN** 40 Ha13
Isola **F** 83 Eb38
Isola 2000 **F** 83 Eb38
Isola del Liri **I** 98 Fd42
Ísola di Capo Rizzuto **I** 109 Gc45
Isperih **BG** 89 Jd38
Ispica **I** 109 Ga48
İspir **TR** 127 Ga19
Issoire **F** 69 Dc36
Issoudun **F** 69 Dc34
Is-sur-Tille **F** 70 Ea33
İstanbul **TR** 103 Kb41
Istiéa **GR** 111 Ja45
Istok **RKS** 87 Hb40
Istra **RUS** 117 Ed10
Istres **F** 82 Dd39
Istria **RO** 89 Ka37
Itéa **GR** 111 Ja45
Itháki **GR** 110 Hc46
Ittiri **I** 97 Ec43
Itzehoe **D** 56 Fa25
Ivacëviçy **BY** 120 Ea13
Ivajlovgrad **BG** 103 Jd41
Ivalo **FIN** 27 Hc05
Ivanava **BY** 120 Ea14
Ivančice **CZ** 65 Gb32
Ivanec **HR** 73 Gb36
Ivane-Puste **UA** 76 Jb32
Ivăneşti **RO** 77 Jd34
Ivangorod **RUS** 47 Ja17

Ivangrad **MNE** 87 Hb40
Ivanić Grad **HR** 74 Gc36
Ivanivci **UA** 76 Jc32
Ivanivka **MD** 77 Kb33
Ivanivka **UA** 126 Fa16
Ivanka pri Dunaji **SK** 74 Gc33
Ivankiv **UA** 121 Ec14
Ivankovo **HR** 86 Gd37
Ivano-Frankivs'k **UA** 76 Ja32
Ivano-Frankivs'k **UA** 124 Ea16
Ivano-Frankove **UA** 67 Hd30
Ivanovka **RUS** 119 Ga09
Ivanovo **BG** 88 Jc38
Ivanovo **RUS** 118 Fa09
Ivanovskoe **RUS** 118 Fb08
Ivanskaja **BIH** 86 Gc37
Ivarrud **N** 33 Ga10
Iveland **N** 42 Fa19
Iveşti **RO** 77 Jd35
Ivjanec **BY** 120 Ea12
Ivje **BY** 120 Ea12
Ivrea **I** 71 Ec36
İvrindi **TR** 103 Ka43
Iyidere **TR** 127 Fd19
Izbica Kujawska **PL** 58 Gd27
Izbiceni **RO** 88 Jb38
Izbišča **BY** 53 Jb24
Izborsk **RUS** 47 Jb20
Izeda **P** 78 Bb39
Izernore **F** 70 Ea35
Izjum **UA** 122 Fb14
Izmajil **UA** 89 Ka36
İzmir **TR** 113 Ka45
Iznalloz **E** 106 Bc45
Izsák **H** 74 Ha35
Izvor **BG** 87 Hd40
Izvor **MK** 101 Hc42
Izvor **SRB** 87 Hc39
Izvoru Dulce **RO** 89 Jd36

J

Jaakonvaara **FIN** 41 Jb12
Jaala **FIN** 41 Hd15
Jablanac **HR** 85 Ga38
Jablanica **BG** 88 Jb39
Jablanica **BIH** 86 Gd39
Jablonec nad Nisou **CZ** 65 Ga30
Jablonica **SK** 66 Gc32
Jabłonka **PL** 67 Ha31
Jabłonowo Pomorskie **PL** 58 Gd26
Jabluniv **UA** 76 Ja32
Jablunkov **CZ** 66 Gd31
Jabugo **E** 105 Ad43
Jabukovac **SRB** 87 Hd38
Jabukovik **SRB** 87 Hd40
Jaca **E** 80 Cc39
Jädraås **S** 38 Gb16
Jadraque **E** 92 Ca40
Jaén **E** 106 Bc44

Jagare **BIH** 86 Gc38
Jagodina **SRB** 87 Hc38
Jahotyn **UA** 121 Ec14
Jajce **BIH** 86 Gc38
Jakabszállás **H** 74 Ha35
Jakalj **SRB** 87 Hb38
Jäkkvik **S** 33 Gb09
Jakobstad **FIN** 34 Ha12
Jakoruda **BG** 101 Ja41
Jakovlevo **RUS** 122 Fa13
Jalance **E** 93 Cb43
Jalasjärvi **FIN** 40 Hb14
Jalta **UA** 126 Fa18
Jambol **BG** 103 Jd40
Jämijärvi **FIN** 40 Hb15
Jäminkipohja **FIN** 40 Hc14
Jämjö **S** 50 Gb22
Jamkino **RUS** 47 Jb19
Jamnice **CZ** 65 Gb32
Jampil' **UA** 125 Eb16
Jämsä **FIN** 40 Hc14
Jämsänkoski **FIN** 40 Hc14
Janja **BIH** 86 Ha38
Janjina **HR** 86 Gd40
Jánoshalma **H** 74 Ha35
Jánosháza **H** 74 Gc34
Jánossomorja **H** 74 Gc34
Janów **PL** 59 Hc26
Janów **PL** 67 Hd30
Janów Lubelski **PL** 67 Hc29
Janowo **PL** 58 Ha26
Janów Podlaski **PL** 59 Hc27
Jånsmåssholmen **S** 33 Ga12
Jantarnyj **RUS** 52 Ha24
Jantra **BG** 88 Jc39
Janville **F** 62 Dc32
Janzé **F** 61 Cd32
Jäppilä **FIN** 41 Hd13
Jaraicejo **E** 91 Bb41
Jaraiz de la Vera **E** 91 Bb41
Jarandilla de la Vera **E** 91 Bb41
Jaransk **RUS** 119 Fc08
Järbo **S** 38 Gb16
Jarcevo **RUS** 117 Ec11
Jard-sur-Mer **F** 68 Cd34
Jaremča **UA** 76 Ja32
Jargeau **F** 69 Dc33
Jarhois **S** 30 Hb08
Järlåsa **S** 45 Gc17
Jarmen **D** 57 Fd25
Jarmolynci **UA** 121 Eb15
Järna **S** 44 Ga17
Järna **S** 45 Gc19
Jarnac **F** 68 Cd35
Jarny **F** 63 Eb31
Jarocin **PL** 58 Gc28
Jaroměř **CZ** 65 Gb30
Jaroměřice nad Rokytnou **CZ** 65 Gb32
Jaroslavl' **RUS** 118 Fa09
Jarosław **PL** 67 Hc30
Jarosławiec **PL** 57 Gb25
Järpen **S** 38 Fd13
Järsnäs **S** 44 Ga20
Järva-Jaani **EST** 47 Hd18

Kalač – Kascjukoviču

Kalač **RUS** 123 Fc13
Kalač- na-Donu **RUS** 123 Fd14
Kalajoki **FIN** 34 Hb11
Kalakoski **FIN** 40 Hb14
Kalamáki **GR** 101 Ja44
Kalamáta **GR** 110 Hd47
Kalambáka **GR** 101 Hd44
Kalambáki **GR** 102 Jb42
Kalana **EST** 46 Hb19
Kalančak **UA** 126 Fa17
Kalándra **GR** 101 Ja43
Kálanos **GR** 110 Hd46
Kalanti **FIN** 40 Ha16
Kälarne **S** 38 Gb13
Kalavárda **GR** 115 Kb47
Kalávrita **GR** 110 Hd46
Kalbe **D** 56 Fc27
Kaldfjord **N** 26 Gc05
Kaledibi **TR** 127 Ga19
Kalérgo **GR** 112 Jc46
Kálimnos **GR** 115 Ka47
Kalinina **RUS** 118 Fb08
Kaliningrad **RUS** 52 Ha24
Kalininsk **RUS** 123 Fd12
Kalinkaviču **BY** 121 Eb13
Kalinovik **BIH** 86 Gd39
Kalipéfki **GR** 101 Hd43
Kalisko **PL** 67 Ha29
Kalisz **PL** 58 Gd28
Kalisz Pomorski **PL** 57 Gb26
Kalithéa **GR** 101 Ja43
Kalitino **RUS** 47 Jb17
Kalivári **GR** 112 Jc46
Kalix **S** 34 Ha09
Kalixforsbron **S** 29 Gd07
Kaljazin **RUS** 117 Ed09
Kalkūne **LV** 53 Ja22
Kall **S** 38 Fd13
Kallaste **EST** 47 Ja18
Kållered **S** 43 Fc20
Kalli **EST** 46 Hc19
Kallinge **S** 50 Gb22
Kallithéa **GR** 101 Hd43
Kallmet **AL** 100 Hb41
Kalloní **GR** 111 Jb47
Kalmar **S** 50 Gb22
Kalmthout **B** 54 Ea28
Kalmykovskij **RUS** 123 Fd14
Kalna **SRB** 87 Hd39
Kalná nad Hronom **SK** 74 Gd33
Kalná Roztoka **SK** 67 Hc32
Kalnciems **LV** 52 Hc21
Kalocsa **H** 74 Ha35
Kalofer **BG** 102 Jb40
Kaló Horio **GR** 112 Jb45
Kalpáki **GR** 101 Hc44
Kalsdorf **A** 73 Gb35
Kaltanenai **LT** 53 Ja23
Kaltenkirchen **D** 56 Fb25
Kaltern **I** 72 Fb35
Kaluga **RUS** 117 Ed11
Kalugerovc **BG** 102 Jb40
Kalundborg **DK** 49 Fc23

Kaluš **UA** 124 Ea16
Kalvåg **N** 36 Ed15
Kalvarija **LT** 52 Hc24
Kälviä **FIN** 34 Hb12
Kalvitsa **FIN** 41 Hd14
Kalvola **FIN** 40 Hc15
Kalynivka **UA** 121 Eb15
Kamáres **GR** 110 Hd46
Kamáres **GR** 111 Jc47
Kamári **GR** 115 Jd48
Kamarino **RUS** 47 Jb19
Kambánis **GR** 101 Ja42
Kámbos **GR** 111 Ja47
Kamčija **BG** 89 Ka39
Kamen **D** 55 Ed28
Kamenec **RUS** 47 Jb18
Kamenica **SRB** 86 Ha38
Kamenice nad Lipou **CZ** 65 Ga32
Kamenka **RUS** 41 Jb16
Kamenka **RUS** 119 Fc11
Kamenka **RUS** 122 Fb13
Kamennogorsk **RUS** 41 Jb15
Kamenný Přívoz **CZ** 65 Ga31
Kameno **BG** 89 Jd39
Kamenskij **RUS** 123 Fd12
Kamensk- Šahtinskij **RUS** 123 Fc14
Kamenz **D** 65 Ga29
Kameškovo **RUS** 118 Fa09
Kamień **PL** 67 Ha29
Kamień Pomorski **PL** 57 Ga25
Kamin'-Kašyrs'kyj **UA** 120 Ea14
Kamišlıkuyu **TR** 128 Gc15
Kam'janec'-Podil's'kyj **UA** 76 Jc32
Kam'janec-Podil's'kyj **UA** 125 Eb16
Kamjaniec **BY** 59 Hd27
Kamjanjuki **BY** 59 Hd27
Kam'janka **UA** 77 Kb34
Kam'janka **UA** 121 Ed15
Kamjanka-Buz'ka **UA** 120 Ea15
Kam'jans'ke **UA** 77 Ka35
Kamlunge **S** 34 Ha09
Kamnik **SLO** 73 Ga36
Kampen **NL** 55 Ec27
Kamskoe Ust'e **RUS** 119 Fd09
Kamyšin **RUS** 123 Fd13
Kanaküla **EST** 47 Hd19
Kanaš **RUS** 119 Fd09
Kańczuga **PL** 67 Hc30
Kándanos **GR** 114 Jb49
Kandava **LV** 52 Hb21
Kandel **D** 63 Ed32
Kandersteg **CH** 71 Ec35
Kandila **GR** 111 Ja46
Kanepi **EST** 47 Ja19
Kanevskaja **RUS** 127 Fc16
Kanfanar **HR** 85 Fd37

Kangaslampi **FIN** 41 Ja14
Kangasniemi **FIN** 41 Hd14
Kangos **S** 30 Ha07
Kangosjärvi **FIN** 30 Ha07
Kaniv **UA** 121 Ec15
Kanjiža **SRB** 75 Hb36
Kankaanpää **FIN** 40 Hb15
Kankainen **FIN** 41 Hd14
Kanlıdivane **TR** 128 Gc17
Kannankoski **FIN** 40 Hc13
Kannus **FIN** 34 Hb12
Kantala **FIN** 41 Hd14
Kantemirovka **RUS** 122 Fb14
Kanturk **IRL** 22 Bd25
Kaolinovo **BG** 89 Jd38
Kaona **SRB** 87 Hb39
Kapandríti **GR** 112 Jb46
Kapellen **B** 54 Ea28
Kapfenberg **A** 73 Gb34
Kapitan Dimitrovo **BG** 89 Jd38
Kaplice **CZ** 65 Ga32
Kaposvár **H** 74 Gd35
Kappeln **D** 49 Fb24
Kappelshamn **S** 45 Gd20
Kappelskär **S** 45 Gd18
Kaprun **A** 72 Fc34
Kapsáli **GR** 111 Ja48
Kapsalos **CY** 128 Gc18
Kapuvár **H** 74 Gc34
Karabiga **TR** 103 Ka42
Karaburun **TR** 103 Kb41
Karaburun **TR** 113 Jd45
Karacabey **TR** 103 Kb42
Karacadağ **TR** 103 Ka40
Karaçaevsk **RUS** 127 Ga17
Karacaköy **TR** 103 Kb41
Karačev **RUS** 121 Ed12
Karacva **TR** 113 Kb46
Karadere **TR** 113 Ka44
Karakaya **TR** 128 Gb15
Karakólithos **GR** 111 Ja45
Karali **RUS** 41 Jb13
Karaman **TR** 128 Gb16
Karamyševo **RUS** 47 Jb19
Karapelit **BG** 89 Jd38
Karapinar **TR** 103 Jd41
Karapınar **TR** 128 Gc15
Kararkút **H** 74 Gd36
Karasjok **N** 27 Hb04
Karatepe **TR** 103 Jd43
Karats **S** 29 Gc08
Karaurgan **TR** 127 Ga19
Karavás **GR** 111 Ja48
Karavómilos **GR** 111 Ja45
Karavostasi **CY** 128 Gc19
Kårböle **S** 38 Ga15
Karcag **H** 75 Hb34
Kardákáta **GR** 110 Hc46
Kardamili **GR** 111 Ja47
Kardašova Řečice **CZ** 65 Ga32
Karditsa **GR** 101 Hd44
Kärdla **EST** 46 Hb18
Kardos **H** 75 Hb35

Kărdžali **BG** 102 Jc41
Kårehamn **S** 51 Gc21
Karesuando **S** 29 Ha06
Kärevete **EST** 47 Hd18
Kargıcak **TR** 128 Gc17
Kargowa **PL** 57 Gb28
Karhukangas **FIN** 35 Hc11
Karhula **FIN** 41 Hd16
Kariá **GR** 111 Ja46
Karianí **GR** 102 Jb42
Karigasniemi **FIN** 27 Hb05
Karijoki **FIN** 40 Ha14
Karine **TR** 113 Ka46
Karis **FIN** 46 Hc17
Káristos **GR** 112 Jc46
Karjaa **FIN** 46 Hc17
Karjala **FIN** 40 Ha16
Karjalohja **FIN** 46 Hc17
Karkkila **FIN** 40 Hc16
Karksi-Nuia **EST** 47 Hd19
Karleby **FIN** 34 Hb12
Karlholmsbruk **S** 45 Gc17
Karlino **PL** 57 Gb25
Karlivka **UA** 122 Fa14
Karlobag **HR** 85 Ga38
Karlovac **HR** 85 Gb37
Karlovássi **TR** 113 Ka46
Karlovice **CZ** 66 Gc31
Karlovka **RUS** 119 Ga11
Karlovo **BG** 102 Jb40
Karlovy Vary **CZ** 65 Fd30
Karlsborg **S** 44 Ga19
Karlshamn **S** 50 Ga22
Karlskoga **S** 44 Ga18
Karlskrona **S** 50 Gb22
Karlsruhe **D** 63 Ed32
Karlstad **S** 44 Fd18
Karlstadt **D** 64 Fa31
Kärnare **BG** 102 Jb40
Karnezéika **GR** 111 Ja47
Karnobat **BG** 89 Jd39
Kärpänkylä **FIN** 35 Ja09
Kárpathos **GR** 115 Kb48
Karpenissi **GR** 110 Hd45
Karpuzlu **TR** 103 Jd42
Kärsämäki **FIN** 35 Hc12
Kārsava **LV** 53 Jb21
Kärsta **S** 45 Gc18
Karstädt **D** 56 Fc26
Karstula **FIN** 40 Hc13
Karsun **RUS** 119 Fd10
Kartal **TR** 103 Kb41
Kartérés **GR** 111 Ja42
Karttula **FIN** 41 Hd13
Kartuzy **PL** 58 Gd25
Karungi **S** 34 Hb09
Karunki **FIN** 34 Hb09
Karup **DK** 48 Fa22
Kärväskylä **FIN** 35 Hc12
Karviná **PL** 66 Gd31
Karvio **FIN** 41 Ja13
Karvoskylä **FIN** 35 Hc12
Kašary **RUS** 123 Fc14
Kascjaneviču **BY** 53 Jb24
Kascjukoviču **BY** 121 Ec12

Kirchheimbolanden – Komsomol'skij

Komsomol'sk Zap. RUS 52 Ha24
Kömürlimaný TR 102 Jc43
Konak SRB 87 Hb37
Konakovo RUS 117 Ed10
Konakpınar TR 103 Kb43
Konare BG 89 Ka38
Konarzyny PL 58 Gc26
Kondolovo BG 103 Ka40
Kondrovo RUS 117 Ed11
Köngas FIN 30 Hb07
Konginkangas FIN 40 Hc13
Kongsberg N 43 Fb18
Kongsmoen N 32 Fd11
Kongsvinger N 43 Fd17
Konice CZ 66 Gc31
Königsbrück D 65 Fd29
Königsbrunn D 72 Fb33
Königsee D 64 Fb30
Königstein D 63 Ed30
Königstein D 65 Ga29
Königswiesen A 73 Ga33
Königswinter D 63 Ec29
Königs Wusterhausen D 57 Fd28
Konin PL 58 Gd28
Kónitsa GR 101 Hc44
Köniz CH 71 Ec34
Konjic BIH 86 Gd39
Könnern D 56 Fc28
Konnevesi FIN 41 Hd13
Konopki PL 58 Ha27
Konotop PL 57 Gb28
Konotop UA 121 Ed14
Końskie PL 67 Ha29
Konsmo N 42 Fa19
Konstancin-Jeziorna PL 59 Hb28
Konstantin BG 88 Jc39
Konstantinovsk RUS 123 Fc15
Konstantinovy Lázně CZ 65 Fd31
Konstantynów PL 59 Hc27
Konstantynów Łódzki PL 58 Ha28
Konstanz D 72 Fa34
Kontiolahti FIN 41 Jb13
Kontiomäki FIN 35 Hd11
Konttajärvi FIN 30 Hb08
Konya TR 128 Gb15
Konz D 63 Ec31
Koosa EST 47 Ja19
Koparnes N 36 Ed14
Kópasker IS 15 Cb05
Kópavogur IS 14 Bc06
Koper SLO 85 Fd37
Kopidlno CZ 65 Gb30
Köping S 44 Gb18
Koplik i Poshtëm AL 100 Ha41
Köpmanholmen S 39 Gc13
Kopor'e RUS 47 Jb17
Koppang N 37 Fc15
Kopparberg S 44 Ga17
Koppelo FIN 27 Hc05

Kopperå N 37 Fd13
Koppom S 43 Fd18
Koprivna BIH 86 Gd37
Koprivnica HR 74 Gc36
Kopřivnice CZ 66 Gd31
Koprivštica BG 102 Jb40
Köprübaşı TR 113 Kb44
Köprülü TR 128 Ga16
Kopyčynci UA 124 Ea16
Korablino RUS 118 Fb11
Korbach D 64 Fa29
Korbeniči RUS 117 Ec08
Korçe AL 101 Hc43
Korčevka RUS 119 Fd10
Korčula HR 86 Gc40
Korec' UA 121 Eb14
Korenevo RUS 121 Ed13
Korenica HR 85 Gb38
Korenovsk RUS 127 Fc16
Korfantów PL 66 Gc30
Korgen N 33 Ga09
Koria FIN 41 Hd16
Korifási GR 110 Hd47
Korinós GR 101 Hd43
Kórinthos GR 111 Ja46
Korita BIH 86 Gd40
Korita MNE 86 Ha40
Korjukivka UA 121 Ec13
Körmen TR 115 Kb47
Körmend H 74 Gc35
Korneuburg A 73 Gb33
Kórnik PL 58 Gc28
Kornofolia GR 103 Jd41
Kornwestheim D 64 Fa32
Koroča RUS 122 Fa13
Koromačno HR 85 Ga37
Koróni GR 110 Hd48
Koronowo PL 58 Gc26
Korop UA 121 Ed13
Körösladány H 75 Hb34
Korosten' UA 121 Eb14
Korostyšiv UA 121 Eb15
Koroviha RUS 118 Fb08
Korpilahti FIN 40 Hc14
Korpilombolo S 30 Ha08
Korpiselkja RUS 41 Jb13
Korpo FIN 46 Ha17
Korppoo FIN 46 Ha17
Korsberga S 50 Ga21
Korskrogen S 38 Gb15
Korsnäs FIN 40 Ha13
Korsør DK 49 Fc24
Korsun'-Ševčenkivs'kyj UA 121 Ec15
Korsvegen N 37 Fc13
Korsvoll N 37 Fb13
Korsze PL 59 Hb25
Korten BG 102 Jc40
Kortesjärvi FIN 40 Hb13
Kórthio GR 112 Jc46
Kortrijk B 62 Dd29
Korucu TR 103 Ka43
Korvala FIN 31 Hc08
Koryčany CZ 66 Gc32
Korycin PL 59 Hc26
Korzybie PL 58 Gc25

Kós GR 115 Kb47
Kosaja Gora RUS 118 Fa11
Kosanica MNE 86 Ha40
Košarovce SK 67 Hc32
Kościan PL 58 Gc28
Kościelec PL 58 Gd28
Kościerzyna PL 58 Gc25
Kose EST 47 Hd18
Košice SK 67 Hb32
Košická Belá SK 67 Hb32
Kosihovce SK 74 Ha33
Kosiv UA 76 Ja32
Kosjerić SRB 87 Hb38
Koška HR 86 Gd37
Koskenpää FIN 40 Hc14
Koski FIN 40 Hb16
Koskolovo RUS 47 Ja17
Koskue FIN 40 Hb14
Koskullskulle S 29 Gd08
Kosmás GR 111 Ja47
Kosmos GR 111 Ja47
Kosovska Mitrovica RKS 87 Hc40
Kosów Lacki PL 59 Hc27
Kosta S 50 Gb22
Kostanjevica na Krki SLO 73 Gb36
Kostelec nad Černými Lesy CZ 65 Ga31
Kostelec na Hané CZ 66 Gc31
Kostenec BG 102 Ja40
Kostinbrod BG 102 Ja40
Kostjantynivka UA 122 Fb15
Kostomłoty PL 66 Gc29
Kostomukša RUS 35 Ja10
Kostopil' UA 120 Ea14
Kostroma RUS 118 Fa08
Kostryna UA 67 Hc32
Kostrzyn PL 57 Ga27
Koszalin PL 57 Gb25
Kőszeg H 74 Gc34
Koszuty PL 58 Gc28
Kotel BG 89 Jd39
Kotel'nikovo RUS 123 Fd14
Kotel'skij RUS 47 Jb17
Kotel'va UA 121 Ed14
Köthen D 56 Fc28
Kotila FIN 35 Hd10
Kotka FIN 41 Hd16
Kotly RUS 47 Jb17
Kotor MNE 100 Ha41
Kotoriba HR 74 Gc35
Kotorsko BIH 86 Gd37
Kotor Varoš BIH 86 Gc38
Kotovo RUS 123 Fd12
Kotovsk RUS 122 Fb12
Kotovs'k UA 77 Ka32
Kotovs'k UA 125 Ec16
Kótronas GR 111 Ja48
Kötschach A 73 Fd35
Kötzting D 65 Fd32
Koufália GR 101 Hd42
Kouklia CY 128 Ga19
Kounávi GR 115 Jd49
Koúndouros GR 112 Jc46
Kounoupitsa GR 112 Jb46

Koutalás GR 111 Jc47
Kouvola FIN 41 Hd16
Kovačevci BG 102 Ja40
Kovačica SRB 87 Hb37
Kovdor RUS 31 Ja06
Kovel' UA 120 Ea14
Kovernino RUS 118 Fb08
Kovero FIN 41 Jb13
Kovrov RUS 118 Fa09
Kovylkino RUS 119 Fc10
Kowal PL 58 Gd27
Kowale Oleckie PL 59 Hc25
Kowary PL 65 Gb30
Kozac'ke UA 77 Kb34
Kozak TR 113 Ka44
Kozáni GR 101 Hd43
Kozel'sk RUS 117 Ed11
Koziegłowy PL 67 Ha30
Kozienice PL 59 Hb28
Kozjatyn UA 121 Eb15
Kozloduj BG 88 Ja38
Kozlovka RUS 119 Fd09
Kozłów PL 67 Ha30
Koźmin PL 58 Gc28
Koźminek PL 58 Gd28
Koźminiec PL 58 Gc28
Koz'modem'jansk RUS 119 Fc09
Kożuchów PL 57 Gb28
Kräckelbäcken S 38 Ga15
Kraddsele S 33 Gb10
Kragenæs DK 49 Fc24
Kragerø N 43 Fb19
Kragujevac SRB 87 Hc38
Krakhella N 36 Ec15
Kräklingbo S 51 Gd21
Krakovec' UA 67 Hd30
Kraków PL 67 Ha30
Krakow am See D 56 Fc26
Kraljevica HR 85 Ga37
Kraljevo SRB 87 Hb39
Kralovice CZ 65 Fd31
Král'ovský Chlmec SK 67 Hc32
Kralupy nad Vltavou CZ 65 Ga30
Kramators'k UA 122 Fb15
Kramfors S 39 Gc13
Kramjanica BY 59 Hd26
Kranídi GR 111 Ja47
Kranj SLO 73 Ga36
Kranjska Gora SLO 73 Fd35
Krapina HR 73 Gb36
Krapinske Toplice HR 73 Gb36
Krapkowice PL 66 Gd30
Kräslava LV 53 Ja22
Krasnae BY 53 Jb24
Krasnaja Gora RUS 121 Ec13
Krasnaja Jaruga RUS 122 Fa13
Krasnaja Poljana RUS 127 Fd17
Krásna nad Hornádom SK 67 Hb32

Kraśnik – Kutjevo

Kraśnik PL 67 Hc29
Krasni Okny UA 77 Ka33
Krasnoarmejsk RUS 118 Fa10
Krasnoarmejsk RUS 123 Fd12
Krasnoarmijs'k UA 122 Fb15
Krasnobród PL 67 Hd30
Krasnodar RUS 127 Fc17
Krasnodon UA 123 Fc15
Krasnoe RUS 52 Hb24
Krasnoe RUS 122 Fa12
Krasnogorodskoe RUS 53 Jb21
Krasnogvardejskoe RUS 127 Fd16
Krasnohorivka UA 122 Fb15
Krásnohorské Podhradie SK 67 Hb32
Krasnohrad UA 122 Fa14
Krasnohvardijs'ke UA 126 Fa17
Krasnojil's'k UA 76 Jb33
Krasnokuts'k UA 122 Fa14
Krasnomajskij RUS 117 Ec09
Krasnopavlivka UA 122 Fa15
Krasnoperekops'k UA 126 Fa17
Krasnopillja UA 122 Fa14
Krasnosielc PL 59 Hb26
Krasnoslobodsk RUS 119 Fc10
Krasnoslobodsk RUS 123 Fd14
Krasnotorovka RUS 52 Ha24
Krasnoznamensk RUS 52 Hc24
Krasnye Baki RUS 118 Fb08
Krasnyj Holm RUS 117 Ed09
Krasnyj Jar RUS 119 Ga10
Krasnyj Kut RUS 123 Ga12
Krasnyj Luč UA 122 Fb15
Krasnystaw PL 67 Hd29
Krastë RKS 100 Hb42
Krasti LV 53 Hd22
Krasyliv UA 121 Eb15
Kratovo MK 101 Hd41
Kražiai LT 52 Hc23
Krefeld D 55 Ec28
Krekenava LT 53 Hd23
Kremenčuk UA 121 Ed15
Kremenec' UA 120 Ea15
Kremidivka MD 77 Kb33
Kremmen D 57 Fd27
Kremna SRB 86 Ha39
Krems A 73 Fd35
Krems A 73 Gb33
Krepoljin SRB 87 Hc38
Krępsko PL 58 Gc26
Kreševo BIH 86 Gd39
Kresk-Królowa PL 59 Hc28
Kresna BG 101 Ja41
Krestcy RUS 117 Eb09

Kréstena GR 110 Hd47
Kretinga LT 52 Hb23
Kreuztal D 63 Ed29
Krëva BY 53 Ja24
Krëva BY 120 Ea12
Kriátsi GR 110 Hd45
Krieglach A 73 Gb34
Kriens CH 71 Ed34
Kríkelos GR 110 Hc45
Krini GR 101 Hd44
Krinides GR 102 Jb42
Kristdala S 50 Gb21
Kristiansand N 42 Fa20
Kristianstad S 50 Ga23
Kristiansund N 36 Fa13
Kristiinankaupunki FIN 40 Ha14
Kristineberg S 33 Gc11
Kristinehamn S 44 Ga18
Kristinestad FIN 40 Ha14
Kriva Feja SRB 87 Hd40
Kriva Palanka MK 101 Hd41
Krive Ozero MD 77 Kb32
Krivodol BG 88 Ja39
Krivolak MK 101 Hd41
Krivorož'e RUS 123 Fc14
Křižanov CZ 65 Gb31
Križevci HR 74 Gc36
Križpolje HR 85 Gb37
Krk HR 85 Ga37
Krnja MNE 86 Ha40
Krnov CZ 66 Gc31
Krobia PL 58 Gc28
Krøderen N 43 Fb17
Krokek S 44 Gb19
Krokilio GR 110 Hd45
Krokom S 38 Ga13
Króksfjarðarnes IS 14 Bc05
Krokvåg S 38 Gb13
Krolevec' UA 121 Ed13
Kroměříž CZ 66 Gc32
Kromy RUS 121 Ed12
Kronach D 64 Fb30
Kronauce LV 52 Hc22
Kronshagen D 56 Fb25
Kronštadt RUS 41 Jb16
Kröpelin D 56 Fc25
Kropotkin RUS 127 Fd16
Krośnice PL 66 Gc29
Krośniewice PL 58 Gd28
Krosno PL 67 Hc31
Krosno Odrzańskie PL 57 Ga28
Krotoszyn PL 58 Gc28
Krško SLO 73 Gb36
Krstac MNE 86 Ha40
Krujë RKS 100 Hb42
Krukenyči UA 67 Hd31
Krukowo PL 59 Hb26
Krumbach D 72 Fb33
Krupa na Vrbasu BIH 86 Gc38
Krupanj SRB 86 Ha38
Krušari BG 89 Ka38
Krusedol Selo SRB 87 Hb37
Kruševac SRB 87 Hc39

Kruševo MK 101 Hc42
Krušovene BG 88 Jb39
Krušovica BG 88 Ja39
Kruszów PL 58 Ha28
Kruszwica PL 58 Gd27
Kruszyna PL 67 Ha29
Kruszyniany PL 59 Hd26
Kruunupyy FIN 34 Hb12
Kryčav BY 121 Ec12
Krylovo RUS 59 Hb25
Krymsk RUS 127 Fc17
Krynica PL 67 Hb31
Krynica Morska PL 58 Gd25
Krynki PL 59 Hd26
Krynyčne UA 77 Ka35
Kryve Ozero UA 125 Ec16
Kryvičy BY 53 Jb24
Kryvsk BY 121 Ec13
Kryvyj Rih UA 125 Ed16
Kryžopil' UA 77 Jd32
Kryžopil' UA 125 Eb16
Krzęcin PL 57 Gb27
Krzeczów PL 66 Gd29
Krzepice PL 66 Gd29
Krzeszyce PL 57 Ga27
Krzywa PL 65 Gb29
Kšenskij RUS 122 Fa13
Księżpol PL 67 Hc30
Kstovo RUS 118 Fb09
Ktísmata GR 100 Hb44
Kubrat BG 88 Jc38
Kučevište MK 101 Hc41
Kučevo SRB 87 Hc38
Kuchary PL 58 Gd28
Kućište RKS 87 Hb40
Küçükbahçe TR 113 Jd45
Küçükkuyu TR 103 Jd43
Kuczbork-Osada PL 58 Ha26
Kudirkos Naumiestis LT 52 Hc24
Kudowa-Zdrój PL 65 Gb30
Kuflew PL 59 Hb28
Kufstein A 72 Fc34
Kugej RUS 127 Fc16
Kuha FIN 35 Hc09
Kühlungsborn D 56 Fc25
Kuhmalahti FIN 40 Hc15
Kuhmo FIN 35 Ja11
Kuhmoinen FIN 40 Hc15
Kuimetsa EST 47 Hd18
Kuivaniemi FIN 34 Hb09
Kuivastu EST 46 Hc19
Kukës AL 100 Hd41
Kuklin PL 58 Ha26
Kukmor RUS 119 Fd08
Kukulje BIH 86 Gc37
Kula BG 87 Hd38
Kula SRB 74 Ha36
Kuldīga LV 52 Hb21
Kulebaki RUS 118 Fb10
Kulen Vakuf BIH 85 Gb38
Kuleši RUS 122 Fa12
Kulevča UA 77 Kb35
Kuliai LT 52 Hb23
Kulmbach D 64 Fc30

Kuloharju FIN 35 Hd09
Kumanovo MK 101 Hc41
Kumielsk PL 59 Hb26
Kumkale TR 103 Jd43
Kumköy TR 103 Kb41
Kumla S 44 Ga18
Kumlinge FIN 46 Ha17
Kummavuopio S 26 Gd05
Kunda EST 47 Hd17
Kungälv S 43 Fc20
Kungsäter S 49 Fd21
Kungsbacka S 49 Fc21
Kungshamn S 43 Fc19
Kungsör S 44 Gb18
Kunhegyes H 75 Hb34
Kun'je UA 122 Fb14
Kunmadaras H 75 Hb34
Kunowo PL 58 Gc28
Kunszentmárton H 75 Hb35
Kunszentmiklós H 74 Ha35
Künzelsau D 64 Fa31
Kuolajärvi RUS 31 Hd07
Kuolio FIN 35 Hd09
Kuopio FIN 41 Hd13
Kuortane FIN 40 Hb13
Kuortti FIN 41 Hd15
Kupiškis LT 53 Hd22
Kup'jans'k UA 122 Fb14
Kup'jans'k- Vuzlovyj UA 122 Fb14
Küplü TR 103 Jd42
Kuprava LV 47 Ja20
Kupres BIH 86 Gc39
Kuražyn UA 76 Jc32
Kurdžinovo RUS 127 Fd17
Kuremäe EST 47 Ja18
Kuressaare EST 46 Hb19
Kurganinsk RUS 127 Fd17
Kurgolovo RUS 47 Ja17
Kurikka FIN 40 Ha14
Kuřim CZ 66 Gc32
Kürkçü TR 128 Gd15
Kurkijoki RUS 41 Jb15
Kurlovskij RUS 118 Fa10
Kurovskoe RUS 118 Fa10
Kurów PL 59 Hc28
Kurowo PL 57 Gb25
Kurravaara S 29 Gd07
Kuršėnai LT 52 Hc22
Kursk RUS 122 Fa13
Kursu FIN 31 Hd08
Kuršumlija SRB 87 Hc39
Kurtakko FIN 30 Hb07
Kuru FIN 40 IIb14
Kurylavčy BY 59 Hd26
Kuşadası TR 113 Ka45
Kušalino RUS 117 Ed09
Kuščevskaja RUS 127 Fc16
Kusel D 63 Ec31
Kusnin RKS 100 Hb41
Kuševanda RUS 35 Ja09
Kušnin RKS 100 Hb41
Kusnyšča UA 59 Hd28
Kustavi FIN 40 Ha16
Kutina HR 86 Gc37
Kutjevo HR 86 Gd37

164

Kutlu-Bukaš **RUS** 119 Ga08
Kutná Hora **CZ** 65 Gb31
Kutno **PL** 58 Ha28
Kuttainen **S** 29 Ha06
Kuttura **FIN** 31 Hc06
Kúty **SK** 66 Gc32
Kuusalu **EST** 47 Hd18
Kuusamo **FIN** 35 Hd09
Kuusankoski **FIN** 41 Hd15
Kuusijärvi **S** 30 Ha08
Kuusjärvi **FIN** 41 Ja13
Kuvaskangas **FIN** 40 Ha15
Kuvšinovo **RUS** 117 Ec10
Kuyucak **TR** 113 Kb45
Kužiai **LT** 52 Hc22
Kuzneck **RUS** 119 Fd10
Kuznečnoe **RUS** 41 Jb15
Kuznecovs'k **UA** 120 Ea14
Kuźnica **PL** 59 Hc26
Kvænangsbotn **N** 26 Gd04
Kværndrup **DK** 49 Fb24
Kvalsund **N** 26 Ha03
Kvam **N** 37 Fb15
Kvanndal **N** 36 Ed16
Kvänum **S** 44 Fd20
Kvédarna **LT** 52 Hb23
Kvelde **N** 43 Fb18
Kvelia **N** 33 Ga11
Kvibille **S** 49 Fd22
Kvikkjokk **S** 29 Gc08
Kvilda **CZ** 65 Fd32
Kvillsfors **S** 50 Gb21
Kvinlog **N** 42 Ed19
Kvissleby **S** 39 Gc14
Kviteseid **N** 42 Fa18
Kwidzyn **PL** 58 Gd26
Kybartai **LT** 52 Hc24
Kyjiv **UA** 121 Ec14
Kyjov **CZ** 66 Gc32
Kyleakin **GB** 16 Cd19
Kyle of Lochalsh **GB** 16 Cd19
Kylestrome **GB** 17 Da18
Kyprinos **GR** 103 Jd41
Kyritz **D** 56 Fc27
Kyrkhult **S** 50 Ga22
Kyrksæterøra **N** 37 Fb13
Kyrkslätt **FIN** 46 Hc17
Kyrksten **S** 44 Ga18
Kyrnyčky **UA** 125 Ec17
Kysucké Nové Mesto **SK** 66 Gd31
Kyyjärvi **FIN** 40 Hc13

L

Laa an der Thaya **A** 65 Gb32
Laage **D** 56 Fc25
Laakajärvi **FIN** 35 Hd12
La Alberca **E** 91 Bb40
La Alberca de Záncara **E** 92 Ca42
La Albuera **E** 90 Ad42
La Algaba **E** 105 Ba44
La Almarcha **E** 92 Ca42

La Almunia de Doña Godina **E** 80 Cb40
Laapinjärvi **FIN** 41 Hd16
Laatzen **D** 56 Fb27
La Bañeza **E** 79 Bc38
La Bassée **F** 62 Dd29
La Baule **F** 60 Cc32
Łabędzie **PL** 57 Gb26
Labenne **F** 80 Cc37
Labin **HR** 85 Ga37
Labinsk **RUS** 127 Fd17
la Bisbal d'Empordà **E** 81 Db40
Labljane **RKS** 87 Hc40
Labouheyre **F** 80 Cc37
La Bourboule **F** 69 Dc36
La Bóveda de Toro **E** 79 Bc39
Labrit **F** 80 Cd37
Labruguiere **F** 81 Db38
Lacanau **F** 68 Cd36
Lacanau-Océan **F** 68 Cc36
La Canourgue **F** 81 Dc37
La Capelle **F** 62 Ea30
La Carlota **E** 105 Bb44
La Carolina **E** 106 Bc44
Lacaune **F** 81 Db38
La Cavalerie **F** 81 Dc38
Lac de Tignes **F** 71 Eb36
La Chaise-Dieu **F** 70 Dd36
La Chapelle-en-Vercors **F** 82 Ea37
La Charité-sur-Loire **F** 70 Dd34
La Chartre-sur-le-Loir **F** 61 Db32
La Châtaigneraie **F** 68 Cd34
La Châtre **F** 69 Db34
La Chaux-de-Fonds **CH** 71 Ec34
Lachen **CH** 71 Ed34
La Chèze **F** 60 Cc31
Lachowo **PL** 59 Hb26
La Ciotat **F** 82 Ea39
La Clayette **F** 70 Dd35
La Clusaz **F** 71 Eb36
Lacock **GB** 24 Da27
Laconi **I** 97 Ed44
La Coruña **E** 78 Ba36
La Côte-Saint-André **F** 70 Ea36
La Couronne **F** 69 Da35
La Courtine-le-Trucq **F** 69 Dc35
Lacu Roşu **RO** 76 Jb34
Lad **H** 74 Gd36
Ląd **PL** 58 Gc28
Ladi **GR** 103 Jd41
Ladispoli **I** 98 Fc41
Laduškin **RUS** 52 Ha24
Ladvozero **RUS** 35 Ja10
Ladyžyn **UA** 125 Ec16
Lærdalsøyri **N** 36 Fa16
Láerma **GR** 115 Kb47
Lævvajokgiedde **N** 27 Hb04
La Fère **F** 62 Dd30

La Ferté-Bernard **F** 61 Db32
La Ferté-Gaucher **F** 62 Dd31
La-Ferté-Macé **F** 61 Da31
La Ferté-Milon **F** 62 Dd31
La Ferté-Saint-Aubin **F** 69 Dc33
La Ferté-Saint-Cyr **F** 69 Db33
La Ferté-sous-Jouarre **F** 62 Dd31
La Flèche **F** 61 Da32
la Font de la Figuera **E** 107 Cb44
La Fuente de San Esteban **E** 91 Bb40
La Gacilly **F** 60 Cc32
La Gallega **E** 79 Ca39
Lagan **S** 50 Ga21
Lage **D** 56 Fa28
La Gineta **E** 92 Ca43
Lagnieu **F** 70 Ea36
Lagny-sur-Marne **F** 62 Dd31
Lagoa **P** 104 Ab43
Lagolovo **RUS** 47 Jb17
Lagonegro **I** 99 Gb44
Lágos **GR** 102 Jc42
Lagos **P** 104 Ab43
Łagów **PL** 57 Gb28
Łagów **PL** 67 Hb29
la Granadella **E** 93 Cd41
La Grande-Motte **F** 82 Dd38
Laguardia **E** 80 Cb38
La Guardia **E** 92 Bd42
Laguarta **E** 80 Cd39
La Guerche-de-Bretagne **F** 61 Cd32
La Guerche-sur-l'Aubois **F** 69 Dc34
Laguiole **F** 81 Dc37
Laguna de Duero **E** 79 Bc39
Laguna de Negrillos **E** 79 Bc38
La Haye-du-Puits **F** 61 Cd30
Lahdepoh'ja **RUS** 41 Jb14
Lahinch **IRL** 18 Bd24
Lahišyn **BY** 120 Ea13
Lahnajärvi **S** 30 Ha08
Lahnstein **D** 63 Ed30
Lahojsk **BY** 53 Jb24
Laholm **S** 49 Fd22
Lahr **D** 71 Ed33
Lahti **FIN** 41 Hd15
Laide **GB** 16 Cd18
L'Aigle **F** 61 Db31
Laignes **F** 70 Ea33
Laigueglia **I** 83 Ec38
L'Aiguillon-sur-Mer **F** 68 Cd34
Laihia **FIN** 40 Ha13
Laiküla **EST** 46 Hc19
Laimoluokta **S** 29 Gd06
Lainio **S** 30 Ha07
Lairg **GB** 17 Da18
Laissac **F** 81 Dc37
Laisvall **S** 33 Gb09

Laitila **FIN** 40 Ha16
Lajkovac **SRB** 87 Hb38
la Jonquera **E** 81 Db40
Lakaträsk **S** 34 Gd09
Lakfors **N** 32 Fd10
Läki **BG** 102 Jb41
Lakinsk **RUS** 118 Fa10
Lakki **GR** 113 Ka46
Lákkoma **GR** 102 Jc42
Lakselv **N** 27 Hb04
Laktaši **BIH** 86 Gc37
Lalapaşa **TR** 103 Jd41
Lálas **GR** 110 Hd46
l'Alcora **E** 93 Cc42
l'Alcúdia **E** 93 Cc43
Lalín **E** 78 Ba37
Lalinde **F** 69 Da36
La Línea de la Concepción **E** 105 Ba46
Laloşu **RO** 88 Ja37
La Loupe **F** 61 Db32
La Louvière **B** 62 Ea29
L'Alpe-d'Huez **F** 83 Eb37
La Machine **F** 70 Dd34
la Maddalena **I** 96 Ed42
Lamarche **F** 71 Eb33
Lamastre **F** 82 Dd37
Lambach **A** 73 Fd33
Lamballe **F** 60 Cc31
Lambesc **F** 82 Ea38
Lámbia **GR** 110 Hd46
Lamego **P** 78 Ad39
l'Ametlla de Mar **E** 93 Cd41
Lamézia Terme-Nicastro **I** 109 Gc45
Lamía **GR** 111 Ja45
Lammhult **S** 50 Ga21
Lammi **FIN** 40 Hc15
La Mothe-Achard **F** 68 Cd33
La Motte **F** 83 Eb38
Lamotte-Beuvron **F** 69 Dc33
Lampeland **N** 43 Fb17
Lampeter **GB** 23 Cc26
La Mure **F** 82 Ea37
Lana **I** 72 Fb35
Lanaja **E** 80 Cc40
Lanark **GB** 21 Da21
La Nava de Ricomalillo **E** 91 Bc41
La Nava de Santiago **E** 91 Ba42
Lancaster **GB** 21 Da24
Lanciano **I** 99 Ga41
Łańcut **PL** 67 Hc30
Landau **D** 63 Ed31
Landau **D** 64 Fc32
Landeck **A** 72 Fb34
Landerneau **F** 60 Cb31
Landeryd **S** 49 Fd21
Landete **E** 93 Cb42
Landivisiau **F** 60 Cb30
Landön **S** 38 Ga13
Landrecies **F** 62 Ea30
Landsberg **D** 72 Fb33
Landsbro **S** 50 Ga21
Landscheid **D** 63 Ec30

Landshut **D** 72 Fc33
Landskrona **S** 49 Fd23
Landvetter **S** 43 Fd20
Langå **DK** 49 Fb22
Långå **S** 38 Fd14
Langadás **GR** 101 Ja42
Langa de Duero **E** 79 Ca39
Långås **S** 49 Fd21
Langeac **F** 69 Dc36
Langeais **F** 69 Da33
Langedijk **NL** 55 Eb26
Längelmäki **FIN** 40 Hc15
Langen **D** 63 Ed30
Langenau **D** 64 Fa32
Langenhagen **D** 56 Fa27
Langenlois **A** 73 Gb33
Langenzenn **D** 64 Fb31
Langesund **N** 43 Fb19
Langevåg **N** 36 Ed14
Langevåg **N** 42 Ec17
Langfjordbotn **N** 26 Gd04
Langholm **GB** 21 Da22
Langnau **CH** 71 Ec34
Langogne **F** 82 Dd37
Langon **F** 68 Cd36
Langres **F** 70 Ea33
Långsele **S** 38 Gb13
Långshyttan **S** 44 Gb17
Långsjöby **S** 33 Gb11
Långträsk **S** 34 Gd10
Lanna **S** 44 Ga18
Länna **S** 45 Gc17
Lannavaara **S** 29 Ha06
Lannemezan **F** 80 Cd38
Lannion **F** 60 Cc30
Länsi-Aure **FIN** 40 Hb14
Lansjärv **S** 30 Ha08
Lanškroun **CZ** 66 Gc31
Lanslebourg-Mont-Cenis **F** 83 Eb37
Lanusei **I** 97 Ed44
Lány **CZ** 65 Ga30
Łany **PL** 66 Gd30
Lanzo Torinese **I** 83 Ec37
Laon **F** 62 Dd30
La Paca **E** 107 Ca45
La Pacaudière **F** 70 Dd35
Lapalisse **F** 70 Dd35
La Palma del Condado **E** 105 Ad44
Lapinlahti **FIN** 35 Hd12
La Plagne **F** 71 Eb36
La Pobla de Segur **E** 81 Da40
La Pola de Gordón **E** 79 Bc37
La Portera **E** 93 Cb43
Lapoş **RO** 88 Jc36
Lapovo **SRB** 87 Hc38
Lappajärvi **FIN** 40 Hb13
Läppe **S** 44 Gb18
Lappeenranta **FIN** 41 Ja15
Lappersdorf **D** 64 Fc32
Lappfjärd **FIN** 40 Ha14
Lappi **FIN** 40 Ha16
Lappohja **FIN** 46 Hb17

Lappoluobbal **N** 26 Ha05
Lappträsk **FIN** 41 Hd16
Lappträsk **S** 34 Hb09
Lappvattnet **S** 34 Gd11
Lappvik **FIN** 46 Hb17
Lapseki **TR** 103 Jd42
Laptevo **RUS** 53 Jb21
Lapua **FIN** 40 Hb13
La Puebla de Cazalla **E** 105 Ba44
La Puebla del Río **E** 105 Ba44
La Puebla de Montalbán **E** 91 Bc41
La Puebla de Valverde **E** 93 Cb42
Lăpuşna **MD** 77 Jd34
Lăpuşna **RO** 76 Jb34
Lapväärtti **FIN** 40 Ha14
Łapy **PL** 59 Hc26
L'Aquila **I** 98 Fd41
Laracha **E** 78 Ba36
Lara de los Infantes **E** 79 Ca39
Laragh **IRL** 19 Cb24
Laragne-Montéglin **F** 82 Ea38
L'Arbresle **F** 70 Ea36
Lärbro **S** 45 Gd20
Larderello **I** 84 Fb40
Laredo **E** 79 Ca37
La Réole **F** 68 Cd36
Largentière **F** 82 Dd37
L'Argentière-la-Bessée **F** 83 Eb37
Largs **GB** 20 Cd21
Lárimna **GR** 111 Ja45
Larino **I** 99 Ga42
Lárissa **GR** 101 Hd44
Larkollen **N** 43 Fc18
Larmor-Plage **F** 60 Cb32
Larnaka **CY** 128 Gc19
Larne **GB** 20 Cc22
La Robla **E** 79 Bc37
La Roca de la Sierra **E** 91 Ba42
La Rochebeaucourt-et-Argentine **F** 69 Da35
La-Roche-Bernard **F** 60 Cc32
La Roche-Chalais **F** 69 Da36
La Roche-en-Ardenne **B** 63 Eb30
La Rochefoucauld **F** 69 Da35
La Rochelle **F** 68 Cd34
La Roche-Posay **F** 69 Db34
La Roche-sur-Foron **F** 71 Eb35
La Roche-sur-Yon **F** 68 Cd33
La Roda **E** 92 Ca43
La Roda de Andalucía **E** 105 Bb45
Larón **E** 78 Bb37
Laroquebrou **F** 69 Db36

Larseng **N** 26 Gc05
Laruns **F** 80 Cd38
Larvik **N** 43 Fb18
Laržanka **UA** 89 Ka36
La Salvetat-sur-Agout **F** 81 Db38
Las Cabezas de San Juan **E** 105 Ba44
la Sénia **E** 93 Cd41
La Seu d'Urgell **E** 81 Da40
La Seyne-sur-Mer **F** 82 Ea39
Łasin **PL** 58 Gd26
Łask **PL** 58 Gd28
Łaskarzew **PL** 59 Hb28
Laskowice **PL** 58 Gd27
Las Navas de la Concepción **E** 105 Ba43
Las Negras **E** 106 Bd46
Las Nieves **E** 105 Ba44
La Solana **E** 92 Bd43
La Souterraine **F** 69 Db35
Lasovo **SRB** 87 Hd39
Las Pedroñeras **E** 92 Ca42
La Spezia **I** 84 Fa38
Låstad **S** 44 Ga19
Lastovo **HR** 86 Gc40
La Suze-sur-Sarthe **F** 61 Da32
Las Ventas con Peña Aguilera **E** 91 Bc42
Las Viñas **E** 106 Bd45
Laterza **I** 99 Gc43
Lathen **D** 55 Ed27
Latheron **GB** 17 Db18
Latina **I** 98 Fc42
Latisana **I** 73 Fd36
Látky **SK** 67 Ha32
La Toba **E** 92 Ca42
La Tour du-Pin **F** 70 Ea36
La Tranche-sur-Mer **F** 68 Cd34
La Tremblade **F** 68 Cd35
La Trimouille **F** 69 Db34
La Trinité-Porhoët **F** 60 Cc31
Latronico **I** 99 Gb44
Lauchhammer **D** 65 Fd29
Lauda-Königshofen **D** 64 Fa31
Lauder **GB** 21 Da21
Laudio **E** 79 Ca38
Ļaudona **LV** 53 Ja21
Lauenburg **D** 56 Fb26
Lauf **D** 64 Fb31
Laufen **D** 73 Fd33
Lauffen (Neckar) **D** 64 Fa32
Laugar **IS** 15 Cb06
Laugarbakki **IS** 14 Bd05
Laugarvatn **IS** 14 Bc07
Laujar de Andarax **E** 106 Bd45
Laukaa **FIN** 40 Hc14
Lauker **S** 34 Gd10
Laukkala **FIN** 35 Hd12
Laukuva **LT** 52 Hb23
Laukvik **N** 26 Gc05

Laukvika **N** 28 Ga07
Launceston **GB** 23 Cc28
La Unión **E** 107 Cb45
Laupheim **D** 72 Fa33
Laurencekirk **GB** 17 Db20
Lauria **I** 99 Gb44
Lausanne **CH** 71 Eb35
Lautaporras **FIN** 40 Hc16
Lauterbach (Hessen) **D** 64 Fa30
Lauterecken **D** 63 Ed31
Lauwersoog **NL** 55 Ec26
Lauzerte **F** 81 Da37
Lavadáki **GR** 110 Hd47
Laval **F** 61 Da32
la Vall d'Uixó **E** 93 Cc42
Lavara **GR** 103 Jd41
Lavardac **F** 80 Cd37
Lavaur **F** 81 Db38
Lávdas **GR** 101 Hc44
Lavelanet **F** 81 Db39
Lavello **I** 99 Gb42
Låveng **N** 32 Fd09
Laveno **I** 71 Ed36
Lavia **FIN** 40 Hb15
La Vieille-Lyre **F** 61 Db31
Lavik **N** 36 Ed15
La Vila Joiosa (Villajoyosa) **E** 94 Cc43
La Voulte-sur-Rhône **F** 82 Ea37
Lavre **P** 90 Ac41
Lavrio **GR** 112 Jb46
Lavrovo **RUS** 117 Ed08
Lavry **RUS** 47 Ja20
Laxå **S** 44 Ga19
Laxbäcken **S** 33 Gb11
Laxford Bridge **GB** 17 Da18
Laž **RUS** 119 Fd08
Lazarevac **SRB** 87 Hb38
Lazarevskoe **RUS** 127 Fc17
Lazaropore **MK** 101 Hc42
Lazdijai **LT** 59 Hc25
Lazdijai **LT** 59 Hc25
Lazuri de Beiuş **RO** 75 Hd35
Łeba **PL** 51 Gc24
Lebach **D** 63 Ec31
Lebane **SRB** 87 Hc40
Le Beausset **F** 82 Ea39
Lebedjan **RUS** 122 Fa12
Lebedyn **UA** 121 Ed14
Le Blanc **F** 69 Db34
Lębork **PL** 58 Gc25
Le Bourg-d'Oisans **F** 83 Eb37
Lebrija **E** 105 Ba44
Le Buisson-de-Cadouin **F** 69 Da36
Le Cateau-Cambrésis **F** 62 Dd30
Le Catelet **F** 62 Dd30
Le Caylar **F** 81 Dc38
Lecce **I** 100 Gd43
Lecco **I** 72 Fa36
Lécera **E** 93 Cc41

Lech **A** 72 Fa34
L'Echalp **F** 83 Eb37
Le Château-d'Oléron **F** 68 Cd34
Le Châtelet **F** 69 Dc34
Le Chesne **F** 62 Ea31
Le Cheylard **F** 82 Dd37
Lechinţa **RO** 76 Ja34
Leči **LV** 52 Hb21
Lecina **E** 80 Cd39
Leciñena **E** 80 Cc40
Leck **D** 48 Fa24
Le Conquet **F** 60 Cb31
Le Creusot **F** 70 Ea34
Le Croisic **F** 60 Cc32
Le Crotoy **F** 62 Dc29
Lectoure **F** 81 Da37
Łęczna **PL** 67 Hc29
Łęczyca **PL** 57 Ga26
Łęczyca **PL** 58 Gd28
Ledesma **E** 78 Bb39
Ledmore **GB** 17 Da18
Le Donjon **F** 70 Dd35
Le Dorat **F** 69 Db34
Lędyczek **PL** 58 Gc26
Leeds **GB** 21 Db24
Leek **GB** 24 Da25
Leek **NL** 55 Ec26
Leenane **IRL** 18 Bd23
Leer **D** 55 Ed26
Leerdam **NL** 55 Eb28
Leesi **EST** 47 Hd17
Leeuwarden **NL** 55 Ec26
Le Faou **F** 60 Cb31
Le Faouët **F** 60 Cb31
Lefkada **FIN** 110 Hc45
Lefkími **GR** 100 Hb44
Lefkógia **GR** 114 Jc49
Lefkónas **GR** 101 Ja42
Lefkoniko **CY** 128 Gc19
Lefkosia **CY** 128 Gb19
Leganés **E** 92 Bd41
Legden **D** 55 Ed28
Legé **F** 68 Cd33
Legionowo **PL** 59 Hb27
Legkovo **RUS** 117 Ed09
Legnago **I** 84 Fb37
Legnano **I** 71 Ed36
Legnica **PL** 65 Gb29
Legnickie Pole **PL** 65 Gb29
Legrad **HR** 74 Gc36
Le Grand-Lucé **F** 61 Db32
Le Grand-Quevilly **F** 61 Db30
Legutiano **E** 80 Cb38
Le Havre **F** 61 Db30
Lehliu-Gară **RO** 89 Jd37
Lehnin **D** 57 Fd28
Lehre **D** 56 Fb27
Lehrte **D** 56 Fb27
Lehtimäki **FIN** 40 Hb13
Leibnitz **A** 73 Gb35
Leicester **GB** 25 Db26
Leichlingen **D** 63 Ec29
Leiden **NL** 55 Eb27
Leie **EST** 47 Hd19

Leikanger **N** 36 Ed14
Leikanger **N** 36 Fa15
Leinefelde **D** 64 Fb29
Leipalingis **LT** 59 Hd25
Leipalingis **LT** 59 Hd25
Leipojärvi **S** 29 Gd08
Leipzig **D** 64 Fc29
Leira **N** 37 Fb16
Leira **N** 37 Fb13
Leirbotn **N** 26 Ha04
Leiria **P** 90 Ac40
Leirmoen **N** 28 Ga08
Leirpollskogen **N** 27 Hc03
Leirvåg **N** 36 Ec16
Leirvik **N** 26 Gd04
Leirvik **N** 42 Ed17
Leirvika **N** 33 Ga09
Leisi **EST** 46 Hb19
Leivonmäki **FIN** 41 Hd14
Leiza **E** 80 Cb38
Lejkowo **PL** 57 Gb25
Lekeitio **E** 80 Cb37
Lekenik **HR** 85 Gb37
Leknes **N** 28 Ga07
Leknes **N** 36 Fa14
Łęknica **PL** 65 Ga29
Leksand **S** 38 Ga16
Leksvik **N** 32 Fc12
Le Lavandou **F** 83 Eb39
Leleasca **RO** 88 Jb37
Le Lion-d'Angers **F** 61 Da32
Lelis **PL** 59 Hb26
Le Locle **CH** 71 Eb34
Le Loroux-Bottereau **F** 68 Cd33
Le Lude **F** 61 Da32
Lelystad **NL** 55 Eb27
Le Malzieu-Ville **F** 81 Dc37
Le Mans **F** 61 Da32
Lembeye **F** 80 Cd38
Le Mêle-sur-Sarthe **F** 61 Db31
Le Merlerault **F** 61 Db31
Lemesos **CY** 128 Gb19
Lemförde **D** 55 Ed27
Lemgo **D** 56 Fa28
Lemland **FIN** 45 Gd17
Lemmenjoki **FIN** 27 Hb05
Lemmer **NL** 55 Ec26
Le Mont-Dore **F** 69 Dc36
Lempäälä **FIN** 40 Hb15
Le Muy **F** 83 Eb39
Lemvig **DK** 48 Fa22
Lena **N** 37 Fc16
Léndas **GR** 115 Jd50
Lendava **SLO** 74 Gc35
Le Neubourg **F** 61 Db31
Lengerich **D** 55 Ed27
Lenggries **D** 72 Fc34
Lengyeltóti **H** 74 Gd35
Lenhovda **S** 50 Gb21
Lenina **BY** 121 Ec13
Lenine **UA** 126 Fb17
Leninogorsk **RUS** 119 Ga09
Leninsk **RUS** 123 Ga13

Leninskij **RUS** 118 Fa11
Lenkivci **UA** 121 Eb15
Lennestadt **D** 63 Ed29
Lens **F** 62 Dd29
Lent'evo **RUS** 117 Ed08
Lenti **H** 74 Gc35
Lentiira **FIN** 35 Ja11
Lentini **I** 109 Ga47
Lentvaris **LT** 53 Hd24
Lenzen **D** 56 Fc26
Leoben **A** 73 Ga34
Leominster **GB** 24 Cd26
León **E** 79 Bc38
Leonding **A** 73 Ga33
Leonessa **I** 84 Fc40
Leonforte **I** 109 Ga47
Leonídio **GR** 111 Ja47
Leopoldsburg **B** 63 Eb29
Leorda **RO** 76 Jc33
Leova **MD** 77 Jd34
Le Palais **F** 60 Cc32
Lepassaare **EST** 47 Ja19
Lepe **E** 105 Ad44
Lepel' **BY** 121 Eb12
Lepoglava **HR** 73 Gb36
Le Pont-de-Beauvoisin **F** 70 Ea36
Le Porge **F** 68 Cd36
Le Portel **F** 62 Dc29
Leppävesi **FIN** 40 Hc14
Leppävirta **FIN** 41 Hd13
Lepşa **RO** 76 Jc35
Le Puy-en-Velay **F** 70 Dd36
Le Quesnoy **F** 62 Ea30
Lera **MK** 101 Hc42
Lerbäck **S** 44 Ga19
Lercara Friddi **I** 108 Fd47
Lerici **I** 84 Fa38
Lerín **E** 80 Cb39
Lerma **E** 79 Bd39
Lermontov **RUS** 119 Fc11
Le Rozier-Peyreleau **F** 81 Dc37
Lerum **S** 43 Fd20
Lervik **N** 43 Fc18
Leş **E** 81 Da39
Leş **RO** 75 Hc34
Les Aix-d'Angillon **F** 69 Dc33
Lešak **RKS** 87 Hb39
Les Andelys **F** 62 Dc31
Lešani **MK** 101 Hc42
Les Arcs **F** 71 Eb36
Le Sauze **F** 83 Eb38
les Borges Blanques **E** 80 Cd40
l'Escala **E** 81 Dc40
L'Escarène **F** 83 Ec39
Lescun **F** 80 Cc38
Les Deux-Alpes **F** 83 Eb37
Les Echelles **F** 70 Ea36
Les Essarts **F** 68 Cd33
Les Eyzies-de-Tayac **F** 69 Da36
Les Herbiers **F** 68 Cd33
Lesjöfors **S** 44 Ga17

Lesko **PL** 67 Hc31
Leskovac **SRB** 87 Hd40
Leskovik **AL** 101 Hc43
Lesneven **F** 60 Cb30
Lesnoe **RUS** 52 Ha24
Lesnoe **RUS** 117 Ec09
Lesnoj **RUS** 52 Ha24
Lesogorskij **RUS** 41 Ja15
Lesparre-Médoc **F** 68 Cd35
L'Esperou **F** 81 Dc38
Lespezi **RO** 76 Jc33
Les Ponts-de-Cé **F** 69 Da33
Les Riceys **F** 70 Ea33
Les Sables-d'Olonne **F** 68 Cc34
Lessay **F** 61 Cd30
Lessebo **S** 50 Gb22
Lessíni **GR** 110 Hc46
Lestijärvi **FIN** 35 Hc12
Les Ulis **F** 62 Dc31
Leszno **PL** 58 Gc28
Létavértes **H** 75 Hc34
Letca **RO** 75 Hd34
Letchworth Garden City **GB** 25 Db27
Letea **RO** 89 Kb36
Le Teil **F** 82 Dd37
Letenye **H** 74 Gc35
Le Thillot **F** 71 Ec33
Letku **FIN** 40 Hb16
Le Touquet-Paris-Plage **F** 62 Dc29
Le Tréport **F** 62 Dc30
Letterfrack **IRL** 18 Bd23
Letterkenny **IRL** 19 Cb21
Letyčiv **UA** 121 Eb15
Leucate-Plage **F** 81 Db39
Leukerbad **CH** 71 Ec35
Leutkirch **D** 72 Fa33
Leutkirch **D** 72 Fa33
Leuven **B** 63 Eb29
Levang **N** 43 Fb19
Levanger **N** 32 Fc12
Levanto **I** 84 Fa38
Leven **GB** 21 Dc24
Le Verdon-sur-Mer **F** 68 Cd35
Leverkusen **D** 63 Ec29
Levet **F** 69 Dc34
Levice **SK** 74 Gd33
Levico Terme **I** 72 Fb36
Levídi **GR** 111 Ja46
Levie **F** 96 Ed41
Levier **F** 71 Eb34
Le Vigan **F** 81 Dc38
Levoča **SK** 67 Hb32
Levroux **F** 69 Db34
Levski **BG** 88 Jb39
Lewes **GB** 25 Db28
Leżajsk **PL** 67 Hc30
Lezay **F** 69 Da34
Lezhë **AL** 100 Hb41
Lézignan-Corbières **F** 81 Db39
Lëzna **BY** 117 Eb11

Leźno – Llanrwst

Leźno **PL** 58 Gd25
Lezoux **F** 70 Dd35
L'gov **RUS** 121 Ed13
L'Hospitalet **E** 95 Da41
L'Hospitalet **F** 81 Da39
Lianokládi **GR** 110 Hd45
Liatorp **S** 50 Ga22
Liberec **CZ** 65 Ga30
Libiąż **PL** 67 Ha30
Libina **CZ** 66 Gc31
Libohovë **AL** 100 Hb44
Libourne **F** 68 Cd36
Libramont-Chevigny **B** 63
  Eb30
Licata **I** 108 Fd48
Lich **D** 64 Fa30
Lichtenau **D** 56 Fa28
Lichtenfels **D** 64 Fb30
Lichtenvoorde **NL** 55 Ec28
Lički Osik **HR** 85 Gb38
Ličko Lešće **HR** 85 Gb38
Lida **BY** 120 Ea12
Liden **S** 38 Gb14
Lidhult **S** 49 Fd22
Lidingö **S** 45 Gc18
Lido di Jesolo **I** 84 Fc37
Lido di Metaponto **I** 99
  Gc43
Lidoríki **GR** 110 Hd45
Lidsjöberg **S** 33 Ga12
Lidzbark **PL** 58 Ha26
Lidzbark Warminski **PL** 58
  Ha25
Liebenwalde **D** 57 Fd27
Lieberose **D** 57 Ga28
Liège **B** 63 Eb29
Lieksa **FIN** 35 Ja12
Lielauce **LV** 52 Hc22
Lielvärde **LV** 53 Hd21
Lienz **A** 72 Fc35
Liepāja **LV** 52 Ha22
Liepene **LV** 46 Hb20
Liepna **LV** 47 Ja20
Lier **B** 62 Ea29
Lierbyen **N** 43 Fb17
Liestal **CH** 71 Ec34
Lieto **FIN** 40 Hb16
Lievestuore **FIN** 41 Hd14
Liévin **F** 62 Dd29
Liezen **A** 73 Ga34
Liffol-le-Grand **F** 63 Eb32
Lifford **IRL** 19 Cb22
Lignano Sabbiadoro **I** 73
  Fd36
Lignières **F** 69 Dc34
Ligny-en-Barrois **F** 63 Eb32
Ligny-le-Châtel **F** 70 Dd33
Ligueil **F** 69 Db33
Lihás **GR** 111 Ja45
Lihoslavl' **RUS** 117 Ed10
Lihovskoj **RUS** 123 Fc15
Lihula **EST** 46 Hc19
Likenäs **S** 38 Fd16
Liknes **N** 42 Ed19

Likovskoe **RUS** 47 Jb18
Lilienfeld **A** 73 Gb33
Lilienthal **D** 56 Fa26
Liljendal **FIN** 41 Hd16
Lilla Edet **S** 43 Fd20
Lillärdal **S** 38 Ga15
Lille **F** 62 Dd29
Lillebonne **F** 61 Db30
Lillehammer **N** 37 Fc16
Lillers **F** 62 Dd29
Lillesand **N** 42 Fa19
Lillestrøm **N** 43 Fc17
Lilli **EST** 47 Hd19
Lillkågeträsk **S** 34 Gd11
Lillo **E** 92 Bd42
Lillselet **S** 30 Ha08
Lima **S** 38 Fd16
Limanáki **GR** 110 Hd46
Limanowa **PL** 67 Hb31
Limavady **GB** 20 Cb21
Limbaži **LV** 47 Hd20
Limburg **D** 63 Ed30
Liménas Géraka **GR** 111
  Ja47
Liménas Hersoníssou **GR**
  115 Jd49
Limerick **IRL** 18 Bd24
Liminka **FIN** 35 Hc10
Limmared **S** 49 Fd21
Límnes **GR** 111 Ja46
Límni **GR** 111 Ja45
Límni Vouliagménis **GR**
  111 Ja46
Limoges **F** 69 Db35
Limone Piemonte **I** 83 Ec38
Limonlu **TR** 128 Gc17
Limoux **F** 81 Db39
Lin **AL** 101 Hc42
Linares **E** 106 Bc44
Linariá **GR** 112 Jc45
Lincoln **GB** 25 Db25
Lind **DK** 48 Fa22
Lindås **N** 36 Ed16
Lindau **D** 72 Fa34
Linde **LV** 53 Hd21
Lindelse **DK** 49 Fb24
Linden **D** 64 Fa30
Lindesberg **S** 44 Ga18
Lindesnes **N** 42 Ed20
Lindome **S** 49 Fc21
Lindos **GR** 115 Kc48
Lindoso **P** 78 Ad38
Lindow **D** 57 Fd27
Lindsdal **S** 50 Gb22
Linevo **RUS** 123 Fd12
Lingbo **S** 38 Gb16
Linge **N** 36 Fa14
Lingen (Ems) **D** 55 Ed27
Linghem **S** 44 Gb19
Linguaglossa **I** 109 Ga47
Linia **PL** 58 Gc25
Linköping **S** 44 Gb19
Linkuva **LT** 52 Hc22
Linlithgow **GB** 21 Da21
Linsell **S** 38 Ga14
Linz **A** 73 Ga33

Linz **D** 63 Ec30
Lipany **SK** 67 Hb32
Lipari **I** 109 Ga46
Lipcani **MD** 76 Jc32
Lipeck **RUS** 122 Fb12
Liperi **FIN** 41 Ja13
Lipiany **PL** 57 Ga27
Lipicy-Zybino **RUS** 122 Fa12
Lipik **HR** 86 Gc37
Lipka **PL** 58 Gc26
Lipki **RUS** 118 Fa11
Lipljan **RKS** 87 Hc40
Lipniak **PL** 59 Hc25
Lipnica **PL** 58 Gc25
Lipnica Murowana **PL** 67
  Hb31
Lipník nad Bečvou **CZ** 66
  Gc31
Lipno **PL** 58 Gd27
Lipolist **SRB** 86 Ha38
Lipova **RO** 75 Hc36
Lipoven'ke **MD** 77 Kb32
Lipovljani **HR** 86 Gc37
Lippstadt **D** 55 Ed28
Lipsk **PL** 59 Hc25
Lipsko **PL** 67 Hb29
Liptovský Hrádok **SK** 67
  Ha32
Lisa Gora **MD** 77 Kb32
Lisboa **P** 90 Ab41
Lisburn **GB** 20 Cc22
Lisdoonvarna **IRL** 18 Bd23
Lisieux **F** 61 Db31
Liskeard **GB** 23 Cc28
Liski **RUS** 122 Fb13
L'Isle-Adam **F** 62 Dc31
L'Isle-en-Dodon **F** 81 Da38
L'Isle-Jourdain **F** 69 Da34
L'Isle-Jourdain **F** 81 Da38
L'Isle-sur-la-Sorgue **F** 82
  Ea38
L'Isle-sur-le-Doubs **F** 71
  Eb34
Lisma **FIN** 30 Hb06
Lismore **IRL** 22 Ca25
Lisnaskea **GB** 20 Cb22
Lišov **CZ** 65 Ga32
List **D** 48 Fa24
Listowel **IRL** 18 Bd24
Lit **S** 38 Ga13
Liteni **RO** 76 Jc33
Litľ **GR** 101 Ja42
Litija **SLO** 73 Ga36
Litóhoro **GR** 101 Hd43
Litoměřice **CZ** 65 Ga30
Litomyšl **CZ** 65 Gb31
Litovel **CZ** 66 Gc31
Litvínov **CZ** 65 Fd30
Livada **RO** 75 Hd33
Livaderó **GR** 101 Hd43
Livaderó **GR** 102 Jb42
Livádi **GR** 111 Jc47
Livadiá **GR** 111 Ja45
Livadohóri **GR** 102 Jc43
Livāni **LV** 53 Ja22
Livari **MNE** 100 Ha41

Livarot **F** 61 Db31
Livera **CY** 128 Gb18
Liverpool **GB** 21 Da24
Livezi **RO** 76 Jc35
Livigno **I** 72 Fa35
Livingston **GB** 21 Da21
Livizile **RO** 76 Ja35
Livno **BIH** 86 Gc39
Livny **RUS** 122 Fa12
Livo **FIN** 35 Hc09
Livorno **I** 84 Fa39
Livron-sur-Drôme **F** 82 Ea37
Liw **PL** 59 Hb27
Lixoúri **GR** 110 Hc46
Lizespasts **LV** 47 Ja20
Lizums **LV** 47 Ja20
Ljachaviċy **BY** 120 Ea13
Ljady **RUS** 47 Jb18
Ljaplëvka **BY** 59 Hd28
Ljaskelja **RUS** 41 Jb14
Ljig **SRB** 87 Hb38
Ljørndalen **N** 37 Fd15
Ljuban' **BY** 121 Eb13
Ljuban' **RUS** 117 Eb08
Ljubar **UA** 121 Eb15
Ljubašivka **MD** 77 Kb32
Ljubešiv **UA** 120 Ea14
Ljubija **BIH** 86 Gc37
Ljubim **RUS** 118 Fa08
Ljubinje **BIH** 86 Gd40
Ljubiš **SRB** 87 Hb39
Ljubljana **SLO** 73 Ga36
Ljuboml' **UA** 67 Hd29
Ljubovija **SRB** 86 Ha38
Ljubuški **BIH** 86 Gd40
Ljubymivka **UA** 122 Fb15
Ljubytino **RUS** 117 Ec09
Ljudinovo **RUS** 121 Ed12
Ljugarn **S** 51 Gd21
Ljung **S** 44 Fd20
Ljunga **S** 44 Gb19
Ljungaverk **S** 38 Gb14
Ljungby **S** 50 Ga22
Ljungbyhed **S** 49 Fd23
Ljungbyholm **S** 50 Gb22
Ljungdalen **S** 38 Fd13
Ljunghusen **S** 49 Fd23
Ljungsbro **S** 44 Gb19
Ljungskile **S** 43 Fc20
Ljusdal **S** 38 Gb15
Ljusfallshammar **S** 44 Gb19
Ljustorp **S** 39 Gc14
Ljutomer **SLO** 73 Gb35
Llagostera **E** 81 Db40
Llanberis **GB** 24 Cd25
Llandeilo **GB** 23 Cc26
Llandovery **GB** 24 Cd26
Llandrindod-Wells **GB** 24
  Cd26
Llandudno **GB** 20 Cd24
Llanelli **GB** 23 Cc26
Llanes **E** 79 Bd37
Llangollen **GB** 24 Cd25
Llangurig **GB** 24 Cd26
Llanidloes **GB** 24 Cd26
Llanrwst **GB** 24 Cd25

Llanwddyn **GB** 24 Cd25
Llanwrtyd Wells **GB** 24 Cd26
Lleida **E** 80 Cd40
Llerena **E** 105 Ba43
Llíria **E** 93 Cc43
Llivynci **UA** 76 Jc32
L'Ile-Rousse **F** 96 Ed40
Llodio **E** 79 Ca38
Lloret de Mar **E** 95 Db41
Llucena **E** 93 Cc42
Llucmajor **E** 95 Db43
Lnáře **CZ** 65 Fd31
Loano **I** 83 Ec38
Löbau **D** 65 Ga29
Lobcovo **RUS** 118 Fa09
Lobenstein **D** 64 Fc30
Löberöd **S** 49 Fd23
Łobez **PL** 57 Gb26
Lobonäs **S** 38 Gb15
Loburg **D** 56 Fc28
Łobżenica **PL** 58 Gc26
Locarno **CH** 71 Ed36
Lochaline **GB** 16 Cd20
Lochboisdale **GB** 16 Cc19
Lochearnhead **GB** 17 Da20
Lochem **NL** 55 Ec27
Loches **F** 69 Db33
Lochgilphead **GB** 16 Cd20
Lochinver **GB** 17 Da18
Lochmaddy **GB** 16 Cc18
Łochów **PL** 59 Hb27
Lochranza **GB** 20 Cd21
Lochvycja **UA** 121 Ed14
Lockerbie **GB** 21 Da22
Löcknitz **D** 57 Ga26
Locminé **F** 60 Cc32
Locri **I** 109 Gc46
Locronan **F** 60 Cb31
Loctudy **F** 60 Cb31
Löderup **S** 50 Ga23
Lodève **F** 81 Dc38
Lodi **I** 84 Fa37
Løding **N** 28 Ga08
Lødingen **N** 28 Gb06
Lodosa **E** 80 Cb39
Lödöse **S** 43 Fc20
Łódź **PL** 58 Ha28
Løfallstrand **N** 42 Ed17
Lofer **A** 72 Fc34
Lofsdalen **S** 38 Fd14
Loftahammar **S** 44 Gb20
Lofthus **N** 42 Ed17
Log **RUS** 123 Fd13
Logatec **SLO** 73 Ga36
Lögdeå **S** 34 Gd12
Lógos **GR** 111 Ja45
Logroño **E** 80 Cb39
Logrosán **E** 91 Bb42
Løgstør **DK** 49 Fb21
Løgumkloster **DK** 48 Fa24
Lohals **DK** 49 Fc24
Lohikoski **FIN** 41 Ja14
Lohiniva **FIN** 30 Hb07
Lohja **FIN** 46 Hc17
Lohmar **D** 63 Ec29
Lohne **D** 55 Ed27

Lohr **D** 64 Fa31
Lohtaja **FIN** 34 Hb12
Loimaa **FIN** 40 Hb16
Loitz **D** 57 Fd25
Loja **E** 105 Bb45
Løken **N** 43 Fc18
Lokeren **B** 62 Ea29
Lokka **FIN** 31 Hc06
Løkken **N** 37 Fb13
Loknja **RUS** 117 Eb10
Lőkösháza **H** 75 Hb35
Lokot' **RUS** 121 Ed13
Loksa **EST** 47 Hd17
Lollar **D** 64 Fa30
Lom **BG** 88 Ja38
Lom **N** 37 Fb15
Lombez **F** 81 Da38
Lomen **N** 37 Fb16
Łomianki **PL** 59 Hb27
Lomma **S** 49 Fd23
Lommel **B** 55 Eb28
Lom nad Rimavicou **SK** 67 Ha32
Lomonosov **RUS** 41 Jb16
Łomża **PL** 59 Hb26
London **GB** 25 Db27
Londonderry **GB** 20 Cb21
Lonevåg **N** 36 Ed16
Longarone **I** 72 Fc36
Longeau **F** 70 Ea33
Longford **IRL** 18 Ca23
Longobucco **I** 109 Gc45
Long Preston **GB** 21 Da24
Longtown **GB** 21 Da22
Longué-Jumelles **F** 69 Da33
Longuyon **F** 63 Eb31
Longwy **F** 63 Eb31
Löningen **D** 55 Ed27
Łoniów **PL** 67 Hb30
Lönsboda **S** 50 Ga22
Lons-le-Saunier **F** 70 Ea35
Lopar **HR** 85 Ga38
Lopătari **RO** 88 Jc36
Lopatino **RUS** 119 Fd11
Lopatovo **RUS** 47 Jb19
Loppa **N** 26 Gd04
Loppi **FIN** 40 Hc16
Lopuhinka **RUS** 47 Jb17
Lora del Río **E** 105 Ba44
Lorca **E** 107 Ca45
Lorch **D** 63 Ed30
Loreto **I** 85 Fd39
Lorgues **F** 83 Eb39
Lorient **F** 60 Cb32
Lőrinci **H** 74 Ha34
Loriol-sur-Drôme **F** 82 Ea37
Lormes **F** 70 Dd33
Lörrach **D** 71 Ec34
Lorris **F** 69 Dc33
Los **S** 38 Ga15
Los Arcos **E** 80 Cb38
Los Barrios **E** 105 Ba46
Los Corrales de Buelna **E** 79 Ca37
Los Cortijos de Arriba **E** 91 Bc42

Losheim **D** 63 Ec31
Łosice **PL** 59 Hc27
Los Navalmorales **E** 91 Bc41
Løsning **DK** 49 Fb23
Los Palacios y Villafranca **E** 105 Ba44
Lossiemouth **GB** 17 Db19
Lostwithiel **GB** 23 Cb28
Los Yébenes **E** 92 Bd42
Løten **N** 37 Fc16
Lotošino **RUS** 117 Ed10
Lotta **RUS** 27 Hc05
Lottigna **CH** 71 Ed35
Löttorp **S** 51 Gc21
Lotyń **PL** 58 Gc26
Loudéac **F** 60 Cc31
Loudun **F** 69 Da33
Loué **F** 61 Da32
Loue **FIN** 34 Hb09
Loughborough **GB** 25 Db26
Loughrea **IRL** 18 Ca23
Louhans **F** 70 Ea35
Louisburgh **IRL** 18 Bd22
Loukíssia **GR** 112 Jb45
Loulé **P** 104 Ac44
Louny **CZ** 65 Fd30
Lourdes **F** 80 Cd38
Loures **P** 90 Ab41
Lourinhã **P** 90 Ab41
Louth **GB** 25 Dc25
Loutrá **GR** 112 Jc46
Loutrá Edipsoú **GR** 111 Ja45
Loutrá Eleftherón **GR** 102 Jb42
Loutráki **GR** 110 Hc45
Loutráki **GR** 111 Ja46
Loutropigí **GR** 110 Hd45
Loutros **GR** 103 Jd42
Louverné **F** 61 Da32
Louvie-Juzon **F** 80 Cd38
Louviers **F** 61 Db31
Louvigné-du-Désert **F** 61 Cd31
Lövånger **S** 34 Ha11
Lövberga **S** 33 Gb12
Loveč **BG** 88 Jb39
Lovere **I** 72 Fa36
Loviisa **FIN** 41 Hd16
Lovisa **FIN** 41 Hd16
Lovište **HR** 86 Gc40
Lövnäs **S** 38 Fd15
Lövnäsvallen **S** 38 Fd15
Lövő **H** 74 Gc34
Lovosice **CZ** 65 Ga30
Lovran **HR** 85 Ga37
Lovreć **HR** 86 Gc39
Lovrin **RO** 75 Hb36
Lövstabruk **S** 45 Gc17
Löwenberg **D** 57 Fd27
Lowestoft **GB** 25 Dd26
Łowicz **PL** 58 Ha28
Loxstedt **D** 56 Fa26
Lož **SLO** 73 Ga36
Loznica **BG** 89 Jd39
Loznica **SRB** 86 Ha38

Lozova **UA** 122 Fa15
Lozoyuela **E** 92 Bd40
Luanco **E** 79 Bc36
Luarca **E** 78 Bb36
Lubaczów **PL** 67 Hd30
Lubań **PL** 65 Gb29
Lubāna **LV** 53 Ja21
Lubartów **PL** 59 Hc28
Lubawa **PL** 58 Ha26
Lübbecke **D** 56 Fa27
Lübben (Spreewald) **D** 57 Ga28
Lübbenau (Spreewald) **D** 57 Ga28
Lübeck **D** 56 Fb25
Lubersac **F** 69 Db36
Lubiąż **PL** 65 Gb29
Lubień Kujawski **PL** 58 Gd27
Lubin **PL** 65 Gb29
Lubjaniki **RUS** 118 Fb10
Lublin **PL** 67 Hc29
Lubliniec **PL** 66 Gd30
Lubniewice **PL** 57 Gb27
Lubny **UA** 121 Ed14
Lubomino **PL** 58 Ha25
Luboń **PL** 58 Gc28
L'ubotín **SK** 67 Hb31
Lubsko **PL** 57 Ga28
Lubuczewo **PL** 58 Gc25
Lubycza Królewska **PL** 67 Hd30
Lübz **D** 56 Fc26
Luca Cernii de Jos **RO** 75 Hd36
Lucca **I** 84 Fa39
Lucena **E** 105 Bb44
Luc-en-Diois **F** 82 Ea37
Lučenec **SK** 74 Ha33
Lucera **I** 99 Ga42
Lüchow **D** 56 Fc27
Lučica **SRB** 87 Hc38
Luc'k **UA** 120 Ea15
Luckau **D** 57 Fd28
Luckenwalde **D** 57 Fd28
Luçon **F** 68 Cd34
Luc-sur-Mer **F** 61 Da30
Ludbreg **HR** 74 Gc36
Lüdenscheid **D** 63 Ed29
Lüdinghausen **D** 55 Ed28
Ludlow **GB** 24 Cd26
Ludomy **PL** 58 Gc27
Luduş **RO** 76 Ja35
Ludvika **S** 44 Ga17
Ludwigsburg **D** 64 Fa32
Ludwigsfelde **D** 57 Fd28
Ludwigshafen **D** 63 Ed31
Ludwigslust **D** 56 Fc26
Ludwigstadt **D** 64 Fc30
Ludza **LV** 53 Jb21
Lug **HR** 74 Ha36
Lugano **CH** 71 Ed36
Lugo **E** 78 Ba36
Lugo **I** 84 Fc38
Lugoj **RO** 75 Hc36
Luh **RUS** 118 Fb09

Luhamaa – Malmbäck

Luhamaa **EST** 47 Ja20
Luhanka **FIN** 40 Hc14
Luhans'k **UA** 122 Fb14
Luhovicy **RUS** 118 Fa10
Luidja **EST** 46 Hb18
Luikonlahti **FIN** 41 Ja13
Luino **I** 71 Ed36
Luizi Călugăra **RO** 76 Jc34
Luka **SRB** 87 Hd38
Lukavac **BIH** 86 Gd38
Lukiv **UA** 67 Hd29
Lukojanov **RUS** 119 Fc10
Lukovit **BG** 88 Jb39
Lukovnikovo **RUS** 117 Ec10
Lukovo **HR** 85 Ga37
Lukovo **MK** 101 Hc42
Łuków **PL** 59 Hc28
Łukta **PL** 58 Ha25
Luleå **S** 34 Ha10
Lüleburgaz **TR** 103 Ka41
Lumbier **E** 80 Cc39
Lumbrales **E** 78 Ba39
Lunca Corbului **RO** 88 Jb37
Lunca de Jos **RO** 76 Jb34
Lund **N** 32 Fd11
Lund **S** 49 Fd23
Lundamo **N** 37 Fc13
Lunde **N** 43 Fb18
Lunde **S** 39 Gc13
Lunderskov **DK** 48 Fa23
Lüneburg **D** 56 Fb26
Lunel **F** 82 Dd38
Lünen **D** 55 Ed28
Lunéville **F** 63 Ec32
Luninec **BY** 120 Ea13
Lunino **RUS** 119 Fc10
Lunna **BY** 59 Hd26
Luopioinen **FIN** 40 Hc15
Luostari **RUS** 27 Hd04
Lurcy-Lévis **F** 69 Dc34
Lure **F** 71 Eb33
Lurgan **GB** 20 Cc22
Lurnfeld **A** 73 Fd35
Lushnjë **RKS** 100 Hb42
Lusignan **F** 69 Da34
Lusigny-sur-Barse **F** 62 Ea32
Luso **P** 78 Ad39
Luspebryggan **S** 29 Gd08
Luss **GB** 20 Cd21
Lussac-les-Châteaux **F** 69 Da34
Lussan **F** 82 Dd38
Lütfiye **TR** 113 Kb44
Lutherstadt Eisleben **D** 64 Fc29
Lutherstadt Wittenberg **D** 57 Fd28
Lütjenburg **D** 56 Fb25
Luton **GB** 25 Db27
Lutuhyne **UA** 122 Fb15
Lututów **PL** 66 Gd29
Luumäki **FIN** 41 Ja15
Luusua **FIN** 31 Hc08
Luvia **FIN** 40 Ha15
Luxembourg **L** 63 Eb31

Luxeuil-les-Bains **F** 71 Eb33
Lużajka **RUS** 41 Ja15
Luzern **CH** 71 Ed34
Luzino **PL** 58 Gc25
Lużki **BY** 53 Jb23
Luz-Saint-Sauveur **F** 80 Cd39
Luzy **F** 70 Dd34
L'viv **UA** 67 Hd30
Lwówek Śląski **PL** 65 Gb29
Lychen **D** 57 Fd26
Lycksele **S** 33 Gc11
Lydney **GB** 24 Cd27
Lyman **UA** 77 Kb35
Lyman **UA** 122 Fa14
Lyme Regis **GB** 24 Cd28
Lymington **GB** 24 Da28
Lyngdal **N** 42 Ed19
Lyngseidet **N** 26 Gd05
Lynton **GB** 23 Cc27
Lyntupy **BY** 53 Ja23
Lyon **F** 70 Ea36
Lyons-la-Forêt **F** 62 Dc30
Lypci **UA** 122 Fa14
Lypova Dolyna **UA** 121 Ed14
Łyse **PL** 59 Hb26
Lysekil **S** 43 Fc20
Lysi **CY** 128 Gc19
Lyskovo **RUS** 119 Fc09
Lysnes **N** 26 Gc05
Lysøysundet **N** 32 Fc12
Lyss **CH** 71 Ec34
Lystrup **DK** 49 Fb22
Lysvik **S** 44 Fd17
Lysyčans'k **UA** 122 Fb14
Lysye Gory **RUS** 123 Fd12
Lytham Saint Anne's **GB** 21 Da24
Lyubimets **BG** 102 Jc41

M

Maam Cross **IRL** 18 Bd23
Maaninka **FIN** 35 Hd12
Maaninkavaara **FIN** 31 Hd08
Maanselkä **FIN** 35 Ja11
Maardu **EST** 46 Hc18
Maarianhamina **FIN** 45 Gd17
Maarja **EST** 47 Ja19
Maasbracht **NL** 63 Eb29
Maaseik **B** 63 Eb29
Maasmechelen **NL** 63 Eb29
Maastricht **NL** 63 Eb29
Mablethorpe **GB** 25 Dc25
Macclesfield **GB** 24 Da25
Macea **RO** 75 Hc35
Maceda **E** 78 Ba37
Macedo de Cavaleiros **P** 78 Ba39
Macerata **I** 85 Fd40
Machault **F** 62 Ea31
Machecoul **F** 68 Cd33
Machynlleth **GB** 24 Cd25
Maciejowice **PL** 59 Hb28
Măcin **RO** 89 Ka36

Macinaggio **F** 96 Ed40
Macomer **I** 97 Ec43
Mâcon **F** 70 Ea35
Macroom **IRL** 22 Bd25
Macugnaga **I** 71 Ec36
Madan **BG** 102 Jc41
Mädängsholm **S** 44 Ga20
Maddaloni **I** 99 Ga43
Maden **TR** 127 Ga19
Madesimo **I** 72 Fa35
Madliena **LV** 53 Hd21
Madona **LV** 53 Ja21
Madonna di Campiglio **I** 72 Fb36
Mädrec **BG** 102 Jc40
Madrid **E** 92 Bd41
Madridejos **E** 92 Bd42
Madrigal de las Altas Torres **E** 91 Bc40
Madrigalejo **E** 91 Bb42
Mădrino **BG** 89 Jd39
Madroñera **E** 91 Bb41
Maël-Carhaix **F** 60 Cc31
Maella **E** 93 Cd41
Mafra **P** 90 Ab41
Magdeburg **D** 56 Fc28
Magenta **I** 71 Ed36
Magganári **GR** 115 Jd47
Maghera **GB** 20 Cc22
Magherani **RO** 76 Jb35
Magione **I** 84 Fc40
Maglaj **BIH** 86 Gd38
Maglavit **RO** 87 Hd38
Maglie **I** 100 Gd44
Măgliż **BG** 102 Jc40
Magnetity **RUS** 31 Ja05
Magnor **N** 43 Fd17
Magny-en-Vexin **F** 62 Dc31
Mágocs **H** 74 Gd35
Maguiresbridge **GB** 20 Cb22
Măgura **RO** 88 Jc36
Măgurele **RO** 88 Jc36
Magyarkeszi **H** 74 Gd35
Mahdalynivka **UA** 122 Fa15
Mahilёv **BY** 121 Eb12
Mahón **E** 95 Dc43
Mahora **E** 92 Ca43
Maials **E** 93 Cd41
Măicănești **RO** 89 Jd36
Maîche **F** 71 Ec34
Maidenhead **GB** 25 Db27
Maidstone **GB** 25 Dd28
Măieruș **RO** 76 Jb35
Mailly-le-Camp **F** 62 Ea32
Mainburg **D** 64 Fc32
Maintenon **F** 62 Dc31
Mainua **FIN** 35 Hd11
Mainz **D** 63 Ed30
Maišiagala **LT** 53 Hd24
Majak Oktjabrja **RUS** 123 Ga13
Majaky **UA** 77 Ka33
Majdan **RUS** 119 Fd09
Majdan **UA** 67 Hd32
Majdanpek **SRB** 87 Hc38

Majilovac **SRB** 87 Hc37
Majkop **RUS** 127 Fd17
Majorskij **RUS** 123 Fd15
Makarovo **RUS** 123 Fc12
Makarska **HR** 86 Gc40
Makijivka **UA** 122 Fb15
Makó **H** 75 Hb35
Makov **SK** 66 Gd31
Makovo **MK** 101 Hc42
Mąkowarsko **PL** 58 Gc26
Maków Mazowiecki **PL** 59 Hb27
Makrakómi **GR** 110 Hd45
Makrany **BY** 59 Hd28
Makrigialós **GR** 115 Ka49
Makrinítsa **GR** 101 Ja44
Makriráhi **GR** 101 Ja44
Maksatiha **RUS** 117 Ed09
Malå **S** 33 Gc10
Malacky **SK** 74 Gc33
Maladzečna **BY** 53 Jb24
Maladzečna **BY** 120 Ea12
Málaga **E** 105 Bb45
Malagón **E** 91 Bc42
Mălăiești **RO** 75 Hd36
Malaja Višera **RUS** 117 Eb09
Mala Kladuša **BIH** 85 Gb37
Malanów **PL** 58 Gd28
Malarrif **IS** 14 Bb05
Malaryta **BY** 59 Hd28
Mala Vyska **UA** 121 Ed15
Malax Maalahti **FIN** 40 Ha13
Malbork **PL** 58 Gd25
Malbuisson **F** 71 Eb34
Malcesine **I** 72 Fb36
Malchin **D** 57 Fd26
Malchow **D** 57 Fd26
Maldegem **B** 54 Ea28
Maldon **GB** 25 Dc27
Matdyty **PL** 58 Ha25
Malè **I** 72 Fb35
Mafe Gacno **PL** 58 Gd26
Máleme **GR** 114 Jb49
Malente **D** 56 Fb25
Malesherbes **F** 62 Dc32
Malestroit **F** 60 Cc32
Malgrat de Mar **E** 95 Db41
Målilla **S** 50 Gb21
Mali Lošinj **HR** 85 Ga38
Maliniec **PL** 58 Gd28
Malinska **HR** 85 Ga37
Maliq **AL** 101 Hc43
Maljiševo **RKS** 87 Hc40
Malkara **TR** 103 Jd42
Malko Tărnovo **BG** 103 Ka40
Mal'kovo **RUS** 53 Jb21
Mallaig **GB** 16 Cd19
Mallaranny **IRL** 18 Bd22
Mallén **E** 80 Cb40
Malles Venosta **I** 72 Fb35
Mallnitz **A** 73 Fd35
Mallow **IRL** 22 Bd25
Mallwyd **GB** 24 Cd25
Malm **N** 32 Fc12
Malmbäck **S** 50 Ga21

Malmberget S 29 Gd08
Malmedy B 63 Eb30
Malmesbury GB 24 Da27
Malmköping S 44 Gb18
Malmö S 49 Fd23
Malmslätt S 44 Gb19
Malmyż RUS 119 Fd08
Maloarhangel'sk RUS 122 Fa12
Maloe BY 59 Hd25
Malojaroslavec RUS 117 Ed11
Małomice PL 65 Gb29
Måløy N 36 Ed14
Malpartida de Plasencia E 91 Bb41
Malpica de Bergantiños E 78 Ad36
Mālpils LV 53 Hd21
Mals im Vinschgau I 72 Fb35
Malta LV 53 Ja21
Malton GB 21 Db24
Małujowice PL 66 Gc30
Malung S 38 Ga16
Malungsfors S 38 Fd16
Maluszyn PL 67 Ha29
Malyn UA 121 Eb14
Mały Płock PL 59 Hb26
Malyševo RUS 118 Fb10
Mamadys RUS 119 Ga08
Mamaia RO 89 Ka37
Mamalyha UA 76 Jc32
Mamers F 61 Db32
Mamonovo RUS 59 Ha25
Mamykovo RUS 119 Ga09
Manacor E 95 Db43
Manamensalo FIN 35 Hd11
Mănăstirea RO 89 Jd37
Mancha Real E 106 Bc44
Manchester GB 21 Da24
Manching D 64 Fc32
Manciano I 84 Fb40
Mandal N 42 Fa20
Mandas I 97 Ed44
Mandráki GR 115 Kb47
Manduria I 100 Gd43
Manerbio I 84 Fa37
Manevyči UA 120 Ea14
Manfredonia I 99 Gb42
Mangalia RO 89 Ka38
Mangen N 43 Fc17
Manger N 36 Ec16
Mangualde P 78 Ad39
Maniago I 72 Fc36
Manisa TR 113 Ka44
Manises E 93 Cc43
Månkarbo S 45 Gc17
Manlleu E 81 Db40
Mannheim D 63 Ed31
Manningtree GB 25 Dc27
Manole BG 102 Jb40
Manoleasa RO 76 Jc32
Manorhamilton IRL 18 Ca22
Manosque F 82 Ea38
Manresa E 81 Da40

Mansfeld D 56 Fc28
Mansfield GB 25 Db25
Mansilla E 79 Bd38
Mansilla E 79 Ca39
Mansilla de las Mulas E 79 Bc38
Mansle F 69 Da35
Mantamádos GR 113 Jd44
Mantes-la-Jolie F 62 Dc31
Mantes-la-Ville F 62 Dc31
Manthiréa GR 111 Ja47
Mantorp S 44 Gb20
Mantova I 84 Fb37
Mäntsälä FIN 40 Hc16
Mänttä FIN 40 Hc14
Manturovo RUS 118 Fb08
Mäntyharju FIN 41 Hd15
Mäntyjärvi FIN 35 Hd09
Mäntyluoto FIN 40 Ha15
Manyas TR 103 Kb43
Manzanares E 92 Bd43
Maó (Mahón) E 95 Dc43
Maqueda E 91 Bc41
Maranello I 84 Fb38
Marans F 68 Cd34
Mărăşeşti RO 77 Jd35
Mărașu RO 89 Ka36
Maratea I 99 Gb44
Marathónas GR 112 Jb46
Marazion GB 23 Cb28
Marbach D 64 Fa32
Marbella E 105 Bb45
Marburg D 64 Fa29
Marcali H 74 Gc35
Marcaltő H 74 Gc34
Marčana HR 85 Fd37
March GB 25 Db26
Marche-en-Famenne B 63 Eb30
Marchena E 105 Ba44
Marchenoir F 61 Db32
Marciac F 80 Cd38
Marciana Marina I 84 Fa40
Marcigny F 70 Dd35
Marcillac-la-Croisille F 69 Db36
Marcinkonys LT 59 Hd25
Marcinkonys LT 59 Hd25
Marck F 54 Dc28
Marco de Canaveses P 78 Ad39
Mardalen N 36 Fa14
Mårdsele S 34 Gd11
Marennes F 68 Cd35
Mareuil-sur-Lay F 68 Cd34
Mar'evka RUS 119 Ga10
Marevo RUS 117 Eb10
Margariti GR 101 Hc44
Margaritove RUS 127 Fc16
Margate GB 25 Dc28
Mărgău RO 75 Hc34
Margecany SK 67 Hb32
Margherita di Savoia I 99 Gb42
Marghita RO 75 Hc34
Margone I 83 Ec37

Margonin PL 58 Gc27
Marhanec' UA 126 Fa16
Mariager DK 49 Fb22
Marialva P 78 Ba39
Mariannelund S 50 Gb21
Mariánské Lázně CZ 65 Fd31
Mariazell A 73 Gb34
Maribo DK 49 Fc24
Maribor SLO 73 Gb35
Mariefred S 45 Gc18
Mariehamn FIN 45 Gd17
Marielund S 33 Gc10
Marielyst DK 49 Fc24
Marienberg D 65 Fd30
Mariés GR 102 Jb42
Mariestad S 44 Ga19
Marignane F 82 Ea39
Marijampolė LT 52 Hc24
Marín E 78 Ad37
Marina di Belvedere I 99 Gb44
Marina di Carrara I 84 Fa38
Marina di Cetraro I 99 Gb44
Marina di Grosseto I 84 Fb40
Marina di Leuca I 100 Ha44
Marina di Pisa I 84 Fa39
Marina di Ragusa I 109 Ga48
Marina di Ravenna I 84 Fc38
Marine de Sisco F 96 Ed40
Marinella I 108 Fc47
Marineo I 108 Fd47
Maringues F 70 Dc35
Marinha Grande P 90 Ac40
Marinka BG 103 Ka40
Mariupol' UA 126 Fb16
Märjamaa EST 46 Hc18
Markabygd N 32 Fc12
Markaryd S 49 Fd22
Market Drayton GB 24 Da25
Market Harborough GB 25 Db26
Market Rasen GB 25 Db25
Market Weighton GB 21 Db24
Markivka MD 77 Kb33
Markivka UA 122 Fb14
Markkina FIN 30 Ha06
Markkleeberg D 64 Fc29
Markópoulo GR 112 Jb46
Markovo BG 103 Jd39
Marksewo PL 59 Hb26
Marktheidenfeld D 64 Fa31
Markt Indersdorf D 72 Fb33
Marktoberdorf D 72 Fb34
Marktredwitz D 64 Fc31
Marl D 55 Ec28
Marlborough GB 24 Da27
Marle F 62 Ea30
Marma S 38 Gb16
Marma S 45 Gc17
Marmande F 81 Da37
Marmara TR 103 Ka42

Marmaraereğlisi TR 103 Ka41
Mármaro GR 113 Jd45
Marnay F 71 Eb34
Marne D 56 Fa25
Marotta I 85 Fd39
Marovac SRB 87 Hc40
Marquise F 62 Dc29
Marradi I 84 Fb38
Marraskoski FIN 30 Hb08
Marsala I 108 Fc47
Maršavicy RUS 47 Jb20
Marsberg D 64 Fa29
Marsciano I 84 Fc40
Marseille F 82 Ea39
Marseille-en-Beauvaisis F 62 Dc30
Marsico Nuovo I 99 Gb43
Märsta S 45 Gc18
Marstal DK 49 Fb24
Marstrand S 43 Fc20
Martelange B 63 Eb30
Mártha GR 115 Jd49
Martigné-Ferchaud F 61 Cd32
Martigny CH 71 Ec35
Martigues F 82 Dd39
Martilla FIN 40 Hb16
Martin SK 66 Gd32
Martina Franca I 100 Gd43
Martinniemi FIN 35 Hc10
Martinšćica HR 85 Ga38
Martinsicuro I 85 Fd40
Martna EST 46 Hc18
Martonvaara FIN 35 Ja12
Martorell E 95 Da41
Martos E 106 Bc44
Martti FIN 31 Hd07
Marvão P 90 Ad41
Marvejols F 81 Dc37
Marvik N 42 Ed18
Maryport GB 21 Da23
Mas de las Matas E 93 Cc41
Masegoso de Tajuña E 92 Ca41
Masfjorden N 36 Ed16
Masi N 26 Ha05
Masku FIN 40 Hb16
Massa I 84 Fa38
Massafra I 99 Gc43
Massa Marittima I 84 Fb40
Massat F 81 Da39
Masseube F 81 Da38
Massiac F 69 Dc36
Mastihári GR 115 Ka47
Masty BY 59 Hd26
Masugnsbyn S 30 Ha07
Måsvik N 26 Gc04
Mátala GR 114 Jc50
Matamala de Almazán E 92 Ca40
Mataró E 95 Db41
Mätäsvaara FIN 35 Ja12
Matching Green GB 25 Db27
Matelica I 85 Fd40

Matera – Mézières-sur-Issoire

Matera I 99 Gc43
Mátészalka H 75 Hc33
Matfors S 38 Gb14
Matha F 68 Cd35
Matíši LV 47 Hd20
Matkasel'kja RUS 41 Jb14
Matosinhos P 78 Ad38
Mátraháza H 74 Ha33
Matrei A 72 Fc35
Mattersburg A 73 Gb34
Mattighofen A 73 Fd33
Matveev Kurgan RUS 123 Fc15
Matyli BY 59 Hd25
Maubeuge F 62 Ea30
Maubourguet F 80 Cd38
Mauléon F 68 Cd33
Mauléon-Licharre F 80 Cc38
Maunu S 29 Ha06
Maura N 43 Fc17
Maure-de-Bretagne F 61 Cd32
Mauriac F 69 Dc36
Mauron F 60 Cc31
Maurs F 81 Db37
Maurvangen N 37 Fb15
Mauterndorf A 73 Fd34
Mauthausen A 73 Ga33
Mauvezin F 81 Da38
Mauzé-sur-le-Mignon F 68 Cd34
Mauzé-sur-le-Mignon F 68 Cd34
Mavas S 28 Gb08
Mavréli GR 101 Hd44
Mavromáta GR 110 Hd45
Mavroúda GR 101 Ja42
Mavrovi Anovi MK 101 Hc41
Măxineni RO 89 Jd36
Maybole GB 20 Cd22
Mayen D 63 Ec30
Mayenne F 61 Da31
Maynooth IRL 19 Cb24
Mayorga E 79 Bc38
Mayrhofen A 72 Fc34
Mazagón E 105 Ad44
Mazamet F 81 Db38
Mazara del Vallo I 108 Fc47
Mazarrón E 107 Ca45
Mažeikiai LT 52 Hb22
Mazières-en-Gâtine F 69 Da34
Mazilmāja LV 52 Hb22
Mazirbe LV 46 Hb20
Mazsalaca LV 47 Hd20
Mazyr BY 121 Eb13
Mazzarino I 109 Ga47
Mcensk RUS 122 Fa12
Meaux F 62 Dd31
Mechelen B 62 Ea29
Mecidiye TR 103 Jd42
Mečka BG 88 Jc38
Mede I 83 Ed37
Medele S 34 Gd11
Medemblik NL 55 Eb26
Medenýči UA 67 Hd31

Medevi S 44 Ga19
Medgidia RO 89 Ka37
Medgyesegyháza H 75 Hb35
Mediaş RO 76 Ja35
Medicina I 84 Fb38
Medinaceli E 92 Ca40
Medina del Campo E 79 Bc39
Medina de Pomar E 79 Ca38
Medina de Ríoseco E 79 Bc39
Medina Sidonia E 105 Ba45
Medininkai LT 53 Ja24
Medulin HR 85 Fd38
Međurečje SRB 87 Hb39
Međurijećje MNE 86 Ha40
Medvedja SRB 87 Hc40
Medvenka RUS 122 Fa13
Medyka UA 67 Hd31
Medze LV 52 Ha22
Medzilaborce SK 67 Hc31
Meerane D 64 Fc30
Megáli Panagía GR 102 Jb43
Megáli Stérna GR 101 Ja42
Megáli Vríssi GR 101 Ja42
Megalohóri GR 101 Hd44
Megálo Horío GR 115 Kb47
Megalópoli GR 110 Hd47
Mégara GR 112 Jb46
Megève F 71 Eb36
Mehamn N 27 Hc02
Mehikoorma EST 47 Ja19
Mehring D 63 Ec31
Mehun-sur-Yèvre F 69 Dc33
Meilen CH 71 Ed34
Meinersen D 56 Fb27
Meinhardt D 64 Fa32
Meiningen D 64 Fb30
Meira E 78 Bb36
Meiringen CH 71 Ed35
Meißen D 65 Fd29
Meitingen D 64 Fb32
Melá GR 112 Jc45
Melaje SRB 87 Hb40
Melalahti FIN 41 Ja13
Melates GR 110 Hc45
Melbu N 28 Ga06
Meldal N 37 Fb13
Meldorf D 56 Fa25
Melegnano I 83 Ed37
Melenci SRB 75 Hb36
Melenki RUS 118 Fb10
Melfi I 99 Gb43
Melgar de Fernamental E 79 Bd38
Melhus N 37 Fc13
Melide E 78 Ba36
Melides P 90 Ab42
Melíki GR 101 Hd43
Melilli I 109 Ga47
Melineşti RO 88 Ja37
Mélissa GR 101 Ja44

Melitopol' UA 126 Fa16
Melito Porto Salvo I 109 Gb47
Melívia GR 101 Ja44
Melk A 73 Gb33
Mellakoski FIN 34 Hb09
Mellansel S 39 Gc13
Mellanström S 33 Gc10
Mellbystrand S 49 Fd22
Melle D 55 Ed27
Melle F 69 Da34
Mellerud S 43 Fd19
Mellrichstadt D 64 Fb30
Melnica SRB 87 Hc38
Melnik BG 101 Ja41
Mělník CZ 65 Ga30
Mel'nikovo RUS 41 Jb15
Melnsils LV 46 Hb20
Mels CH 72 Fa34
Melsungen D 64 Fa29
Meltaus FIN 30 Hb08
Melton Mowbray GB 25 Db26
Meltosjärvi FIN 30 Hb08
Melun F 62 Dc32
Melvich GB 17 Db18
Membrio E 91 Ba41
Memmingen D 72 Fa33
Mena UA 121 Ec13
Menaggio I 71 Ed36
Menai Bridge GB 20 Cd24
Mende F 81 Dc37
Mendeleevsk RUS 119 Ga08
Menden D 55 Ed28
Mendrisio CH 71 Ed36
Menemen TR 113 Ka45
Menen B 62 Dd29
Meneou CY 128 Gc19
Menesjärvi FIN 27 Hb05
Menfi I 108 Fc47
Mengen D 72 Fa33
Mengeš SLO 73 Ga36
Mengíbar E 106 Bc44
Menídi GR 110 Hc45
Mentana I 98 Fc41
Menton F 83 Ec39
Menzelinsk RUS 119 Ga08
Meppel NL 55 Ec27
Meppen D 55 Ed27
Mequinenza E 93 Cd41
Mer F 69 Db33
Meråker N 37 Fd13
Meran I 72 Fb35
Merano I 72 Fb35
Merasjärvi S 30 Ha07
Mercato Saraceno I 84 Fc39
Merdrignac F 60 Cc31
Merefa UA 122 Fa14
Merei RO 88 Jc36
Méribel F 71 Eb36
Meričleri BG 102 Jc40
Mérida E 91 Ba42
Mérignac F 68 Cd36
Mérihas GR 111 Jc47
Merijärvi FIN 34 Hb11
Merikarvia FIN 40 Ha15

Meri-Pori FIN 40 Ha15
Merkinė LT 59 Hd25
Merkinė LT 59 Hd25
Mernye H 74 Gd35
Mersch L 63 Eb31
Merseburg D 64 Fc29
Mersin TR 128 Gd16
Mērsrags LV 52 Hc21
Merthyr Tydfil GB 24 Cd26
Mértola P 104 Ac43
Méru F 62 Dc31
Měry BY 53 Jb22
Merzig D 63 Ec31
Mesagne I 100 Gd43
Meschede D 63 Ed29
Meselefors S 33 Gb11
Mesihovina BIH 86 Gc39
Meslay-du-Maine F 61 Da32
Mesohóri GR 101 Hd44
Mesopotamiá GR 101 Hc43
Mesopótamo GR 110 Hc45
Messaure S 29 Gd08
Messelt N 37 Fc15
Messina I 109 Gb46
Messini GR 110 Hd47
Messinó GR 111 Ja46
Meßkirch D 72 Fa33
Messolóngi GR 110 Hd46
Messongí GR 100 Hb44
Mesta BG 101 Ja41
Mestá GR 113 Jd45
Mestanza E 106 Bc43
Mesti GR 102 Jc42
Město Albrechtice CZ 66 Gc30
Město Touškov CZ 65 Fd31
Mestre I 84 Fc37
Mesvres F 70 Dd34
Metajna HR 85 Ga38
Metamorfósi GR 111 Ja47
Méthana GR 112 Jb46
Methóni GR 110 Hd48
Metković HR 86 Gd40
Metlika SLO 73 Gb36
Metóhi GR 112 Jb45
Metsäkylä FIN 35 Hd10
Metsküla EST 46 Hb19
Métsovo GR 101 Hc44
Mettlach D 63 Ec31
Metz F 63 Eb31
Metzingen D 64 Fa32
Meulan F 62 Dc31
Meuselwitz D 64 Fc29
Meydancik TR 127 Ga18
Meyenburg D 56 Fc26
Meymac F 69 Db36
Meyrueis F 81 Dc37
Meyzieu F 70 Ea36
Mézapos GR 111 Ja48
Mezdra BG 88 Ja39
Mężenin PL 59 Hc26
Mežica SLO 73 Ga35
Mézières-en-Brenne F 69 Db34
Mézières-sur-Issoire F 69 Da35

Mézin F 80 Cd37
Mezőberény H 75 Hb35
Mezőcsát H 75 Hb33
Mezőkovácsháza H 75 Hb35
Mezőkövesd H 75 Hb33
Mézos F 80 Cc37
Mežotne LV 52 Hc22
Mezőtúr H 75 Hb34
Miajadas E 91 Ba42
Miastko PL 58 Gc25
Michajlovskoe RUS 119 Fc09
Michalin PL 58 Gd27
Michalovce SK 67 Hc32
Michelstadt D 64 Fa31
Micleşti RO 77 Jd34
Mičurinsk RUS 122 Fb12
Mičurinskoe RUS 41 Jb16
Middelburg NL 54 Ea28
Middelfart DK 49 Fb23
Middelharnis NL 54 Ea28
Middlesbrough GB 21 Db23
Midhurst GB 24 Da28
Midleton IRL 22 Bd25
Midsund N 36 Fa13
Miechów PL 67 Ha30
Miedźno PL 66 Gd29
Międzychód PL 57 Gb27
Międzylesie PL 66 Gc30
Międzyrzec Podlaski PL 59 Hc28
Międzyrzecz PL 57 Gb27
Międzywodzie PL 57 Ga25
Międzyzdroje PL 57 Ga25
Miehikkälä FIN 41 Ja16
Miélan F 80 Cd38
Mielec PL 67 Hb30
Mieraslompolo FIN 27 Hc04
Miercurea-Ciuc RO 76 Jb35
Miercurea Sibiului RO 88 Ja36
Mieres E 79 Bc37
Mierojokki N 26 Ha05
Miesbach D 72 Fc34
Mieszków PL 58 Gc28
Mieszkowice PL 57 Ga27
Mietoinen FIN 40 Ha16
Mifol AL 100 Hb43
Migennes F 70 Dd33
Miglionico I 99 Gc43
Mihăeşti RO 88 Jb38
Mihail Kogălniceanu RO 89 Ka37
Mihailovca MD 77 Ka33
Mihailovca MD 77 Ka34
Mihajlov RUS 118 Fa11
Mihajlovka RUS 123 Fd13
Mihajlovo BG 88 Ja39
Mihalkovo BG 102 Jb41
Miheşu de Câmpie RO 76 Ja35
Mihnevo RUS 118 Fa10
Mikašēvičy BY 121 Eb13
Mikaszówka PL 59 Hc25
Mikeļtornis LV 46 Hb20
Mikkeli FIN 41 Hd14

Mikkelvik N 26 Gc04
Mikolaivka MD 77 Kb32
Mikołajki PL 59 Hb25
Mikołów PL 66 Gd30
Mikonos GR 113 Jd46
Mikre BG 88 Jb39
Mikulov CZ 66 Gc32
Miladinovci MK 101 Hc41
Milagro E 80 Cb39
Miłakowo PL 58 Ha25
Milano I 71 Ed36
Milas TR 113 Kb46
Milazzo I 109 Gb46
Miléa GR 101 Hc44
Milešovo SRB 74 Ha36
Milestone IRL 18 Ca24
Mileto I 109 Gb46
Milevsko CZ 65 Ga31
Milford GB 25 Db28
Milford Haven GB 23 Cc26
Milići BIH 86 Ha38
Milicz PL 66 Gc29
Milín CZ 65 Ga31
Militello I 109 Ga47
Militsa GR 110 Hd48
Millas F 81 Db39
Millau F 81 Dc38
Millerovo RUS 123 Fc14
Millom GB 21 Da23
Milltown Malbay IRL 18 Bd24
Milmersdorf D 57 Fd27
Milna HR 86 Gc40
Mílos GR 111 Jc47
Milot RKS 100 Hb42
Milówka PL 67 Ha31
Miltenberg D 64 Fa31
Milton Keynes GB 25 Db27
Mimizan F 80 Cc37
Mimoň CZ 65 Ga30
Mina de São Domingos P 104 Ac43
Mindelheim D 72 Fb33
Minden D 56 Fa27
Minehead GB 23 Cc27
Mineral'nye Vody RUS 127 Ga16
Minervino Murge I 99 Gb42
Minglanilla E 93 Cb42
Mingorría E 91 Bc40
Minićevo SRB 87 Hd39
Minsk BY 120 Ea12
Mińsk Mazowiecki PL 59 Hb28
Mintlaw GB 17 Db19
Minturno I 98 Fd42
Miomo F 96 Ed40
Mionica SRB 87 Hb38
Mioveni RO 88 Jb37
Mira E 93 Cb42
Mira I 84 Fc37
Mira P 90 Ac39
Miramas F 82 Dd39
Mirambeau F 68 Cd35
Miramont-de-Guyenne F 69 Da36

Miranda de Ebro E 79 Ca38
Miranda do Douro P 78 Bb39
Mirande F 80 Cd38
Mirandela P 78 Ba39
Mirandola I 84 Fb37
Mirano I 84 Fc37
Mircze PL 67 Hd29
Mirebeau F 69 Da34
Mirebeau-sur-Bèze F 70 Ea34
Mirecourt F 63 Eb32
Mirepoix F 81 Db39
Mireşti MD 77 Jd34
Mírina GR 102 Jc43
Mirne UA 77 Kb34
Mirosławiec PL 57 Gb26
Mirotice CZ 65 Ga31
Mirovice CZ 65 Ga31
Mirow D 57 Fd26
Mírtos GR 115 Jd49
Mischii RO 88 Ja38
Misi FIN 31 Hc08
Miskolc H 75 Hb33
Mišnjak HR 85 Ga38
Misso EST 47 Ja20
Misterbianco I 109 Ga47
Misterhult S 50 Gb21
Mistretta I 109 Ga47
Mitchelstown IRL 22 Bd25
Míthimna GR 113 Jd44
Mítikas GR 110 Hc45
Mitrašinci MK 101 Hd41
Mitrofanovka RUS 122 Fb14
Mitrovo SRB 87 Hc39
Mittådalen S 38 Fd14
Mittenwald D 72 Fb34
Mittersill A 72 Fc34
Mitterteich D 64 Fc31
Mittweida D 65 Fd29
Mizil RO 88 Jc36
Mjadzel BY 53 Jb23
Mjadzel BY 120 Ea12
Mjakiševo RUS 53 Jb21
Mjaksa RUS 117 Ed08
Mjölby S 44 Ga20
Mjönäs S 44 Fd17
Mjøndalen N 43 Fb18
Mladá Boleslav CZ 65 Ga30
Mladá Vožice CZ 65 Ga31
Mladenovac SRB 87 Hb38
Mława PL 58 Ha26
Mlebniko RUS 119 Fd08
Mlinište BIH 86 Gd38
Młodasko PL 57 Gb27
Młogoszyn PL 58 Ha28
Młynary PL 58 Ha25
Młynarze PL 59 Hb26
Mlyniv UA 120 Ea15
Mníšek nad Hnilcom SK 67 Hb32
Mo N 43 Fc17
Moacşa RO 76 Jc35
Moara Vlăsiei RO 88 Jc37

Moate IRL 18 Ca23
Mochy PL 57 Gb28
Mociu RO 76 Ja34
Möckern D 56 Fc28
Mockfjärd S 44 Ga17
Modane F 83 Eb37
Modena I 84 Fb38
Modica I 109 Ga48
Modigliana I 84 Fb38
Modliborzyce PL 67 Hc29
Mödling A 73 Gb33
Modriča BIH 86 Gd37
Modugno I 99 Gc42
Moelv N 37 Fc16
Moen N 26 Gc05
Moers D 55 Ec28
Moffat GB 21 Da22
Moftin RO 75 Hd33
Mogadouro P 78 Ba39
Mogili RUS 53 Jb21
Mogilno PL 58 Gc27
Mogliano Veneto I 72 Fc36
Mogosoaia RO 88 Jc37
Moguer E 105 Ad44
Mohács H 74 Gd36
Mohed S 38 Gb16
Moheda S 50 Ga21
Mohelnice CZ 66 Gc31
Möhnesee D 55 Ed28
Mohora H 74 Ha33
Mohyliv-Podil's'kyj UA 77 Jd32
Mohyliv-Podil's'kyj UA 125 Eb16
Moi N 42 Ed19
Moineşti RO 76 Jc35
Mo i Rana N 33 Ga09
Mõisaküla EST 47 Hd19
Moisiovaara FIN 35 Ja10
Moissac F 81 Da37
Mojácar E 107 Ca45
Mojados E 79 Bc39
Möklinta S 44 Gb17
Mokobody PL 59 Hc27
Mokre PL 58 Gc25
Mokren BG 89 Jd39
Mokrous RUS 119 Ga11
Mokšan RUS 119 Fc11
Mol B 63 Eb29
Mola di Bari I 99 Gc42
Mold GB 24 Cd25
Moldava nad Bodvou SK 67 Hb32
Molde N 36 Fa13
Molėtai LT 53 Hd23
Molfetta I 99 Gc42
Moliden S 39 Gc13
Molina E 93 Cb41
Molina de Segura E 107 Cb44
Molinella I 84 Fb38
Molkom S 44 Ga18
Mollerussa E 80 Cd40
Mölln D 56 Fb26
Mölltorp S 44 Ga19

173

Molodi – Morskoj

Molodi RUS 47 Jb19
Mólos GR 111 Ja45
Moloskovicy RUS 47 Jb17
Molsheim F 63 Ec32
Molunat HR 100 Gd41
Mombuey E 78 Bb38
Momčilgrad BG 102 Jc41
Mommark DK 49 Fb24
Mon S 33 Ga11
Monaco MC 83 Ec39
Monaghan IRL 19 Cb22
Monaši UA 77 Kb34
Monasterace Marina I 109 Gc46
Monastir I 97 Ed44
Monastyrščina RUS 121 Ec12
Monastyryšče UA 121 Ec15
Monastyrys'ka UA 124 Ea16
Moncada E 93 Cc43
Moncalieri I 83 Ec37
Moncalvo I 83 Ed37
Monção P 78 Ad37
Mönchengladbach D 63 Ec29
Monchique P 104 Ab43
Moncontour F 60 Cc31
Mondéjar E 92 Bd41
Mondello I 108 Fd46
Mondim de Basto P 78 Ad38
Mondolfo I 85 Fd39
Mondoñedo E 78 Bb36
Mondoubleau F 61 Db32
Mondovi I 83 Ec38
Mondragone I 98 Fd42
Mondriz E 78 Bb36
Mondsee A 73 Fd33
Moneasa RO 75 Hc35
Monein F 80 Cd38
Monemvassiá GR 111 Ja48
Monesterio E 105 Ba43
Moneymore GB 20 Cb22
Monfalcone I 73 Fd36
Monforte P 90 Ad41
Monheim D 64 Fb32
Moniatis CY 128 Gb19
Möniste EST 47 Ja20
Monistrol-d'Allier F 70 Dd36
Monistrol-sur-Loire F 70 Dd36
Mońki PL 59 Hc26
Monmouth GB 24 Cd26
Monolíthio GR 101 Hc44
Monólithos GR 115 Kb48
Monopoli I 99 Gc43
Monóvar E 107 Cb44
Monreal del Campo E 93 Cb41
Monreale I 108 Fd46
Monroy E 91 Ba41
Monroyo E 93 Cc41
Mons B 62 Ea29
Monsanto P 91 Ba40
Monsaraz P 90 Ad42
Monschau D 63 Ec29

Monselice I 84 Fc37
Mönsterås S 50 Gb21
Montagnac F 81 Dc38
Montagnana I 84 Fb37
Montaigu F 68 Cd33
Montalbán E 93 Cc41
Montalcino I 84 Fb40
Montalegre P 78 Ba38
Montalivet-les-Bains F 68 Cd35
Montalto di Castro I 98 Fb41
Montalto Uffogo I 109 Gb45
Montamarta E 78 Bb39
Montana BG 88 Ja39
Montargil P 90 Ac41
Montargis F 62 Dc32
Montauban F 81 Da37
Montauban-de-Bretagne F 61 Cd31
Montbard F 70 Ea33
Montbazon F 69 Db33
Montbéliard F 71 Ec34
Montblanc E 95 Da41
Montbrison F 70 Dd36
Montbron F 69 Da35
Montceau-les-Mines F 70 Ea34
Montchanin F 70 Ea34
Montcuq F 81 Da37
Mont-Dauphin F 83 Eb37
Mont-de-Marsan F 80 Cd37
Montdidier F 62 Dd30
Montealegre del Castillo E 93 Cb43
Monte Argentario-Porto San Stefano I 98 Fb41
Montebelluna I 72 Fc36
Montecatini Terme I 84 Fb39
Montecchio Emilia I 84 Fa38
Montecchio Maggiore I 84 Fb37
Montech F 81 Da37
Montefiascone I 84 Fc40
Monteforte de Lemos E 78 Ba37
Montefrío E 106 Bc45
Montehermoso E 91 Ba40
Montélimar F 82 Dd37
Montella I 99 Ga43
Montellano E 105 Ba45
Montemor-o-Novo P 90 Ac42
Montendre F 68 Cd35
Montepulciano I 84 Fb40
Montereau F 62 Dd32
Monteriggioni I 84 Fb39
Monterosso al Mare I 84 Fa38
Monterotondo I 98 Fc41
Monte San Savino I 84 Fb39
Monte Sant'Angelo I 99 Gb42
Montesilvano I 99 Ga41
Montesquieu-Volvestre F 81 Da38

Montevarchi I 84 Fb39
Montfaucon-d'Argonne F 63 Eb31
Montfaucon-en-Velay F 70 Dd36
Montguyon F 68 Cd36
Monthey CH 71 Ec35
Monti I 97 Ed43
Montichiari I 84 Fa37
Monticiano I 84 Fb40
Montier-en-Der F 62 Ea32
Montignac F 69 Da36
Montigny F 63 Eb31
Montigny-le-Roi F 71 Eb33
Montigny-sur-Aube F 70 Ea33
Montijo E 91 Ba42
Montijo P 90 Ac41
Montilla E 105 Bb44
Montivilliers F 61 Db30
Mont-Louis F 81 Db39
Montluçon F 69 Dc35
Montluel F 70 Ea36
Montmarault F 69 Dc35
Montmédy F 63 Eb31
Montmirail F 62 Dd31
Montmoreau-Saint-Cybard F 69 Da35
Montmorency F 62 Dc31
Montmorillon F 69 Db34
Montoire-sur-le-Loir F 61 Db32
Montón E 80 Cb40
Montoro E 106 Bc44
Montpellier F 81 Dc38
Montpon-Ménestérol F 69 Da36
Montréjeau F 80 Cd38
Montreuil F 62 Dc29
Montreuil-Bellay F 69 Da33
Montreux CH 71 Ec35
Montrevel-en-Bresse F 70 Ea35
Montrichard F 69 Db33
Montrond-les-Bains F 70 Dd36
Montrose GB 17 Db20
Montroy E 93 Cb43
Mont-Saint-Aignan F 61 Db30
Montsalvy F 81 Dc37
Montségur F 81 Db39
Montseny E 81 Db40
Montsûrs F 61 Da32
Montuïri E 95 Db43
Monza I 71 Ed36
Monzón E 80 Cd40
Moosburg D 72 Fc33
Mór H 74 Gd34
Mora E 92 Bd42
Mora P 90 Ac41
Mora S 38 Ga16
Mora de Rubielos E 93 Cc42
Morąg PL 58 Ha25
Mórahalom H 74 Ha36

Morakovo MNE 86 Ha40
Morakowo PL 58 Gc27
Móra la Nova E 93 Cd41
Moral de Calatrava E 92 Bd43
Moraleja E 91 Ba40
Morărești RO 88 Jb37
Moratalla E 107 Ca44
Moravița RO 87 Hc37
Morávka CZ 66 Gd31
Moravská Třebová CZ 66 Gc31
Moravské Budějovice CZ 65 Gb32
Moravské Lieskové SK 66 Gd32
Moravský Beroun CZ 66 Gc31
Moravský Krumlov CZ 65 Gb32
Morawica PL 67 Hb29
Morbach D 63 Ec31
Mörbylånga S 50 Gb22
Morcenx F 80 Cc37
Morcone I 99 Ga42
Mordelles F 61 Cd32
Mordoğan TR 113 Ka45
Mordovo RUS 122 Fb12
Mordy PL 59 Hc27
Mor'e RUS 117 Eb08
Morecambe GB 21 Da24
Moreda E 106 Bc45
Morée F 61 Db32
Morella E 93 Cc41
Moreni RO 88 Jb37
Mores I 97 Ed43
Moreton-in-Marsh GB 24 Da26
Moret-sur-Loing F 62 Dd32
Moreuil F 62 Dd30
Morez F 71 Eb35
Morfou CY 128 Gb19
Morges CH 71 Eb35
Morgins CH 71 Ec35
Morgongåva S 45 Gc17
Morgos RO 75 Hd35
Morhange F 63 Ec32
Moriani-Plage F 96 Ed41
Morjärv S 34 Ha09
Morki RUS 119 Fd08
Mörkret S 38 Fd15
Morlaàs F 80 Cd38
Morlaix F 60 Cb30
Mörlunda S 50 Gb21
Morón de Almazán E 92 Ca40
Morón de la Frontera E 105 Ba44
Morottaja FIN 31 Hd08
Morozeni MD 77 Jd33
Morozovsk RUS 123 Fc14
Morpeth GB 21 Db22
Mörrum S 50 Ga22
Moršansk RUS 118 Fb11
Mörsil S 38 Ga13
Morskoj RUS 52 Ha24

Mörskom FIN 41 Hd16
Morsovo RUS 118 Fb11
Mørsvik N 28 Gb07
Mortagne-au-Perche F 61 Db31
Mortagne-sur-Sèvre F 68 Cd33
Mortain F 61 Da31
Mortara I 83 Ed37
Mortrée F 61 Da31
Morzine F 71 Eb35
Morzyczyn PL 57 Ga26
Mosal'sk RUS 117 Ed11
Mosbach D 64 Fa31
Mosby N 42 Fa19
Mosfellsbær IS 14 Bc07
Moshófito GR 101 Hc44
Mosina PL 58 Gc28
Mosjøen N 32 Fd10
Mosko BIH 86 Gd40
Moskosel S 34 Gd09
Moskva RUS 117 Ed10
Moslavina Podravska HR 74 Gd36
Mosonmagyaróvár H 74 Gc33
Moss N 43 Fc18
Most CZ 65 Fd30
Mostar BIH 86 Gd39
Móstoles E 92 Bd41
Mostovskoj RUS 127 Fd17
Mosty PL 59 Hd28
Mostys'ka UA 67 Hd31
Mota del Cuervo E 92 Bd42
Mota del Marqués E 79 Bc39
Motala S 44 Ga19
Moţca RO 76 Jc33
Motherwell GB 21 Da21
Motilla del Palancar E 92 Ca42
Motril E 106 Bc45
Motru RO 87 Hd37
Moudon CH 71 Eb35
Moúdros GR 102 Jc43
Mougins F 83 Eb39
Mouhijärvi FIN 40 Hb15
Moulins F 70 Dd34
Mountain Ash GB 24 Cd26
Mount Bellew IRL 18 Ca23
Mountbenger GB 21 Da22
Mountmellick IRL 18 Ca24
Moura P 105 Ad43
Mourão P 90 Ad42
Mourenx F 80 Cc38
Mourmelon-le-Grand F 62 Ea31
Mouscron B 62 Dd29
Moustiers-Ste-Marie F 83 Eb38
Mouthe F 71 Eb35
Moutier CH 71 Ec34
Moûtiers F 71 Eb36
Moutsoúna GR 115 Jd47
Mouy F 62 Dc31
Mouzáki GR 101 Hd44

Mouzon F 63 Eb31
Movila Miresii RO 89 Jd36
Moviliţa RO 88 Jc37
Moyuela E 93 Cc41
Mozăceni RO 88 Jb37
Možajsk RUS 117 Ed10
Možga RUS 119 Ga08
Mozirje SLO 73 Ga36
Mozuli RUS 53 Jb21
Mrągowo PL 59 Hb25
Mrčajevci SRB 87 Hb39
Mrežičko MK 101 Hd42
Mrkonjić Grad BIH 86 Gc38
Mrkopalj HR 85 Ga37
Mrzeżyno PL 57 Gb25
Mšanec' UA 67 Hc31
Mscislav BY 121 Ec12
Mšenélázně CZ 65 Ga30
Mučkapskij RUS 123 Fc12
Muckross IRL 22 Bd25
Mudanya TR 103 Kb42
Muel E 80 Cc40
Mügeln D 65 Fd29
Mühlacker D 63 Ed32
Mühldorf D 72 Fc33
Mühlhausen D 64 Fb29
Muhovo BG 102 Jb40
Mukačeve UA 67 Hd32
Mula E 107 Ca44
Mülheim (Ruhr) D 55 Ec28
Mulhos FIN 35 Hc10
Mulhouse F 71 Ec33
Müllheim D 71 Ec33
Mullingar IRL 19 Cb23
Müllrose D 57 Ga28
Mullsjö S 44 Ga20
Multia FIN 40 Hc14
Munaðarnes IS 14 Bd04
Münchberg D 64 Fc30
Müncheberg D 57 Ga27
München D 72 Fc33
Mundesley GB 25 Dd26
Mundford GB 25 Dc26
Munera E 92 Ca43
Mungia E 80 Cb37
Muniesa E 93 Cc41
Munka-Ljungby S 49 Fd22
Munkebo DK 49 Fb23
Munkedal S 43 Fc19
Munkfors S 44 Fd17
Münsingen D 72 Fa33
Münster CH 71 Ed35
Münster D 55 Ed28
Munster D 56 Fb27
Munster F 71 Ec33
Munteni RO 77 Jd35
Münzkirchen A 73 Fd33
Muodoslompolo S 30 Ha07
Muonio FIN 30 Ha07
Muradiye TR 113 Ka44
Murat F 69 Dc36
Muratlı TR 103 Ka41
Murato F 96 Ed40
Murau A 73 Ga34
Muravera I 97 Ed44
Murça P 78 Ba39

Murcia E 107 Cb45
Mur-de-Barrez F 81 Dc37
Mur-de-Bretagne F 60 Cc31
Mureck A 73 Gb35
Mürefte TR 103 Ka42
Muret F 81 Da38
Murgeni RO 77 Jd35
Murgia E 79 Ca38
Murighiol RO 89 Ka36
Murjek S 34 Gd09
Murmaši RUS 31 Ja05
Murnau D 72 Fb34
Muro E 95 Db43
Muro del Alcoy E 107 Cb44
Muro Lucano I 99 Gb43
Murom RUS 118 Fb10
Muros E 78 Ad36
Murrhardt D 64 Fa32
Murska Sobota SLO 73 Gb35
Mursko Središće HR 74 Gc35
Murten CH 71 Ec34
Murter HR 85 Gb39
Mürzzuschlag A 73 Gb34
Muša RUS 119 Fd08
Musorka RUS 119 Ga10
Musselburgh GB 21 Da21
Mussidan F 69 Da36
Mussomeli I 108 Fd47
Mussy-sur-Seine F 70 Ea33
Mustafakemalpaşa TR 103 Kb42
Mustér CH 71 Ed35
Mustjala EST 46 Hb19
Mustla EST 47 Hd19
Mustvee EST 47 Ja18
Muszyna PL 67 Hb31
Mut TR 128 Gb17
Mutovaara FIN 35 Ja09
Muurame FIN 40 Hc14
Muurasjärvi FIN 35 Hc12
Muurola FIN 30 Hb08
Muxía E 78 Ad36
Muzillac F 60 Cc32
Mychajlivka UA 126 Fa16
Myckelgensjö S 33 Gc12
Myczków PL 67 Hc31
Myjava SK 66 Gc32
Mykolajiv UA 67 Hd31
Mykolajiv UA 125 Ed16
Mykolajivka UA 126 Fa17
Myllykoski FIN 41 Hd16
Mynämäki FIN 40 Ha16
Myrdal N 36 Fa16
Myre N 28 Ga06
Myre N 28 Gb05
Myrhorod UA 121 Ed14
Myrland N 28 Gb06
Myrlandshaugen N 28 Gb06
Myrmoen N 37 Fd14
Myronivka UA 121 Ec15
Myrskylä FIN 41 Hd16
Myrtou CY 128 Gb18
Myrviken S 38 Ga13
Mysen N 43 Fc18

Myślenice PL 67 Ha31
Myślibórz PL 57 Ga27
Myslivka UA 67 Hd32
Mysovka RUS 52 Hb24
Myszków PL 67 Ha30
Myszyniec PL 59 Hb26
Mytilíni GR 113 Jd44
Mytišči RUS 117 Ed10
Mýtna SK 74 Ha33

N

Naantali FIN 40 Hb16
Naarva FIN 41 Jb12
Naas IRL 19 Cb24
Näätämö FIN 27 Hc04
Nabburg D 64 Fc31
Naberežny Čelny RUS 119 Ga08
Nabuvoll N 37 Fc14
Náchod CZ 65 Gb30
Nadarzyce PL 57 Gb26
Nådendal FIN 40 Hb16
Nadežda UA 77 Kb34
Nădlac RO 75 Hb36
Nadvirna UA 76 Ja32
Nadvirna UA 124 Ea16
Nærbø N 42 Ed19
Næstved DK 49 Fc24
Náfpaktos GR 110 Hd46
Náfplio GR 111 Ja47
Nagajbakovo RUS 119 Ga08
Naggen S 38 Gb14
Nagłowice PL 67 Ha30
Nagor'e RUS 117 Ed09
Nagu Nauvo FIN 46 Ha17
Nagyatád H 74 Gc36
Nagybajom H 74 Gc35
Nagyhalász H 75 Hc33
Nagyigmánd H 74 Gd34
Nagykanizsa H 74 Gc35
Nagykáta H 74 Ha34
Nagykörös H 74 Ha34
Nagylak RO 75 Hb36
Nagyszénás H 75 Hb35
Nahačiv UA 67 Hd30
Naila D 64 Fc30
Nairn GB 17 Da19
Najac F 81 Db37
Nájera E 79 Ca39
Naklik PL 67 Hc30
Nakło nad Notecią PL 58 Gc26
Nakskov DK 49 Fc24
Nalbant RO 89 Ka36
Nal'čik RUS 127 Ga17
Nälden S 38 Ga13
Nałęczów PL 67 Hc29
Nálepkovo SK 67 Hb32
Näljänkä FIN 35 Hd10
Nalžovské Hory CZ 65 Fd32
Náměšť nad Oslavou CZ 65 Gb32
Námestovo SK 67 Ha31
Nämpnäs FIN 40 Ha14

Namsos N 32 Fc11
Namsskogan N 32 Fd11
Namur B 63 Eb29
Namysłów PL 66 Gc29
Nancy F 63 Eb32
Nangis F 62 Dd32
Nanterre F 62 Dc31
Nantes F 68 Cd33
Nanteuil-le-Haudouin F 62 Dd31
Nantua F 70 Ea35
Nantwich GB 24 Da25
Náousa GR 115 Jd47
Náoussa GR 101 Hd43
Napoli I 98 Fd43
När S 51 Gd21
Narač BY 53 Ja23
Narač BY 53 Ja24
Narač BY 120 Ea12
Narberth GB 23 Cc26
Narbonne F 81 Dc39
Nardò I 100 Gd44
Narečenski bani BG 102 Jb41
Narew PL 59 Hc26
Narewka PL 59 Hd26
Narkaus FIN 35 Hc09
Narken S 30 Ha08
Narman TR 127 Ga19
Narni I 98 Fc41
Naro-Fominsk RUS 117 Ed10
Narovlja BY 121 Eb13
Närpes FIN 40 Ha14
Närpiö FIN 40 Ha14
Nartkala RUS 127 Ga17
Narva EST 47 Ja17
Narva-Jõesuu EST 47 Ja17
Närvijoki FIN 40 Ha14
Narvik N 28 Gb06
Naryškino RUS 121 Ed12
Nås S 44 Ga17
Năsăud RO 76 Ja34
Nasavrky CZ 65 Gb31
Nasbinals F 81 Dc37
Našice HR 86 Gd37
Nasielsk PL 59 Hb27
Naso I 109 Ga46
Nassau D 63 Ed30
Nässjö S 44 Ga20
Nastola FIN 41 Hd15
Näsviken S 38 Gb15
Natalinci SRB 87 Hb38
Nattavaara S 29 Gd08
Nättraby S 50 Gb22
Naturno I 72 Fb35
Naturns I 72 Fb35
Nauders A 72 Fb35
Nauen D 57 Fd27
Naujoji Akmenė LT 52 Hc22
Naumburg D 64 Fc29
Naumovskij RUS 123 Fd15
Naustdal N 36 Ed15
Nautijaur S 29 Gc08
Nautsi RUS 27 Hd05
Nava E 79 Bc37

Navacerrada E 92 Bd40
Navahermosa E 91 Bc42
Navahrudak BY 120 Ea13
Navalcarnero E 92 Bd41
Navalmanzano E 92 Bd40
Navalmanzano E 92 Bd40
Navalmoral de la Mata E 91 Bb41
Navalvillar de Pela E 91 Bb42
Navan IRL 19 Cb23
Navapolack BY 117 Eb11
Navarcles E 81 Da40
Navarrenx F 80 Cc38
Navarrés E 93 Cb43
Navascués E 80 Cc39
Navas del Madroño E 91 Ba41
Navasëlki BY 121 Eb13
Navašino RUS 118 Fb10
Nävekvarn S 44 Gb19
Navelgas E 78 Bb36
Navia E 78 Bb36
Navlja RUS 121 Ed12
Năvodari RO 89 Ka37
Navoloki RUS 118 Fa09
Náxos GR 115 Jd47
Nay F 80 Cd38
Nazaré P 90 Ac40
Nazilli TR 113 Kb45
Ndroq RKS 100 Hb42
Néa Aghíalos GR 101 Ja44
Néa Artáki GR 112 Jb45
Néa Epídavros GR 111 Ja46
Néa Fókea GR 101 Ja43
Néa Ionía GR 101 Ja44
Néa Kalikrátia GR 101 Ja43
Néa Mihanióna GR 101 Ja43
Néa Moudania GR 101 Ja43
Néa Péramos GR 102 Jb42
Neápoli GR 101 Hc43
Neápoli GR 111 Ja48
Neápoli GR 115 Jd49
Neath GB 23 Cc26
Néa Triglia GR 101 Ja43
Néa Zíhni GR 102 Jb42
Nebiler TR 113 Ka44
Nebolči RUS 117 Ec08
Neckargemünd D 63 Ed31
Neckarsulm D 64 Fa32
Nedelišće HR 73 Gb35
Nederweert NL 55 Eb28
Neðribær IS 14 Bc04
Nedryhajliv UA 121 Ed14
Nedstrand N 42 Ed18
Negotin SRB 87 Hd38
Negotino MK 101 Hd42
Negraşi RO 88 Jb37
Nègrepelisse F 81 Db37
Negreşti RO 77 Jd34
Negreşti-Oaş RO 75 Hd33
Negru Vodă RO 89 Ka38
Nehaevskij RUS 123 Fc13
Neja RUS 118 Fb08
Nekla PL 58 Gc27
Nekrasovskoe RUS 118 Fa09

Nelaug N 42 Fa19
Nelidovo RUS 117 Ec10
Nellim FIN 27 Hc05
Nelson GB 21 Da24
Neman RUS 52 Hb24
Nemenčinė LT 53 Ja24
Nemours F 62 Dc32
Nemšová SK 66 Gd32
Nemyriv UA 67 Hd30
Nemyriv UA 121 Eb15
Nenagh IRL 18 Ca24
Nenitoúria GR 113 Jd45
Néo Erásmio GR 102 Jc42
Neohóri GR 101 Hd44
Néo Monastíri GR 101 Hd44
Néo Petrítsi GR 101 Ja42
Néos Marmarás GR 102 Jb43
Néos Skopós GR 101 Ja42
Nepolje RKS 87 Hb40
Nepomuk CZ 65 Fd31
Neptun RO 89 Ka38
Nérac F 81 Da37
Neratovice CZ 65 Ga30
Nerehta RUS 118 Fa09
Nereju RO 76 Jc35
Neresheim D 64 Fb32
Nereta LV 53 Hd22
Nergnäset S 34 Ha10
Neringa-Nida LT 52 Ha23
Nerja E 106 Bc45
Nerl' RUS 117 Ed09
Nérondes F 69 Dc34
Nerpio E 107 Ca44
Nerušaj UA 77 Kb35
Nerva E 105 Ad43
Nervi I 83 Ed38
Nes N 36 Fa15
Nes N 37 Fb16
Nesbyen N 37 Fb16
Nesebăr BG 89 Ka39
Nesflaten N 42 Ed17
Nesheim N 36 Ed16
Nesjahverfi IS 15 Cb08
Neskaupstaður IS 15 Cc07
Neslandsvatn N 43 Fb19
Nesle F 62 Dd30
Nesna N 32 Fd09
Nesodden N 43 Fc18
Nestáni GR 111 Ja47
Nestavoll N 37 Fb14
Nesterov RUS 52 Hc24
Nestiary RUS 119 Fc09
Nesttun N 36 Ed16
Nesvik N 42 Ed18
Nettetal D 55 Ec28
Nettuno I 98 Fc42
Neubrandenburg D 57 Fd26
Neubukow D 56 Fc25
Neuburg an der Donau D 64 Fb32
Neuchâtel CH 71 Ec34
Neuenhagen D 57 Fd27
Neuenhaus D 55 Ec27
Neuenkirchen D 56 Fb26
Neuf-Brisach F 71 Ec33

Neufchâteau B 63 Eb30
Neufchâteau F 63 Eb32
Neufchâtel-en-Bray F 62 Dc30
Neufchâtel-sur-Aisne F 62 Ea31
Neuhaus D 56 Fb26
Neuhaus D 64 Fb30
Neuhof D 64 Fa30
Neuillé-Pont-Pierre F 69 Db33
Neukirchen A 72 Fc34
Neulengbach A 73 Gb33
Neum BIH 86 Gd40
Neumarkt A 73 Ga35
Neumarkt in der Oberpfalz D 64 Fc32
Neumarkt-Sankt Veit D 72 Fc33
Neumünster D 56 Fb25
Neunburg D 64 Fc31
Neung-sur-Beuvron F 69 Dc33
Neunkirchen A 73 Gb34
Neunkirchen D 63 Ec31
Neuruppin D 57 Fd27
Neusiedl A 74 Gc33
Neuss D 63 Ec29
Neustadt D 56 Fb25
Neustadt D 64 Fb30
Neustadt (Aisch) D 64 Fb31
Neustadt (Donau) D 64 Fc32
Neustadt (Orla) D 64 Fc30
Neustadt (Weinstraße) D 63 Ed31
Neustadt/Dosse D 56 Fc27
Neustadt am Rübenberg D 56 Fa27
Neustadt-Glewe D 56 Fc26
Neustift A 72 Fb34
Neustrelitz D 57 Fd26
Neutraubling D 64 Fc32
Neu-Ulm D 72 Fa33
Neuvic F 69 Dc36
Neuville-aux-Bois F 62 Dc32
Neuville-de-Poitou F 69 Da34
Neuville-sur-Saône F 70 Ea35
Neuvy-sur-Barangeon F 69 Dc33
Neuwied D 63 Ed30
Neveklov CZ 65 Ga31
Nevel' RUS 117 Eb11
Nevers F 70 Dd34
Nevesinje BIH 86 Gd40
Nevestino BG 87 Hd40
Nevinnomyssk RUS 127 Fd16
Nevlunghavn N 43 Fb19
Nevskoe RUS 52 Hc24
Newark-on-Trent GB 25 Db25
Newbridge IRL 19 Cb24
Newbury GB 24 Da27

Newcastle GB 20 Cc23
Newcastle-under-Lyme GB 24 Da25
Newcastle upon Tyne GB 21 Db23
Newcastle West IRL 18 Bd24
Newhaven GB 25 Db28
Newmarket GB 25 Dc27
Newport GB 24 Cd27
Newport GB 24 Da28
Newport GB 24 Da25
Newport Pagnell GB 25 Db26
Newquay GB 23 Cb28
New Romney GB 25 Dc28
New Ross IRL 22 Ca25
Newry GB 20 Cc23
Newton Abbot GB 23 Cc28
Newtonmore GB 17 Da19
Newton Stewart GB 20 Cd22
Newtown GB 24 Cd25
Newtownabbey GB 20 Cc22
Newtownards GB 20 Cc22
Newtown Saint Boswells GB 21 Da22
Newtownstewart GB 20 Cb22
Nexø DK 50 Ga24
Nezvys'ko UA 76 Jb32
Nianfors S 38 Gb15
Nibe DK 49 Fb21
Nicaj-Shalë AL 100 Hb41
Nice F 83 Eb39
Nicgale LV 53 Ja22
Nicosia I 109 Ga47
Nicotera I 109 Gb46
Niculiţel RO 89 Ka36
Nidda D 64 Fa30
Nidderau D 64 Fa30
Nidri GR 110 Hc45
Nidzica PL 58 Ha26
Niebüll D 48 Fa24
Niedalino PL 57 Gb25
Niederaula D 64 Fa29
Niederbronn-les-Bains F 63 Ec32
Niedrzwica Duża PL 67 Hc29
Nielisz PL 67 Hc29
Niemce PL 67 Hc29
Niemisel S 34 Ha09
Nienburg D 56 Fa27
Nierstein D 63 Ed31
Niesky D 65 Ga29
Nieuwegein NL 55 Eb27
Nieuwpoort B 54 Dd28
Niewęgłosz PL 59 Hc28
Niezabyszewo PL 58 Gc25
Niğde TR 128 Gd15
Nigríta GR 101 Ja42
Nijar E 106 Bd46
Nijkerk NL 55 Eb27
Nijmegen NL 55 Ec28
Nijverdal NL 55 Ec27
Níkea GR 101 Hd44

Nikel' RUS 27 Hd04
Nikifóros GR 102 Jb42
Nikitas GR 102 Jb43
Nikkaluokta S 29 Gc07
Nikolaevka RUS 119 Fd10
Nikolaevo BG 102 Jc40
Nikolaevo RUS 47 Jb19
Nikolaevo RUS 123 Fd13
Nikol'sk RUS 119 Fd10
Nikopol BG 88 Jb38
Nikopol' UA 126 Fa16
Nikópoli GR 110 Hc45
Nikšić MNE 86 Ha40
Nilivaara S 30 Ha08
Nilsiä FIN 35 Hd12
Nîmes F 82 Dd38
Nin HR 85 Ga38
Ninove B 62 Ea29
Niort F 68 Cd34
Niš SRB 87 Hc39
Nisa P 90 Ad41
Niscemi I 109 Ga48
Niška Banja SRB 87 Hd39
Nisko PL 67 Hc30
Nisou CY 128 Gb19
Nisporeni MD 77 Jd33
Nissedal N 42 Fa18
Nissi EST 46 Hc18
Nissilä FIN 35 Hd12
Nitaure LV 53 Hd21
Nitra SK 74 Gd33
Nitrianske Pravno SK 66 Gd32
Nittedal N 43 Fc17
Nittenau D 64 Fc32
Nivala FIN 35 Hc12
Nivelles B 62 Ea29
Nivenskoe RUS 52 Ha24
Nižná Boca SK 67 Ha32
Nižnekamsk RUS 119 Ga08
Nižnij Novgorod RUS 118 Fb09
Nižyn UA 121 Ec14
Nizza Monferrato I 83 Ed37
Njasviž BY 120 Ea13
Njivice HR 85 Ga37
Njurundabommen S 39 Gc14
Noailles F 62 Dc31
Noci I 99 Gc43
Nodeland N 42 Fa20
Nödinge-Nol S 43 Fc20
Nœux-les-Mines F 62 Dd29
Nogales E 91 Ba42
Nogarejas E 78 Bb38
Nogent F 71 Eb33
Nogent-le-Roi F 62 Dc31
Nogent-le-Rotrou F 61 Db32
Nogent-sur-Seine F 62 Dd32
Noginsk RUS 118 Fa10
Noguera E 93 Cb41
Nohfelden D 63 Ec31
Noia E 78 Ad36
Noirétable F 70 Dd35
Noirmoutier-en-l'Île F 68 Cc33

Nokia FIN 40 Hb15
Nola I 99 Ga43
Nolay F 70 Ea34
Nomeny F 63 Eb32
Nomitsís GR 111 Ja48
Nonancourt F 61 Db31
Nonantola I 84 Fb38
Nontron F 69 Da35
Nonza F 96 Ed40
Noordwijk aan Zee NL 55 Eb27
Noormarkku FIN 40 Ha15
Nora S 44 Ga18
Norberg S 44 Gb17
Norcia I 85 Fd40
Nordagutu N 43 Fb18
Nordborg DK 49 Fb24
Nordby DK 48 Fa23
Nordby DK 49 Fb23
Norddal N 36 Ed15
Norden D 55 Ed26
Nordenham D 56 Fa26
Norderstedt D 56 Fb26
Nordfjordeid N 36 Ed14
Nordfold N 28 Ga07
Nordhausen D 64 Fb29
Nordholz D 56 Fa25
Nordhorn D 55 Ed27
Nordingrå S 39 Gc13
Nordkjosbotn N 26 Gc05
Nördlingen D 64 Fb32
Nordmaling S 34 Gd12
Nordmark S 44 Ga18
Nordmela N 28 Gb05
Nordøyvågen N 32 Fd09
Nordre Osen N 37 Fc16
Nord-Sel N 37 Fb15
Noresund N 43 Fb17
Norheimsund N 36 Ed16
Norråker S 33 Gb11
Norra Tresund S 33 Gb11
Norrbäck S 33 Gc11
Nørre Aaby DK 49 Fb23
Nørre Alslev DK 49 Fc24
Nørre Nebel DK 48 Fa23
Nørre Vorupør DK 48 Fa21
Norrfjärden S 34 Ha10
Norrfors S 33 Gc12
Norrhult S 50 Ga21
Norrköping S 44 Gb19
Norrsundet S 39 Gc16
Norrtälje S 45 Gd18
Nors DK 48 Fa21
Norsholm S 44 Gb19
Norsjö S 34 Gd11
Northallerton GB 21 Db23
Northampton GB 25 Db26
North Berwick GB 21 Db21
Northeim D 56 Fb28
North Kessock GB 17 Da19
Northleach GB 24 Da27
North Walsham GB 25 Dd26
Nortorf D 56 Fb25
Nort-sur-Erdre F 61 Cd32
Norwich GB 25 Dc26
Nosivka UA 121 Ec14

Nosovo RUS 47 Jb20
Nossebro S 43 Fd20
Nössemark S 43 Fc18
Nossen D 65 Fd29
Noszolop H 74 Gc34
Noto I 109 Ga48
Notodden N 43 Fb18
Nottingham GB 25 Db25
Növa EST 46 Hc18
Nova Borova UA 121 Eb14
Nová Bystřice CZ 65 Ga32
Novačene BG 88 Ja39
Novaci MK 101 Hc42
Novaci RO 88 Ja37
Nova Crnja SRB 75 Hb36
Nova Gorica SLO 73 Fd36
Nova Gradiška HR 86 Gc37
Novaja Derevnja RUS 52 Hb24
Novaja Ladoga RUS 117 Eb08
Novaja Ruda BY 59 Hd25
Nova Kachovka UA 126 Fa16
Novalja HR 85 Ga38
Novalukoml' BY 121 Eb12
Nova Odesa UA 125 Ed16
Novara I 71 Ed36
Nova Topola BIH 86 Gc37
Nova Ušycja UA 125 Eb16
Nova Varoš SRB 87 Hb39
Nova Vodolaha UA 122 Fa14
Nova Zagora BG 102 Jc40
Nové Hrady CZ 65 Ga32
Novellara I 84 Fb37
Nové Město nad Metují CZ 65 Gb30
Nové Město na Moravě CZ 65 Gb31
Nové Zámky SK 74 Gd33
Novgorod RUS 117 Eb09
Novgorodka RUS 47 Jb20
Novhorodka UA 121 Ed15
Novhorod-Sivers'kyj UA 121 Ed13
Novi Bečej SRB 75 Hb36
Novi Bilokorovyči UA 121 Eb14
Novi Grad BIH 86 Gd37
Novigrad HR 85 Fd37
Novigrad-Podravski HR 74 Gc36
Novi Iskăr BG 102 Ja40
Novi Ligure I 83 Ed37
Novion-Porcien F 62 Ea31
Novi Pazar BG 89 Jd38
Novi Pazar SRB 87 Hb40
Novi Sad SRB 86 Ha37
Novi Sanžary UA 121 Ed15
Novi Vinodolski HR 85 Ga37
Novoaleksandrovsk RUS 127 Fd16
Novoanninskij RUS 123 Fc13
Novoarchanhel's'k UA 121 Ec15

Novoazovs'k **UA** 126 Fb16
Novočeboksarsk **RUS** 119 Fc09
Novočerkassk **RUS** 123 Fc15
Novocimljanskaja **RUS** 123 Fd14
Novofedorivka **UA** 125 Ed17
Novohrad-Volyns'kyj **UA** 121 Eb14
Novokašpirskij **RUS** 119 Ga10
Novokrasne **MD** 77 Kb32
Novokubansk **RUS** 127 Fd16
Novokujbyševsk **RUS** 119 Ga10
Novo Mesto **SLO** 73 Ga36
Novomičurinsk **RUS** 118 Fa11
Novomihajlovskij **RUS** 127 Fc17
Novomoskovsk **RUS** 118 Fa11
Novomoskovs'k **UA** 122 Fa15
Novomykolajivka **UA** 122 Fa15
Novomykolajivka **UA** 125 Ed17
Novomyrhorod **UA** 121 Ed15
Novonikolaevskij **RUS** 123 Fc13
Novooleksijivka **UA** 126 Fa17
Novopavlovsk **RUS** 127 Ga17
Novopokrovka **UA** 122 Fa15
Novopokrovskaja **RUS** 127 Fd16
Novopskov **UA** 122 Fb14
Novorossijsk **RUS** 127 Fc17
Novoržev **RUS** 117 Eb10
Novošahtinsk **RUS** 123 Fc15
Novoselci **BG** 103 Jd40
Novosel'e **RUS** 47 Jb19
Novoselec **BG** 102 Jc40
Novoselivs'ke **UA** 126 Fa17
Novo Selo **BG** 88 Jc39
Novo Selo **BG** 101 Hd41
Novo Selo **BIH** 86 Gd37
Novoselycia **UA** 76 Jb32
Novosokol'niki **RUS** 117 Eb10
Novotroickoe **RUS** 119 Fc10
Novotrojic'ke **UA** 126 Fa17
Novotulka **RUS** 123 Ga12
Novoukrajinka **UA** 125 Ed16
Novoul'janovsk **RUS** 119 Fd10
Novouzensk **RUS** 123 Ga12
Novovolyns'k **UA** 67 Hd29
Novska **HR** 86 Gc37
Nový Bor **CZ** 65 Ga30
Novycja **UA** 76 Ja32
Novy Dvor **BY** 59 Hd26
Novy Dvor **BY** 59 Hd25
Novyi Oskol **RUS** 122 Fb13
Novyj Buh **UA** 125 Ed16
Nový Jičín **CZ** 66 Gd31
Novyj Rozdil **UA** 67 Hd31
Nowa Brzeźnica **PL** 66 Gd29

Nowa Cerekwia **PL** 66 Gd30
Nowa Dęba **PL** 67 Hc30
Nowa Karczma **PL** 58 Gd25
Nowa Ruda **PL** 65 Gb30
Nowa Słupia **PL** 67 Hb29
Nowa Sól **PL** 57 Gb28
Nowa Wieś **PL** 59 Hb26
Nowa Wieś Ełcka **PL** 59 Hc25
Nowa Wieś Lęborska **PL** 58 Gc25
Nowe Miasteczko **PL** 57 Gb28
Nowe Miasto **PL** 58 Ha27
Nowe Miasto nad Pilicą **PL** 58 Ha28
Nowe Warpno **PL** 57 Ga26
Nowinka **PL** 59 Hc25
Nowogard **PL** 57 Ga26
Nowogród **PL** 59 Hb26
Nowogród Bobrzański **PL** 57 Gb28
Nowo Miasto nad Wartą **PL** 58 Gc28
Nowosiółki **PL** 67 Hd30
Nowy Duninów **PL** 58 Ha27
Nowy Dwór **PL** 65 Gb29
Nowy Dwór Gdański **PL** 58 Gd25
Nowy Dwór Mazowiecki **PL** 59 Hb27
Nowy Korczyn **PL** 67 Hb30
Nowy Sącz **PL** 67 Hb31
Nowy Staw **PL** 58 Gd25
Nowy Targ **PL** 67 Ha31
Nowy Tomyśl **PL** 57 Gb28
Nowy Żmigród **PL** 67 Hb31
Noyant **F** 69 Da33
Noyers **F** 70 Dd33
Noyon **F** 62 Dd30
Nozay **F** 61 Cd32
Nucet **RO** 75 Hd35
Nudol' **RUS** 117 Ed10
Nudyže **UA** 59 Hd28
Nuenen **NL** 55 Eb28
Nufǎru **RO** 89 Ka36
Nuijamaa **FIN** 41 Ja15
Nuits-Saint-Georges **F** 70 Ea34
Nules **E** 93 Cc42
Nummela **FIN** 40 Hc16
Nummi **FIN** 40 Hc16
Nummijärvi **FIN** 40 Hb14
Nuneaton **GB** 24 Da26
Nunnanen **FIN** 30 Hb06
Nuorgam **FIN** 27 Hc04
Nuoro **I** 97 Ed43
Núpsstaður **IS** 15 Ca08
Nurlat **RUS** 119 Ga09
Nurmes **FIN** 35 Ja12
Nurmijärvi **FIN** 35 Ja12
Nurmijärvi **FIN** 40 Hc16
Nurmo **FIN** 40 Hb13
Nürnberg **D** 64 Fb31
Nürtingen **D** 64 Fa32
Nuşfalau **RO** 75 Hd34

Nusnäs **S** 38 Ga16
Nuupas **FIN** 35 Hc09
Nuvvus **FIN** 27 Hb04
Nyåker **S** 34 Gd12
Nybergsund **N** 37 Fd16
Nyborg **DK** 49 Fb24
Nyborg **S** 34 Ha09
Nybro **S** 50 Gb22
Nyékládháza **H** 75 Hb33
Nyergesújfalu **H** 74 Gd34
Nyhammar **S** 44 Ga17
Nýidalur **IS** 15 Ca07
Nyírábrány **H** 75 Hc34
Nyíradony **H** 75 Hc33
Nyírbátor **H** 75 Hc33
Nyírbéltek **H** 75 Hc33
Nyíregyháza **H** 75 Hc33
Nyirmada **H** 75 Hc33
Nyírtelek **H** 75 Hc33
Nykøbing F **DK** 49 Fc24
Nykøbing M **DK** 48 Fa21
Nykøbing S **DK** 49 Fc23
Nyköping **S** 45 Gc19
Nykroppa **S** 44 Ga18
Nykvarn **S** 45 Gc18
Nyland **S** 39 Gc13
Nymburk **CZ** 65 Ga30
Nynäshamn **S** 45 Gc19
Nyneset **N** 32 Fd11
Nyon **CH** 71 Eb35
Nyons **F** 82 Ea38
Nýřany **CZ** 65 Fc31
Nyrud **N** 27 Hd05
Nysa **PL** 66 Gc30
Nysäter **S** 43 Fd18
Nystad **FIN** 40 Ha16
Nysted **DK** 49 Fc24
Nyvoll **N** 26 Ha04
Nyžni Sirohozy **UA** 126 Fa16
Nyžni Torhaji **UA** 126 Fa16
Nyžni Vorota **UA** 67 Hd32
Nyžn'ohirs'kyj **UA** 126 Fa17

O

Oakham **GB** 25 Db26
Oban **GB** 16 Cd20
O Barco **E** 78 Bb37
Obbnäs **FIN** 46 Hc17
Obbola **S** 34 Gd12
Öbektaş **TR** 128 Gc15
Obeliai **LT** 53 Ja22
Oberammergau **D** 72 Fb34
Oberhausen **D** 55 Ec28
Oberkirch **D** 63 Ed32
Obernai **F** 63 Ec32
Obernburg **D** 64 Fa31
Oberndorf **A** 73 Fd33
Oberndorf **D** 71 Ed33
Oberpullendorf **A** 74 Gc34
Oberstdorf **D** 72 Fa34
Obertyn **UA** 76 Ja32
Oberviechtach **D** 64 Fc31
Oberwart **A** 73 Gb34
Óbidos **P** 90 Ac41

Obninsk **RUS** 117 Ed11
Obodivka **UA** 77 Ka32
Obojan' **RUS** 122 Fa13
Obolon' **UA** 121 Ed15
Oborniki **PL** 58 Gc27
Oborniki Śląskie **PL** 66 Gc29
Oborowo **PL** 58 Gd27
Obory **CZ** 65 Ga31
Obrenovac **SRB** 87 Hb38
Obrež **HR** 73 Gb36
Obrovac **HR** 85 Gb38
Obruk **TR** 128 Gc15
Obsza **PL** 67 Hc30
Obzor **BG** 89 Ka39
Obžyle **UA** 77 Ka32
Očakiv **UA** 125 Ed17
Ocaña **E** 92 Bd41
Očeretuvate **UA** 126 Fa16
Ochsenfurt **D** 64 Fa31
Ochsenhausen **D** 72 Fa33
Ochtrup **D** 55 Ed27
Ochtyrka **UA** 121 Ed14
Ocieka **PL** 67 Hb30
Ockelbo **S** 38 Gb16
Ocland **RO** 76 Jb35
Ocna Mureş **RO** 76 Ja35
Ocna Sibiului **RO** 88 Ja36
Ocnele Mari **RO** 88 Ja37
Ocniţa **MD** 76 Jc32
Ocoliş **RO** 75 Hd35
Ödåkra **S** 49 Fd22
Odda **N** 42 Ed17
Odden Færgehavn **DK** 49 Fc23
Odder **DK** 49 Fb23
Odeceixe **P** 104 Ab43
Odemira **P** 104 Ab43
Ödemiş **TR** 113 Kb45
Odensbacken **S** 44 Gb18
Odense **DK** 49 Fb23
Oderzo **I** 72 Fc36
Odesa **UA** 77 Kb34
Odesa **UA** 125 Ec17
Odincovo **RUS** 117 Ed10
Odobasca **RO** 88 Jc36
Odobeşti **RO** 77 Jd35
Odolanów **PL** 66 Gc29
Odoorn **NL** 55 Ec27
Odorheiu Secuiesc **RO** 76 Jb35
Odry **CZ** 66 Gd31
Odrzywół **PL** 58 Ha28
Ødsted **DK** 49 Fb23
Odžaci **SRB** 86 Ha37
Odžak **BIH** 86 Gd37
Oebisfelde **D** 56 Fb27
Ǿekény **H** 74 Ha34
Oelsnitz **D** 64 Fc30
Oettingen **D** 64 Fb32
Oetz **A** 72 Fb34
Offenbach **D** 63 Ed30
Offenburg **D** 63 Ed32
Ogošte **RKS** 87 Hc40
Ogre **LV** 53 Hd21
Ogrodniki **PL** 59 Hc25
Ogrodzieniec **PL** 67 Ha30

Ogulin HR 85 Gb37
Ohrid MK 101 Hc42
Öhringen D 64 Fa32
Oijärvi FIN 35 Hc09
Oikarainen FIN 31 Hc08
Oisemont F 62 Dc30
Oitti FIN 40 Hc16
Öja FIN 34 Hb12
Öje S 38 Ga16
Öjebyn S 34 Ha10
Ojos Negros E 93 Cb41
Ojrzeń PL 58 Ha27
Öjung S 38 Gb15
Okartowo PL 59 Hb25
Okehampton GB 23 Cc28
Okkelberg N 37 Fc13
Okovcy RUS 117 Ec10
Okrzeja PL 59 Hc28
Oksbøl DK 48 Fa23
Øksfjord N 26 Gd04
Okstad N 37 Fc13
Oktjabr'sk RUS 119 Ga10
Oktjabr'skij RUS 123 Fd14
Okučani HR 86 Gc37
Okulovka RUS 117 Ec09
Ólafsfjörður IS 15 Ca05
Ólafsvik IS 14 Bb05
Olaine LV 52 Hc21
Olargues F 81 Dc38
Oława PL 66 Gc29
Olbernhau D 65 Fd30
Olbia I 96 Ed42
Oldeide N 36 Ed14
Olden N 36 Fa15
Olden S 33 Ga12
Oldenburg D 55 Ed26
Oldenburg in Holstein D 56 Fb25
Oldenzaal NL 55 Ec27
Olderdalen N 26 Gd05
Olderfjord N 27 Hb03
Oldervik N 26 Gc04
Oldham GB 21 Da24
Oldmeldrum GB 17 Db19
Olecko PL 59 Hc25
Oleggio I 71 Ed36
Oleiros P 90 Ad40
Oleksandrija UA 121 Ed15
Oleksandrivka MD 77 Kb32
Oleksandrivka UA 121 Ed15
Oleksandrivka UA 121 Ed15
Oleksandrivka UA 122 Fb15
Oleksandrivka UA 125 Ed17
Ølen N 42 Ed17
Olenino RUS 117 Ec10
Olenivka UA 125 Ed17
Oleśnica PL 66 Gc29
Olesno PL 66 Gd29
Oleszno PL 67 Ha29
Oleszyce PL 67 Hd30
Olevs'k UA 121 Eb14
Olfen D 55 Ed28
Ølgod DK 48 Fa23
Olhão P 104 Ac44
Olhava FIN 35 Hc10
Ol'hi RUS 118 Fb11

Ol'hovatka RUS 122 Fb13
Ol'hovka RUS 123 Fd13
Oliena I 97 Ed43
Olimbía GR 110 Hd47
Olimp RO 89 Ka37
Olimpiáda GR 102 Jb42
Olite E 80 Cb39
Oliva E 94 Cc44
Oliva de la Frontera E 105 Ad43
Oliveira de Azeméis P 78 Ad39
Oliveira do Hospital P 90 Ad40
Olivenza E 90 Ad42
Olivet F 62 Dc32
Olkusz PL 67 Ha30
Ollerton GB 25 Db25
Olmedo E 79 Bc39
Olmeto F 96 Ed41
Olofström S 50 Ga22
Olomouc CZ 66 Gc31
Olovo BIH 86 Gd38
Olpe D 63 Ed29
Ol'ša RUS 117 Ec11
Olsberg D 63 Ed29
Olshammar S 44 Ga19
Olszamy PL 59 Hb28
Olszanka PL 59 Hc25
Olsztyn PL 58 Ha25
Olsztynek PL 58 Ha26
Olszyna PL 57 Ga28
Oltedal N 42 Ed18
Olten CH 71 Ed34
Olteniţa RO 89 Jd38
Oltina RO 89 Jd37
Oltu TR 127 Ga19
Oltuš BY 59 Hd28
Olukpınar TR 128 Gb17
Olur TR 127 Ga19
Olustvere EST 47 Hd19
Ólvega E 80 Cb40
Olvera E 105 Ba45
Ólymbos GR 115 Kb48
Omagh GB 20 Cb22
Omali GR 101 Hc43
Omarska BIH 86 Gc37
Omegna I 71 Ed36
Omiš HR 86 Gc39
Ommen NL 55 Ec27
Omurtag BG 89 Jd39
Onda E 93 Cc42
Ondarroa E 80 Cb37
Oneşti RO 76 Jc35
Onich GB 16 Cd20
Ontinyent E 107 Cb44
Ontojoki FIN 35 Ja11
Ontur E 107 Ca44
Onuškis LT 53 Hd22
Oostburg NL 54 Ea28
Oostende B 54 Dd28
Oosterend NL 55 Eb26
Oosterhout NL 55 Eb28

Oosterwolde NL 55 Ec26
Oostkapelle NL 54 Ea28
Oost-Vlieland NL 55 Eb26
Opaka BG 88 Jc38
Oparić SRB 87 Hc39
Opatija HR 85 Ga37
Opatów PL 66 Gd29
Opatów PL 67 Hb29
Opava CZ 66 Gd31
Ope S 38 Ga13
Opišnja UA 121 Ed14
Opličići BIH 86 Gd40
Opočka RUS 53 Jb21
Opoczno PL 67 Ha29
Opole PL 66 Gd30
Opol'e RUS 47 Jb17
Opole Lubelskie PL 67 Hc29
Opovo SRB 87 Hb37
Oppdal N 37 Fb14
Oppenheim D 63 Ed31
Opsa BY 53 Ja23
Opuzen HR 86 Gd40
Ora I 72 Fb35
Oradea RO 75 Hc34
Orahova BIH 86 Gc37
Orahovac RKS 87 Hb40
Orahovačko Polje BIH 86 Gd38
Orahovica BIH 86 Gd38
Orahovica HR 86 Gd37
Oraison F 82 Ea38
Orajärvi FIN 30 Hb08
Orange F 82 Dd38
Oranienburg D 57 Fd27
Oranmore IRL 18 Bd23
Orăştie RO 75 Hd36
Oraşu Nou RO 75 Hd33
Oravainen FIN 40 Ha13
Oraviţa RO 87 Hc37
Oravská Lesná SK 67 Ha31
Oravská Polhora SK 67 Ha31
Oravský Podzámok SK 67 Ha31
Orbassano I 83 Ec37
Orbeasca RO 88 Jb38
Orbec F 61 Db31
Orbetello I 98 Fb41
Örbyhus S 45 Gc17
Orce E 106 Bd45
Orchowo PL 58 Gd27
Orcières F 83 Eb37
Ordes E 78 Ba36
Ordu TR 127 Fc19
Orduña E 79 Ca38
Ordžonikidze UA 126 Fa16
Ordžonikidzevskij RUS 127 Ga17
Orea E 93 Cb41
Orebić HR 86 Gc40
Örebro S 44 Ga18
Oredež RUS 117 Eb09
Öregrund S 45 Gc17
Orehovno RUS 47 Jb18
Orehovo-Zuevo RUS 118 Fa10
Orel RUS 47 Ja18

Orel RUS 121 Ed12
Ören TR 113 Kb46
Orense E 78 Ba37
Orestiada GR 103 Jd41
Öreström S 33 Gc12
Orford GB 25 Dc27
Organyà E 81 Da40
Orgaz E 92 Bd42
Orgelet F 70 Ea35
Órgiva E 106 Bc45
Orgosolo I 97 Ed43
Orhei MD 77 Ka33
Orhomenós GR 111 Ja45
Oria E 106 Bd45
Orichiv UA 126 Fa16
Orihuela E 107 Cb44
Orijahovo BG 88 Ja38
Orimattila FIN 41 Hd16
Ório GR 112 Jb45
Oriolo I 99 Gc44
Orissaare EST 46 Hb19
Oristano I 97 Ec44
Őriszentpéter H 74 Gc35
Orivesi FIN 40 Hc15
Ørje N 43 Fc18
Orkanger N 37 Fc13
Örkelljunga S 49 Fd22
Orlea RO 88 Jb38
Orléans F 62 Dc32
Orleşti RO 88 Ja37
Orlivka UA 89 Ka36
Orlja BY 59 Hd25
Orlov Gaj RUS 123 Ga12
Orlovskij RUS 123 Fd15
Orly F 62 Dc31
Ormea I 83 Ec38
Órmos Panórmou GR 112 Jc46
Ormož SLO 73 Gb35
Ormskirk GB 21 Da24
Ornans F 71 Eb34
Ørnes N 28 Ga08
Orneta PL 58 Ha25
Örnsköldsvik S 39 Gc13
Oropesa E 91 Bb41
Orosei I 97 Ed43
Orosháza H 75 Hb35
Oroszlány H 74 Gd34
Orpesa E 93 Cc42
Orrefors S 50 Gb22
Orrliden S 38 Fd16
Orrviken S 38 Ga13
Orša BY 121 Eb12
Orsa S 38 Ga16
Oršac BIH 85 Gb38
Orşova RO 87 Hd37
Ørsta N 36 Ed14
Örsundsbro S 45 Gc18
Ortakaraören TR 128 Ga16
Ortakent TR 113 Kb46
Ortaklar TR 113 Kb45
Ortaköy TR 103 Jd42
Ortaköy TR 127 Ga19
Orta Nova I 99 Gb42
Orta San Giulio I 71 Ed36
Orte I 98 Fc41

Orthez F 80 Cc38
Ortigueira E 78 Ba36
Ortisei I 72 Fc35
Ortnevik N 36 Ed15
Orto F 96 Ed41
Ortona I 99 Ga41
Ortrand D 65 Fd29
Orvault F 68 Cd33
Orvieto I 84 Fc40
Orzesze PL 66 Gd30
Orzinuovi I 84 Fa37
Orživ UA 120 Ea14
Oržycja UA 121 Ed15
Orzysz PL 59 Hb25
Os N 37 Fc14
Osby S 50 Ga22
Oschatz D 65 Fd29
Oschersleben D 56 Fc28
Oschiri I 97 Ed43
Ose N 42 Fa18
Osečina SRB 86 Ha38
Osen N 32 Fc11
Osenovlag BG 88 Ja39
Osieczna PL 58 Gc28
Osieczno PL 57 Gb27
Osiek PL 58 Gd26
Osijek HR 74 Ha36
Osimo I 85 Fd39
Osinów PL 57 Ga27
Osjaków PL 66 Gd29
Osječenica MNE 86 Ha40
Oskarshamn S 50 Gb21
Oskarström S 49 Fd22
Os'kino RUS 122 Fb13
Oslo N 43 Fc17
Os'mino RUS 47 Jb18
Ösmo S 45 Gc19
Osmolda UA 76 Ja32
Osnabrück D 55 Ed27
Ośno Lubuskie PL 57 Ga27
Osor HR 85 Ga38
Osorno la Mayor E 79 Bd38
Osøyro N 42 Ed17
Oss NL 55 Eb28
Ossa de Montiel E 92 Bd43
Östansjö S 44 Ga19
Ostaškov RUS 117 Ec10
Ostatija SRB 87 Hb39
Östavall S 38 Gb14
Østby N 37 Fd16
Osterburg D 56 Fc27
Osterburken D 64 Fa31
Österbybruk S 45 Gc17
Österbymo S 44 Gb20
Österforse S 38 Gb13
Osterhofen D 65 Fd32
Osterholz-Scharmbeck D 56 Fa26
Øster Hurup DK 49 Fb21
Osterode D 56 Fb28
Östersund S 38 Ga13
Östervåla S 45 Gc17
Östhammar S 45 Gc17
Östmark S 44 Fd17
Ostra RO 76 Jb33
Ostrava CZ 66 Gd31

Ostren i madhë RKS 100 Hb42
Ostritz D 65 Ga29
Ostróda PL 58 Ha26
Ostrogožsk RUS 122 Fb13
Ostroh UA 120 Ea15
Ostrołęka PL 59 Hb26
Ostrov CZ 65 Fd30
Ostrov RO 89 Jd37
Ostrov RO 89 Ka36
Ostrov RUS 47 Jb20
Ostrowice PL 57 Gb26
Ostrowiec Świętokrzyski PL 67 Hb29
Ostrowieczno PL 58 Gc28
Ostrowite PL 58 Gd27
Ostrów Lubelski PL 59 Hc28
Ostrów Mazowiecka PL 59 Hb27
Ostrów Wielkopolski PL 58 Gc28
Ostrožac BIH 85 Gb37
Ostrzeszów PL 66 Gd29
Ostuni I 100 Gd43
Ostvik S 34 Gd11
Osuna E 105 Bb44
Oswestry GB 24 Cd25
Oświęcim PL 67 Ha30
Osypenko UA 126 Fb16
Otaci MD 77 Jd32
Otanmäki FIN 35 Hd11
Oțelu Roșu RO 75 Hd36
Otepää EST 47 Ja19
Oteren N 26 Gc05
Oteşti de Jos RO 88 Ja37
Otištić HR 86 Gc39
Otnes N 37 Fc15
Otok HR 86 Gc39
Otok HR 86 Ha37
Otorowo PL 57 Gb27
Otradnaja RUS 127 Fd17
Otradnyj RUS 119 Ga10
Otranto I 100 Ha44
Otrokovice CZ 66 Gc32
Otta N 37 Fb15
Ottenby S 50 Gb22
Otterbäcken S 44 Ga19
Otterburn GB 21 Db22
Otterndorf D 56 Fa25
Otterup DK 49 Fb23
Ottobrunn D 72 Fc33
Otwock PL 59 Hb28
Otynja UA 76 Ja32
Ouddorp NL 54 Ea28
Oudenaarde B 62 Ea29
Oude Pekela NL 55 Ed26
Oughterard IRL 18 Bd23
Ouistreham F 61 Da30
Oulainen FIN 35 Hc11
Oulu FIN 35 Hc10
Oulunsalo FIN 35 Hc10
Oundle GB 25 Db26
Ouranoúpoli GR 102 Jb43
Ourense E 78 Ba37
Ourique P 104 Ac43

Outakoski FIN 27 Hb04
Outokumpu FIN 41 Ja13
Ouzouer-sur-Loire F 69 Dc33
Ovacık TR 127 Ga19
Ovacık TR 128 Gc17
Ovada I 83 Ed38
Ovanåker S 38 Gb15
Ovar P 78 Ad39
Ovča SRB 87 Hb37
Overath D 63 Ec29
Øverdalen N 36 Fa14
Øvergård N 26 Gc05
Överhörnäs S 39 Gc13
Överkalix S 34 Ha09
Överlida S 49 Fd21
Övermark FIN 40 Ha14
Overpelt B 63 Eb29
Övertorneå S 34 Hb09
Överturingen S 38 Ga14
Överum S 44 Gb20
Ovidiopol' UA 77 Kb34
Ovidiopol' UA 125 Ec17
Ovidiu RO 89 Ka37
Oviedo E 79 Bc37
Øvre Årdal N 36 Fa15
Øvre Rendal N 37 Fc15
Övre Soppero S 29 Gd06
Ovruč UA 121 Eb14
Owińska PL 58 Gc27
Oxelösund S 45 Gc19
Oxford GB 24 Da27
Oxie S 49 Fd23
Øye N 36 Fa16
Oyonnax F 70 Ea35
Øyslebø N 42 Fa20
Oyten D 56 Fa26
Ozalj HR 85 Gb37
Ożarów PL 67 Hb29
Özbaşı TR 113 Kb46
Ózd H 75 Hb33
Ožďany SK 74 Ha33
Oženna PL 67 Hb31
Ožerel'e RUS 118 Fa11
Ozerki RUS 119 Fc09
Ozerki RUS 119 Fd10
Ozerki RUS 119 Fd11
Ozersk RUS 59 Ha25
Ozery RUS 118 Fa11
Ozieri I 97 Ed43
Ozimek PL 66 Gd30
Ozorków PL 58 Ha28

P

Paakkola FIN 34 Hb09
Paavola FIN 35 Hc11
Pabianice PL 58 Ha28
Pabradė LT 53 Ja23
Pačelma RUS 119 Fc11
Pachino I 109 Ga48
Pacov CZ 65 Ga31
Pacy-sur-Eure F 62 Dc31
Paczków PL 66 Gc30
Padarosk BY 59 Hd26

Padasjoki FIN 40 Hc15
Padej SRB 75 Hb36
Paderborn D 56 Fa28
Padina RO 89 Jd37
Padova I 84 Fc37
Padrón E 78 Ad36
Padstow GB 23 Cb28
Padsville BY 53 Jb23
Padul E 106 Bc45
Pafos CY 128 Ga19
Pag HR 85 Ga38
Pagėgiai LT 52 Hb24
Pagelażiai LT 53 Hd23
Pagny-sur-Moselle F 63 Eb32
Pahraničny BY 59 Hd26
Paide EST 47 Hd18
Paignton GB 23 Cc28
Paimbœuf F 60 Cc32
Paimio FIN 40 Hb16
Paimpol F 60 Cc30
Paisley GB 20 Cd21
Paitasjärvi S 29 Ha06
Pāiušeni RO 75 Hc35
Pajala S 30 Ha08
Pajęczno PL 66 Gd29
Páka H 74 Gc35
Pakrac HR 86 Gc37
Pakruojis LT 52 Hc22
Paks H 74 Ha35
Palačany BY 53 Jb24
Palafrugell E 81 Dc40
Palagonia I 109 Ga47
Palaichori CY 128 Gb19
Palaiseau F 62 Dc31
Palamás E 101 Hd44
Palamós E 81 Dc40
Palanga LT 52 Ha23
Palárikovo SK 74 Gd33
Palas de Rei E 78 Ba37
Palatna RKS 87 Hc40
Palau I 96 Ed42
Palazzolo Acreide I 109 Ga48
Palazzolo sull'Oglio I 72 Fa36
Paldiski EST 46 Hc18
Pale BIH 86 Gd39
Paleh RUS 118 Fb09
Palékastro GR 115 Ka49
Palencia E 79 Bd39
Paleohóra GR 114 Jd49
Paleohóri GR 101 Hd44
Paleokastrítsa GR 100 Hb44
Paleópoli GR 102 Jc42
Paleópoli GR 112 Jc46
Palermo I 108 Fd46
Palestrina I 98 Fc41
Pálháza H 67 Hc32
Paligrad MK 101 Hc41
Palin H 74 Gc35
Palinuro I 99 Gb44
Paliochori GR 111 Jc47
Palioúri GR 102 Jb43
Paliouriá GR 101 Hd44
Páliros GR 111 Ja48

Perísta – Pļaviņas

Perísta **GR** 110 Hd45
Perithóri **GR** 110 Hd46
Perivólia **GR** 111 Ja47
Perleberg **D** 56 Fc26
Perloja **LT** 59 Hd25
Perloja **LT** 59 Hd25
Pernik **BG** 102 Ja40
Perniö **FIN** 46 Hb17
Pernitz **A** 73 Gb33
Péronne **F** 62 Dd30
Perpignan **F** 81 Db39
Perros-Guirec **F** 60 Cc30
Persbo **S** 44 Ga17
Perstorp **S** 49 Fd22
Perth **GB** 17 Da20
Pertoúli **GR** 101 Hd44
Pertteli **FIN** 40 Hb16
Pertuis **F** 82 Ea38
Pertunmaa **FIN** 41 Hd15
Perugia **I** 84 Fc40
Perušić **HR** 85 Gb38
Pervomaisc **MD** 77 Kb34
Pervomajs'k **MD** 77 Kb32
Pervomajsk **RUS** 119 Fc10
Pervomajs'k **UA** 125 Ec16
Pervomajskij **RUS** 118 Fb11
Pervomajskoe **RUS** 41 Jb16
Pervomajskoe **RUS** 119 Ga11
Pervomajs'kyj **UA** 122 Fa14
Pesaro **I** 84 Fc39
Pesčanokopskoe **RUS** 127 Fd16
Pescara **I** 99 Ga41
Pescasseroli **I** 98 Fd41
Peschiera del Garda **I** 84 Fb37
Pescia **I** 84 Fb39
Pescina **I** 98 Fd41
Pesco Sannita **I** 99 Ga42
Peshkopi **AL** 100 Hb41
Pesiökylä **FIN** 35 Hd10
Pesmes **F** 71 Eb34
Pesočani **MK** 101 Hc42
Peso da Régua **P** 78 Ba39
Pessac **F** 68 Cd36
Peštera **BG** 102 Jb41
Peştişani **RO** 87 Hd37
Pestovo **RUS** 117 Ec09
Pestravka **RUS** 119 Ga10
Petäiskylä **FIN** 35 Ja12
Petäjäskoski **FIN** 34 Hb09
Petäjävesi **FIN** 40 Hc14
Petalax Petolahti **FIN** 40 Ha13
Petalidi **GR** 110 Hd47
Peterborough **GB** 25 Db26
Peterhead **GB** 17 Dc19
Peterlee **GB** 21 Db23
Petersfield **GB** 24 Da28
Petilia Policastro **I** 109 Gc45
Petín **E** 78 Bb37
Pet'ki **BY** 59 Hd27
Petkula **FIN** 31 Hc07
Petra **GR** 113 Jd44
Petralia-Sottana **I** 108 Ga47

Petran **AL** 100 Hb43
Petreni **MD** 77 Jd32
Petrič **BG** 101 Ja42
Petrila **RO** 88 Ja36
Petrinja **HR** 85 Gb37
Petrivka **MD** 77 Kb33
Petrivka **UA** 77 Ka34
Petrivka **UA** 121 Ec14
Petropavlivka **UA** 122 Fa15
Petropavlovka **RUS** 123 Fc13
Petroşani **RO** 88 Ja36
Petrova **RO** 76 Ja33
Petrovac **SRB** 87 Hc38
Petrovice **CZ** 65 Ga31
Petrovo **RUS** 117 Ec09
Petrovsk **RUS** 119 Fd11
Petrovskoe **RUS** 41 Jb15
Petrovskoe **RUS** 118 Fa09
Petrovskoe **RUS** 122 Fb12
Petrykav **BY** 121 Eb13
Petsikko **FIN** 27 Hc04
Petsmo **FIN** 40 Ha13
Petuški **RUS** 118 Fa10
Peuilly-sur-Claise **F** 69 Db34
Peurasuvanto **FIN** 31 Hc06
Peyrat-le-Château **F** 69 Db35
Peyrehorade **F** 80 Cc37
Pézenas **F** 81 Dc38
Pezens **F** 81 Db38
Pezinok **SK** 74 Gc33
Pfaffenhofen **D** 72 Fc33
Pfarrkirchen **D** 73 Fd33
Pforzheim **D** 63 Ed32
Pfronten **D** 72 Fb34
Pfullendorf **D** 72 Fa33
Pfungstadt **D** 63 Ed31
Phals-bourg **F** 63 Ec32
Philippeville **B** 62 Ea30
Piacenza **I** 84 Fa37
Piana di Albanesi **I** 108 Fd46
Pias **P** 105 Ad43
Piaseczno **PL** 59 Hb28
Piasek **PL** 66 Gd30
Piaski **PL** 67 Hc29
Piątek **PL** 58 Ha28
Piatra **RO** 88 Jb38
Piatra-Neamţ **RO** 76 Jc34
Piatra-Olt **RO** 88 Ja38
Piazza Armerina **I** 109 Ga47
Pičaevo **RUS** 118 Fb11
Pickering **GB** 21 Db24
Picquigny **F** 62 Dc30
Piedimonte Matese **I** 99 Ga42
Piedrabuena **E** 91 Bc42
Piedrahita **E** 91 Bb40
Piekary Śląskie **PL** 66 Gd30
Pieksämäki **FIN** 41 Hd14
Pielavesi **FIN** 35 Hd12
Pieniężno **PL** 58 Ha25
Pienza **I** 84 Fb40
Pierre-Buffière **F** 69 Db35
Pierre-de-Bresse **F** 70 Ea34
Pierrefonds **F** 62 Dd31

Pierrefort **F** 69 Dc36
Pierrelatte **F** 82 Dd37
Piešťany **SK** 66 Gd32
Pieszyce **PL** 66 Gc30
Pietarsaari **FIN** 34 Ha12
Pietrasanta **I** 84 Fa39
Pietroşani **RO** 88 Jc38
Pieve di Cadore **I** 72 Fc35
Pieve San Stefano **I** 84 Fc39
Pigés **GR** 101 Hc44
Pihtipudas **FIN** 35 Hc12
Piippola **FIN** 35 Hc11
Pikalevo **RUS** 117 Ec08
Pikasilla **EST** 47 Hd19
Piła **PL** 58 Gc26
Pilas **E** 105 Ad44
Pilawa **PL** 59 Hb28
Pilgrimstad **S** 38 Ga13
Pilis **H** 74 Ha34
Pilisvörösvár **H** 74 Ha34
Pílos **GR** 110 Hd47
Piltene **LV** 52 Hb21
Pilvlškiai **LT** 52 Hc24
Pilzno **PL** 67 Hb30
Pímpió **S** 30 Ha08
Pınarbaşi **TR** 128 Gb16
Pınarcık **TR** 113 Kb46
Pinarello **F** 96 Ed41
Pınarhisar **TR** 103 Ka41
Pincehely **H** 74 Gd35
Pinczów **PL** 67 Hb30
Pinerolo **I** 83 Ec37
Pineto **I** 85 Fd40
Piney **F** 62 Ea32
Pinhão **P** 78 Ba39
Pinhel **P** 78 Ba39
Pinkafeld **A** 73 Gb34
Pinneberg **D** 56 Fb26
Pino **F** 96 Ed40
Pinoso **E** 107 Cb44
Pinos-Puente **E** 106 Bc45
Pinsk **BY** 120 Ea14
Pintamo **FIN** 35 Hd09
Pinto **E** 92 Bd41
Pioltikasvaara **S** 29 Gd07
Piombino **I** 84 Fa40
Pionerskij **RUS** 52 Ha24
Pionki **PL** 59 Hb28
Piotrków Trybunalski **PL** 67 Ha29
Pipirig **RO** 76 Jb34
Pipriac **F** 61 Cd32
Piran **SLO** 85 Fd37
Pirčiupiai **LT** 53 Hd24
Pirdop **BG** 102 Jb40
Pireás **GR** 112 Jb46
Pirgadikia **GR** 102 Jb43
Pirgí **GR** 100 Hb44
Pirgío **GR** 113 Jd45
Pírgos **GR** 110 Hd47
Pirin **BG** 101 Ja41
Pirki **BY** 121 Ec14
Pirkkala **FIN** 40 Hb15
Pirmasens **D** 63 Ec31
Pirna **D** 65 Ga29

Pirot **SRB** 87 Hd39
Pirovac **HR** 85 Gb39
Pirsógiani **GR** 101 Hc43
Pirttikoski **FIN** 31 Hc08
Pirttikylä **FIN** 40 Ha14
Pirttimäki **FIN** 35 Hd11
Pisa **I** 84 Fa39
Pišča **UA** 59 Hd28
Piščana **UA** 77 Ka32
Piščanka **UA** 77 Jd32
Pisciotta **I** 99 Gb44
Piscu **RO** 89 Jd36
Písek **CZ** 65 Ga32
Pisogne **I** 72 Fa36
Píso Livádi **GR** 115 Jd47
Pissos **F** 80 Cd37
Pissouri **CY** 128 Gb19
Pisticci **I** 99 Gc43
Pistoia **I** 84 Fb39
Pisz **PL** 59 Hb26
Piteå **S** 34 Ha10
Pitelino **RUS** 118 Fb10
Piteşti **RO** 88 Jb37
Pithiviers **F** 62 Dc32
Pitigliano **I** 84 Fb40
Pitkälahti **FIN** 41 Hd13
Pitkovo **RUS** 41 Jb15
Pitlochry **GB** 17 Da20
Pitomača **HR** 74 Gc36
Pitvaros **H** 75 Hb35
Pivka **SLO** 73 Ga36
Piwniczna-Zdrój **PL** 67 Hb31
Piżma **RUS** 119 Fc08
Pizzighettone **I** 84 Fa37
Pizzo **I** 109 Gb45
Pizzoli **I** 98 Fd41
Pjaozero **RUS** 35 Ja09
Pjatigorsk **RUS** 127 Ga17
P'jatychatky **UA** 121 Ed15
Plabennec **F** 60 Cb30
Pláka **GR** 102 Jc43
Plakotí **GR** 101 Hc44
Planá nad Labem **CZ** 65 Ga32
Plancoët **F** 61 Cd31
Plandište **SRB** 87 Hc37
Plan-du-Var **F** 83 Eb38
Plášľovce **SK** 74 Gd33
Plasencia **E** 91 Bb41
Plaški **HR** 85 Gb37
Platamónas **GR** 101 Ja43
Platamónas **GR** 102 Jb42
Platania **GR** 101 Ja44
Platánia **GR** 110 Hd47
Plátanos **GR** 110 Hd45
Plátanos **GR** 114 Jb49
Platariá **GR** 100 Hb44
Platis Gialós **GR** 111 Jc47
Platís Gialós **GR** 113 Jd46
Plattling **D** 65 Fd32
Plau **D** 56 Fc26
Plauen **D** 64 Fc30
Plav **MNE** 87 Hb40
Plavecký Mikuláš **SK** 74 Gc33
Pļaviņas **LV** 53 Hd21

Prylęk **PL** 67 Hb30
Pryluky **UA** 121 Ed14
Prymors'k **UA** 126 Fb16
Pryozerne **UA** 77 Ka35
Przasnysz **PL** 59 Hb26
Przechlewo **PL** 58 Gc26
Przedbórz **PL** 67 Ha29
Przemyśl **PL** 67 Hc31
Przeworsk **PL** 67 Hc30
Przewóz **PL** 65 Ga29
Przybiernów **PL** 57 Ga26
Przyborowice **PL** 58 Ha27
Przyłęki **PL** 58 Gc27
Przystawy **PL** 57 Gb25
Przysucha **PL** 67 Hb29
Przytoczno **PL** 59 Hc28
Przytuty **PL** 59 Hc26
Psahná **GR** 112 Jb45
Psará **GR** 113 Jd45
Psarádes **GR** 101 Hc42
Psári **GR** 111 Ja46
Psebaj **RUS** 127 Fd17
Pskov **RUS** 47 Jb19
Pszczyna **PL** 66 Gd31
Pszów **PL** 66 Gd31
Ptolemaída **GR** 101 Hd43
Ptuj **SLO** 73 Gb35
Ptujska Gora **SLO** 73 Gb36
Pučež **RUS** 118 Fb09
Púchov **SK** 66 Gd32
Pucioasa **RO** 88 Jb36
Pučišća **HR** 86 Gc39
Puck **PL** 51 Gd24
Puçol **E** 93 Cc43
Pudasjärvi **FIN** 35 Hc10
Puebla de Alcocer **E** 91 Bb42
Puebla de Don Fadrique **E** 106 Bd44
Puebla de Don Rodrigo **E** 91 Bc42
Puebla de Guzmán **E** 105 Ad43
Puebla de Lillo **E** 79 Bc37
Puebla de Sanabria **E** 78 Bb38
Puebla de Trives **E** 78 Ba37
Puente-Genil **E** 105 Bb44
Puente la Reina **E** 80 Cb38
Puente la Reina de Jaca **E** 80 Cc39
Puentelarrá **E** 79 Ca38
Puerto de San Vicente **E** 91 Bb42
Puertollano **E** 92 Bc43
Puerto Lumbreras **E** 107 Ca45
Puerto Real **E** 105 Ad45
Puerto Rey **E** 91 Bb42
Pufeşti **RO** 77 Jd35
Pugačev **RUS** 119 Ga11
Puget-Ville **F** 82 Ea39
Puhos **FIN** 35 Hd10
Puhos **FIN** 41 Jb14
Pui **RO** 75 Hd36
Puiatu **EST** 47 Hd19

Puieşti **RO** 77 Jd34
Puigcerdà **E** 81 Da40
Puig-reig **E** 81 Da40
Puiseaux **F** 62 Dc32
Pukalaidun **FIN** 40 Hb16
Pukavik **S** 50 Ga22
Pukë **AL** 100 Hb41
Pula **HR** 85 Fd37
Pula **I** 97 Ed45
Pulaj **AL** 100 Ha41
Puławy **PL** 67 Hc29
Pulju **FIN** 30 Hb06
Pulkkila **FIN** 35 Hc11
Pulkkinen **FIN** 34 Hb12
Pulpí **E** 107 Ca45
Pulsano **I** 100 Gd43
Pulsnitz **D** 65 Ga29
Pulsnitz **D** 65 Ga29
Pulsujärvi **S** 29 Gd06
Pułtusk **PL** 59 Hb27
Pumpėnai **LT** 53 Hd22
Punkaharju **FIN** 41 Jb14
Punta Križa **HR** 85 Ga38
Punta Umbría **E** 105 Ad44
Puokio **FIN** 35 Hd10
Puolanka **FIN** 35 Hd10
Puoltsa **S** 29 Gd07
Puottaure **S** 34 Gd09
Purchena **E** 106 Bd45
Purdoški **RUS** 119 Fc10
Purmerend **NL** 55 Eb27
Puškino **RUS** 123 Ga12
Puškinskie Gory **RUS** 47 Jb20
Püspökladány **H** 75 Hb34
Pustoška **RUS** 117 Eb11
Putbus **D** 57 Fd25
Putignano **I** 99 Gc43
Putlitz **D** 56 Fc26
Puttgarden **D** 56 Fc25
Putyvl' **UA** 121 Ed13
Puumala **FIN** 41 Ja15
Puurmani **EST** 47 Hd19
Puy l'Evêque **F** 81 Da37
Puzači **RUS** 122 Fa13
Pwllheli **GB** 23 Cc25
Pyhäjärvi **FIN** 27 Hb05
Pyhäjärvi **FIN** 31 Hc07
Pyhäjärvi **FIN** 35 Hc12
Pyhäjoki **FIN** 34 Hb11
Pyhäkylä **FIN** 35 Hd10
Pyhäntä **FIN** 35 Hc11
Pyhäntä **FIN** 35 Hd11
Pyhäranta **FIN** 40 Ha16
Pyhäselkä **FIN** 41 Jb13
Pyhtää **FIN** 41 Hd16
Þykkvibær **IS** 14 Bc07
Pyla-sur-Mer **F** 68 Cc36
Pylkönmäki **FIN** 40 Hc13
Pynjany **UA** 67 Hd31
Pyrill **IS** 14 Bc06
Pyrjatyn **UA** 121 Ed14
Pyrzyce **PL** 57 Ga26
Pyskowice **PL** 66 Gd30
Pytalovo **RUS** 47 Jb20
Pyttis **FIN** 41 Hd16
Pyzdry **PL** 58 Gc28

Q

Qafëzez **AL** 101 Hc43
Quafmollë **RKS** 100 Hb42
Quakenbrück **D** 55 Ed27
Quarré-les-Tombes **F** 70 Dd33
Quarteira **P** 104 Ac44
Quartu Sant'Elena **I** 97 Ed45
Quedlinburg **D** 56 Fb28
Querfurt **D** 64 Fc29
Quesada **E** 106 Bd44
Questembert **F** 60 Cc32
Quiberon **F** 60 Cc32
Quick born **D** 56 Fb26
Quillan **F** 81 Db39
Quimper **F** 60 Cb31
Quimperlé **F** 60 Cb31
Quingey **F** 71 Eb34
Quintana de Castillo **E** 79 Bc37
Quintana del Puente **E** 79 Bd39
Quintanar de la Orden **E** 92 Bd42
Quintanar del Rey **E** 92 Ca43
Quintin **F** 60 Cc31
Quinto **E** 80 Cc40
Quiroga **E** 78 Ba37

R

Raabs **A** 65 Gb32
Raahe **FIN** 34 Hb11
Rääkkylä **FIN** 41 Ja13
Raanujärvi **FIN** 30 Hb08
Raattama **FIN** 30 Hb06
Rab **HR** 85 Ga38
Rabac **HR** 85 Ga37
Rábafüzes **HR** 73 Gb35
Rábahidvég **H** 74 Gc35
Rabka-Zdroj **PL** 67 Ha31
Râbniţa **MD** 77 Ka32
Rača **SRB** 87 Hc40
Râcaciuni **RO** 76 Jc35
Racalmuto **I** 108 Fd47
Răcăşdia **RO** 87 Hc37
Racconigi **I** 83 Ec37
Rachiv **UA** 76 Ja33
Rachiv **UA** 124 Ea16
Raciąż **PL** 58 Ha27
Racibórz **PL** 66 Gd30
Račičy **BY** 59 Hc25
Račja Vas **HR** 85 Ga37
Racksund **S** 33 Gc09
Radakowice **PL** 66 Gc29
Radalj **SRB** 86 Ha38
Radaškovičy **BY** 53 Jb24
Radaškovičy **BY** 120 Ea12
Rădăuţi **RO** 76 Jb33
Rădăuţi-Prut **RO** 76 Jc32
Radeberg **D** 65 Fd29
Radebeul **D** 65 Fd29

Radeburg **D** 65 Fd29
Radechiv **UA** 67 Hd29
Radechiv **UA** 120 Ea15
Radenci **SLO** 73 Gb35
Radenthein **A** 73 Fd35
Radijovce **MK** 101 Hc41
Radilovo **BG** 102 Jb41
Radisne **MD** 77 Kb33
Radlje ob Dravi **SLO** 73 Gb35
Radnevo **BG** 102 Jc40
Radom **PL** 67 Hb29
Radomicko **PL** 57 Ga28
Radomir **BG** 102 Ja40
Radomsko **PL** 67 Ha29
Radomyšl' **UA** 121 Eb14
Radomyšl nad Sanem **PL** 67 Hc29
Radomyśl Wielki **PL** 67 Hb30
Radovan **RO** 88 Ja38
Radovec **BG** 103 Jd40
Radoviš **MK** 101 Hd41
Radovljica **SLO** 73 Ga36
Radstadt **A** 73 Fd34
Radun' **BY** 59 Hd25
Radviliškis **LT** 52 Hc23
Radymno **PL** 67 Hc30
Radzanów **PL** 58 Ha27
Radziejów **PL** 58 Gd27
Radzyń Chełmiński **PL** 58 Gd26
Radzyń Podlaski **PL** 59 Hc28
Raesfeld **D** 55 Ec28
Rafína **GR** 112 Jb46
Raftópoulo **GR** 110 Hd45
Ragaciems **LV** 52 Hc21
Ragusa **I** 109 Ga48
Rahačov **BY** 121 Eb13
Rahden **D** 56 Fa27
Raheste **EST** 46 Hc19
Rain **D** 64 Fb32
Raippaluoto **FIN** 40 Ha13
Raippo **FIN** 41 Ja15
Raisdorf **D** 56 Fb25
Raisio **FIN** 40 Hb16
Raivala **FIN** 40 Hb14
Raja-Jooseppi **FIN** 31 Hc06
Rajakoski **RUS** 27 Hd05
Rájec-Jestřebí **CZ** 66 Gc31
Rajec Poduchowny **PL** 59 Hb28
Rajgród **PL** 59 Hc25
Rajka **H** 74 Gc33
Rakaca **H** 75 Hb33
Rakkestad **N** 43 Fc18
Rakovica **BG** 87 Hd39
Rakovica **HR** 85 Gb37
Rakovník **CZ** 65 Fd31
Rakovski **BG** 102 Jb40
Rakvere **EST** 47 Hd18
Rama-Prozor **BIH** 86 Gd39
Rambervillers **F** 63 Ec32
Rambouillet **F** 62 Dc31
Rameški **RUS** 117 Ed09

Ramnäs **S** 44 Gb18
Râmnicelu **RO** 89 Jd36
Râmnicu Sărăt **RO** 89 Jd36
Râmnicu Vâlcea **RO** 88 Ja37
Ramsele **S** 38 Gb13
Ramsey **GBM** 20 Cd23
Ramsgate **GB** 25 Dc28
Ramsjö **S** 38 Gb14
Ramstein **D** 63 Ec31
Ramvik **S** 39 Gc14
Ramygala **LT** 53 Hd23
Randalstown **GB** 20 Cc22
Randazzo **I** 109 Ga47
Rånddalen **S** 38 Fd14
Randers **DK** 49 Fb22
Randijaur **S** 29 Gc08
Randsverk **N** 37 Fb15
Rånea **S** 34 Ha09
Ranemsletta **N** 32 Fd11
Rankweil **A** 72 Fa34
Rannoch Station **GB** 17 Da20
Ransta **S** 44 Gb18
Rantasalmi **FIN** 41 Ja14
Rantsila **FIN** 35 Hc11
Ranua **FIN** 35 Hc09
Raon-l'Etape **F** 63 Ec32
Rapallo **I** 83 Ed38
Räpina **EST** 47 Ja19
Rapla **EST** 46 Hc18
Rapperswil **CH** 71 Ed34
Räsåker **S** 38 Gb13
Râșcani **MD** 76 Jc32
Rașcov **MD** 77 Jd32
Raseiniai **LT** 52 Hc23
Raška **SRB** 87 Hb39
Râșnov **RO** 88 Jb36
Rasova **RO** 89 Ka37
Rasovo **BG** 88 Ja39
Rasskazovo **RUS** 123 Fc12
Rastatt **D** 63 Ed32
Rastede **D** 55 Ed26
Rasti **FIN** 30 Hb07
Rätan **S** 38 Ga14
Ratasjärvi **FIN** 30 Hb08
Rathdrum **IRL** 19 Cb24
Rathenow **D** 56 Fc27
Rathfriland **GB** 20 Cc23
Rathmore **IRL** 22 Bd25
Rathnew **IRL** 19 Cb24
Ratíškovice **CZ** 66 Gc32
Ratne **UA** 59 Hd28
Ratne **UA** 120 Ea14
Ratten **A** 73 Gb34
Rättvik **S** 38 Ga16
Ratuș **MD** 77 Jd33
Ratzeburg **D** 56 Fb26
Raubling **D** 72 Fc34
Raudeberg **N** 36 Ed14
Raudlia **N** 33 Ga09
Raufarhöfn **IS** 15 Cc05
Raufoss **N** 37 Fc16
Rauland **N** 42 Fa17
Rauma **FIN** 40 Ha16
Rauna **LV** 47 Hd20
Râu Sadului **RO** 88 Ja36

Răuseni **RO** 76 Jc33
Rautalampi **FIN** 41 Hd13
Rautavaara **FIN** 35 Ja12
Rautjärvi **FIN** 41 Jb14
Ravanusa **I** 108 Fd47
Rava Rus'ka **UA** 67 Hd30
Ravenna **I** 84 Fc38
Ravensburg **D** 72 Fa33
Ravna Gora **HR** 85 Ga37
Ravnaja **SRB** 86 Ha38
Ravne na Koroškem **SLO** 73 Ga35
Ravno Bučje **SRB** 87 Hd39
Rawa Mazowiecka **PL** 58 Ha28
Rawicz **PL** 66 Gc29
Ražanka **BY** 59 Hd25
Războieni **RO** 76 Jc34
Razbojna **SRB** 87 Hc39
Razdol **BG** 101 Ja41
Răzeni **MD** 77 Ka34
Razgrad **BG** 89 Jd38
Razlog **BG** 101 Ja41
Reading **GB** 24 Da27
Réalmont **F** 81 Db38
Rebirechioulet **F** 81 Da38
Rebordelo **P** 78 Ba38
Recanati **I** 85 Fd39
Recaș **RO** 75 Hc36
Recea **RO** 88 Jb36
Recess **IRL** 18 Bd23
Recey-sur-Ource **F** 70 Ea33
Recklinghausen **D** 55 Ed28
Recoaro Terme **I** 72 Fb36
Rèčyca **BY** 121 Ec13
Recz **PL** 57 Gb26
Ręczno **PL** 67 Ha29
Reda **PL** 51 Gd24
Redange-sur-Attert **L** 63 Eb30
Redcar **GB** 21 Db23
Redditch **GB** 24 Da26
Redea **RO** 88 Ja38
Redkino **RUS** 117 Ed10
Redon **F** 60 Cc32
Redondela **I** 78 Ad37
Redondo **P** 90 Ad42
Redruth **GB** 23 Cb28
Rędzikowo **PL** 58 Gc25
Rędziny **PL** 67 Ha29
Rees **D** 55 Ec28
Regalbuto **I** 109 Ga47
Regen **D** 65 Fd32
Regensburg **D** 64 Fc32
Regenstauf **D** 64 Fc32
Reggio di Calabria **I** 109 Gb46
Reggio Nell'emilia **I** 84 Fb38
Reghin **RO** 76 Ja34
Reghiu **RO** 76 Jc35
Regínio **GR** 111 Ja45
Reguengos de Monsaraz **P** 90 Ad42
Rehau **D** 64 Fc30
Rehburg-Loccum **D** 56 Fa27
Reichenbach **D** 64 Fc30

Reichshoffen **F** 63 Ed32
Reife **N** 29 Gc06
Reigate **GB** 25 Db28
Reims **F** 62 Ea31
Reinach **CH** 71 Ed34
Reinbek **D** 56 Fb26
Reinberg **D** 57 Fd25
Reine **N** 28 Fd07
Reinheim **D** 64 Fa31
Reinosa **E** 79 Bd37
Reinsvik **N** 36 Fa13
Reinsvoll **N** 37 Fc16
Reisjärvi **FIN** 35 Hc12
Reit im Winkel **D** 72 Fc34
Rejmyre **S** 44 Gb19
Rejowiec **PL** 67 Hd29
Rejštejn **CZ** 65 Fd32
Rekavice **BIH** 86 Gc38
Relleu **E** 94 Cc44
Remagen **D** 63 Ec30
Remda **RUS** 47 Ja19
Remeskylä **FIN** 35 Hc12
Remiremont **F** 71 Ec33
Remontnoe **RUS** 123 Ga15
Remscheid **D** 63 Ec29
Rémuzat **F** 82 Ea37
Rena **N** 37 Fc16
Rencēni **LV** 47 Hd20
Renda **LV** 52 Hb21
Rende **I** 109 Gb45
Rendína **GR** 101 Ja42
Rendsburg **D** 56 Fb25
Reni **UA** 89 Ka36
Renko **FIN** 40 Hc16
Rennebu **N** 37 Fb13
Rennes **F** 61 Cd31
Renningen **D** 63 Ed32
Rensjön **S** 29 Gd07
Renträsk **S** 34 Gd10
Reola **EST** 47 Ja19
Rep'evka **RUS** 122 Fb13
Repojoki **FIN** 30 Hb06
Reposaari **FIN** 40 Ha15
Repvåg **N** 27 Hb03
Requena **E** 93 Cb43
Réquista **F** 81 Db38
Reșadiye **TR** 115 Kb47
Resen **MK** 101 Hc42
Rešetylivka **UA** 121 Ed15
Reșița **RO** 87 Hc37
Reszel **PL** 59 Hb25
Retford **GB** 25 Db25
Rethel **F** 62 Ea31
Rethem **D** 56 Fa27
Réthimno **GR** 114 Jc49
Retiers **F** 61 Cd32
Rétság **H** 74 Ha33
Retuerta del Bullaque **E** 91 Bc42
Retz **A** 65 Gb32
Reus **E** 93 Cd41
Reuterstadt Stavenhagen **D** 57 Fd26
Reutlingen **D** 64 Fa32
Reutte **A** 72 Fb34
Revel **F** 81 Db38

Revfülöp **H** 74 Gc35
Revigny-sur-Ornain **F** 62 Ea32
Revin **F** 62 Ea30
Řevnice **CZ** 65 Ga31
Revsnes **N** 28 Gb06
Revúca **SK** 67 Ha32
Reyðarfjörður **IS** 15 Cc07
Reykhólar **IS** 14 Bc05
Reykholt **IS** 14 Bc07
Reykholt **IS** 14 Bc06
Reykjadiskur **IS** 15 Ca05
Reykjahlið **IS** 15 Cb06
Reykjanes **IS** 14 Bc04
Reykjavík **IS** 14 Bc06
Rezé **F** 68 Cd33
Rēzekne **LV** 53 Ja21
Rezovo **BG** 103 Ka40
Rgotina **SRB** 87 Hd38
Rhayader **GB** 24 Cd26
Rheda-Wiedenbrück **D** 55 Ed28
Rheinau **D** 63 Ed32
Rheine **D** 55 Ed27
Rheinfelden **D** 71 Ec34
Rheinsberg **D** 57 Fd27
Rheinstetten **D** 63 Ed32
Rhiconich **GB** 17 Da18
Rhinow **D** 56 Fc27
Rho **I** 71 Ed36
Rhondda **GB** 24 Cd27
Riákia **GR** 101 Hd43
Riala **S** 45 Gc18
Riaño **E** 79 Bd37
Rians **F** 82 Ea39
Riaza **E** 92 Bd40
Ribadavia **E** 78 Ba37
Ribadelago **E** 78 Bb38
Ribadeo **E** 78 Bb36
Ribadesella **E** 79 Bd37
Ribarica **BG** 102 Jb40
Ribarska Banja **SRB** 87 Hc39
Ribe **DK** 48 Fa23
Ribécourt **F** 62 Dd30
Ribera **I** 108 Fd47
Ribérac **F** 69 Da36
Ribnica **BIH** 86 Gd38
Ribnica **SLO** 73 Ga36
Ribnitz-Damgarten **D** 57 Fd25
Říčany **CZ** 65 Ga31
Riccia **I** 99 Ga42
Riccione **I** 84 Fc39
Richelieu **F** 69 Da33
Richmond **GB** 21 Db23
Richmond **GB** 25 Db27
Ricobayo **E** 78 Bb39
Ridderkerk **NL** 55 Eb28
Ried im Innkreis **A** 73 Fd33
Riedlingen **D** 72 Fa33
Riesa **D** 65 Fd29
Riesi **I** 108 Fd47
Rietavas **LT** 52 Hb23
Rieti **I** 98 Fc41
Rietschen **D** 65 Ga29

Rieumes F 81 Da38
Rieupeyroux F 81 Db37
Riez F 82 Ea38
Riga LV 52 Hc21
Rignac F 81 Db37
Riguldi EST 46 Hc18
Riihikoski FIN 40 Hb16
Riihimäki FIN 40 Hc16
Rijeka HR 85 Ga37
Rijssen NL 55 Ec27
Riksgränsen S 29 Gc06
Rila BG 101 Ja41
Rimavská Sobota SK 74 Ha33
Rimbo S 45 Gc18
Rimforsa S 44 Gb20
Rimini I 84 Fc38
Rímnio GR 101 Hd43
Rindal N 37 Fb13
Rindbø N 28 Gb06
Ringamåla S 50 Ga22
Ringarum S 44 Gb20
Ringaskiddy IRL 22 Bd25
Ringe DK 49 Fb24
Ringebu N 37 Fc15
Ringkøbing DK 48 Fa22
Ringsted DK 49 Fc23
Ringwood GB 24 Da28
Rinia GR 112 Jc46
Rintala RUS 41 Jb15
Rinteln D 56 Fa28
Rio GR 110 Hd46
Rio Frio P 78 Bb38
Riom F 69 Dc35
Rio Maior P 90 Ac41
Riom-ès-Montagnes F 69 Dc36
Rionero in Vulture I 99 Gb43
Rioz F 71 Eb34
Ripač BIH 85 Gb38
Ripanj SRB 87 Hb38
Ripky UA 121 Ec13
Ripoll E 81 Db40
Ripon GB 21 Db24
Riposto I 109 Gb47
Riquewihr F 71 Ec33
Risbäck S 33 Gb11
Riscle F 80 Cd38
Riska N 42 Ed18
Risnes N 42 Ed19
Risør N 43 Fb19
Risoul 1850 F 83 Eb37
Risøyhamn N 28 Gb05
Rissa N 32 Fc12
Rissna S 38 Gb13
Risti EST 46 Hc18
Ristiina FIN 41 Hd15
Ristijärvi FIN 35 Hd11
Ristilä FIN 41 Hd14
Ritsem S 28 Gb07
Ritterhude D 56 Fa26
Riumar E 93 Cd41
Riva del Garda I 72 Fb36
Rive-de-Gier F 70 Dd36
Rivesaltes F 81 Db39
Rivne UA 120 Ea14

Rivne UA 125 Ed16
Rivoli I 83 Ec37
Rize TR 127 Ga19
Rizokarpaso CY 128 Gc18
Rjabovskij RUS 123 Fc13
Rjazan' RUS 118 Fa11
Rjazanka RUS 123 Fc12
Rjažsk RUS 118 Fb11
Rjukan N 42 Fa17
Roa E 79 Bd39
Roa N 43 Fc17
Roanne F 70 Dd35
Röbäck S 34 Gd12
Röbel D 57 Fd26
Robertsfors S 34 Gd12
Robledo E 92 Ca43
Röblingen D 64 Fc29
Rocamadour F 69 Db36
Roccadaspide I 99 Gb43
Rocca Imperiale I 99 Gc44
Roccamena I 108 Fd47
Roccastrada I 84 Fb40
Roccella Ionica I 109 Gc46
Rochdale GB 21 Da24
Rochechouart F 69 Da35
Rochefort B 63 Eb30
Rochefort F 68 Cd34
Rocheservière F 68 Cd33
Rochester GB 25 Db28
Rochlitz D 65 Fd29
Ročov CZ 65 Fd30
Rocroi F 62 Ea30
Rødberg N 43 Fb17
Rødbyhavn DK 49 Fc24
Rödeby S 50 Gb22
Rødekro DK 48 Fa24
Rodel GB 16 Cc18
Roden NL 55 Ec26
Rodez F 81 Dc37
Rodi Garganico I 99 Gb41
Roding D 64 Fc32
Rodna RO 76 Ja33
Rodniki RUS 118 Fa09
Rodolívos GR 102 Jb42
Ródos GR 115 Kc47
Rødsjøen N 32 Fc12
Rødvig DK 49 Fd24
Roela EST 47 Hd18
Roermond NL 63 Ec29
Roeselare B 62 Dd29
Roești RO 88 Ja37
Roetgen D 63 Ec29
Rogač HR 85 Gb39
Rogačevka RUS 122 Fb13
Rogačica SRB 86 Ha38
Rogaška Slatina SLO 73 Gb36
Rogatica BIH 86 Ha39
Rogliano I 109 Gc45
Rognan N 28 Gb08
Rogne N 37 Fb16
Rogovo RUS 47 Jb20
Rogowo PL 58 Gc27
Rogoźniczka PL 59 Hc28
Rogoźno PL 58 Gc27
Rohan F 60 Cc31

Rohožník SK 74 Gc33
Rohrbach A 73 Ga33
Rohrbach-lès-Bitche F 63 Ec32
Rohuküla EST 46 Hc18
Rohuneeme EST 46 Hc17
Roismala FIN 40 Hb15
Roissy F 62 Dd31
Roja LV 46 Hb20
Rojão P 90 Ad40
Röjdåfors S 44 Fd17
Rokiciny PL 58 Ha28
Rokiškis LT 53 Hd22
Roknäs S 34 Gd10
Rokycany CZ 65 Fd31
Rokytne UA 121 Eb14
Rolde NL 55 Ec26
Rolfs S 34 Ha09
Rolfstorp S 49 Fd21
Roma I 98 Fc41
Roma S 51 Gd21
Roman BG 88 Ja39
Roman RO 76 Jc34
Românești RO 76 Jc33
Romanshorn CH 72 Fa34
Romans-sur-Isère F 82 Ea37
Romilly-sur-Seine F 62 Dd32
Romny UA 121 Ed14
Romodan UA 121 Ed14
Romorantin-Lanthenay F 69 Db33
Romsey GB 24 Da28
Rönäs S 33 Ga10
Roncesvalles E 80 Cc38
Ronchamp F 71 Eb33
Ronciglione I 98 Fc41
Ronda E 105 Ba45
Rønde DK 49 Fb22
Ronehamn S 51 Gd21
Rõngu EST 47 Hd19
Rønne DK 50 Ga24
Ronneby S 50 Gb22
Ronnenberg D 56 Fa27
Rönnliden S 33 Gc10
Rönnöfors S 33 Ga12
Ronse B 62 Ea29
Roosendaal NL 54 Ea28
Ropczyce PL 67 Hb30
Ropotovo MK 101 Hc42
Roquefort F 80 Cd37
Roquesteron F 83 Eb38
Roquetas de Mar E 106 Bd46
Roquetes E 93 Cd41
Rore BIH 86 Gc38
Røros N 37 Fc12
Rorschach CH 72 Fa34
Rørvik N 32 Fc11
Rørvika N 37 Fc13
Ros' BY 59 Hd26
Rošal' RUS 118 Fa10
Rosal de la Frontera E 105 Ad43
Rosans F 82 Ea38
Rosarno I 109 Gb46

Roscales E 79 Bd38
Roščino RUS 41 Jb16
Roscoff F 60 Cb30
Roscommon IRL 18 Ca23
Roscrea IRL 18 Ca24
Rose MNE 100 Ha41
Rosendal N 42 Ed17
Rosengarten D 56 Fb26
Rosenheim D 72 Fc33
Roses E 81 Dc40
Roseto degli Abruzzi I 85 Fd40
Roșia RO 75 Hc35
Roșia de Secaș RO 76 Ja35
Roșia Nouă RO 75 Hd35
Rosica BG 89 Ka38
Rosice CZ 65 Gb32
Rosignano Marittimo I 84 Fa39
Rosignano Solvay I 84 Fa39
Roșiori RO 75 Hc34
Roșiori de Vede RO 88 Jb38
Roskilde DK 49 Fc23
Roslavl' RUS 121 Ec12
Rosolini I 109 Ga48
Rosoman MK 101 Hd42
Rosporden F 60 Cb31
Rossano I 99 Gc44
Rossija RUS 117 Ec11
Rosslare IRL 23 Cb25
Rosslare Harbour IRL 23 Cb25
Roßlau D 56 Fc28
Rossön S 33 Gb12
Ross-on-Wye GB 24 Cd26
Rossoš' RUS 122 Fb13
Rostock D 56 Fc25
Rostov RUS 118 Fa09
Rostov- na-Donu RUS 123 Fc15
Rostrenen F 60 Cc31
Røsvik N 28 Gb07
Rosvik S 34 Ha10
Rot S 38 Ga16
Rota E 105 Ad45
Rot am See D 64 Fa32
Rotenburg D 64 Fa29
Rotenburg (Wümme) D 56 Fa26
Roth D 64 Fb32
Rothenburg ob der Tauber D 64 Fb31
Rotherham GB 25 Db25
Rothesay GB 20 Cd21
Rothwell GB 21 Db24
Rotondella I 99 Gc44
Rottenburg D 63 Ed32
Rottenburg D 64 Fc32
Rotterdam NL 55 Eb27
Rottne S 50 Ga21
Rottneros S 44 Fd18
Rottweil D 71 Ed33
Rötz D 64 Fc31
Roubaix F 62 Dd29
Roudnice nad Labem CZ 65 Ga30

Rouen – Saint Anne

Rouen **F** 61 Db30
Rougemont **F** 71 Eb34
Rouillac **F** 69 Da35
Roulans **F** 71 Eb34
Roussillon **F** 70 Ea36
Roussilon **F** 82 Ea38
Rovaniemi **FIN** 31 Hc08
Rovato **I** 72 Fa36
Roveň **SK** 67 Hc32
Roven'ki **RUS** 122 Fb14
Rovereto **I** 72 Fb36
Roverud **N** 43 Fd17
Rovigo **I** 84 Fc37
Rovinari **RO** 87 Hd37
Rovinj **HR** 85 Fd37
Rovnoe **RUS** 123 Fd12
Rów **PL** 57 Ga27
Rowy **PL** 51 Gc24
Royal Tunbridge Wells **GB** 25 Db28
Royan **F** 68 Cd35
Roye **F** 62 Dd30
Røyken **N** 43 Fc18
Røyrvik **N** 33 Ga11
Royston **GB** 25 Db27
Roza **BG** 103 Jd40
Rožaj **MNE** 87 Hb40
Różan **PL** 59 Hb27
Rozay-en-Brie **F** 62 Dd32
Rozdil'na **UA** 125 Ec17
Rozdol'ne **UA** 126 Fa17
Rozdyl'na **MD** 77 Kb33
Rožencovo **RUS** 119 Fc08
Rozivka **UA** 126 Fb16
Rožmitál pod Třemšínem **CZ** 65 Fd31
Rožňava **SK** 67 Hb32
Rožnov pod Radhoštěm **CZ** 66 Gd31
Rozogi **PL** 59 Hb26
Rožok **RUS** 118 Fb09
Rozoy-sur-Serre **F** 62 Ea30
Rozprza **PL** 67 Ha29
Roztoky **CZ** 65 Ga30
Rožyšče **UA** 120 Ea14
Rrogozhinë **RKS** 100 Hb42
Rtiščevo **RUS** 119 Fc11
Ruba **BY** 117 Eb11
Rubbestadneset **N** 42 Ec17
Rubiás **E** 78 Bb36
Rucăr **RO** 88 Jb36
Rucava **LV** 52 Ha22
Ruciane-Nida **PL** 59 Hb26
Ruda **S** 50 Gb21
Ruda Śląska **PL** 66 Gd30
Rude **HR** 73 Gb36
Rüdersdorf **D** 57 Fd27
Rüdesheim **D** 63 Ed30
Rudilla **E** 93 Cc41
Rudinka **HR** 85 Ga38
Rūdiškės **LT** 53 Hd24
Rudkøbing **DK** 49 Fb24
Rudky **UA** 67 Hd31
Rudna Glava **SRB** 87 Hd38
Rudnik **BG** 89 Ka39
Rudnik **SRB** 87 Hb38

Rudniki **PL** 66 Gd29
Rudnja **RUS** 117 Eb11
Rudo **BIH** 86 Ha39
Rudolstadt **D** 64 Fc30
Rue **F** 62 Dc29
Rueda **E** 79 Bc39
Ruen **BG** 89 Jd39
Ruffec **F** 69 Da35
Rugāji **LV** 53 Ja21
Rugby **GB** 24 Da26
Rugles **F** 61 Db31
Ruguj **RUS** 117 Eb08
Ruhan' **RUS** 121 Ec12
Ruhland **D** 65 Fd29
Ruidera **E** 92 Bd43
Rūjiena **LV** 47 Hd20
Ruka **FIN** 31 Hd08
Ruma **SRB** 86 Ha37
Rumboci **BIH** 86 Gd39
Rumburk **CZ** 65 Ga29
Rumia **PL** 51 Gd24
Rumilly **F** 71 Eb36
Rumšiškės **LT** 53 Hd24
Runcorn **GB** 24 Da25
Rundfloen **N** 37 Fd16
Rundvik **S** 39 Gd13
Rungsted **DK** 49 Fd23
Runtuna **S** 45 Gc19
Ruokojärvi **FIN** 30 Hb07
Ruokolahti **FIN** 41 Ja15
Ruokto **S** 29 Gc08
Ruovesi **FIN** 40 Hb14
Rupe **HR** 85 Gb39
Rupea **RO** 76 Jb35
Ruse **BG** 88 Jc38
Rusele **S** 33 Gc11
Rushden **GB** 25 Db26
Ruskeala **RUS** 41 Jb14
Rusksele **S** 33 Gc11
Rusnė **LT** 52 Hb23
Rüsselsheim **D** 63 Ed30
Russelv **N** 26 Gd04
Russkij Kameškir **RUS** 119 Fd11
Russnes **N** 27 Hb03
Rust **A** 74 Gc34
Rusterfjelbma **N** 27 Hc03
Ruszów **PL** 65 Ga29
Rute **E** 105 Bb44
Rüthen **D** 55 Ed28
Ruthin **GB** 24 Cd25
Rutigliano **I** 99 Gc42
Rutka-Tartak **PL** 59 Hc25
Rutledalen **N** 36 Ed15
Ruukki **FIN** 35 Hc11
Ruuvaoja **FIN** 31 Hd07
Ruvo di Puglia **I** 99 Gc42
Ruza **RUS** 117 Ed10
Ruzaevka **RUS** 119 Fc10
Ružany **BY** 120 Ea13
Ružomberok **SK** 67 Ha32
Ry **DK** 49 Fb22
Rybačij **RUS** 52 Ha24
Rybczewice **PL** 67 Hc29
Rybinsk **RUS** 117 Ed09
Rybnik **PL** 59 Hc26

Rybnik **PL** 66 Gd30
Rybno **PL** 59 Hb25
Rybnoe **RUS** 118 Fa11
Rychłocice **PL** 66 Gd29
Rychnowo **PL** 58 Ha26
Rychtal **PL** 66 Gc29
Rychwał **PL** 58 Gd28
Ryd **S** 50 Ga22
Rydaholm **S** 50 Ga21
Ryde **GB** 24 Da28
Rydet **S** 49 Fc21
Rydsnäs **S** 44 Ga20
Rydzewo **PL** 59 Hb26
Rye **GB** 25 Dc28
Rykene **N** 42 Fa19
Ryki **PL** 59 Hc28
Ryl'sk **RUS** 121 Ed13
Rymań **PL** 57 Gb25
Rymanów **PL** 67 Hc31
Rýmařov **CZ** 66 Gc31
Rymättylä **FIN** 46 Ha17
Ryn **PL** 59 Hb25
Rypefjord **N** 26 Ha03
Rypin **PL** 58 Ha26
Rysjedalsvika **N** 36 Ed15
Rytinki **FIN** 35 Hd09
Rząśnik **PL** 59 Hb27
Rzecznica **PL** 58 Gc26
Rzepin **PL** 57 Ga28
Rzeszów **PL** 67 Hc30
Ржев **RUS** 117 Ec10
Ržyščiv **UA** 121 Ec15

S

Sääksjärvi **FIN** 40 Hb13
Saalfeld **D** 64 Fc30
Saalfelden am Steinernen Meer **A** 73 Fd34
Saarbrücken **D** 63 Ec31
Saarburg **D** 63 Ec31
Sääre **EST** 46 Hb20
Saari **FIN** 41 Jb14
Saarijärvi **FIN** 40 Hc13
Saariselkä **FIN** 31 Hc06
Saarivaara **FIN** 35 Ja10
Saarlouis **D** 63 Ec31
Saas Fee **CH** 71 Ec36
Šabac **SRB** 86 Ha37
Sabadell **E** 95 Da41
Šabany **RUS** 47 Jb20
Sabarat **F** 81 Da39
Sabatinivka **UA** 77 Ka32
Sabaudia **I** 98 Fc42
Sabbioneta **I** 84 Fa37
Sabile **LV** 52 Hb21
Sabiñánigo **E** 80 Cd39
Sabinov **SK** 67 Hb32
Šabla **BG** 89 Ka38
Sablé-sur-Sarthe **F** 61 Da32
Saborsko **HR** 85 Gb37
Sabres **F** 80 Cd37
Sabugal **P** 91 Ba40
Säby **S** 44 Ga20
Sacecorbo **E** 92 Ca41

Sacedón **E** 92 Ca41
Săcel **RO** 76 Ja33
Săcele **RO** 88 Jb36
Săcele **RO** 89 Ka37
Săceni **RO** 88 Jb38
Sacile **I** 72 Fc36
Šack **BY** 120 Ea13
Šack **RUS** 118 Fb11
Šac'k **UA** 59 Hd28
Sacoşu Turcesc **RO** 75 Hc36
Săcueni **RO** 75 Hc34
Sada **E** 78 Ba36
Sádaba **E** 80 Cc39
Sadala **EST** 47 Ja18
Sadova **RO** 88 Ja38
Sadovo **BG** 102 Jb40
Sadovoe **RUS** 123 Ga14
Sæbø **N** 36 Fa14
Sæby **DK** 49 Fb21
Săedinenie **BG** 102 Jb40
Săedinenie **BG** 102 Jc40
Saelices **E** 92 Ca42
Sævareid **N** 42 Ed17
Safara **P** 105 Ad43
Säffle **S** 43 Fd18
Saffron Walden **GB** 25 Db27
Safonovo **RUS** 117 Ec11
Sâg **RO** 75 Hd34
Sagadi **EST** 47 Hd17
Sagard **D** 57 Fd25
Sagone **F** 96 Ed41
Sagres **P** 104 Ab43
Sagunt (Sagunto) **E** 93 Cc43
Sagvåg **N** 42 Ed17
Sahagún **E** 79 Bc38
Saharna Nouă **MD** 77 Ka33
Sahechores **E** 79 Bc38
Sahin **TR** 103 Jd42
Šahty **RUS** 123 Fc15
Šahun'ja **RUS** 119 Fc08
Šahy **SK** 74 Ha33
Saija **FIN** 31 Hd07
Saillans **F** 82 Ea37
Saint-Affrique **F** 81 Dc38
Saint-Agrève **F** 82 Dd37
Saint-Aignan **F** 69 Db33
Saint Albans **GB** 25 Db27
Saint-Amand-en-Puisaye **F** 70 Dd33
Saint-Amand-les-Eaux **F** 62 Dd29
Saint-Amand-Montrond **F** 69 Dc34
Saint-Ambroix **F** 82 Dd38
Saint-Amé **F** 71 Ec33
Saint-Amour **F** 70 Ea35
Saint-André-de-Cubzac **F** 68 Cd36
Saint-André-de-l'Eure **F** 61 Db31
Saint-André-les-Alpes **F** 83 Eb38
Saint Andrews **GB** 21 Db21
Saint Anne **GBA** 61 Cd29

Salantai **LT** 52 Hb22
Salas **E** 79 Bc36
Salas de los Infantes **E** 79 Ca39
Sălătrucu **RO** 88 Ja36
Salbris **F** 69 Dc33
Salcia **RO** 87 Hd38
Salcia **RO** 88 Jb38
Šalčininkai **LT** 53 Ja24
Sălcuţa **MD** 77 Ka34
Saldaña **E** 79 Bd38
Saldus **LV** 52 Hb21
Salemi **I** 108 Fc47
Sälen **S** 38 Fd16
Salerno **I** 99 Ga43
Salers **F** 69 Dc36
S'Algar **E** 95 Dc43
Salgótarján **H** 74 Ha33
Salhus **N** 36 Ed16
Sali **HR** 85 Ga39
Salihler **TR** 103 Jd43
Salihli **TR** 113 Kb45
Salihorsk **BY** 120 Ea13
Salins-les-Bains **F** 71 Eb34
Salisbury **GB** 24 Da28
Sălişte **RO** 88 Ja36
Salla **FIN** 31 Hd08
Sallanches **F** 71 Eb36
Sallent **E** 81 Da40
Salme **EST** 46 Hb20
Salmenkylä **FIN** 40 Hb14
Salmerón **E** 92 Ca41
Salmijärvi **RUS** 27 Hd04
Salò **I** 72 Fb36
Salo **FIN** 40 Hb16
Salon-de-Provence **F** 82 Ea38
Salonta **RO** 75 Hc35
Salsbruket **N** 32 Fd11
Salses-le-Château **F** 81 Db39
Sal'sk **RUS** 123 Fd15
Salsomaggiore Terme **I** 84 Fa37
Saltash **GB** 23 Cc28
Saltburn-by-the-Sea **GB** 21 Db23
Saltvik **FIN** 45 Gd17
Saluzzo **I** 83 Ec37
Salvatierra-Agurain **E** 80 Cb38
Salvatierra de los Barros **E** 91 Ba42
Şalyhyne **UA** 121 Ed13
Salzburg **A** 73 Fd34
Salzgitter **D** 56 Fb28
Salzkotten **D** 56 Fa28
Salzwedel **D** 56 Fc27
Samachvalaviçy **BY** 120 Ea12
Samara **RUS** 119 Ga10
Samarina **GR** 101 Hc43
Sâmbăta **RO** 75 Hc35
Sambir **UA** 67 Hd31
Sambuca di Sicilia **I** 108 Fd47

Sámi **GR** 110 Hc46
Sämi **EST** 47 Hd17
Sămica **BG** 102 Jb41
Şamlı **TR** 103 Kb43
Samobor **HR** 73 Gb36
Samoëns **F** 71 Eb35
Samofalovka **RUS** 123 Fd13
Samokov **BG** 102 Ja40
Samolva **RUS** 47 Ja19
Samos **SRB** 87 Hb37
Sámos **TR** 113 Ka46
Samothráki **GR** 102 Jc42
Samro **RUS** 47 Jb18
Samsun **TR** 127 Fc19
Samtens **D** 57 Fd25
Sanadinovo **BG** 88 Jb39
Sânandrei **RO** 75 Hc36
Sanary-sur-Mer **F** 82 Ea39
San Bartolomé de la Torre **E** 105 Ad44
San Bartolomeo in Galdo **I** 99 Ga42
San Benedetto del Tronto **I** 85 Fd40
San Benedetto Po **I** 84 Fb37
San Cataldo **I** 100 Gd43
Sancerre **F** 69 Dc33
Sanchidrián **E** 91 Bc40
San Clemente **E** 92 Ca42
Sancoins **F** 69 Dc34
San Cristóbal de Entreviñas **E** 79 Bc38
Sancti-Spíritus **E** 91 Bb40
Sançursk **RUS** 119 Fc08
Sand **N** 42 Ed18
Sand **N** 43 Fc17
Sandane **N** 36 Ed15
San Daniele del Friuli **I** 73 Fd36
Sandanski **BG** 101 Ja41
Sandata **RUS** 127 Fd16
Sandbach **GB** 24 Da25
Sande **D** 55 Ed26
Sande **N** 36 Ed15
Sandefjord **N** 43 Fb18
Sandgerði **IS** 14 Bb06
Sand in Taufers **I** 72 Fc35
Sandnes **N** 42 Ed18
Sandnessjøen **N** 32 Fd09
Sandomíri **GR** 110 Hd46
Sandomierz **PL** 67 Hb29
Sândominic **RO** 76 Jb34
San Donà di Piave **I** 72 Fc36
Sandovo **RUS** 117 Ed09
Sandøysund **N** 43 Fb18
Šandrivka **UA** 122 Fa15
Sandsele **S** 33 Gc10
Sandstad **N** 32 Fb12
Sandvik **S** 51 Gc21
Sandvika **N** 32 Fd12
Sandvika **N** 33 Ga11
Sandviken **S** 38 Gb16
Sandvikvåg **N** 42 Ed17
Sandwich **GB** 25 Dc28
Sandy **GB** 25 Db27
San Elia a Pianisi **I** 99 Ga42

San Esteban de Gormaz **E** 79 Ca39
San Ferdinando di Puglia **I** 99 Gb42
San Fernando **E** 105 Ad45
San Fratello **I** 109 Ga46
Sangaste **EST** 47 Ja19
San Gavino Monreale **I** 97 Ec44
Sângeorgiu de Pădure **RO** 76 Jb35
Sângeorz-Băi **RO** 76 Ja34
Sângera **MD** 77 Ka34
Sângerei **MD** 77 Jd33
Sangerhausen **D** 64 Fc29
Sângeru **RO** 88 Jc36
San Gimignano **I** 84 Fb39
Sanginkylä **FIN** 35 Hc10
San Giovanni in Fiore **I** 109 Gc45
San Giovanni in Persiceto **I** 84 Fb38
San Giovanni Rotondo **I** 99 Gb42
San Giovanni Valdarno **I** 84 Fb39
Sangis **S** 34 Hb09
San Giuliano Terme **I** 84 Fa39
Sangla **EST** 47 Hd19
Sangüesa **E** 80 Cc39
San Javier **E** 107 Cb45
San José **E** 106 Bd46
Sankavak **TR** 128 Gc17
Sankt Andrä **A** 73 Ga35
Sankt Anna **S** 44 Gb19
Sankt Anton **A** 72 Fa34
Sankt Gallen **CH** 72 Fa34
Sankt Georgen **D** 71 Ed33
Sankt Gilgen **A** 73 Fd34
Sankt Goar **D** 63 Ed30
Sankt Ingbert **D** 63 Ec31
Sankt Jakob **A** 72 Fc35
Sankt Johann **A** 73 Fd34
Sankt Johann **A** 72 Fc34
Sankt Margrethen **CH** 72 Fa34
Sankt Michaelisdonn **D** 56 Fa25
Sankt Moritz **CH** 72 Fa35
Sankt-Peterburg **RUS** 41 Jb16
Sankt-Peterburg **RUS** 117 Eb08
Sankt Peter-Ording **D** 56 Fa25
Sankt Pölten **A** 73 Gb33
Sankt Ulrich **I** 72 Fc35
Sankt Valentin **A** 73 Ga33
Sankt Veit an der Glan **A** 73 Ga35
Sankt Vika **S** 45 Gc19
Sankt-Vith **B** 63 Ec30
Sankt Wendel **D** 63 Ec31
San Leonardo de Yagüe **E** 79 Ca39

San Lorenzo de Calatrava **E** 106 Bc43
San Lorenzo de El Escorial **E** 92 Bd40
San Lorenzo de la Parrilla **E** 92 Ca42
Sanlúcar de Barrameda **E** 105 Ad45
Sanlúcar de Guadiana **E** 104 Ac43
San Lucido **I** 109 Gb45
Sanluri **I** 97 Ed44
San Marco in Lamis **I** 99 Gb42
San Marino **RSM** 84 Fc39
Sânmartin **RO** 76 Jc35
San Martín del Pimpollar **E** 91 Bc41
San Martín de Montalbán **E** 91 Bc42
San Martín de Valdeiglesias **E** 91 Bc41
San Martino di Castrozza **I** 72 Fc36
San Miguel de Salinas **E** 107 Cb45
Sânmihaiu de Câmpie **RO** 76 Ja34
San Miniato **I** 84 Fb39
Sänna **EST** 47 Ja20
San Nicandro Garganico **I** 99 Gb41
Sânnicolau Mare **RO** 75 Hb36
Sanniki **PL** 58 Ha27
Sanok **PL** 67 Hc31
Šanovo **BG** 102 Jc40
San Pedro **E** 92 Ca43
San Pedro del Pinatar **E** 107 Cb45
San Pellegrino Terme **I** 72 Fa36
Sanquhar **GB** 21 Da22
San Quirico d'Orcia **I** 84 Fb40
Sanremo **I** 83 Ec39
San Roque **E** 105 Ba46
San Salvo **I** 99 Ga41
San Sebastián **E** 80 Cb38
San Sebastián de los Reyes **E** 92 Bd41
Sansepolcro **I** 84 Fc39
San Severino Marche **I** 85 Fd40
San Severo **I** 99 Gb42
Sanski Most **BIH** 86 Gc38
San Stefano di Camastra **I** 109 Ga46
Santa Amalia **E** 91 Ba42
Santa Bárbara de Casa **E** 105 Ad43
Santa Cesarea Terme **I** 100 Ha44
Santa Clara-a-Velha **P** 104 Ab43
Santa Coloma de Queralt **E** 95 Da41

Santa Comba **E** 78 Ad36
Santa Croce Camarina **I** 109 Ga48
Santa Cruz de Campezo **E** 80 Cb38
Santa Cruz de Mudela **E** 92 Bd43
Santadi **I** 97 Ec45
Santa Eufemia **E** 105 Bb43
Santa Eugenia (Ribeira) **E** 78 Ad37
Santa Eulalia **E** 93 Cb41
Santa Eulália **P** 90 Ad42
Santa Eulària des Riu **E** 94 Cd44
Santa Fé **E** 106 Bc45
Sant' Agata di Militello **I** 109 Ga46
Santa Margherita **I** 97 Ec45
Santa Maria **CH** 72 Fa35
Santa María de la Peña **E** 80 Cc39
Santa Maria del Calmí **E** 95 Db43
Santa María del Páramo **E** 79 Bc38
Santa María la Real de Nieva **E** 92 Bd40
Santa Marinella **I** 98 Fb41
Santa Marta **E** 91 Ba42
Santana da Serra **P** 104 Ac43
Santander **E** 79 Ca37
Sant'Andrea Frius **I** 97 Ed44
Sant'Angelo dei Lombardi **I** 99 Gb43
Sant'Angelo Lodigia **I** 84 Fa37
Sant'Antioco **I** 97 Ec45
Sant Antoni de Portmany **E** 94 Cd44
Sant'Antonio di Santadi **I** 97 Ec44
Santanyí **E** 95 Db44
Santa Olalla del Cala **E** 105 Ba43
Santa Pau **E** 81 Db40
Santa Pola **E** 107 Cb44
Sant' Arcangelo **I** 99 Gc44
Santarcangelo di Romagna **I** 84 Fc39
Santarém **P** 90 Ac41
Santa-Severa **F** 96 Ed40
Santa Teresa di Riva **I** 109 Gb47
Santa Teresa Gallura **I** 96 Ed42
Sant Carles de la Ràpita **E** 93 Cd42
Sant Carles de Peralta **E** 94 Cd44
Sant Celoni **E** 95 Db41
San Teodoro **I** 97 Ed43
Santeramo in Colle **I** 99 Gc43
Santesteban **E** 80 Cc38

Sant' Eufemia Lamezia **I** 109 Gc45
Sant Feliu de Guíxols **E** 95 Db41
Sant Francesc de Formentera **E** 94 Cd44
Santhià **I** 83 Ed37
Santiago de Alcántara **E** 90 Ad41
Santiago de Compostela **E** 78 Ad36
Santiago do Cacém **P** 90 Ab42
Santibánez de la Sierra **E** 91 Bb40
Santillana del Mar **E** 79 Ca37
Santisteban del Puerto **E** 106 Bd44
Sant Joan d'Alacant **E** 107 Cb44
Sant Llorenç de Morunys **E** 81 Da40
Sant Mateu **E** 93 Cc42
Santo Domingo de la Calzada **E** 79 Ca38
Santo Domingo de Silos **E** 79 Ca39
Santoña **E** 79 Ca37
Santo Tirso **P** 78 Ad38
Santu Lussurgiu **I** 97 Ec43
San Vicente de Alcántara **E** 90 Ad41
San Vicente de la Barquera **E** 79 Bd37
San Vincenzo **I** 84 Fa40
San Vito **I** 97 Ed44
San Vito al Tagliamento **I** 73 Fd36
San Vito dei Normanni **I** 100 Gd43
San Vito lo Capo **I** 108 Fc46
Sanxenxo Sangenjo **E** 78 Ad37
Sanza **I** 99 Gb44
São Brás de Alportel **P** 104 Ac44
São João da Madeira **P** 78 Ad39
São Marcos da Serra **P** 104 Ac43
São Martinho de Angueira **P** 78 Bb39
Saorge **F** 83 Ec38
São Teotónio **P** 104 Ab43
Sápai **GR** 102 Jc42
Sapernoe **RUS** 41 Jb15
Sapožok **RUS** 118 Fb11
Sapri **I** 99 Gb44
Sara **FIN** 40 Hb14
Sarabikulovo **RUS** 119 Ga09
Saraby **N** 26 Ha03
Sarai **RUS** 118 Fb11
Säräisniemi **FIN** 35 Hd11
Saraiu **RO** 89 Ka37
Sarajärvi **FIN** 35 Hd09

Sarajevo **BIH** 86 Gd39
Sarakína **GR** 101 Hd43
Sarakína **GR** 101 Hd44
Sarakiní **GR** 101 Hd42
Saramon **F** 81 Da38
Saranci **BG** 102 Ja40
Sáránd **H** 75 Hc34
Sarandë **AL** 100 Hb44
Saransk **RUS** 119 Fc10
Sarantáporo **GR** 101 Hd43
Šarašova **BY** 59 Hd27
Sarata **UA** 77 Kb35
Sărăteni **MD** 77 Ka34
Saratov **RUS** 123 Fd12
Saray **TR** 103 Ka41
Sarbinowo **PL** 57 Gb25
Sárbograd **H** 74 Gd35
Sardara **I** 97 Ec44
Šarečensk **RUS** 31 Ja07
S'Arenal **E** 95 Db43
Šarengrad **HR** 86 Ha37
Šarhorod **UA** 125 Eb16
Saria **GR** 115 Kb48
Sarıköy **TR** 103 Ka42
Sariñena **E** 80 Cd40
Sariveliler **TR** 128 Gb17
Sariyer **TR** 103 Kb41
Šar'ja **RUS** 117 Eb08
Šar'ja **RUS** 118 Fb08
Sarkadkeresztúr **H** 75 Hc35
Särkelä **FIN** 31 Hd07
Särkijarvi **FIN** 30 Ha07
Şarköy **TR** 103 Ka42
Sarlat-la-Canéda **F** 69 Da36
Sărmaşag **RO** 75 Hd34
Särna **S** 38 Fd15
Sarnaki **PL** 59 Hc27
Sarnano **I** 85 Fd40
Sarnen **CH** 71 Ed35
Sarnico **I** 72 Fa36
Sarno **I** 99 Ga43
Sarny **UA** 120 Ea14
Särö **S** 49 Fc21
Saronída **GR** 111 Jb47
Saronída **GR** 112 Jb46
Saronno **I** 71 Ed36
Sárosd **H** 74 Gd35
Sárospatak **H** 75 Hc33
Šarovce **SK** 74 Gd33
Sarpsborg **N** 43 Fc18
Sarralbe **F** 63 Ec32
Sarrebourg **F** 63 Ec32
Sarreguemines **F** 63 Ec32
Sarre-Union **F** 63 Ec32
Sarria **E** 78 Ba37
Sartène **F** 96 Ed42
Sárti **GR** 102 Jb43
Saruhanlı **TR** 113 Ka44
Sárvár **H** 74 Gc34
Särvsjön **S** 38 Fd14
Sarzana **I** 84 Fa38
Sarzeau **F** 60 Cc32
Sarzedas **P** 90 Ad40
Sa Savina **E** 94 Cd44
Sásd **H** 74 Gd36

Sasino **PL** 51 Gc24
Sasovo **RUS** 118 Fb10
Sassari **I** 97 Ec43
Sassnitz **D** 57 Fd25
Sassoferrato **I** 84 Fc39
Sasso Marconi **I** 84 Fb38
Sassuolo **I** 84 Fb38
Sástago **E** 80 Cc40
Šaštín-Stráže **SK** 66 Gc32
Såtenäs **S** 43 Fd19
Säter **S** 38 Ga14
Säter **S** 44 Gb17
Sātiņi **LV** 52 Hb22
Sátoraljaújhely **H** 75 Hc33
Satovča **BG** 102 Jb41
Sattanen **FIN** 31 Hc07
Satu Mare **RO** 75 Hd33
Šatura **RUS** 118 Fa10
Saucats **F** 68 Cd36
Sauclières **F** 81 Dc38
Sauda **N** 42 Ed17
Sauðárkrókur **IS** 15 Ca05
Saue **EST** 46 Hc18
Saugues **F** 81 Dc37
Saujon **F** 68 Cd35
Sauland **N** 43 Fb18
Săuleşti **RO** 88 Ja37
Saulieu **F** 70 Dd34
Saulkrasti **LV** 52 Hc21
Sault **F** 82 Ea38
Saumur **F** 69 Da33
Saunajärvi **FIN** 35 Ja11
Sauveterre-de-Béarn **F** 80 Cc38
Sauveterre-de-Guyenne **F** 68 Cd36
Sauvo **FIN** 46 Hb17
Sauxillanges **F** 69 Dc36
Sauzé-Vaussais **F** 69 Da34
Sävar **S** 34 Gd12
Sävärşin **RO** 75 Hc36
Sävast **S** 34 Ha09
Savaştepe **TR** 103 Ka43
Savenay **F** 61 Cd32
Säveni **RO** 76 Jc33
Saverdun **F** 81 Da38
Saverne **F** 63 Ec32
Savigliano **I** 83 Ec37
Savignano sul Rubicone **I** 84 Fc38
Savikylä **FIN** 35 Ja12
Şavirii Vechi **MD** 77 Jd32
Savitaipale **FIN** 41 Ja15
Šavnik **MNE** 86 Ha40
Savona **I** 83 Ed38
Savonlinna **FIN** 41 Ja14
Savonranta **FIN** 41 Ja14
Savran **UA** 77 Ka32
Sävsjö **S** 50 Ga21
Savukoski **FIN** 31 Hd07
Sawin **PL** 67 Hd29
Saxmundham **GB** 25 Dc27
Saxnäs **S** 33 Ga11
Säyneinen **FIN** 35 Ja12
Scaër **F** 60 Cb31
Scăeşti **RO** 88 Ja38

Scalasaig – Şevketiye

Scalasaig **GB** 16 Cc20
Scalea **I** 99 Gb44
Scanno **I** 98 Fd41
Scansano **I** 84 Fb40
Scanzano Ionico **I** 99 Gc43
Scarborough **GB** 21 Dc24
Scarinish **GB** 16 Cc20
Scarriff **IRL** 18 Ca24
Sčekino **RUS** 118 Fa11
Schaffhausen **CH** 71 Ed33
Schagen **NL** 55 Eb26
Scharbeutz **D** 56 Fb25
Schärding **A** 73 Fd33
Scheeßel **D** 56 Fa26
Scheibbs **A** 73 Ga33
Scheifling **A** 73 Ga34
Scheßlitz **D** 64 Fb31
Scheveningen **NL** 54 Ea27
Schiermonnikoog **NL** 55 Ec26
Schiffdorf **D** 56 Fa26
Schiltach **D** 71 Ed33
Schio **I** 72 Fb36
Schirmeck **F** 63 Ec32
Schitu Duca **RO** 77 Jd34
Schitu Goleşti **RO** 88 Jb36
Schladming **A** 73 Fd34
Schlanders **I** 72 Fb35
Schleiden **D** 63 Ec30
Schleiz **D** 64 Fc30
Schleswig **D** 49 Fb24
Schleusingen **D** 64 Fb30
Schlieben **D** 57 Fd28
Schlitz **D** 64 Fa30
Schlüchtern **D** 64 Fa30
Schmalkalden **D** 64 Fb30
Schneverdingen **D** 56 Fb26
Schönberg **D** 56 Fb25
Schönberg **D** 56 Fb25
Schöne beck **D** 56 Fc28
Schongau **D** 72 Fb33
Schöningen **D** 56 Fb28
Schönsee **D** 64 Fc31
Schopfheim **D** 71 Ec33
Schörfling **A** 73 Fd33
Schorndorf **D** 64 Fa32
Schramberg **D** 71 Ed33
Schrobenhausen **D** 64 Fb32
Schruns **A** 72 Fa34
Schwaan **D** 56 Fc25
Schwabach **D** 64 Fb31
Schwäbisch Gmünd **D** 64 Fa32
Schwäbisch Hall **D** 64 Fa32
Schwabmünchen **D** 72 Fb33
Schwaigern **D** 64 Fa32
Schwalmstadt **D** 64 Fa29
Schwalmtal **D** 64 Fa30
Schwandorf **D** 64 Fc32
Schwanewede **D** 56 Fa26
Schwarmstedt **D** 56 Fa27
Schwarzenbek **D** 56 Fb26
Schwaz **A** 72 Fc34
Schwechat **A** 74 Gc33
Schwedt **D** 57 Ga27
Schweich **D** 63 Ec30

Schweinfurt **D** 64 Fb30
Schwerin **D** 56 Fc26
Schwerte **D** 55 Ed28
Schwetzingen **D** 63 Ed31
Schwyz **CH** 71 Ed34
Sciacca **I** 108 Fc47
Scicli **I** 109 Ga48
Ščigry **RUS** 122 Fa13
Scilla **I** 109 Gb46
Ścinawa **PL** 65 Gb29
Scoarţa **RO** 88 Ja37
Scorniceşti **RO** 88 Jb37
Ščors **UA** 121 Ec13
Scourie **GB** 17 Da18
Scrabster **GB** 17 Db18
Ščučyn **BY** 59 Hd25
Sculeni **MD** 77 Jd33
Scunthorpe **GB** 25 Db25
Scuol **CH** 72 Fa35
Scutaru **RO** 76 Jc35
Ščyrec' **UA** 67 Hd31
Seahouses **GB** 21 Db22
Seamer **GB** 21 Dc24
Šebekino **RUS** 122 Fa14
Sebeş **RO** 88 Ja36
Sebež **RUS** 53 Jb21
Sebiş **RO** 75 Hc35
Sebnitz **D** 65 Ga29
Secemin **PL** 67 Ha29
Sečenovo **RUS** 119 Fc09
Seclin **F** 62 Dd29
Secondigny **F** 69 Da34
Seda **LT** 52 Hb22
Sedan **F** 62 Ea30
Séderon **F** 82 Ea38
Sedini **I** 96 Ed42
Sedlčany **CZ** 65 Ga31
Šeduva **LT** 52 Hc23
Sędziszów **PL** 67 Ha30
Seefeld **A** 72 Fb34
Seehausen **D** 56 Fc27
Seelow **D** 57 Ga27
Sées **F** 61 Db31
Seferihisar **TR** 113 Ka45
Şegarcea **RO** 88 Ja38
Segorbe **E** 93 Cc42
Segovia **E** 92 Bd40
Segré **F** 61 Cd32
Segura **P** 91 Ba41
Segura de la Sierra **E** 106 Bd44
Segura de León **E** 105 Ba43
Seia **P** 90 Ad40
Şeica Mare **RO** 76 Ja35
Seilhac **F** 69 Db36
Seinäjoki **FIN** 40 Hb13
Seini **RO** 76 Hd33
Seirijai **LT** 59 Hd25
Seirijai **LT** 59 Hd25
Sejny **PL** 59 Hc25
Şękowa **PL** 67 Hb31
Šeksna **RUS** 117 Ed08
Sekulovo **BG** 89 Jd38
Selargius **I** 97 Ed45
Şelaru **RO** 88 Jb37
Selb **D** 64 Fc30

Selbekken **N** 37 Fc13
Selbitz **D** 64 Fc30
Selbu **N** 37 Fc13
Selby **GB** 21 Db24
Sel'co **RUS** 47 Jb19
Selçuk **TR** 113 Ka45
Selde **DK** 48 Fa21
Sélestat **F** 71 Ec33
Selet **S** 34 Gd10
Selevac **SRB** 87 Hb38
Selfoss **IS** 14 Bc07
Seligenstadt **D** 64 Fa30
Selimiye **TR** 113 Kb46
Selimpaşa **TR** 103 Kb41
Selište **SRB** 87 Hd38
Seližarovo **RUS** 117 Ec10
Seljaküla **EST** 46 Hc18
Seljatyn **UA** 76 Jb33
Seljatyn **UA** 124 Ea16
Selje **N** 36 Ed14
Seljebø **N** 37 Fb13
Seljord **N** 42 Fa18
Selkirk **GB** 21 Da22
Selles-sur-Cher **F** 69 Db33
Selongey **F** 70 Ea33
Selsjön **S** 39 Gc13
Seltjärn **S** 39 Gc13
Semenivka **UA** 121 Ec13
Semenov **RUS** 118 Fb09
Semënovka **RUS** 123 Fd13
Semerdžievo **BG** 88 Jc38
Semikarakorsk **RUS** 123 Fc15
Semiluki **RUS** 122 Fb13
Šemordan **RUS** 119 Fd08
Šempeter **SLO** 73 Ga36
Sempujärvi **FIN** 34 Hb09
Semur-en-Auxois **F** 70 Ea33
Senden **D** 72 Fa33
Şendreni **RO** 89 Jd36
Senec **SK** 74 Gc33
Senftenberg **D** 65 Ga29
Senica **SK** 66 Gc32
Senigallia **I** 85 Fd39
Senj **HR** 85 Ga37
Senkaya **TR** 127 Ga19
Senlis **F** 62 Dd31
Sennecey-le-Grand **F** 70 Ea34
Sennen **GB** 23 Ca28
Sennybridge **GB** 24 Cd26
Senohrad **SK** 74 Ha33
Senokos **BG** 89 Ka38
Senonches **F** 61 Db31
Senorbì **I** 97 Ed44
Senovo **BG** 88 Jc38
Sens **F** 62 Dd32
Senta **SRB** 75 Hb36
Separeva Banja **BG** 102 Ja40
Šepelevo **RUS** 41 Jb16
Šepetivka **UA** 121 Eb15
Sępólno Krajeńskie **PL** 58 Gc26
Sępopol **PL** 59 Hb25
Septemvri **BG** 102 Jb40

Sepúlveda **E** 92 Bd40
Serafimoviè **RUS** 123 Fd13
Seraing **B** 63 Eb29
Serdobsk **RUS** 119 Fc11
Serebrjanskij **RUS** 47 Jb18
Sereď **SK** 74 Gd33
Seredžius **LT** 52 Hc24
Seregno **I** 71 Ed36
Šeremet'evka **RUS** 119 Ga08
Séres **GR** 101 Ja42
Serfaus **A** 72 Fb34
Sergač **RUS** 119 Fc09
Sergiev Posad **RUS** 118 Fa10
Sergines **F** 62 Dd32
Sérifos **GR** 111 Jc47
Sermaize-les-Bains **F** 62 Ea32
Sermehin **MK** 101 Hd42
Sernancelhe **P** 78 Ba39
Sernur **RUS** 119 Fd08
Serock **PL** 59 Hb27
Serón **E** 106 Bd45
Serón de Nágima **E** 80 Cb40
Seròs **E** 80 Cd40
Serpa **P** 104 Ac43
Serpuhov **RUS** 117 Ed11
Serracapriola **I** 99 Ga41
Serra de Outes **E** 78 Ad36
Serradilla **E** 91 Bb41
Serra San Bruno **I** 109 Gc46
Serres **F** 82 Ea37
Serrières **F** 70 Ea36
Sertã **P** 90 Ad40
Sertolovo **RUS** 41 Jb16
Sérvia **GR** 101 Hd43
Sesimbra **P** 90 Ab42
Seskarö **S** 34 Hb09
Sessa Aurunca **I** 98 Fd42
Sestimo **BG** 102 Ja40
Sesto Fiorentino **I** 84 Fb39
Sesto San Giovanni **I** 71 Ed36
Sestriere **I** 83 Eb37
Sestri Levante **I** 83 Ed38
Sestroreck **RUS** 41 Jb16
Sesvete **HR** 73 Gb36
Šėta **LT** 53 Hd23
Sète **F** 81 Dc39
Setermoen **N** 29 Gc06
Setraki **RUS** 123 Fc14
Settimo Torinese **I** 83 Ec37
Settle **GB** 21 Da24
Setúbal **P** 90 Ac42
Seui **I** 97 Ed44
Seurre **F** 70 Ea34
Sevaster **AL** 100 Hb43
Sevastopol' **UA** 126 Fa18
Ševčenkove **UA** 122 Fa14
Sevenoaks **GB** 25 Db28
Séverac-le-Château **F** 81 Dc37
Sevettijarvi **FIN** 27 Hc04
Sevilla **E** 105 Ba44
Şevketiye **TR** 103 Ka43

Skara – Sola

Skara **S** 44 Fd19
Skarberget **N** 28 Gb06
Skärblacka **S** 44 Gb19
Skardet **N** 26 Gd04
Skardet **N** 33 Ga09
Skare **N** 42 Ed17
Skåre **N** 44 Fd18
Skärhamn **S** 43 Fc20
Skarness **N** 43 Fc17
Skärplinge **S** 45 Gc17
Skärså **S** 39 Gc15
Skarsvåg **N** 27 Hb02
Skarvsjöby **S** 33 Gb11
Skaryszew **PL** 67 Hb29
Skarżysko-Kamienna **PL** 67 Hb29
Skattkärr **S** 44 Ga18
Skattungbyn **S** 38 Ga16
Skatval **N** 37 Fc13
Skaudvilė **LT** 52 Hc23
Skaulo **S** 29 Gd07
Skawina **PL** 67 Ha31
Skeby **S** 44 Fd19
Skeda **S** 44 Gb20
Skedshult **S** 44 Gb20
Skedsmokorset **N** 43 Fc17
Skee **S** 43 Fc19
Skegness **GB** 25 Dc25
Skei **N** 32 Fd10
Skei **N** 36 Ed15
Skei **N** 37 Fb13
Skellefteå **S** 34 Gd11
Skelleftehamn **S** 34 Ha11
Skender Vakuf **BIH** 86 Gc38
Skene **S** 49 Fd21
Skepasti **GR** 114 Jc49
Skerries **IRL** 19 Cb24
Ski **N** 43 Fc18
Skibbereen **IRL** 22 Bc25
Skibotn **N** 26 Gd05
Skidal' **BY** 59 Hd25
Skien **N** 43 Fb18
Skien **N** 43 Fb18
Skierbieszów **PL** 67 Hd29
Skierniewice **PL** 58 Ha28
Skillingaryd **S** 50 Ga21
Skinnskatteberg **S** 44 Gb18
Skipton **GB** 21 Da24
Skirmantiškė **LT** 52 Hc23
Skive **DK** 48 Fa22
Skjelstad **N** 32 Fd12
Skjern **DK** 48 Fa23
Skjervøy **N** 26 Gd04
Skjold **N** 26 Gc05
Skjolden **N** 36 Fa15
Skjønhaug **N** 43 Fc18
Šklov **BY** 121 Eb12
Skoczów **PL** 66 Gd31
Škofja Loka **SLO** 73 Ga36
Škofljica **SLO** 73 Ga36
Skógar **IS** 14 Bc08
Skoghall **S** 44 Fd18
Skogn **N** 32 Fc12
Skoki **PL** 58 Gc27
Skole **UA** 67 Hd31
Skollenborg **N** 43 Fb18

Skopiá **GR** 111 Ja45
Skopin **RUS** 118 Fa11
Skopje **MK** 101 Hc41
Skórcz **PL** 58 Gd26
Skorków **PL** 67 Ha29
Skorodnoe **RUS** 122 Fa13
Skorogoszcz **PL** 66 Gc30
Skoroszyce **PL** 66 Gc30
Skorovatn **N** 32 Fd11
Skørping **DK** 49 Fb21
Skortsinós **GR** 111 Ja47
Skotterud **N** 43 Fd17
Skoulikariá **GR** 110 Hc45
Skoúrta **GR** 112 Jb46
Skövde **S** 44 Ga19
Skrá **GR** 101 Hd42
Skrad **HR** 85 Ga37
Skradin **HR** 85 Gb39
Skreia **N** 37 Fc16
Skrīveri **LV** 53 Hd21
Skrolsvika **N** 28 Gb05
Skrunda **LV** 52 Hb21
Skule **S** 39 Gc13
Skulgam **N** 26 Gc04
Skulsk **PL** 58 Gd27
Skulte **LV** 46 Hc20
Skultorp **S** 44 Ga20
Skultuna **S** 44 Gb18
Skuodas **LT** 52 Hb22
Skurup **S** 49 Fd23
Skurv **S** 50 Gb22
Skutari **AL** 100 Ha41
Skutskär **S** 39 Gc16
Skutvika **N** 28 Ga07
Skverbai **LT** 53 Hd22
Skvyra **UA** 121 Ec15
Skwierzyna **PL** 57 Gb27
Skyttmon **S** 38 Gb13
Skyttorp **S** 45 Gc17
Slabada **BY** 53 Jb24
Slagelse **DK** 49 Fc23
Slagnäs **S** 33 Gc10
Slănčev Briag **BG** 89 Ka39
Slancy **RUS** 47 Ja18
Slane **IRL** 19 Cb23
Slănic **RO** 88 Jc36
Slănic-Moldova **RO** 76 Jc35
Slano **HR** 86 Gd40
Slaný **CZ** 65 Ga30
Slatina **BIH** 86 Gc38
Slatina **HR** 74 Gd36
Slatina **RO** 88 Ja37
Slatina **SRB** 86 Ha38
Slatina-Timiş **RO** 87 Hd37
Slattum **N** 43 Fc17
Slavharad **BY** 121 Ec12
Slavičín **CZ** 66 Gd32
Slavikai **LT** 52 Hc24
Slavinja **SRB** 87 Hd39
Slavjansk na-Kubani **RUS** 127 Fc17
Slavkoviči **RUS** 47 Jb20
Slavonice **CZ** 65 Gb32
Slavonski Brod **HR** 86 Gd37
Slavonski Šamac **HR** 86 Gd37

Slavsk **RUS** 52 Hb24
Slavs'ke **UA** 67 Hd32
Slavuta **UA** 121 Eb15
Sławatycze **PL** 59 Hd28
Sławno **PL** 57 Gb25
Śleśin **PL** 58 Gd27
Slidre **N** 37 Fb16
Sligachan **GB** 16 Cd19
Sligo **IRL** 18 Ca22
Slisenvaara **RUS** 41 Jb14
Šlissel'burg **RUS** 117 Eb08
Slite **S** 45 Gd20
Slivata **BG** 87 Hd38
Sliven **BG** 89 Jd39
Slivnica **BG** 102 Ja40
Slivo Pole **BG** 88 Jc38
Słomniki **PL** 67 Ha30
Slonim **BY** 120 Ea13
Slovenj Gradec **SLO** 73 Ga35
Slovenska Bistrica **SLO** 73 Gb35
Slovenska L'upča **SK** 67 Ha32
Slovinka **RUS** 118 Fb08
Slov'jans'k **UA** 122 Fb15
Słubice **PL** 57 Ga28
Sluck **BY** 120 Ea13
Slunj **HR** 85 Gb37
Słupca **PL** 58 Gc28
Słupia **PL** 67 Hb30
Słupno **PL** 58 Ha27
Słupsk **PL** 58 Gc25
Slussfors **S** 33 Gb10
Smålandsstenar **S** 49 Fd21
Smalininkai **LT** 52 Hc24
Smaljan'dca **BY** 59 Hd27
Smaljaviču **BY** 121 Eb12
Smârdioasa **RO** 88 Jc38
Smarhon' **BY** 53 Ja24
Smarhon' **BY** 120 Ea12
Šmarje pri Jelšah **SLO** 73 Gb36
Smeberg **S** 43 Fc19
Smedby **S** 50 Gb22
Smederevo **SRB** 87 Hb38
Smedjebacken **S** 44 Gb17
Śmierdnica **PL** 57 Ga26
Śmigiel **PL** 57 Gb28
Smila **UA** 121 Ed15
Smiltene **LV** 47 Hd20
Smjadovo **BG** 89 Jd39
Smogulec **PL** 58 Gc27
Šmojlovo **RUS** 47 Jb20
Smołdzino **PL** 51 Gc24
Smolenice **SK** 74 Gc33
Smolensk **RUS** 117 Ec11
Smoljan **BG** 102 Jb41
Smolnik **PL** 67 Hc31
Smolsko **BG** 102 Ja40

Smože **UA** 67 Hd32
Smygehamn **S** 49 Fd24
Šmykove **UA** 77 Kb32
Smyšljaevsk **RUS** 119 Ga10
Snåsa **N** 32 Fd12
Snedsted **DK** 48 Fa21
Sneek **NL** 55 Ec26
Sneem **IRL** 22 Bc25
Snihurivka **UA** 125 Ed16
Snillfjord **N** 37 Fb13
Snina **SK** 67 Hc32
Snjatyn **UA** 76 Jb32
Snjatyn **UA** 124 Ea16
Snøfjord **N** 26 Ha03
Soanlahti **RUS** 41 Jb13
Soave **I** 84 Fb37
Sobibór **PL** 59 Hd28
Sobinka **RUS** 118 Fa10
Sobolevo **RUS** 118 Fb11
Sobótka **PL** 67 Hb29
Sobra **HR** 86 Gd40
Sobrance **SK** 67 Hc32
Søby **DK** 49 Fb24
Sochaczew **PL** 58 Ha28
Soči **RUS** 127 Fd17
Socodor **RO** 75 Hc35
Socuéllamos **E** 92 Bd42
Sodankylä **FIN** 31 Hc07
Söderåkra **S** 50 Gb22
Söderbärke **S** 44 Gb17
Söderfors **S** 45 Gc17
Söderhamn **S** 39 Gc16
Söderköping **S** 44 Gb19
Södertälje **S** 45 Gc18
Södervik **S** 45 Gd18
Södra Sunderbyn **S** 34 Ha10
Södra Tresund **S** 33 Gb11
Södra Vi **S** 44 Gb20
Soest **D** 55 Ed28
Sofádes **GR** 101 Hd44
Sofija **BG** 102 Ja40
Sofijivka **UA** 121 Ed15
Šofjanga **RUS** 35 Ja09
Sögel **D** 55 Ed27
Sogndal **N** 36 Fa15
Sohós **GR** 101 Ja42
Soignies **B** 62 Ea29
Şoimi **RO** 75 Hc35
Soini **FIN** 40 Hb13
Soissons **F** 62 Dd31
Sokal' **UA** 67 Hd30
Sokal' **UA** 120 Ea15
Söke **TR** 113 Kb46
Sokna **N** 43 Fb17
Soknedal **N** 37 Fc13
Soko Banja **SRB** 87 Hc39
Sokol **RUS** 117 Ed08
Sokolac **BIH** 86 Ha39
Sokółka **PL** 59 Hc26
Sokołów Małopolski **PL** 67 Hc30
Sokołów Podlaski **PL** 59 Hc27
Sokoły **PL** 59 Hc26
Sokyrjany **UA** 76 Jc32
Sola **N** 42 Ec18

Solana del Pino E 106 Bc43
Solares E 79 Ca37
Solberg S 33 Gc12
Solca RO 76 Jb33
Sol'cy RUS 117 Eb09
Şoldăneşti MD 77 Ka32
Sölden A 72 Fb35
Solec Kujawski PL 58 Gd26
Solënoe RUS 123 Fd15
Solenzara F 96 Ed41
Solihull GB 24 Da26
Solingen D 63 Ec29
Sollebrunn S 43 Fd20
Sollefteå S 39 Gc13
Sollentuna S 45 Gc18
Sóller E 95 Db43
Sollihøgda N 43 Fc17
Solncevo RUS 122 Fa13
Solnečnogorsk RUS 117
Ed10
Solnice CZ 65 Gb30
Šolohovskij RUS 123 Fc14
Solone UA 122 Fa15
Solonţ RO 76 Jc34
Solothurn CH 71 Ec34
Solotvyn UA 76 Ja32
Solotvyna UA 76 Ja33
Sølsnes N 36 Fa14
Solsona E 81 Da40
Solsvik N 36 Ec16
Solt H 74 Ha35
Soltau D 56 Fb27
Soltvadkert H 74 Ha35
Solvarbo S 44 Gb17
Sölvesborg S 50 Ga23
Soly BY 53 Ja24
Sol y Nieve E 106 Bc45
Soma TR 113 Ka44
Somaén E 92 Ca40
Somain F 62 Dd29
Sombor SRB 74 Ha36
Şomcuta Mare RO 75 Hd34
Somero FIN 40 Hb16
Somianki PL 59 Hb27
Sömmerda D 64 Fb29
Sommersete N 27 Hd03
Sommesous F 62 Ea32
Sommières F 82 Dd38
Somogyvár H 74 Gd35
Somonino PL 58 Gd24
Sompolno PL 58 Gd27
Soncillo E 79 Ca38
Sondalo I 72 Fa35
Søndeled N 43 Fb19
Sønderborg DK 49 Fb24
Sønder Nissum DK 48 Fa22
Sønder Omme DK 48 Fa23
Sondershausen D 64 Fb29
Søndersø DK 49 Fb23
Søndervig DK 48 Fa22
Sondrio I 71 Ed34
Son en Breugel NL 55 Eb28
Sonkajärvi FIN 35 Hd12
Sonkovo RUS 117 Ed09
Sonneberg D 64 Fb30
Sonseca E 91 Bc42

Sonthofen D 72 Fa34
Sontra D 64 Fa29
Sopot PL 58 Gd25
Sopot SRB 87 Hb38
Sopotnica MK 101 Hc42
Sopron H 74 Gc34
Sora I 98 Fd42
Söråker S 39 Gc14
Sorano I 84 Fb40
Sorbas E 106 Bd45
Sörbygden S 38 Gb14
Sore F 80 Cd37
Søre Moen N 32 Fd12
Soresina I 84 Fa37
Sør-Flatanger N 32 Fc11
Sörforsa S 38 Gb15
Sorgono I 97 Ed44
Sorgues-l'Ouvèze F 82
Dd38
Sør-Gutvika N 32 Fd11
Soria E 79 Ca39
Sørkjosen N 26 Gd04
Sørland N 28 Fd07
Sørli N 33 Ga12
Sörmjöle S 34 Gd12
Sornac F 69 Db35
Sorø DK 49 Fc23
Soroca MD 77 Jd32
Soroč'i Gory RUS 119 Fd09
Sørreisa N 26 Gc05
Sorrento I 99 Ga43
Sørrollnes N 28 Gb06
Sorsakoski FIN 41 Hd13
Sorsele S 33 Gc10
Sorso I 97 Ec43
Sørstraumen N 26 Gd04
Sort E 81 Da39
Sortavala RUS 41 Jb14
Sortland N 28 Gb06
Sør-Tverrfjord N 26 Gd04
Sørumsand N 43 Fc17
Sørvær N 26 Gd03
Sørvågen N 28 Fd07
Sörvattnet S 38 Fd14
Sørvika N 37 Fd14
Sösdala S 49 Fd23
Sos del Rey Católico E 80
Cc39
Sosedka RUS 119 Fc11
Sosnenskij RUS 117 Ed11
Sosnicy RUS 47 Jb17
Sosnove UA 120 Ea14
Sosnovka RUS 118 Fb11
Sosnovka RUS 119 Fd08
Sosnovo RUS 41 Jb16
Sosnovyj Bor RUS 47 Jb17
Sosnowica PL 59 Hc28
Sosnowiec PL 67 Ha30
Sospel F 83 Ec39
Šoštanj SLO 73 Ga35
Šoška RUS 119 Fd15
Sotasæter N 36 Fa15
Sotillo de la Adrada E 91
Bc41
Sotkamo FIN 35 Hd11
Soto del Barco E 79 Bc36

Sotogrande E 105 Ba46
Sottunga FIN 46 Ha17
Soufflenheim F 63 Ed32
Soufli GR 103 Jd41
Souillac F 69 Db36
Souilly F 63 Eb31
Soulac-sur-Mer F 68 Cd35
Soúli GR 111 Ja46
Soulópoulo GR 101 Hc44
Sourpi GR 111 Ja45
Sousceyrac F 69 Db36
Sousel P 90 Ad41
Soustons F 80 Cc37
Southampton GB 24 Da28
Southend-on-Sea GB 25
Dc27
South Molton GB 23 Cc27
Southport GB 21 Da24
South Shields GB 21 Db23
Southwold GB 25 Dd27
Souvigny F 69 Dc34
Sovata RO 76 Jb35
Soverato I 109 Gc46
Sovetsk RUS 52 Hb24
Sovetskaja RUS 123 Fc14
Sovetskaja RUS 127 Fd17
Sovetskij RUS 41 Ja16
Sovetskij RUS 119 Fd08
Sovetskoe RUS 127 Ga17
Sowczyce PL 66 Gd29
Sowia Góra PL 57 Gb27
Sozopol BG 103 Ka40
Spa B 63 Eb30
Spalding GB 25 Db26
Spálené Poříčí CZ 65 Fd31
Sparbu N 32 Fc12
Sparreholm S 44 Gb19
Spárti GR 111 Ja47
Spas-Klepiki RUS 118 Fa10
Spasovo BG 89 Ka38
Spassk- Rjazanskij RUS
118 Fb11
Spean Bridge GB 16 Cd19
Spentrup DK 49 Fb22
Spétses GR 111 Ja47
Speyer D 63 Ed31
Spezzano Albanese I 99
Gc44
Spezzano della Sila I 109
Gc45
Spiddle IRL 18 Bd23
Spiez CH 71 Ec35
Spijkenisse NL 54 Ea28
Spilimbergo I 73 Fd36
Spiljani MNE 87 Hb40
Spilsby GB 25 Dc25
Spinazzola I 99 Gb43
Špindlerův Mlýn CZ 65
Gb30
Spirovo RUS 117 Ec09
Spišská Belá SK 67 Hb32
Spittal an der Drau A 73
Fd35
Spitz A 73 Gb33
Spjelkavik N 36 Fa14
Split HR 86 Gc39

Splügen CH 72 Fa35
Spodsbjerg DK 49 Fb24
Špogi LV 53 Ja22
Špola UA 121 Ec15
Spoleto I 84 Fc40
Spotorno I 83 Ed38
Spremberg D 65 Ga29
Şpring RO 76 Ja35
Springe D 56 Fa28
Sproge S 51 Gc21
Spuž MNE 86 Ha40
Squillace I 109 Gc45
Squinzano I 100 Gd43
Srb HR 85 Gb38
Srbac BIH 86 Gc37
Srbica RKS 87 Hc40
Srbobran SRB 74 Ha36
Srbovac RKS 87 Hc40
Srdiečko SK 67 Ha32
Srebărna BG 89 Jd37
Srebrenica BIH 86 Ha38
Srebrenik BIH 86 Gd38
Sredec BG 102 Jc40
Sredec BG 103 Jd40
Śrem PL 58 Gc28
Sremska Mitrovica SRB 86
Ha37
Sremski Karlovci SRB 87
Hb37
Sribne UA 121 Ed14
Środa Wielkopolska PL 58
Gc28
Srokowo PL 59 Hb25
Stachanov UA 122 Fb15
Stachy CZ 65 Fd32
Staðarskáli IS 14 Bd06
Stade D 56 Fa26
Stadskanaal NL 55 Ed26
Stadthagen D 56 Fa27
Stadtlohn D 55 Ec28
Staffanstorp S 49 Fd23
Stafford GB 24 Da25
Stahnsdorf D 57 Fd27
Staicele LV 47 Hd20
Stakkvik N 26 Gc04
Stakliškės LT 53 Hd24
Stalbe LV 47 Hd20
Ställdalen S 44 Ga17
Staloluokta S 28 Gb08
Stalon S 33 Gb11
Stalowa Wola PL 67 Hc30
Stambolijski BG 102 Jb40
Stamford GB 25 Db26
Stamford Bridge GB 21
Db24
Stamnes N 36 Ed16
Stamsund N 28 Ga07
Stânceni RO 76 Jb34
Stånga S 51 Gd21
Stange N 37 Fc16
Stanhope GB 21 Db23
Stanica Bagaevskaja RUS
123 Fc15
Stanišić SRB 74 Ha36
Staňkov CZ 65 Fd31
Stanovoe RUS 122 Fa12

Stans – Stropkov

Stans **CH** 71 Ed34
Stanyčno- Luhans'ke **UA** 123 Fc14
Staphorst **NL** 55 Ec27
Staporków **PL** 67 Hb29
Stara **PL** 67 Ha29
Stara Caryčanka **UA** 77 Kb34
Starachowice **PL** 67 Hb29
Staraja Russa **RUS** 117 Eb09
Stara Kiszewa **PL** 58 Gd25
Stara Moravica **SRB** 74 Ha36
Stara Novalja **HR** 85 Ga38
Stara Pazova **SRB** 87 Hb37
Stara Rečka **BG** 88 Jc39
Stara Reka **BG** 88 Jc39
Stara Ušycja **UA** 76 Jc32
Stara Vyživka **UA** 59 Hd28
Stara Zagora **BG** 102 Jc40
Stare Dolistowo **PL** 59 Hc26
Stare Jeżewo **PL** 59 Hc26
Stare Kiełbonki **PL** 59 Hb26
Stare Strącze **PL** 57 Gb28
Stargard Szczeciński **PL** 57 Ga26
Stårheim **N** 36 Ed14
Starica **RUS** 117 Ec10
Starica **RUS** 121 Ed12
Starigrad **HR** 86 Gc40
Starnberg **D** 72 Fb33
Starobil's'k **UA** 122 Fb14
Starobin **BY** 120 Ea13
Starodub **RUS** 121 Ec13
Starogard **PL** 57 Gb26
Starogard Gdański **PL** 58 Gd25
Starojur'evo **RUS** 118 Fb11
Starokostjantyniv **UA** 121 Eb15
Starominskaja **RUS** 127 Fc16
Staro Nagoričane **MK** 101 Hd41
Staro Petrovo Selo **HR** 86 Gd37
Starosel **BG** 102 Jb40
Staro Selo **BG** 88 Jc38
Starotitarovskaja **RUS** 126 Fb17
Starožilovo **RUS** 118 Fa11
Stary Dzierzgoń **PL** 58 Gd25
Staryi Oskol **RUS** 122 Fa13
Staryja Darohi **BY** 121 Eb13
Staryj Sambir **UA** 67 Hd31
Staßfurt **D** 56 Fc28
Staszów **PL** 67 Hb30
Stathelle **N** 43 Fb18
Staume **N** 36 Ed15
Stavanger **N** 42 Ed18
Stave **SRB** 86 Ha38
Stavelot **B** 63 Eb30
Stavern **N** 43 Fb19
Stavky **UA** 67 Hd29

Stavre **S** 38 Ga14
Stavrodrómi **GR** 110 Hd46
Stavropol' **RUS** 127 Fd16
Stavrós **GR** 101 Ja42
Stavroskiádi **GR** 101 Hc44
Stavroúpoli **GR** 102 Jb42
Stawiski **PL** 59 Hb26
Stawiszyn **PL** 58 Gd28
Steenbergen **NL** 54 Ea28
Steenvoorde **F** 62 Dd29
Steenwijk **NL** 55 Ec27
Stefan Karadža **BG** 89 Jd38
Ştefan-Vodă **MD** 77 Kb34
Steffisburg **CH** 71 Ec35
Stege **DK** 49 Fc24
Stegna **PL** 58 Gd25
Ştei **RO** 75 Hd35
Steķi **LV** 53 Ja21
Stein **D** 64 Fb31
Steinach **A** 72 Fb34
Steinach **D** 64 Fb30
Stein am Rhein **CH** 71 Ed34
Steinau **D** 64 Fa30
Steine **N** 28 Ga06
Steinfeld **D** 55 Ed27
Steinfurt **D** 55 Ed27
Steinhagen **D** 57 Fd25
Steinheim **D** 56 Fa28
Steinkjer **N** 32 Fc12
Steinshamn **N** 36 Fa13
Steinsstaðabyggð **IS** 15 Ca06
Stekenjokk **S** 33 Ga11
Stenay **F** 63 Eb31
Stendal **D** 56 Fc27
Stende **LV** 52 Hb21
Štěnovice **CZ** 65 Fd31
Stensele **S** 33 Gb11
Stenstorp **S** 44 Fd20
Stenträsk **S** 34 Gd09
Stenudden **S** 33 Gc09
Stenungsund **S** 43 Fc20
Stepanci **MK** 101 Hc42
Štepivka **UA** 121 Ed14
Stepnica **PL** 57 Ga26
Stepnoe Matjunico **RUS** 119 Fd10
Stepojevac **SRB** 87 Hb38
Sterdyń-Osada **PL** 59 Hc27
Sternberg **D** 56 Fc26
Šternberk **CZ** 66 Gc31
Stérnes **GR** 114 Jc49
Sterzing **I** 72 Fb35
Stęszew **PL** 58 Gc28
Stevenage **GB** 25 Db27
Steyr **A** 73 Ga33
Stężyca **PL** 58 Gc25
Stigen **S** 43 Fc19
Stigliano **I** 99 Gb43
Stigtomta **S** 44 Gb19
Stilida **PL** 111 Ja45
Stilo **I** 109 Gc46
Štimlje **RKS** 87 Hc40
Stinăpari **RO** 87 Hc37
Štip **MK** 101 Hd41
Stíra **GR** 112 Jb46

Stirling **GB** 21 Da21
Štítary **CZ** 65 Gb32
Štítnik **SK** 67 Hb32
Stjørdal **N** 37 Fc13
Stockach **D** 71 Ed33
Stockaryd **S** 50 Ga21
Stockbridge **GB** 24 Da28
Stockerau **A** 73 Gb33
Stockholm **S** 45 Gc18
Stockport **GB** 24 Da25
Stockton-on-Tees **GB** 21 Db23
Stoczek Lukowski **PL** 59 Hc28
Stod **CZ** 65 Fd31
Stöde **S** 38 Gb14
Stødi **N** 33 Ga09
Stöðvarfjörður **IS** 15 Cc08
Stoholm **DK** 48 Fa22
Stoke-on-Trent **GB** 24 Da25
Stokkseyri **IS** 14 Bc07
Stokkvågen **N** 32 Fd09
Stokmarknes **N** 28 Ga06
Stolac **BIH** 86 Gd40
Stolin **BY** 120 Ea14
Stollberg **D** 65 Fd30
Stöllet **S** 44 Fd17
Stoloiceni **MD** 77 Jd34
Stómio **GR** 101 Ja44
Stone **GB** 24 Da25
Stonehaven **GB** 17 Db20
Stonglandet **N** 28 Gb05
Stopnica **PL** 67 Hb30
Storå **S** 44 Ga18
Stora Blåsjön **S** 33 Ga11
Storberg **S** 33 Gc10
Storby **FIN** 45 Gd17
Stordalen **N** 36 Fa14
Stordalen **S** 29 Gc06
Stordalselv **N** 26 Gc05
Storebro **S** 50 Gb21
Store Heddinge **DK** 49 Fd24
Storekorsnes **N** 26 Ha04
Storelv **N** 26 Ha03
Store Molvik **N** 27 Hc03
Støren **N** 37 Fc13
Storfors **S** 44 Ga18
Storforshei **N** 33 Ga09
Storjola **S** 33 Ga11
Storjord **N** 28 Gb08
Storjorda **N** 28 Ga08
Storkow **D** 57 Ga28
Storlien **S** 38 Fd13
Stornoway **GB** 16 Cd18
Storožynec' **UA** 76 Jb32
Storožynec' **UA** 124 Ea16
Storslett **N** 26 Gd04
Storstein **N** 26 Gd04
Storsteinnes **N** 26 Gc05
Storuman **S** 33 Gb11
Storvorde **DK** 49 Fb21
Storvreta **S** 45 Gc17
Stöten **S** 38 Fd16
Stovbcy **BY** 120 Ea13
Støvring **DK** 49 Fb21
Stowięcino **PL** 58 Gc25

Stowmarket **GB** 25 Dc27
Stow-on-the-Wold **GB** 24 Da27
Strabane **GB** 20 Cb22
Stradella **I** 83 Ed37
Straelen **D** 55 Ec28
Strakonice **CZ** 65 Fd32
Straldža **BG** 103 Jd40
Stralki **BY** 53 Jb22
Stralsund **D** 57 Fd25
Strambino **I** 71 Ec36
Strâmtura **RO** 76 Ja33
Stranda **N** 36 Fa14
Strandby **DK** 49 Fb21
Strandebarm **N** 42 Ed17
Strangford **GB** 20 Cc23
Strängnäs **S** 45 Gc18
Strångsjö **S** 44 Gb19
Stranraer **GB** 20 Cd22
Strasbourg **F** 63 Ec32
Strasburg **D** 57 Fd26
Strășeni **MD** 77 Ka33
Straßwalchen **A** 73 Fd33
Stratford-upon-Avon **GB** 24 Da26
Stratinista **GR** 101 Hc44
Stratinska **BIH** 86 Gc38
Stratóni **GR** 102 Jb43
Strátos **GR** 110 Hc45
Stratton **GB** 23 Cc27
Straubing **D** 64 Fc32
Straumen **N** 26 Gc05
Straumen **N** 28 Ga08
Straumen **N** 28 Gb08
Straumen **N** 32 Fc12
Straumsnes **N** 28 Ga06
Strausberg **D** 57 Ga27
Stražica **BG** 88 Jc39
Strážný **CZ** 65 Fd32
Štrba **SK** 67 Ha32
Štrbské Pleso **SK** 67 Ha32
Strečno **SK** 66 Gd32
Strehaia **RO** 87 Hd37
Strekov **SK** 74 Gd33
Strelča **BG** 102 Jb40
Strelkino **RUS** 47 Jb20
Strenči **LV** 47 Hd20
Stresa **I** 71 Ed36
Strezimirovci **SRB** 87 Hd40
Strezovce **RKS** 87 Hc40
Stříbro **CZ** 65 Fd31
Strilky **UA** 67 Hd31
Strimasund **S** 33 Ga09
Strimonikó **GR** 101 Ja42
Strmica **HR** 85 Gb38
Strofiliá **GR** 111 Ja45
Stromeferry **GB** 16 Cd19
Stromiec **PL** 59 Hb28
Stromness **GB** 17 Db17
Strömsbruk **S** 39 Gc15
Strömsnäsbruk **S** 49 Fd22
Strömstad **S** 43 Fc19
Strömsund **S** 33 Gb12
Strongoli **I** 109 Gc45
Strontian **GB** 16 Cd20
Stropkov **SK** 67 Hc31

Százhalombatta – Tenja

Százhalombatta **H** 74 Ha34
Szczawne **PL** 67 Hc31
Szczawnica **PL** 67 Hb31
Szczebrzeszyn **PL** 67 Hc29
Szczecin **PL** 57 Ga26
Szczecinek **PL** 58 Gc26
Szczekociny **PL** 67 Ha30
Szczerców **PL** 66 Gd29
Szczuczyn **PL** 59 Hc26
Szczurowa **PL** 67 Hb30
Szczytno **PL** 59 Hb26
Szécsény **H** 74 Ha33
Szederkény **H** 74 Gd36
Szeged **H** 75 Hb35
Székely **H** 75 Hc33
Székesfehérvár **H** 74 Gd34
Székkutas **H** 75 Hb35
Szekszárd **H** 74 Gd35
Szendrő **H** 75 Hb33
Szentendre **H** 74 Ha34
Szentes **H** 75 Hb35
Szentlőrinc **H** 74 Gd36
Szepietowo **PL** 59 Hc27
Szerencs **H** 75 Hb33
Szigetvár **H** 74 Gd36
Szilvásvárad **H** 75 Hb33
Szin **H** 67 Hb32
Szklarska Poręba **PL** 65 Gb30
Szolnok **H** 75 Hb34
Szombathely **H** 74 Gc34
Szprotawa **PL** 65 Gb29
Sztabin **PL** 59 Hc25
Sztum **PL** 58 Gd25
Szubin **PL** 58 Gc27
Szydłów **PL** 67 Hb30
Szydłowiec **PL** 67 Hb29
Szypliszki **PL** 59 Hc25

T

Taalintehdas **FIN** 46 Hb17
Tábara **E** 78 Bb38
Taberg **S** 44 Ga20
Tabernas **E** 106 Bd45
Tablate **E** 106 Bc45
Tábor **CZ** 65 Ga31
Tabuenca **E** 80 Cb40
Täby **S** 45 Gc18
Tachov **CZ** 64 Fc31
Tacinskij **RUS** 123 Fc14
Tafalla **E** 80 Cb39
Täfteå **S** 34 Gd12
Ţaga **RO** 76 Ja34
Tagaj **RUS** 119 Fd10
Taganrog **RUS** 123 Fc15
Taggia **I** 83 Ec39
Tagliacozzo **I** 98 Fd41
Tahkuna **EST** 46 Hb18
Tahta **RUS** 127 Fd16
Taicy **RUS** 47 Jb17
Tain **GB** 17 Da18
Tain-l'Hermitage **F** 82 Ea37
Tairove **UA** 77 Kb34
Taivalkoski **FIN** 35 Hd09
Taivassalo **FIN** 40 Ha16

Talačyn **BY** 121 Eb12
Talarrubias **E** 91 Bb42
Talavera de la Reina **E** 91 Bc41
Taldom **RUS** 117 Ed10
Talgarth **GB** 24 Cd26
Tallard **F** 83 Eb38
Tallåsen **S** 38 Gb15
Tällberg **S** 38 Ga16
Tallinn **EST** 46 Hc18
Talloires **F** 71 Eb36
Tallsjö **S** 33 Gc12
Talluskylä **FIN** 41 Hd13
Talmont-Saint-Hilaire **F** 68 Cd34
Tal'ne **UA** 121 Ec15
Talovaja **RUS** 122 Fb13
Talsi **LV** 52 Hb21
Tamala **RUS** 119 Fc11
Tamames **E** 91 Bb40
Tamanhos **P** 78 Ba39
Tamarite de Litera **E** 80 Cd40
Tamási **H** 74 Gd35
Tambov **RUS** 122 Fb12
Tammisaari **FIN** 46 Hb17
Tampere **FIN** 40 Hb15
Tamsalu **EST** 47 Hd18
Tamsweg **A** 73 Fd34
Tamworth **GB** 24 Da26
Tana bru **N** 27 Hd03
Ţăndărei **RO** 89 Jd37
Tandsbyn **S** 38 Ga13
Tandsjöborg **S** 38 Ga15
Tångaberg **S** 49 Fc21
Tangen **N** 37 Fc16
Tangerhütte **D** 56 Fc27
Tangermünde **D** 56 Fc27
Tanhua **FIN** 31 Hc07
Tankavaara **FIN** 31 Hc06
Tännäs **S** 38 Fd14
Tannay **F** 70 Dd33
Tänndalen **S** 38 Fd14
Tannila **FIN** 35 Hc10
Tanum **N** 43 Fc17
Tanumshede **S** 43 Fc19
Taormina **I** 109 Gb47
Tapa **EST** 47 Hd18
Tapia de Casariego **E** 78 Bb36
Tápiószele **H** 74 Ha34
Tapizë **RKS** 100 Hb42
Tapolca **H** 74 Gc35
Taraclia **MD** 77 Ka34
Taraclia **MD** 77 Ka35
Tarancón **E** 92 Bd42
Taranto **I** 99 Gc43
Tarare **F** 70 Dd35
Tarašča **UA** 121 Ec15
Tarascon **F** 82 Dd38
Tarascon-sur-Ariège **F** 81 Da39
Tarazona **E** 80 Cb39
Tarazona de la Mancha **E** 92 Ca43

Tarbert **GB** 16 Cd20
Tarbert **GB** 16 Cd18
Tarbert **GB** 20 Cd21
Tarbert **IRL** 18 Bd24
Tarbes **F** 80 Cd38
Tarcento **I** 73 Fd36
Tarczyn **PL** 59 Hb28
Tärendö **S** 30 Ha08
Târgovişte **RO** 88 Jb37
Târgovište **BG** 89 Jd39
Târgu Bujor **RO** 77 Jd35
Târgu Cărbunești **RO** 88 Ja37
Târgu Frumos **RO** 76 Jc33
Târgu Gânguleşti **RO** 88 Ja37
Târgu Jiu **RO** 87 Hd37
Târgu Lăpuş **RO** 76 Ja34
Târgu Mureş **RO** 76 Ja35
Târgu-Neamţ **RO** 76 Jc34
Târgu Ocna **RO** 76 Jc35
Târgu Secuiesc **RO** 76 Jc35
Târguşor **RO** 89 Ka37
Tarifa **E** 105 Ba46
Târlişua **RO** 76 Ja34
Tarm **DK** 48 Fa23
Tärnaby **S** 33 Ga10
Tarna-lelesz **H** 75 Hb33
Tarna Mare **RO** 75 Hd33
Tärnamo **S** 33 Ga10
Târnăveni **RO** 76 Ja35
Tarnobrzeg **PL** 67 Hb30
Tarnogród **PL** 67 Hc30
Tarnov **SK** 67 Hb31
Târnova **RO** 75 Hc35
Tarnów **PL** 67 Hb30
Tarnowskie Góry **PL** 66 Gd30
Tärnsjö **S** 44 Gb17
Tårnvika **N** 28 Ga07
Tarporley **GB** 24 Da25
Tarquinia **I** 98 Fb41
Tarragona **E** 95 Da41
Tàrrega **E** 81 Da40
Tårs **DK** 49 Fc24
Tartas **F** 80 Cc37
Tărtăşeşti **RO** 88 Jc37
Tartaul de Salcie **MD** 77 Ka35
Tartu **EST** 47 Ja19
Tarusa **RUS** 117 Ed11
Tarutyne **UA** 77 Ka34
Tarvin **GB** 24 Da25
Tarvisio **I** 73 Fd35
Tåsjö **S** 33 Gb12
Taşkent **TR** 128 Ga16
Taşlıc **MD** 77 Ka33
Tăşnad **RO** 75 Hd34
Taşucu **TR** 128 Gc17
Tata **H** 74 Gd34
Tatabánya **H** 74 Gd34
Tătărăştii de Jos **RO** 88 Jb37
Tataháza **H** 74 Ha36
Tatanovo **RUS** 118 Fb11
Tătăranu **RO** 89 Jd36

Tatarbunary **UA** 77 Kb35
Tatarbunary **UA** 125 Ec17
Tatarlı **TR** 128 Gc15
Tatlıkuyu **TR** 128 Gc15
Tau **N** 42 Ed18
Tauberbischofsheim **D** 64 Fa31
Taucha **D** 64 Fc29
Taufkirchen **D** 72 Fc33
Taulov **DK** 49 Fb23
Taunton **GB** 24 Cd27
Taurianova **I** 109 Gb46
Taurisano **I** 100 Gd44
Tauste **E** 80 Cc40
Tavaklı İsk. **TR** 103 Jd43
Tavelsjö **S** 34 Gd12
Tavernes de la Valldigna **E** 93 Cc43
Tavíkovice **CZ** 65 Gb32
Tavira **P** 104 Ac44
Tavistock **GB** 23 Cc28
Tayfur **TR** 103 Jd42
Tayinloan **GB** 20 Cc21
Tazlău **RO** 76 Jc34
Tczew **PL** 58 Gd25
Tczów **PL** 67 Hb29
Teaca **RO** 76 Ja34
Teano **I** 98 Fd42
Teba **E** 105 Bb45
Tebay **GB** 21 Da23
Teberda **RUS** 127 Ga17
Techirghiol **RO** 89 Ka37
Tecuci **RO** 77 Jd35
Tegelträsk **S** 33 Gc12
Tegernsee **D** 72 Fc34
Teignmouth **GB** 23 Cc28
Teiuş **RO** 76 Ja35
Tejkovo **RUS** 118 Fa09
Tekirdağ **TR** 103 Ka41
Telč **CZ** 65 Gb32
Telciu **RO** 76 Ja34
Teleneşti **MD** 77 Jd33
Telese **I** 99 Ga42
Telford **GB** 24 Da25
Telfs **A** 72 Fb34
Telgte **D** 55 Ed28
Tellejåkk **S** 34 Gd09
Tel'manove **UA** 122 Fb15
Telšiai **LT** 52 Hb22
Teltow **D** 57 Fd27
Tembleque **E** 92 Bd42
Temerin **SRB** 87 Hb37
Temmes **FIN** 35 Hc11
Tempio Pausania **I** 96 Ed42
Templemore **IRL** 18 Ca24
Templin **D** 57 Fd26
Temrjuk **RUS** 126 Fb17
Tenala **FIN** 46 Hb17
Tenby **GB** 23 Cc26
Tendilla **E** 92 Ca41
Tenec **RUS** 47 Jb20
Tenhola **FIN** 46 Hb17
Tenhult **S** 44 Ga20
Tenja **HR** 86 Ha37

Tenterden GB 25 Dc28
Teofipol' UA 120 Ea15
Teovo MK 101 Hc41
Tepasto FIN 30 Hb06
Tepelenë AL 100 Hb43
Teplice CZ 65 Fd30
Teploe RUS 118 Fa11
Tepsa FIN 30 Hb07
Terälahti FIN 40 Hb15
Teramo I 85 Fd40
Ter Apel NL 55 Ed26
Teratyn PL 67 Hd29
Terbuny RUS 122 Fa12
Terebovlja UA 120 Ea15
Teremia Mare RO 75 Hb36
Teren'ga RUS 119 Fd10
Tergnier F 62 Dd30
Terlizzi I 99 Gc42
Termachivka UA 121 Eb14
Terme TR 127 Fc19
Terme di Lurisia I 83 Ec38
Termini Imerese I 108 Fd46
Termoli I 99 Ga41
Terneuzen NL 54 Ea28
Terni I 84 Fc40
Ternitz A 73 Gb34
Ternopil' UA 120 Ea15
Terpnés GR 101 Hc44
Terracina I 98 Fd42
Terråk N 32 Fd11
Terralba I 97 Ec44
Terrassa E 95 Da41
Teruel E 93 Cb42
Tervakoski FIN 40 Hc16
Tervel BG 89 Jd38
Tervo FIN 41 Hd13
Tervola FIN 34 Hb09
Tešanj BIH 86 Gd38
Tešel BG 102 Jb41
Tešica SRB 87 Hc39
Teslić BIH 86 Gd38
Tét H 74 Gc34
Tetbury GB 24 Da27
Teterow D 57 Fd26
Teteven BG 88 Jb39
Tetijiv UA 121 Ec15
Tetovo BG 88 Jc38
Tetovo MK 101 Hc41
Teulada I 97 Ec45
Teulada-Moraira E 94 Cc44
Teuva FIN 40 Ha14
Tewkesbury GB 24 Da26
Thann F 71 Ec33
Thaon-les-Vosges F 71 Eb33
Thássos GR 102 Jb42
The Mumbles GB 23 Cc27
Theológos GR 111 Ja45
Thermo GR 110 Hd45
Thesprotikó GR 110 Hc45
Thessaloníki GR 101 Ja43
Thetford GB 25 Dc26
Thiene I 72 Fb36
Thiers F 70 Dd35
Thiesi I 97 Ec43
Thionville F 63 Eb31

Thíra GR 115 Jd48
Thirsk GB 21 Db24
Thisted DK 48 Fa21
Thíva GR 111 Ja45
Thiviers F 69 Da35
Thizy F 70 Dd35
Tholária GR 115 Jd47
Thonon-les-Bains F 71 Eb35
Thorne GB 21 Db24
Thornhill GB 21 Da22
Thorsminde DK 48 Fa22
Thouars F 69 Da33
Thrapston GB 25 Db26
Thueyts F 82 Dd37
Thuir F 81 Db39
Thun CH 71 Ec35
Thurles IRL 18 Ca24
Thursby GB 21 Da23
Thurso GB 17 Db18
Thury-Harcourt F 61 Da31
Thusis CH 72 Fa35
Thyborøn DK 48 Fa22
Tibana RO 77 Jd34
Tibro S 44 Ga19
Tiča BG 89 Jd39
Tidaholm S 44 Ga20
Tidan S 44 Ga19
Tiel NL 55 Eb28
Tielt B 62 Ea29
Tienen B 63 Eb29
Tierp S 45 Gc17
Tigharry GB 16 Cc18
Tighina MD 77 Ka34
Tihoreck RUS 127 Fc16
Tihvin RUS 117 Eb08
Tikkakoski FIN 40 Hc14
Tilaj H 74 Gc35
Tilburg NL 55 Eb28
Tilbury GB 25 Db28
Til-Châtel F 70 Ea33
Tileagd RO 76 Hc34
Tillberga S 44 Gb18
Tilža LV 53 Ja21
Tim RUS 122 Fa13
Timashevsk RUS 127 Fc16
Timfristós GR 110 Hd45
Timişoara RO 75 Hc36
Timmele S 44 Fd20
Timohino RUS 117 Ec08
Timošino RUS 118 Fb08
Timrå S 39 Gc14
Tineo E 79 Bc36
Tinglev DK 48 Fa24
Tingsryd S 50 Ga22
Tingstäde S 45 Gd20
Tingvoll N 37 Fb13
Tinlot B 63 Eb30
Tínos GR 112 Jc46
Tinqueux F 62 Ea31
Tinténiac F 61 Cd31
Tinůži LV 53 Hd21
Tione di Trento I 72 Fb36
Tipasoja FIN 35 Ja11
Tipperary IRL 18 Ca24
Tiranë RKS 100 Hb42
Tirano I 72 Fa36

Tiraspol MD 77 Ka34
Tire TR 113 Kb45
Tirebolu TR 127 Fd19
Tirkšliai LT 52 Hb22
Tírnavos GR 101 Hd44
Tirrenia I 84 Fa39
Tirschenreuth D 64 Fc31
Tišća BIH 86 Ha38
Tišnov CZ 65 Gb31
Tisovec SK 67 Ha32
Tisvildeleje DK 49 Fc23
Tiszabecs H 75 Hd33
Tiszacsege H 75 Hb33
Tiszacsermely H 75 Hc33
Tiszadada H 75 Hb33
Tiszaföldvár H 75 Hb35
Tiszafüred H 75 Hb34
Tiszakécske H 75 Hb35
Tiszaluc H 75 Hb33
Tiszaújváros H 75 Hb33
Tiszavasvári H 75 Hb33
Titisee-Neustadt D 71 Ed33
Titran N 32 Fb12
Titu RO 88 Jb37
Tivat MNE 100 Ha41
Tiverton GB 23 Cc28
Tivoli I 98 Fc41
Tizzano F 86 Ed42
Tjačiv UA 75 Hd33
Tjæreborg DK 48 Fa23
Tjällmo S 44 Gb19
Tjåmotis S 29 Gc08
Tjautjas N 29 Gd07
Tjeldnes N 28 Gb06
Tjentište BIH 86 Ha39
Tjøtta N 32 Fd10
Tłuchowo PL 58 Ha27
Tłuszcz PL 59 Hb27
Tobarra E 107 Ca44
Tobercurry IRL 18 Ca22
Tobermory GB 16 Cd20
Toblach I 72 Fc35
Töcksfors S 43 Fc18
Todi I 84 Fc40
Todireşti RO 76 Jb33
Todorići BIH 86 Gc38
Todtnau D 71 Ed33
Tofta S 49 Fd21
Tofta S 51 Gc21
Tofte N 43 Fc18
Töftedal S 43 Fc19
Toftlund DK 48 Fa24
Tohmajärvi FIN 41 Jb13
Tohmo FIN 31 Hc08
Toholampi FIN 34 Hb12
Toijala FIN 40 Hb15
Toivakka FIN 41 Hd14
Toivala FIN 41 Hd13
Tokaj H 75 Hc33
Tokarevka RUS 122 Fb12
Tokmak UA 126 Fa16
Toledo E 91 Bc41
Tolentino I 85 Fd40
Tolfa I 98 Fc41
Tolga N 37 Fc14
Tol'jatti RUS 119 Ga10

Tollarp S 50 Ga23
Tolmezzo I 73 Fd35
Tolmin SLO 73 Fd36
Tolosa E 80 Cb38
Tolva FIN 31 Hd08
Tomakivka UA 126 Fa16
Tomar P 90 Ac40
Tomarovka RUS 122 Fa14
Tomaševac SRB 87 Hb37
Tomašpil' UA 77 Jd32
Tomašpil' UA 125 Eb16
Tomaszów Lubelski PL 67 Hd30
Tomaszów Mazowiecki PL 58 Ha28
Tomelilla S 50 Ga23
Tomelloso E 92 Bd43
Tomeşti RO 75 Hd36
Tomeşti RO 77 Jd33
Tomintoul GB 17 Db19
Tomislavgrad BIH 86 Gc39
Tømmerneset N 28 Gb07
Tømmervåg N 36 Fa13
Tompa H 74 Ha36
Tomrefjord N 36 Fa14
Tonara I 97 Ed44
Tonbridge GB 25 Db28
Tondela P 78 Ad39
Tønder DK 48 Fa24
Tongeren B 63 Eb29
Tongue GB 17 Da18
Tonkino RUS 119 Fc08
Tonnay-Boutonne F 68 Cd34
Tonnay-Charente F 68 Cd34
Tonneins F 81 Da37
Tonnerre F 70 Dd33
Tönning D 56 Fa25
Tonšaevo RUS 119 Fc08
Tønsberg N 43 Fb18
Tonstad N 42 Ed19
Tonya TR 127 Fd19
Topczewo PL 59 Hc27
Toplet RO 87 Hd37
Topli Do SRB 87 Hd39
Toplita RO 76 Jb34
Topola SRB 87 Hb38
Topolčani MK 101 Hc42
Topol'čany SK 66 Gd32
Topolog RO 89 Ka36
Topoloveni RO 88 Jb37
Topolovgrad BG 103 Jd40
Topolovo BG 102 Jc41
Toponica SRB 87 Hb38
Toporu RO 88 Jc38
Topusko HR 85 Gb37
Torà E 93 Da40
Torbalı TR 113 Ka45
Tordesillas E 79 Bc39
Töre S 34 Ha09
Töreboda S 44 Ga19
Torekov S 49 Fd22
Torelló E 81 Db40
Toreno E 78 Bb37
Torfjanovka RUS 41 Ja16
Torgåsmon S 38 Fd16

Torgau – Tuhala

Torgau **D** 65 Fd29
Torgelow **D** 57 Ga26
Torhout **B** 54 Dd28
Torigni-sur-Vire **F** 61 Da30
Torija **E** 92 Ca41
Toril **E** 93 Cb42
Torino **I** 83 Ec37
Tormac **RO** 75 Hc36
Törmänen **FIN** 27 Hc05
Tornal'a **SK** 75 Hb33
Torneträsk **S** 29 Gd06
Tornio **FIN** 34 Hb09
Tornjoš **SRB** 74 Ha36
Toro **E** 79 Bc39
Törökbalint **H** 74 Ha34
Törökszentmiklós **H** 75 Hb34
Torony **H** 74 Gc34
Toropec **RUS** 117 Eb10
Torošino **RUS** 47 Jb19
Torpo **N** 37 Fb16
Torpshammar **S** 38 Gb14
Torquay **GB** 23 Cc28
Torrão **P** 90 Ac42
Torre Annunziata **I** 99 Ga43
Torrebeleña **E** 92 Ca40
Torreblanca **E** 93 Cc42
Torrecampo **E** 105 Bb43
Torrecilla en Cameros **E** 79 Ca39
Torre de la Higuera **E** 105 Ad44
Torre del Greco **I** 99 Ga43
Torre de Moncorvo **P** 78 Ba39
Torre de'Passeri **I** 98 Fd41
Torredonjimeno **E** 106 Bc44
Torrejón de Ardoz **E** 92 Bd41
Torrelaguna **E** 92 Bd40
Torrelavega **E** 79 Ca37
Torremaggiore **I** 99 Gb42
Torremolinos **E** 105 Bb45
Torremormojón **E** 79 Bc39
Torrent **E** 93 Cc43
Torre-Pacheco **E** 107 Cb45
Torre Pellice **I** 83 Ec37
Torrequemada **E** 91 Ba41
Torres Novas **P** 90 Ac41
Torres Vedras **P** 90 Ab41
Torrevieja **E** 107 Cb45
Torri del Benaco **I** 72 Fb36
Torriglia **I** 83 Ed38
Torrijas **E** 93 Cb42
Torrijos **E** 91 Bc41
Tørring **DK** 49 Fb23
Tørring **N** 32 Fc12
Torrington **GB** 23 Cc27
Torroella de Montgrí **E** 81 Dc40
Torsåker **S** 44 Gb17
Torsås **S** 50 Gb22
Torsborg **S** 38 Fd14
Torsby **S** 44 Fd17
Torshälla **S** 44 Gb18
Tórtoles de Esgueva **E** 79 Bd39

Tortolì **I** 97 Ed44
Tortona **I** 83 Ed37
Tortorici **I** 109 Ga46
Tortosa **E** 93 Cd41
Torul **TR** 127 Fd19
Toruń **PL** 58 Gd27
Torup **S** 49 Fd21
Törva **EST** 47 Hd19
Toržok **RUS** 117 Ec10
Torzym **PL** 57 Ga28
Tosbotn **N** 32 Fd10
Toslak **TR** 128 Ga17
Tosno **RUS** 117 Eb08
Töstamaa **EST** 46 Hc19
Tostedt **D** 56 Fb26
Totana **E** 107 Ca45
Totebo **S** 44 Gb20
Tôtes **F** 61 Db30
Tótkomlós **H** 75 Hb35
Tøtlandsvik **N** 42 Ed18
Totnes **GB** 23 Cc28
Toucy **F** 70 Dd33
Toul **F** 63 Eb32
Toulon **F** 82 Ea39
Toulon-sur-Arroux **F** 70 Dd34
Toulouse **F** 81 Da38
Tourcoing **F** 62 Dd29
Tourlaville **F** 61 Cd30
Tournai **B** 62 Dd29
Tournon-d'Agenais **F** 81 Da37
Tournon-sur-Rhône **F** 82 Ea37
Tournus **F** 70 Ea35
Tours **F** 69 Db33
Toury **F** 62 Dc32
Tovarkovskij **RUS** 118 Fa11
Tovarnik **HR** 86 Ha37
Tovste **UA** 76 Jb32
Töysä **FIN** 40 Hb13
Trabanca **E** 78 Bb39
Traben-Trarbach **D** 63 Ec30
Trabzon **TR** 127 Fd19
Tragacete **E** 93 Cb41
Trahiá **GR** 111 Ja47
Traiskirchen **A** 73 Gb33
Tralee **IRL** 18 Bc24
Tramore **IRL** 22 Ca25
Trần **BG** 87 Hd40
Tranås **S** 44 Ga20
Tranemo **S** 49 Fd21
Tranent **GB** 21 Da21
Trani **I** 99 Gc42
Tranøya **N** 28 Gb07
Transtrand **S** 38 Fd16
Trapani **I** 108 Fc46
Trasacco **I** 98 Fd41
Traun **A** 73 Ga33
Traunreut **D** 72 Fc33
Traunstein **D** 72 Fc33
Travemünde **D** 56 Fb25
Travnik **BIH** 86 Gd38
Travo **F** 96 Ed41
Trawniki **PL** 67 Hc29
Trbovlje **SLO** 73 Ga36

Trebbin **D** 57 Fd28
Třebíč **CZ** 65 Gb32
Trebinje **BIH** 86 Gd40
Trebisacce **I** 99 Gc44
Trebišov **SK** 67 Hc32
Treblinka **PL** 59 Hb27
Trebnje **SLO** 73 Ga36
Třeboň **CZ** 65 Ga32
Trecate **I** 83 Ed37
Treffurt **D** 64 Fb29
Tregaron **GB** 24 Cd26
Trégastel-Plage **F** 60 Cc30
Tréguier **F** 60 Cc30
Trehörningsjö **S** 33 Gc12
Treignac **F** 69 Db35
Trekljano **BG** 87 Hd40
Trélazé **F** 69 Da33
Trelleborg **S** 49 Fd24
Tremezzo **I** 71 Ed36
Tremp **E** 81 Da40
Trenčín **SK** 66 Gd32
Trento **I** 72 Fb36
Tresfjord **N** 36 Fa14
Trespaderne **E** 79 Ca38
Tretten **N** 37 Fc15
Treuchtlingen **D** 64 Fb32
Treuenbrietzen **D** 57 Fd28
Treviglio **I** 72 Fa36
Treviso **I** 72 Fc36
Tribunj **HR** 85 Gb39
Tricarico **I** 99 Gb43
Tricase **I** 100 Ha44
Tridubi **MD** 77 Kb32
Trieben **A** 73 Ga34
Trier **D** 63 Ec31
Trieste **I** 73 Fd36
Trie-sur-Baïse **F** 80 Cd38
Trifeşti **RO** 77 Jd33
Trignac **F** 60 Cc32
Trigono **GR** 101 Hc43
Tríkala **GR** 101 Hd44
Trikéri **GR** 111 Ja45
Trillo **E** 92 Ca41
Trim **IRL** 19 Cb23
Trinatopoli **I** 99 Gb42
Trino **I** 83 Ed37
Triora **I** 83 Ec38
Trípoli **GR** 111 Ja47
Trivento **I** 99 Ga42
Trjavna **BG** 88 Jc39
Trnava **SK** 74 Gc33
Trnovo **BIH** 86 Gd39
Tročany **SK** 67 Hb32
Trödje **S** 39 Gc16
Troekurovo **RUS** 118 Fb11
Trofaiach **A** 73 Ga34
Trofors **N** 33 Ga10
Trogir **HR** 85 Gb39
Troglan Bara **SRB** 87 Hc38
Troia **I** 99 Gb42
Tróia **P** 90 Ab42
Troickaja **RUS** 127 Fc17
Troic'ke **MD** 77 Kb32
Troisdorf **D** 63 Ec29
Troiţa Nouă **MD** 77 Ka34

Trojaci **MK** 101 Hd42
Trojan **BG** 88 Jb39
Trollhättan **S** 43 Fd20
Tromsø **N** 26 Gc05
Tromvik **N** 26 Gc04
Trondheim **N** 37 Fc13
Troon **GB** 20 Cd21
Troøyen **N** 37 Fc13
Tropea **I** 109 Gb46
Trosa **S** 45 Gc19
Troškas **LV** 53 Ja21
Troškūnai **LT** 53 Hd23
Trosna **RUS** 121 Ed12
Trostan' **RUS** 121 Ec13
Trostberg **D** 72 Fc33
Trostjanec' **UA** 121 Ed14
Trostjanskij **RUS** 123 Fc13
Trouville-sur-Mer **F** 61 Db30
Trowbridge **GB** 24 Cd27
Troyes **F** 62 Ea32
Trsa **MNE** 86 Ha40
Tršće **HR** 85 Ga37
Trstenik **SRB** 87 Hc39
Trubčevsk **RUS** 121 Ed13
Trubetčino **RUS** 122 Fb12
Trud **BG** 102 Jb40
Trujillo **E** 91 Bb41
Trumieje **PL** 58 Gd26
Trun **F** 61 Da31
Truro **GB** 23 Cb28
Truşeşti **RO** 76 Jc33
Trustrup **DK** 49 Fc22
Trutnov **CZ** 65 Gb30
Tryškiai **LT** 52 Hb22
Tržac **BIH** 85 Gb37
Trzcianka **PL** 57 Gb27
Trzcianne **PL** 59 Hc26
Trzciel **PL** 57 Gb28
Trzebiatów **PL** 57 Gb25
Trzebień **PL** 65 Gb29
Trzebinia **PL** 67 Ha30
Trzebnica **PL** 66 Gc29
Trzemeszno **PL** 58 Gc27
Trzydnik Duży **PL** 67 Hc29
Tsepélovo **GR** 101 Hc44
Tsjernobyl **UA** 121 Ec14
Tuam **IRL** 18 Ca23
Tuapse **RUS** 127 Fc17
Tubbergen **NL** 55 Ec27
Tübingen **D** 64 Fa32
Tubize **B** 62 Ea29
Tuchan **F** 81 Db39
Tuchola **PL** 58 Gc26
Tuchów **PL** 67 Hb31
Tučovo **RUS** 117 Ed10
Tuczna **PL** 59 Hd28
Tuczno **PL** 57 Gb27
Tuczno **PL** 57 Gb26
Tudela **E** 80 Cb39
Tudela de Duero **E** 79 Bc39
Tudu **EST** 47 Ja18
Tudulinna **EST** 47 Ja18
Tuéjar **E** 93 Cb42
Tufeni **RO** 88 Jb37
Tugotino **RUS** 47 Jb19
Tuhala **EST** 46 Hc18

Tuhkala **RUS** 35 Ja09
Tui **E** 78 Ad37
Tuin **MK** 101 Hc41
Tūja **LV** 46 Hc20
Tukums **LV** 52 Hc21
Tula **RUS** 118 Fa11
Tulare **SRB** 87 Hc40
Tulcea **RO** 89 Ka36
Tul'čyn **UA** 125 Eb16
Tulgheş **RO** 76 Jb34
Tuliszków **PL** 58 Gd28
Tullamore **IRL** 18 Ca24
Tulle **F** 69 Db36
Tulln **A** 73 Gb33
Tullow **IRL** 19 Cb24
Tułowice **PL** 66 Gc30
Tulppio **FIN** 31 Hd06
Tulsk **IRL** 18 Ca23
Tuma **RUS** 118 Fb10
Tumba **S** 45 Gc18
Tunadal **S** 39 Gc14
Tungozero **RUS** 35 Ja09
Tunstall **GB** 21 Da23
Tuntsa **FIN** 31 Hd07
Tupicino **RUS** 47 Jb18
Turčianske Teplice **SK** 66 Gd32
Turda **RO** 76 Ja35
Turégano **E** 92 Bd40
Turek **PL** 58 Gd28
Tureni **RO** 76 Ja35
Turgutlu **TR** 113 Kb45
Turgutreıs **TR** 115 Kb47
Türi **EST** 47 Hd18
Turijs'k **UA** 120 Ea14
Turís **E** 93 Cb43
Turiščevo **RUS** 121 Ed12
Turka **UA** 67 Hd31
Türkeli **TR** 103 Ka42
Túrkeve **H** 75 Hb34
Turksad **RUS** 127 Ga16
Turku **FIN** 40 Hb16
Turnhout **B** 55 Eb28
Türnitz **A** 73 Gb33
Turnov **CZ** 65 Ga30
Turnu **RO** 75 Hc35
Turnu Măgurele **RO** 88 Jb38
Turoś **PL** 59 Hb26
Turriff **GB** 17 Db19
Turtel **MK** 101 Hd41
Turtola **FIN** 30 Hb08
Turzovka **SK** 66 Gd31
Tuscania **I** 98 Fb41
Tutaev **RUS** 118 Fa09
Tutin **SRB** 87 Hb40
Tutova **RO** 77 Jd35
Tutrakan **BG** 89 Jd38
Tuttlingen **D** 71 Ed33
Tuulos **FIN** 40 Hc15
Tuupovaara **FIN** 41 Jb13
Tuusniemi **FIN** 41 Ja13
Tuusula **FIN** 40 Hc16
Tuutisjärvi **RUS** 31 Ja08
Tuža **RUS** 119 Fc08
Tuzi **MNE** 100 Ha41
Tuzla **BIH** 86 Ha38

Tuzly **UA** 77 Kb35
Tuzly **UA** 125 Ec17
Tvååker **S** 49 Fd21
Tväråsund **S** 34 Gd12
Tvärdica **BG** 88 Jc39
Tvardiţa **MD** 77 Ka35
Tvedestrand **N** 43 Fb19
Tveitsund **N** 42 Fa18
Tver' **RUS** 117 Ed10
Tverrvika **N** 28 Ga08
Tving **S** 50 Gb22
Tvrdošín **SK** 67 Ha31
Twardogóra **PL** 66 Gc29
Twello **NL** 55 Ec27
Twistringen **D** 56 Fa27
Tychowo **PL** 57 Gb25
Tychy **PL** 66 Gd30
Tyczyn **PL** 67 Hc30
Tyfors **S** 44 Ga17
Tykocin **PL** 59 Hc26
Tylawa **PL** 67 Hc31
Tylkowo **PL** 58 Ha26
Tylösand **S** 49 Fd22
Tymkove **MD** 77 Ka32
Tyndrum **GB** 16 Cd20
Tynemouth **GB** 21 Db23
Tyngsjö **S** 44 Ga17
Tyniec **PL** 67 Ha31
Týniště nad Orlicí **CZ** 65 Gb30
Týn nad Vltavou **CZ** 65 Ga32
Tynset **N** 37 Fc14
Tyringe **S** 49 Fd22
Tyristrand **N** 43 Fb17
Tyrnävä **FIN** 35 Hc11
Tyrnyauz **RUS** 127 Ga17
Tyškivka **UA** 125 Ec16
Tysnes **N** 42 Ed17
Tyssebotn **N** 36 Ed16
Tyssedal **N** 42 Ed17
Tystberga **S** 45 Gc19
Tyszowce **PL** 67 Hd29
Tytuvėnai **LT** 52 Hc23
Tywyn **GB** 24 Cd25
Tzermiádo **GR** 115 Jd49

Ub **SRB** 87 Hb38
Úbeda **E** 106 Bc44
Überlingen **D** 72 Fa33
Ubieszyn **PL** 67 Hc30
Ubl'a **SK** 67 Hc32
Ubli **MNE** 86 Ha40
Ubrique **E** 105 Ba45
Ucero **E** 79 Ca39
Üçharman **TR** 128 Gc16
Uchte **D** 56 Fa27
Uckfield **GB** 25 Db28
Üçpınar **TR** 128 Ga16
Uda **RO** 88 Jb37
Udačnoe **RUS** 123 Ga14
Udbina **HR** 85 Gb38
Uddevalla **S** 43 Fc19
Uddheden **S** 44 Fd17

Uden **NL** 55 Eb28
Udine **I** 73 Fd36
Udomlja **RUS** 117 Ec09
Ueckermünde **D** 57 Ga26
Uelzen **D** 56 Fb27
Uetersen **D** 56 Fb26
Uetze **D** 56 Fb27
Uffenheim **D** 64 Fb31
Ugåle **LV** 52 Hb21
Ugao **SRB** 87 Hb40
Ugärčin **BG** 88 Jb39
Ugíjar **E** 106 Bc45
Ugine **F** 71 Eb36
Uglič **RUS** 117 Ed09
Ugljan **HR** 85 Ga38
Ugra **RUS** 117 Ed11
Uherské Hradiště **CZ** 66 Gc32
Uherský Brod **CZ** 66 Gc32
Uhniv **UA** 67 Hd30
Uig **GB** 16 Cd18
Uimaharju **FIN** 41 Jb12
Uithuizen **NL** 55 Ec26
Uivar **RO** 75 Hb36
Ujeździec Mały **PL** 66 Gc29
Újfehértó **H** 75 Hc33
Ujma **PL** 58 Gd27
Ujście **PL** 58 Gc27
Ukiernica **PL** 57 Ga26
Ukmergė **LT** 53 Hd23
Ukrajina **UA** 121 Eb15
Ulan Ėrge **RUS** 123 Ga15
Ulanów **PL** 67 Hc30
Ulbroka **LV** 52 Hc21
Ulcinj **MNE** 100 Ha41
Ulefoss **N** 43 Fb18
Uleila del Campo **E** 106 Bd45
Ulfborg **DK** 48 Fa22
Úlibice **CZ** 65 Gb30
Ulieş **RO** 76 Jb35
Ul'janovka **MD** 77 Kb32
Ul'janovka **MD** 77 Kb32
Ul'janovka **UA** 125 Ec16
Uljanovo **RUS** 52 Hb24
Uljanovsk **RUS** 119 Fd09
Ullånger **S** 39 Gc13
Ullapool **GB** 17 Da18
Ullared **S** 49 Fd21
Ullatti **S** 30 Ha08
Ullava **FIN** 34 Hb12
Ulldecona **E** 93 Cd42
Ullerslev **DK** 49 Fb23
Ulm **D** 72 Fa33
Ulmu **RO** 89 Jd36
Ulricehamn **S** 44 Fd20
Ulrika **S** 44 Gb20
Ulriksfors **S** 33 Gb12
Ulsteinvik **N** 36 Ed14
Ulukışla **TR** 128 Gd15
Uluköy **TR** 103 Jd43
Ulvåker **S** 44 Ga19
Ulverston **GB** 21 Da23
Ulvik **N** 36 Fa16
Ulvila **FIN** 40 Ha15
Ulvsvåg **N** 28 Gb07

Umag **HR** 85 Fd37
Uman' **UA** 121 Ec15
Umbertide **I** 84 Fc40
Umčari **SRB** 87 Hb38
Umeå **S** 34 Gd12
Umgransele **S** 33 Gc11
Umka **SRB** 87 Hb38
Umurbey **TR** 103 Jd43
Umurga **LV** 47 Hd20
Umurlu **TR** 113 Kb45
Unari **FIN** 30 Hb07
Uncastillo **E** 80 Cc39
Undenäs **S** 44 Ga19
Undersåker **S** 38 Fd13
Uneča **RUS** 121 Ec13
Ungheni **MD** 77 Jd33
Ungheni **RO** 88 Jb37
Unguriņi **LV** 47 Hd19
Unichowo **PL** 58 Gc25
Uničov **CZ** 66 Gc31
Uniejów **PL** 58 Gd28
Unisław **PL** 58 Gd26
Unna **D** 55 Ed28
Unnaryd **S** 49 Fd21
Unterhaching **D** 72 Fc33
Ünye **TR** 127 Fc19
Upa **EST** 46 Hb19
Upinniemi **FIN** 46 Hc17
Upolokša **RUS** 31 Ja06
Upplands-Väsby **S** 45 Gc18
Uppsala **S** 45 Gc17
Ura-Vajgurore **AL** 100 Hb43
Urbania **I** 84 Fc39
Urbino **I** 84 Fc39
Uren **RUS** 119 Fc08
Urganlı **TR** 113 Kb45
Uria **RO** 76 Ja34
Uriž **UA** 67 Hd31
Urjala **FIN** 40 Hb16
Urjupinsk **RUS** 123 Fc13
Urk **NL** 55 Ec27
Urla **TR** 113 Ka45
Urlaţi **RO** 88 Jc36
Urlingford **IRL** 18 Ca24
Urmary **RUS** 119 Fd09
Uroševac **RKS** 101 Hc41
Ursviken **S** 34 Ha11
Urszulewo **PL** 58 Ha27
Urzędów **PL** 67 Hc29
Urziceni **RO** 88 Jc37
Uržum **RUS** 119 Fd08
Ušačy **BY** 117 Eb11
Usadišče **RUS** 117 Ec08
Usagre **E** 105 Ba43
Uschodni **BY** 120 Ea12
Usedom **D** 57 Ga26
Usingen **D** 63 Ed30
Usk **GB** 24 Cd27
Uskoplje (Gornji Vakuf) **BIH** 86 Gd39
Uslar **D** 56 Fa28
Usman' **RUS** 122 Fb12
Usovo **RUS** 119 Fc11
Ussel **F** 69 Dc36
Uster **CH** 71 Ed34
Ust'Džeguta **RUS** 127 Fd17

Ustibar – Varhaug

Ustibar **BIH** 86 Ha39
Ustikolina **BIH** 86 Ha39
Ústí nad Labem **CZ** 65 Ga30
Ústí nad Orlicí **CZ** 65 Gb31
Ustiprača **BIH** 86 Ha39
Ustjužna **RUS** 117 Ec08
Ustka **PL** 58 Gc25
Ustʻ-Labinsk **RUS** 127 Fc17
Ustʻ-Luga **RUS** 47 Ja17
Ustovo **BG** 102 Jb41
Ustrem **BG** 103 Jd40
Ustroń **PL** 66 Gd31
Ustronie Morskie **PL** 57
  Gb25
Ustrzyki Dolne **PL** 67 Hc31
Ustyluh **PL** 67 Hd29
Usvjaty **RUS** 117 Eb11
Utajärvi **FIN** 35 Hc10
Utåker **N** 42 Ed17
Utansjö **S** 39 Gc14
Utena **LT** 53 Ja23
Utiel **E** 93 Cb43
Utne **N** 36 Ed16
Utrecht **NL** 55 Eb27
Utrera **E** 105 Ba44
Utsjoki **FIN** 27 Hc04
Uttoxeter **GB** 24 Da25
Utvin **RO** 75 Hc36
Utvorda **N** 32 Fc11
Uukuniemi **FIN** 41 Jb14
Uurainen **FIN** 40 Hc14
Uusikaarlepyy **FIN** 34 Ha12
Uusikaupunki **FIN** 40 Ha16
Úvaly **CZ** 65 Ga31
Uvarovo **RUS** 123 Fc12
Uvdal **N** 43 Fb17
Uzdowo **PL** 58 Ha26
Uzerche **F** 69 Db36
Uzès **F** 82 Dd38
Užhorod **UA** 67 Hc32
Užice **SRB** 87 Hb39
Uzlovaja **RUS** 118 Fa11
Užovka **RUS** 119 Fc10
Uzuncaburç **TR** 128 Gc17
Uzunköprü **TR** 103 Jd41
Uzunkuyu **TR** 128 Gb15
Užventis **LT** 52 Hc23
Uzyn **UA** 121 Ec15

Vääkio **FIN** 35 Hd10
Vaala **FIN** 35 Hd11
Vaalajärvi **FIN** 31 Hc07
Vaalimaa **FIN** 41 Ja16
Vaaraslahti **FIN** 35 Hd12
Vaasa **FIN** 40 Ha13
Vabalninkas **LT** 53 Hd22
Vabre **F** 81 Db38
Vác **H** 74 Ha34
Vacha **D** 64 Fb29
Väckelsång **S** 50 Ga22
Vadheim **N** 36 Ed15
Vadsø **N** 27 Hd03
Vadstena **S** 44 Ga19

Vadu Crișului **RO** 75 Hc34
Vaduz **FL** 72 Fa34
Vågaholmen **N** 28 Ga08
Vågåmo **N** 37 Fb15
Vaggeryd **S** 50 Ga21
Vagnhärad **S** 45 Gc19
Vägsele **S** 33 Gc11
Vähäkyrö **FIN** 40 Ha13
Vahto **FIN** 40 Hb16
Vaihingen (Enz) **D** 64 Fa32
Vailly-sur-Sauldre **F** 69 Dc33
Vainikkala **FIN** 41 Ja15
Vaiņode **LV** 52 Hb22
Vaison-la-Romaine **F** 82 Ea38
Vajszló **H** 74 Gd36
Vakfıkebir **TR** 127 Fd19
Vakıf **TR** 103 Jd42
Valaam **RUS** 41 Jb14
Vålådalen **S** 38 Fd13
Valandovo **MK** 101 Hd42
Valaská Belá **SK** 66 Gd32
Valašská Polanka **CZ** 66
  Gd32
Valašské Meziříčí **CZ** 66
  Gd31
Vålberg **S** 44 Fd18
Valbo **S** 38 Gb16
Valbonæ **AL** 100 Hb41
Vălčedrăm **BG** 88 Ja39
Vălčidol **BG** 89 Jd38
Valdagno **I** 72 Fb36
Valdahon **F** 71 Eb34
Valdaj **RUS** 117 Ec09
Valdefuentes **E** 91 Ba42
Valdelagua **E** 92 Bd41
Valdeltormo **E** 93 Cd41
Valdemārpils **LV** 52 Hb21
Valdemarsvik **S** 44 Gb20
Valdemeca **E** 93 Cb42
Valdemoro **E** 92 Bd41
Valdenoceda **E** 79 Ca38
Valdepeñas **E** 92 Bd43
Valdepeñas de Jaén **E** 106
  Bc44
Valderas **E** 79 Bc38
Val de Reuil **F** 61 Db31
Valderrobres **E** 93 Cd41
Val dʻIsère **F** 71 Eb36
Valdobbiadene **I** 72 Fc36
Valea Ierii **RO** 75 Hd35
Valea lui Mihai **RO** 75 Hc34
Valea Mare-Pravăț **RO** 88
  Jb36
Valea Mărului **RO** 77 Jd35
Valea Perjei **MD** 77 Ka34
Valea Sării **RO** 76 Jc35
Valea Ursului **RO** 76 Jc34
Valea Uzului **RO** 76 Jc35
Valejkiđki **BY** 53 Ja24
Valença do Minho **P** 78
  Ad37
Valençay **F** 69 Db33
Valence **F** 81 Da37
Valence **F** 82 Ea37
Valence-sur-Baïse **F** 81
  Da37

València **E** 93 Cc43
Valencia de Alcántara **E**
  90 Ad41
Valencia de Don Juan **E** 79
  Bc38
Valenciennes **F** 62 Ea29
Vălenii de Munte **RO** 88
  Jc36
Valeni-Stânișoara **RO** 76
  Jb33
Valensole **F** 82 Ea38
Valentano **I** 84 Fb40
Valenza **I** 83 Ed37
Våler **N** 37 Fc16
Valeria **E** 92 Ca42
Valevåg **N** 42 Ed17
Valga **EST** 47 Hd20
Valguarnera Caropepe **I** 109
  Ga47
Valíra **GR** 110 Hd47
Vălișoara **RO** 75 Hd35
Văliug **RO** 87 Hc37
Valjevo **SRB** 87 Hb38
Valka **LV** 47 Hd20
Valkeakoski **FIN** 40 Hc15
Valkeala **FIN** 41 Hd15
Valkenswaard **NL** 55 Eb28
Valko **FIN** 41 Hd16
Valkom **FIN** 41 Hd16
Valky **UA** 122 Fa14
Valla **S** 44 Gb19
Valladolid **E** 79 Bc39
Vallargärdet **S** 44 Fd18
Valldemossa **E** 95 Db43
Valle **N** 42 Fa18
Valle de Cabuérniga **E** 79
  Bd37
Vallentuna **S** 45 Gc18
Vallgrund **FIN** 40 Ha13
Vallon-Pont-dʻArc **F** 82 Dd37
Vallorbe **CH** 71 Eb35
Valls **E** 95 Da41
Vallsta **S** 38 Gb15
Vallvik **S** 39 Gc16
Valmanya **E** 81 Db39
Valmiera **LV** 47 Hd20
Valognes **F** 61 Cd30
VALØY **N** 32 Fc11
Valožyn **BY** 120 Ea12
Valpaços **P** 78 Ba38
Valpovo **HR** 74 Gd36
Valréas **F** 82 Ea37
Valset **N** 32 Fb12
Valsjöbyn **S** 33 Ga12
Val-Thorens **F** 71 Eb36
Valtimo **FIN** 35 Ja12
Valtournenche **I** 71 Ec36
Valujki **RUS** 122 Fb14
Valverde de Júcar **E** 92
  Ca42
Valverde del Camino **E** 105
  Ad43
Valverde de Leganés **E** 90
  Ad42
Valverde del Fresno **E** 91
  Ba40

Vama **RO** 76 Jb33
Vamberk **CZ** 65 Gb30
Vamdrup **DK** 48 Fa23
Våmhus **S** 38 Ga16
Vamlingbo **S** 51 Gc21
Vammala **FIN** 40 Hb15
Vampula **FIN** 40 Hb16
Vana-Kuuste **EST** 47 Ja19
Vânatori **RO** 76 Jb35
Vânatori **RO** 87 Hd38
Vändra **EST** 47 Hd19
Vändträsk **S** 34 Ha09
Vandžiogala **LT** 52 Hc23
Vāne **LV** 52 Hb21
Vänersborg **S** 43 Fd19
Vangaži **LV** 53 Hd21
Vängel **S** 33 Gb12
Vangsnes **N** 36 Ed15
Vänjaurträsk **S** 33 Gc12
Vânju Mare **RO** 87 Hd38
Vannareid **N** 26 Gc04
Vännäs **S** 34 Gd12
Vännäsberget **S** 34 Ha09
Vännäsby **S** 34 Gd12
Vannes **F** 60 Cc32
Vansbro **S** 44 Ga17
Vänsjö **S** 38 Ga15
Vanttauskoski **FIN** 31 Hc08
Vanvikan **N** 32 Fc12
Vara **S** 43 Fd20
Varades **F** 68 Cd33
Varakļāni **LV** 53 Ja21
Varallo **I** 71 Ed36
Vărăncău **MD** 77 Ka33
Varangerbotn **N** 27 Hc03
Varapaeva **BY** 53 Jb23
Varaždin **HR** 73 Gb36
Varaždinske Toplice **HR** 74
  Gc36
Varazze **I** 83 Ed38
Varberg **S** 49 Fd21
Vărbica **BG** 89 Jd39
Varde **DK** 48 Fa23
Várda **GR** 110 Hd46
Vardø **N** 27 Hd03
Vårdö **FIN** 46 Ha17
Varekil **S** 43 Fc20
Varel **D** 55 Ed26
Varėna **LT** 59 Hd25
Varėna **LT** 59 Hd25
Varena I **LT** 59 Hd25
Varena I **LT** 59 Hd25
Varengeville-sur-Mer **F** 61
  Db30
Varennes-en-Argonne **F** 62
  Ea31
Varennes-sur-Allier **F** 70
  Dd35
Vareš **BIH** 86 Gd38
Varese **I** 71 Ed36
Varese Ligure **I** 84 Fa38
Vârfu Câmpului **RO** 76 Jc33
Vârfurile **RO** 75 Hd35
Vårgårda **S** 43 Fd20
Vargön **S** 43 Fd19
Varhaug **N** 42 Ec19

Varilhes – Vetsikko

Varilhes **F** 81 Da39
Váris **GR** 101 Hd43
Varkaus **FIN** 41 Ja14
Varmahlíð **IS** 15 Ca05
Värmlandsbro **S** 44 Fd18
Varna **BG** 89 Ka39
Värnamo **S** 50 Ga21
Varniai **LT** 52 Hb23
Varnja **EST** 47 Ja19
Varnjany **BY** 53 Ja24
Varnsdorf **CZ** 65 Ga29
Varoška Rijeka **BIH** 85 Gb37
Varpaisjärvi **FIN** 35 Hd12
Várpalota **H** 74 Gd34
Vărşag **RO** 76 Jb35
Vărşand **RO** 75 Hc35
Vărşec **BG** 88 Ja39
Vărşilo **BG** 103 Ka40
Vartdal **N** 36 Ed14
Vartius **FIN** 35 Ja10
Vârtop **RO** 88 Ja38
Värtsilä **FIN** 41 Jb13
Varva **UA** 121 Ed14
Varvara **BG** 102 Jb40
Varzi **I** 83 Ed37
Varzy **F** 70 Dd33
Vasa **FIN** 40 Ha13
Vasalemma **EST** 46 Hc18
Vásárosnamény **H** 75 Hc33
Vasil'evo **RUS** 47 Jb20
Vasil'evo **RUS** 119 Fd09
Vasiliki **GR** 110 Hc45
Vaškai **LT** 52 Hc22
Vaskelovo **RUS** 41 Jb16
Vaskivesi **FIN** 40 Hb14
Vasknarva **EST** 47 Ja18
Vaslui **RO** 77 Jd34
Vassilika **GR** 101 Ja43
Vassilikó **GR** 112 Jb45
Vassilikós **GR** 110 Hc47
Vasstrand **N** 26 Gc05
Västansjö **S** 33 Ga10
Västbacka **S** 38 Ga15
Västerås **S** 44 Gb18
Västerhaninge **S** 45 Gc18
Västervik **S** 44 Gb20
Vasto **I** 99 Ga41
Våstra **S** 45 Gc18
Västra Ämtervik **S** 44 Fd18
Vasvár **H** 74 Gc35
Vasylivka **UA** 126 Fa16
Vasyl'kiv **UA** 121 Ec15
Vasyl'kivka **UA** 122 Fa15
Vasyščeve **UA** 122 Fa14
Vaţa de Jos **RO** 75 Hd35
Vatan **F** 69 Db33
Váthi **GR** 101 Ja42
Vathí **GR** 115 Ka47
Vatla **EST** 46 Hc19
Vatne **N** 36 Fa14
Vatra **MD** 77 Ka33
Vatra Dornei **RO** 76 Jb34
Vatra Moldoviţei **RO** 76 Jb33
Vättlax **FIN** 46 Hb17
Vatutine **UA** 121 Ec15

Vaucouleurs **F** 63 Eb32
Vaudrey **F** 71 Eb34
Vau i Dejës **AL** 100 Hb41
Vaukalata **BY** 53 Jb23
Vauvert **F** 82 Dd38
Väversunda **S** 44 Ga20
Vavkavysk **BY** 59 Hd26
Vaxholm **S** 45 Gc18
Växjö **S** 50 Ga21
Våxtorp **S** 49 Fd22
Vayrac **F** 69 Db36
Vechelde **D** 56 Fb28
Vechta **D** 55 Ed27
Vecinos **E** 91 Bb40
Veclaicene **LV** 47 Ja20
Vecpiebalga **LV** 53 Hd21
Vecses **H** 74 Ha34
Vecumnieki **LV** 53 Hd21
Veddige **S** 49 Fd21
Vedea **RO** 88 Jc38
Vedevåg **S** 44 Gb18
Vedjeön **S** 33 Gb12
Vedrovo **RUS** 118 Fb08
Veendam **NL** 55 Ec26
Veenendaal **NL** 55 Eb27
Veere **EST** 46 Hb19
Vegadeo **E** 78 Bb36
Vegarienza **E** 79 Bc37
Vegårshei **N** 42 Fa19
Veghel **NL** 55 Eb28
Veglie **I** 100 Gd43
Vegusdal **N** 42 Fa19
Vehmaa **FIN** 40 Ha16
Vehmersalmi **FIN** 41 Ja13
Vehu **FIN** 40 Hc13
Veidnes **N** 27 Hb03
Veisiejai **LT** 59 Hc25
Veisiejai **LT** 59 Hc25
Veitsiluoto **FIN** 34 Hb09
Vejdelevka **RUS** 122 Fb14
Vejen **DK** 48 Fa23
Vejer de la Frontera **E** 105 Ad45
Vejle **DK** 49 Fb23
Vejprty **CZ** 65 Fd30
Vekilski **BG** 89 Jd38
Vela Luka **HR** 86 Gc40
Velanídia **GR** 111 Jb48
Vel'aty **SK** 67 Hc32
Velbert **D** 63 Ec29
Velden **A** 73 Ga35
Veldhoven **NL** 55 Eb28
Velēna **LV** 47 Ja20
Velenje **SLO** 73 Ga36
Veles **MK** 101 Hd41
Velestino **GR** 101 Ja44
Vélez Blanco **E** 107 Ca45
Vélez-Málaga **E** 105 Bb45
Vélez Rubio **E** 107 Ca45
Velika **GR** 110 Hd47
Velika **HR** 86 Gd37
Velika Gorica **HR** 73 Gb36
Velika Kladuša **HR** 85 Gb37
Velika Plana **SRB** 87 Hc38
Velika Plana **SRB** 87 Hc39
Velika Slatina **RKS** 87 Hc40

Veliki Dal'nik **UA** 77 Kb34
Velikie Luki **RUS** 117 Eb10
Veliki Gradište **SRB** 87 Hc37
Veliki Grđevac **HR** 74 Gc36
Veliki Kupci **SRB** 87 Hc39
Veliki Preslav **BG** 89 Jd39
Veliki Radinci **SRB** 86 Ha37
Veliki Šiljegovac **SRB** 87 Hc39
Veliki Zdenci **HR** 74 Gc36
Veliko Tărnovo **BG** 88 Jc39
Velimlje **MNE** 86 Ha40
Velingrad **BG** 102 Jb41
Veliž **RUS** 117 Eb11
Veljun **HR** 85 Gb37
Velká Bíteš **CZ** 65 Gb32
Vel'ké Kapušany **SK** 67 Hc32
Velké Losiny **CZ** 66 Gc31
Velké Meziříčí **CZ** 65 Gb32
Velký Bor **CZ** 65 Fd31
Vel'ký Krtíš **SK** 74 Ha33
Vel'ký Šariš **SK** 67 Hb32
Velletri **I** 98 Fc42
Vellinge **S** 49 Fd23
Velventós **GR** 101 Hd43
Velyka Lepetycha **UA** 126 Fa16
Velyka Mychajlivka **MD** 77 Kb33
Velyka Pysarivka **UA** 122 Fa14
Velyki Dederkaly **UA** 120 Ea15
Velyki Mosty **UA** 67 Hd30
Velykoploske **UA** 77 Ka33
Velykyj Bereznyj **UA** 67 Hc32
Velykyj Burluk **UA** 122 Fa14
Vemb **DK** 48 Fa22
Vemdalen **S** 38 Ga14
Venafro **I** 98 Fd42
Venarey-les Laumes **F** 70 Ea33
Venčane **SRB** 87 Hb38
Vence **F** 83 Eb39
Venda Nova **P** 78 Ba38
Vendas Novas **P** 90 Ac42
Vendeuvre-sur-Barse **F** 62 Ea32
Vendôme **F** 61 Db32
Venec **BG** 89 Jd38
Veneheitto **FIN** 35 Hc11
Venev **RUS** 118 Fa11
Venezia **I** 84 Fc37
Vénissieux **F** 70 Ea36
Venjan **S** 38 Ga16
Venlo **NL** 55 Ec28
Vennesla **N** 42 Fa19
Vennesund **S** 32 Fd10
Venosa **I** 99 Gb43
Venray **NL** 55 Ec28
Venta **LT** 52 Hb22
Venta de Ballerías **E** 80 Cd40

Venta de Baños **E** 79 Bd39
Ventimiglia **I** 83 Ec39
Ventspils **LV** 52 Hb21
Vera **E** 107 Ca45
Verbania **I** 71 Ed36
Verbier **CH** 71 Ec35
Vercelli **I** 83 Ed37
Verchnjadzvinsk **BY** 53 Jb22
Verchnje Syn'ovydne **UA** 67 Hd31
Verchn'odniprovs'k **UA** 121 Ed15
Verdalsøra **N** 32 Fc12
Verden (Aller) **D** 56 Fa27
Verdun **F** 63 Eb31
Verdun-sur-le-Doubs **F** 70 Ea34
Vergato **I** 84 Fb38
Vergt **F** 69 Da36
Verhnetulomskij **RUS** 31 Ja05
Véria **GR** 101 Hd43
Verín **E** 78 Ba38
Verinsko **BG** 102 Ja40
Veriora **EST** 47 Ja19
Verl **D** 56 Fa28
Vermenton **F** 70 Dd33
Vernazza **I** 84 Fa38
Verneuil-sur-Avre **F** 61 Db31
Vernon **F** 62 Dc31
Vero **F** 96 Ed41
Verona **I** 84 Fb37
Versailles **F** 62 Dc31
Versmold **D** 55 Ed28
Vertelim **RUS** 119 Fc10
Vertijivka **UA** 121 Ec14
Vertjačij **RUS** 123 Fd14
Vertus **F** 62 Ea31
Verviers **B** 63 Eb29
Vervins **F** 62 Ea30
Vesanka **FIN** 40 Hc14
Vesanto **FIN** 41 Hd13
Ves'egonsk **RUS** 117 Ed08
Vesele **UA** 126 Fa16
Veselij Kut **UA** 77 Ka35
Veselí nad Lužnicí **CZ** 65 Ga32
Veselí nad Moravou **CZ** 66 Gc32
Veselynove **UA** 125 Ed16
Vešenskaja **RUS** 123 Fc13
Vesoul **F** 71 Eb33
Vessigebro **S** 49 Fd21
Vestby **N** 43 Fc18
Vesterli **N** 28 Ga08
Vesterø Havn **DK** 49 Fc21
Vestnes **N** 36 Fa14
Vestre Jakobselv **N** 27 Hc03
Veszprém **H** 74 Gd34
Veţel **RO** 75 Hd36
Veteli **FIN** 34 Hb12
Vetlanda **S** 50 Ga21
Vetluga **RUS** 118 Fb08
Vetrişoaia **RO** 77 Jd34
Větrný Jeníkov **CZ** 65 Gb31
Vetsikko **FIN** 27 Hc04

Veulettes-sur-Mer – Villeneuve

Veulettes-sur-Mer **F** 61 Db30
Veurne **B** 54 Dd28
Vevelstad **N** 32 Fd10
Vevey **CH** 71 Eb35
Vévi **GR** 101 Hd42
Veynes **F** 82 Ea37
Vézelay **F** 70 Dd33
Viadana **I** 84 Fa37
Viana **E** 80 Cb39
Viana de Bolo **E** 78 Ba38
Viana do Alentejo **P** 90 Ac42
Viana do Castelo **P** 78 Ad38
Vianden **L** 63 Eb30
Vianen **NL** 55 Eb27
Viareggio **I** 84 Fa39
Vias **F** 81 Dc39
Vibble **S** 45 Gc20
Viborg **DK** 49 Fb22
Vibo Valentia **I** 109 Gb46
Vibraye **F** 61 Db32
Vic **E** 81 Db40
Vicdessos **F** 81 Da39
Vic-en-Bigorre **F** 80 Cd38
Vicenza **I** 84 Fb37
Vichy **F** 70 Dd35
Vic-le-Comte **F** 69 Dc36
Vic-le-Fesq **F** 82 Dd38
Vico **F** 96 Ed41
Vicovu de Jos **RO** 76 Jb33
Vic-sur-Cère **F** 69 Dc36
Victoria **RO** 77 Jd33
Victoria **RO** 88 Jb36
Vičuga **RUS** 118 Fb09
Vidamlja **BY** 59 Hd27
Vidauban **F** 83 Eb39
Videbæk **DK** 48 Fa22
Videle **RO** 88 Jc38
Videsæter **N** 36 Fa15
Vidice **CZ** 65 Fd31
Vidigueira **P** 90 Ac42
Vidin **BG** 87 Hd38
Vidiškiai **LT** 53 Hd23
Vidsel **S** 34 Gd09
Vidzy **BY** 53 Ja23
Viechtach **D** 65 Fd32
Vieki **FIN** 35 Ja12
Viekšniai **LT** 52 Hb22
Vielha **E** 81 Da39
Vielsalm **B** 63 Eb30
Vienne **F** 70 Ea36
Vieremä **FIN** 35 Hd12
Viernheim **D** 63 Ed31
Viersen **D** 63 Ec29
Vierzon **F** 69 Dc33
Viesite **LV** 53 Hd22
Vieste **I** 99 Gb41
Vietas **S** 29 Gc07
Vif **F** 82 Ea37
Vigeland **N** 42 Ed20
Vigevano **I** 83 Ed37
Vignola **I** 84 Fb38
Vigo **E** 78 Ad37
Vigrestad **N** 42 Ec19
Vihanti **FIN** 35 Hc11

Vihiers **F** 69 Da33
Vihtari **FIN** 41 Ja13
Vihti **FIN** 40 Hc16
Vīïaka **LV** 47 Jb20
Viiala **FIN** 40 Hb15
Viira **EST** 46 Hb19
Viisarimäki **FIN** 41 Hd14
Viişoara **RO** 76 Jc34
Viitasaari **FIN** 40 Hc13
Viitna **EST** 47 Hd17
Viivikonna **EST** 47 Ja17
Vík **IS** 14 Bd08
Vik **S** 50 Ga23
Vika **S** 38 Ga16
Vikajärvi **FIN** 31 Hc08
Vikanes **N** 36 Ed16
Vikarbyn **S** 38 Ga16
Vikedal **N** 42 Ed18
Viken **S** 49 Fd22
Vikersund **N** 43 Fb17
Vikevåg **N** 42 Ed18
Vikhammer **N** 37 Fc13
Vikno **UA** 76 Jb32
Vikran **N** 26 Gc05
Viksjö **S** 39 Gc14
Viksøyri **N** 36 Ed16
Vila de Rei **P** 90 Ad40
Vila do Bispo **P** 104 Ab43
Vila Flor **P** 78 Ba39
Vilafranca del Maestrat **E** 93 Cc42
Vilafranca del Penedès **E** 95 Da41
Vila Franca de Xira **P** 90 Ac41
Vilagarcía de Arousa **E** 78 Ad37
Vilalba **E** 78 Ba36
Viļāni **LV** 53 Ja21
Vila Nova de Famalição **P** 78 Ad38
Vila Nova de Foz Côa **P** 78 Ba39
Vila Nova de Milfontes **P** 104 Ab43
Vila Nova de Paiva **P** 78 Ad39
Vilanova i la Geltrú **E** 95 Da41
Vila Pouca de Aguiar **P** 78 Ba38
Vilar **P** 78 Ba39
Vila Real **P** 78 Ba39
Vila-real (Villareal de los Infantes) **E** 93 Cc42
Vila Real de Santo Antonio **P** 104 Ac43
Vilar Formoso **P** 91 Ba40
Vila Velha de Ródão **P** 90 Ad41
Vila Verde de Ficalho **P** 105 Ad43
Vila Viçosa **P** 90 Ad42
Vilches **E** 106 Bc44
Vildbjerg **DK** 48 Fa22
Vilejka **BY** 53 Jb24

Vilejka **BY** 120 Ea12
Vilhelmina **S** 33 Gb11
Viljandi **EST** 47 Hd19
Vilkaviškis **LT** 52 Hc24
Vilkija **LT** 52 Hc24
Villablino **E** 78 Bb37
Villacañas **E** 92 Bd42
Villacarillo **E** 106 Bd44
Villacarriedo **E** 79 Ca37
Villacastín **E** 91 Bc40
Villach **A** 73 Fd35
Villacidro **I** 97 Ec44
Villada **E** 79 Bc38
Villa del Río **E** 106 Bc44
Villadiego **E** 79 Bd38
Villafranca del Bierzo **E** 78 Bb37
Villafranca de los Barros **E** 91 Ba42
Villafranca de los Caballeros **E** 92 Bd42
Villafranca di Verona **I** 84 Fb37
Villafranco del Guadalquivir **E** 105 Ad44
Villaharta **E** 105 Bb43
Villahermosa **E** 92 Bd43
Villahoz **E** 79 Bd39
Villalba **E** 78 Ba36
Villalón de Campos **E** 79 Bc38
Villalpando **E** 79 Bc39
Villamalea **E** 93 Cb43
Villamanrique **E** 92 Bd43
Villamartín **E** 105 Ba45
Villamayor **E** 80 Cc40
Villamayor de Santiago **E** 92 Bd42
Villandraut **F** 68 Cd36
Villa Nova de Cerveira **P** 78 Ad37
Villanubla **E** 79 Bc39
Villanueva de Alcorón **E** 92 Ca41
Villanueva de Argaño **E** 79 Bd38
Villanueva de Córdoba **E** 105 Bb43
Villanueva de Gállego **E** 80 Cc40
Villanueva de la Fuente **E** 92 Bd43
Villanueva de la Jura **E** 92 Ca43
Villanueva de la Serena **E** 91 Bb42
Villanueva de la Sierra **E** 91 Ba40
Villanueva de las Torres **E** 106 Bd45
Villanueva del Campo **E** 79 Bc38
Villanueva del Fresno **E** 90 Ad42
Villanueva del Huerva **E** 80 Cc40

Villanueva de los Castillejos **E** 105 Ad43
Villanueva de los Infantes **E** 92 Bd43
Villanueva del Río y Minas **E** 105 Ba44
Villány **H** 74 Gd36
Villapalacios **E** 92 Bd43
Villaputzu **I** 97 Ed44
Villard-de-Lans **F** 82 Ea37
Villardeciervos **E** 78 Bb38
Villar de Domingo García **E** 92 Ca41
Villardefrades **E** 79 Bc39
Villar del Arzobispo **E** 93 Cb42
Villar del Rey **E** 91 Ba42
Villarejo de Fuentes **E** 92 Ca42
Villarejo de Salvanés **E** 92 Bd41
Villarente **E** 79 Bc38
Villarmayor **E** 78 Bb39
Villarrín de Campos **E** 79 Bc39
Villarrobledo **E** 92 Ca43
Villarroya de la Sierra **E** 80 Cb40
Villarrubia de los Ojos **E** 92 Bd42
Villars **CH** 71 Ec35
Villars-les-Dombes **F** 70 Ea35
Villarta de los Montes **E** 91 Bc42
Villasalto **I** 97 Ed44
Villasana de Mena **E** 79 Ca37
Villa San Giovanni **I** 109 Gb46
Villa Santa Maria **I** 99 Ga41
Villasimius **I** 97 Ed45
Villaviciosa **E** 79 Bc36
Villaviciosa de Córdoba **E** 105 Bb43
Villedieu-les-Poêles **F** 61 Da31
Villedieu-sur-Indre **F** 69 Db34
Villefort **F** 82 Dd37
Villefranche-de-Conflent **F** 81 Db39
Villefranche-de-Lauragais **F** 81 Db38
Villefranche-de-Rouergue **F** 81 Db37
Villefranche-du-Périgord **F** 81 Da37
Villefranche-sur-Cher **F** 69 Db33
Villefranche-sur-Mer **F** 83 Ec39
Villefranche-sur-Saône **F** 70 Ea35
Villena **E** 107 Cb44
Villeneuve **F** 81 Db37

204

Villeneuve-lès-Avignon F 82 Dd38
Villeneuve-sur-Lot F 81 Da37
Villeneuve-sur-Yonne F 62 Dd32
Villeréal F 69 Da36
Villers-Bocage F 61 Da30
Villers-Bocage F 62 Dd30
Villers-Bretonneux F 62 Dd30
Villers-Cotterêts F 62 Dd31
Villersexel F 71 Eb33
Villerupt F 63 Eb31
Villeurbanne F 70 Ea36
Villiers-Saint-Georges F 62 Dd32
Villingen-Schwenningen D 71 Ed33
Vilnius LT 53 Hd24
Vil'njans'k UA 122 Fa15
Vil'nohirs'k UA 121 Ed15
Vilppula FIN 40 Hc14
Vil'šanka UA 77 Jd32
Vil'šany UA 122 Fa14
Vilsbiburg D 72 Fc33
Vilshofen D 65 Fd32
Vimianzo E 78 Ad36
Vimeiro P 90 Ad42
Vimioso P 78 Bb39
Vimmerby S 44 Gb20
Vimoutiers F 61 Db31
Vimpeli FIN 40 Hb13
Vinac BIH 86 Gc38
Vinaròs E 93 Cd42
Vindeln S 34 Gd12
Vinderup DK 48 Fa22
Vindrej RUS 119 Fc10
Vinga RO 75 Hc36
Vingåker S 44 Gb19
Vinhais P 78 Ba38
Vinica MK 101 Hd41
Vinište BG 88 Ja39
Vinje N 36 Ed16
Vinje N 37 Fb13
Vinkovci HR 86 Ha37
Vinnycja UA 121 Eb15
Vinograd BG 88 Jc39
Vinon-sur-Verdon F 82 Ea38
Vinslöv S 50 Ga23
Vinsternes N 37 Fb13
Vinstra N 37 Fb15
Vipiteno I 72 Fb35
Vir HR 85 Ga38
Viranşehir TR 128 Gd17
Virbalis LT 52 Hc24
Vire F 61 Da31
Vireši LV 47 Ja20
Virginia IRL 19 Cb23
Virkby FIN 46 Hc17
Virkkala FIN 46 Hc17
Virklund DK 49 Fb22
Virojoki FIN 41 Ja16
Virolahden FIN 41 Ja16
Virovitica HR 74 Gc36
Virpazar MNE 100 Ha41

Virrat FIN 40 Hb14
Virsbo S 44 Gb17
Virserum S 50 Gb21
Virtaniemi FIN 27 Hc05
Virtasalmi FIN 41 Hd14
Virton B 63 Eb31
Virtsu EST 46 Hc19
Virttaa FIN 40 Hb16
Vis HR 85 Gb40
Visaginas LT 53 Ja23
Visalaukė LT 53 Hd23
Visby S 45 Gc20
Visé B 63 Eb29
Višegrad BIH 86 Ha39
Viseu P 78 Ad39
Vişeu de Sus RO 76 Ja33
Višgorodok RUS 47 Jb20
Višina RO 88 Jb38
Viskafors S 43 Fd20
Vislanda S 50 Ga22
Viďneva BY 53 Ja24
Viso del Marqués E 106 Bc43
Visoki Dečani RKS 87 Hb40
Visoko BIH 86 Gd39
Visp CH 71 Ec35
Vissefjärda S 50 Gb22
Visselhövede D 56 Fa27
Vistabella del Maestrat E 93 Cc42
Vistheden S 34 Gd10
Vištytis LT 52 Hc24
Visuvesi FIN 40 Hb14
Vitberget S 34 Gd09
Viterbo I 98 Fc41
Vitez BIH 86 Gd38
Vithkuq AL 101 Hc43
Vitigudino E 78 Bb39
Vitina RKS 101 Hc41
Vitolište MK 101 Hd42
Vitoria E 80 Cb38
Vitré F 61 Cd32
Vitrolles F 82 Ea39
Vitry-le-François F 62 Ea32
Vitteaux F 70 Ea33
Vittel F 71 Eb33
Vittjärv S 34 Ha09
Vittoria I 109 Ga48
Vittorio Veneto I 72 Fc36
Vittsjö S 49 Fd22
Vitvattnet S 34 Ha09
Viù I 83 Ec37
Vivario F 96 Ed41
Viveiro E 78 Bb36
Viviers F 82 Dd37
Vivonne F 69 Da34
Vize TR 103 Ka41
Vizille F 82 Ea37
Viziru RO 89 Jd36
Vizovice CZ 66 Gd32
Vizzini I 109 Ga48
Vjalikija Matykaly BY 59 Hd27
Vjartsilja RUS 41 Jb13

Vjatskie Poljany RUS 119 Ga08
Vjatskoe RUS 118 Fa08
Vjaz'ma RUS 117 Ec11
Vjazniki RUS 118 Fb09
Vlădeni RO 76 Jc33
Vlădeni RO 76 Jc33
Vladimir MNE 100 Ila41
Vladimir RUS 118 Fa10
Vladimirovo BG 88 Ja39
Vlad Ţepeş RO 89 Jd37
Vlagtwedde NL 55 Ed26
Vlaháta GR 110 Hc46
Vlaháva GR 101 Hd44
Vlahiá GR 112 Jb45
Vlăhiţa RO 76 Jb35
Vlasenica BIH 86 Ha38
Vlašim CZ 65 Ga31
Vlaşin RO 88 Jc38
Vlasotince SRB 87 Hd40
Vlissingen NL 54 Ea28
Vlkolínec SK 67 Ha32
Vlorë AL 100 Hb43
Vlotho D 56 Fa28
Vöcklabruck A 73 Fd33
Vodice HR 85 Gb39
Vodňany CZ 65 Ga32
Vodnjan HR 85 Fd37
Vodskov DK 49 Fb21
Voerde D 55 Ec28
Voghera I 83 Ed37
Vohburg D 64 Fc32
Vohenstrauß D 64 Fc31
Võhma EST 46 Hb19
Võhma EST 47 Hd19
Voikoski FIN 41 Hd15
Voineasa RO 88 Ja36
Voineasa RO 88 Ja38
Voineşti RO 88 Jb37
Voiron F 70 Ea36
Võiste EST 46 Hc19
Voiteg RO 75 Hc36
Voitsberg A 73 Ga35
Vojens DK 48 Fa23
Vojinka UA 126 Fa17
Vojnić HR 85 Gb37
Vojnica RUS 35 Ja10
Vojnika BG 103 Jd40
Vojnovo BG 89 Jd38
Vojutyči UA 67 Hd31
Voknavolok RUS 35 Ja10
Volary CZ 65 Fd32
Volčki RUS 122 Fb12
Volda N 36 Ed14
Volga RUS 117 Ed09
Volgodonsk RUS 123 Fd15
Volgograd RUS 123 Fd14
Volgorečensk RUS 118 Fa09
Volgsele S 33 Gb11
Volhov RUS 117 Ec11
Volintiri MD 77 Ka34
Volissós GR 113 Jd45
Volkach D 64 Fb31
Völkermarkt A 73 Ga35
Volkovo RUS 47 Jb20

Vollsjö S 49 Fd23
Volnovacha UA 122 Fb15
Voločajevskij RUS 123 Fd15
Voločys'k UA 120 Ea15
Volodarka UA 121 Ec15
Volodarsk RUS 118 Fb09
Volodymyrec' UA 120 Ea14
Volodymyr-Volyns'kyj UA 67 Hd29
Vologda RUS 117 Ed08
Volokolamsk RUS 117 Ed10
Volokonovka RUS 122 Fb13
Vólos GR 101 Ja44
Vološča UA 67 Hd31
Volosjanka UA 67 Hd32
Volosovo RUS 47 Jb17
Volotovo RUS 122 Fb13
Volovec' UA 67 Hd32
Völs A 72 Fb34
Vol'sk RUS 119 Ga11
Volterra I 84 Fb39
Voltri I 83 Ed38
Voltti FIN 40 Hb13
Volvic F 69 Dc35
Volyně CZ 65 Fd32
Volžsk RUS 119 Fd09
Volžskij RUS 123 Fd13
Vonešta Voda BG 88 Jc39
Vónitsa GR 110 Hc45
Võnnu EST 47 Ja19
Vopnafjörður IS 15 Cc06
Vorbasse DK 48 Fa23
Vordingborg DK 49 Fc24
Vorey F 70 Dd36
Vormsele S 33 Gc11
Vorniceni RO 76 Jc33
Vorochta UA 76 Ja32
Voroneţ RO 76 Jb33
Voronež RUS 122 Fb13
Voronovo RUS 47 Jb18
Vorožba UA 121 Ed13
Vorsma RUS 118 Fb09
Võru EST 47 Ja20
Voshod RUS 123 Ga14
Voskresensk RUS 118 Fa10
Voskresenskoe RUS 117 Ed09
Voskresenskoe RUS 119 Fc08
Voss N 36 Ed16
Võsu EST 47 Hd17
Votice CZ 65 Ga31
Voúdia GR 111 Jc47
Vouillé F 69 Da34
Vouliagméni GR 112 Jb46
Vourkári GR 112 Jc46
Vouzela P 78 Ad39
Vouziers F 62 Ea31
Vovčans'k UA 122 Fa14
Voves F 62 Dc32
Voxna S 38 Gb15
Vöyri FIN 40 Ha13
Voznesens'k UA 125 Ed16
Voznesenskoe RUS 118 Fb10
Vrå DK 49 Fb21